W9-BWB-153

FISHING
IN
SOUTHERN
CALIFORNIA

Eighth Edition

The Complete Guide

Ken Albert

ISBN 0-934061-41-6

ISBN 0-934061-41-6

9 780934 061414   90000

Cover Design:	Electric Art Studios Mountain View, CA	Maps by:	JS & K MapGraphics Aptos, CA
Printed by:	Delta Printing Solutions Valencia, CA.	Typesetting by:	Laura Spray Colorado Springs, CO
Thanks to:	Jim Matthews for his help in updating this book		

Marketscope
Huntington Beach, Ca. 92605
(714) 375-9888

"The leading publisher of fishing books
for California anglers"

Great Books *(for more details see p. 236)*

Fishing in Northern California

Marketscope publishes the bestselling **Fishing in Northern California** (8 1/2 x 11 inches, 240 pages). It includes "How To Catch" sections on all freshwater fish as well as salmon, steelhead, sturgeon, shad, kokanee, lingcod, clams, sharks, rock crab, crawdads, stripers, etc. Plus, there are sections on all major NorCal fishing waters (over 50 lakes, the Delta, Coastal Rivers, Valley Rivers, Mountain Trout and the Pacific Ocean). All these waters are mapped in detail!

Fishing in Southern California

Marketscope also publishes the bestselling **Fishing in Southern California** (8 1/2 x 11 inches, 240 pages). It includes "How To Catch" sections on all freshwater fish as well as barracuda, bonito, calico bass, grunion, halibut, marlin, sea bass and yellowtail. Plus, there are sections on major SoCal fishing waters (45 lakes, the Salton Sea, Colorado River, Mountain Trout and the Pacific Ocean).All these waters are mapped in detail!

Bass Fishing in California

At last, a bass fishing book just for Californians—both beginners and veterans. This book explains in detail how to catch more and larger bass in California's unique waters. But, most valuable, it includes a comprehensive guide, with maps, to 40 of California's best bass lakes, up and down the state. 8 1/2 x 11, 240 pages.

Trout Fishing in California

Trout fishing is special in California and now there is a special book for the California trout anglers. It covers, in detail, how to catch trout in lakes or streams, with line, bait or flies, by trolling, casting or still fishing, from boat or shore. And even better for California anglers, this is a guide to the best trout waters all over the state. Detailed info and precise maps are featured. 8 1/2 x 11, 252 pages.

Saltwater Fishing in California

California is blessed with over 800 miles of Pacific Ocean coastline. This is a marvelous resource for all Golden State anglers. And now there is a book that covers it all. Surf fishing. Kelp fishing. Harbor and Bay fishing. Poke poling. And more. Don't go saltwater fishing without it. Both veteran anglers and beginners are finding this book a necessity. It explains, in detail, how to catch albacore, barracuda, bass, bonito, halibut, rockfish, sharks, salmon, stripers, yellowtail and striped marlin. And there is a large "How-To and Where-To" Guide for hot spots all along the coast. And don't be without the Saltwater Sportfish I.D. Section. This book has become a standard because it explains in simple, straightforward language how to catch fish in the Pacific, off California. 8 1/2 x 11, 256 pages.

Order your Copies Today!

	Price	Sales Tax	Total Price	Qty	Total Amount
___ **Fishing in Northern California**	$14.95	$ .95	$15.90	___	_____
___ **Fishing in Southern California**	$14.95	$ .95	$15.90	___	_____
___ **Bass Fishing in California**	$14.95	$ .95	$15.90	___	_____
___ **Trout Fishing in California**	$14.95	$ .95	$15.90	___	_____
___ **Saltwater Fishing in California**	$14.95	$ .95	$15.90	___	_____

Postage & Handling (1st book $1.75; no charge on 2 or more books) . . . . _____ *

Check Enclosed . . . . _____

*Special Offer (order 2 books, any combination, and we'll pay **all** postage & handling)

Name_____   Address_____

Send Your Order To: **Marketscope, P.O. Box 3118, HUNTINGTON BEACH, CA 92605**
(Permission is granted to xerox this page.)

Contents

continued . . .

Contents (continued)

Specials

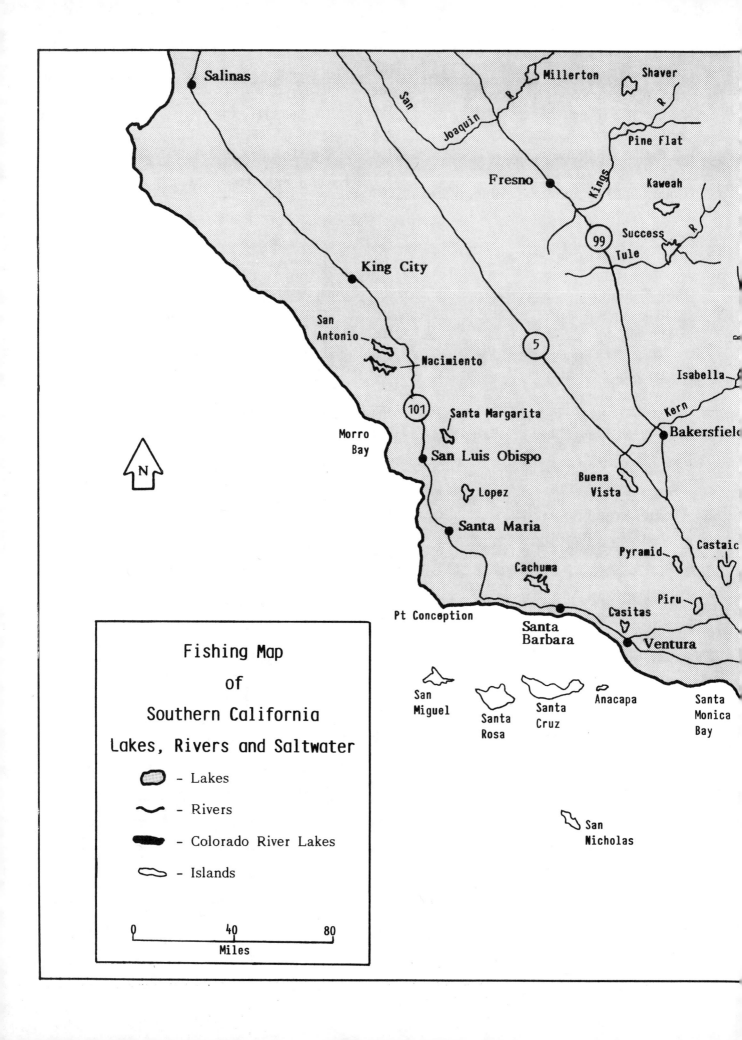

Salinas

San
Joaquin

Millerton   Shaver

Pine Flat

Fresno   Kings   Kaweah

King City

99   Success
Tule

San
Antonio

Nacimiento

5

101   Isabella

Santa Margarita   Kern

Morro
Bay   San Luis Obispo   Bakersfield

Lopez   Buena
Vista

Santa Maria   Castaic

Pyramid

Cachuma   Piru

Casitas
Pt Conception   Santa
Barbara   Ventura

N

San
Miguel

Santa
Rosa   Santa
Cruz   Anacapa   Santa
Monica
Bay

San
Nicholas

Fishing Map

of

Southern California

Lakes, Rivers and Saltwater

- Lakes

- Rivers

- Colorado River Lakes

- Islands

0   40   80

Miles

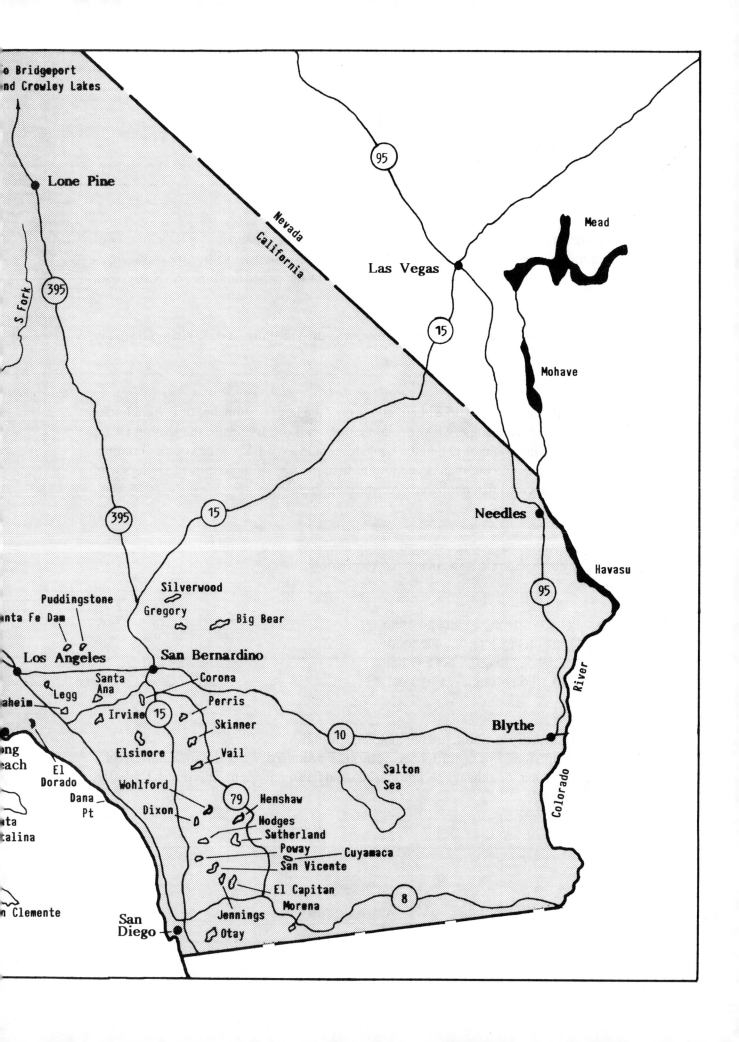

Ramblings . . .

Sometimes when a book is layed out, a wonderful thing happens. It's the luxury of having a page that the author can call his own, to use for a dedication, acknowledgements, personal reflections, etc. Well, that's what happened this time. So here goes...

- This book is dedicated to my mother, who died recently. You'll always be in my thoughts and in my actions.

- Marketscope has worked hard and is now the largest publisher of fishing books for California anglers. A special thanks to all our friends in the fishing tackle marketing business and in the bookstore trade. We'll keep the cookies coming. Also, we send our thanks and gratitude to the tens of thousands of anglers who have decided that our books are worth buying.

- The ultimate fishing experience may not be to "take a limit," but rather to catch and release as many fish as possible.

- Eat all day long . . . not possible.
  Drink all day long . . . not good.
  Sex all day long . . . not any more.
  Fish all day long . . . why not!

- And finally to Carol, my wife and best friend—
  In previous books, in the dedication, I promised we'd do something really important for a change . . . I promised we'd fish more often. This time let's really, really do it!

Take a Kid Fishing—One Story

My thirteen-year-old son Bruce had been after me for months to go fishing with him in tiny Lake Freedom, about four miles from our home. He'd heard at school that kids had caught some nice bass there. So late one Saturday afternoon we loaded our rowboat in the pick-up and drove to the lake.

I took my big, old metal tackle box. It had been my father's box and was packed with everything that was "state of the art" in the 1930's. He was killed in an industrial accident when I was a teenager. I inherited his love for fishing and his big, metal tackle box.

All the lures that my father used 40 and 50 years ago to entice the lunker bass are still in that metal box. But actually I hardly ever use any of his lures, since they're almost antiques and I don't want to lose them. Besides, I score most with spinnerbaits and plastic worms. This is what Bruce and I were using at Lake Freedom and we were getting skunked. The sun had set and I was ready to go home for dinner.

For some reason Bruce looked into his grandfather's tackle box and spotted an old red bucktail with three small fish-shaped flashers that protected the hook. "Dad, why don't you try this? It's sort of like a spinnerbait, isn't it?" he asked.

"Yea, I guess it is," I responded as I continued to work my worm."

"Come on, try it. Let's see how it swims."

"Okay, we'll give it a try."

I decided to humor him so I put it on and pulled it beside the boat to watch the action. "It looks pretty good. Like a spinnerbait," I said. Bruce agreed.
My first cast with this well-built relic landed near some overhanging branches. When I began my retrieve, the line stiffened and my rod arched. "Damn, I've snagged an underwater branch," I said under my breath. I was upset. I didn't want to lose that lure. For some reason, I didn't want to lose anything from the old, metal tackle box. But then the snag began to "run" and take line against my drag. What do you know, I had a strike on the first cast of a lure that hadn't been in the water since before World War II.

We landed the bass. It was a beauty. Bruce couldn't resist the temptation to say, "See Dad, I told you so. Those old lures are good."

"They sure are," I said, grinning.

Then we agreed that the fish should be released. Lake Freedom needed that bass, and we needed to know that it was alive and well. After all, it and that old lure performed 3 minor miracles. It was that old lure that gave Bruce and I a wonderful moment together. That old lure made me cherish my father's tackle box even more. And, it tied together a grandfather and grandson who never knew each other, except for a few moments at Lake Freedom.

Bruce switched to one of his grandfather's spinnerbait-like lures and we each made a few more casts into the twilight. Then Bruce said, "Dad, let's go home. I don't want to risk losing this lure. We can't see the overhanging branches." I nodded and we rowed to shore.

During the drive home, Bruce chattered about how to tell Mom our fishing story, and how to convince her with no fish as proof. But I was thinking about something else. I was thinking that someday Bruce would be a loving keeper of that big metal tackle box and those old lures.

*See the "Teaching Kids How to Fish" section starting on page **14***

About this Expanded and Updated Edition

The man who will use his skill and constructive imagination to see how much he can give for a dollar, instead of how little he can give for a dollar, is bound to succeed.

Henry Ford

Henry Ford delivered an awful lot for each dollar in his Model A and Model T automobiles. And we're believers in Henry's philosophy. So we've worked very hard and long to "see how much we can give for a dollar" in developing this book. There is much more "How to Fish" info. There is way more "Where to Fish" coverage. More lakes, rivers, streams and saltwater. More maps and illustrations. More of everything. Quite simply, this expanded and updated edition is bigger and better. And guess what? It has the same cover price as the previous edition!

The Editor

Fishing Success

In the previous editions of this book we proclaimed that fishing is great in Southern California. Well, guess what? **Fishing is still great**.

There are thousands of lakes, streams and reservoirs, many very accessible to metropolitan areas. Then there are the big inland fisheries like the Salton Sea and Lake Havasu. And last but not least, there are the hundreds of miles of coastline, offshore islands and Baja waters. Anglers here are fortunate to have an immense variety of quality fishing opportunities:

- Rainbow, golden and brown trout in Sierra lakes and streams.

- Largemouth bass, trout, striper, catfish, crappie and bluegill in numerous lakes and reservoirs.

- Surfperch, bass, bonito, barracuda, halibut and croakers in coastal inshore waters.

- Yellowtail, albacore, rockfish, marlin and lingcod in the Pacific.

- Corvina, sargo and tilapia in the Salton Sea.

- Bass, striper, trout, catfish and panfish in the Colorado River Lakes.

- Wahoo, dorado and other exotics in the Pacific off Baja.

And most of this great fishing is accessible, quite simple and requires only modestly priced tackle. An added benefit—fishing is a wonderful way to share the outdoor experience with family or friends.

But the immense variety of the Southern California fishing experience does raise many questions, some major, others just puzzling:

- What size hook (or line) do I use for trout (or catfish)?

- Where are the bass hot spots at Casitas or Hodges?

- How do I catch striper in Havasu or Pyramid?

- If I catch a halibut (or catfish, or a . . .), how do I clean it?

- When is the hot halibut season in Santa Monica Bay?

- What is a spinnerbait?

- Can I fish for bass from shore at Lower Otay?

- Where are the best spots to fish at the Salton Sea?

- How do I clean and cook a corvina?

Fishing in Southern California answers all these questions and many, many more. For all of the types of fish and different locations, it tells how to fish, where to fish and when to fish. It tells what equipment, tackle, rigs, bait and lures to use, how to clean and preserve your catch, and how to cook each fish.

But there are common elements to fishing success. Elements that apply to many Southern California angling situations, from mountain trouting to saltwater pier fishing. And that's what this first chapter is all about.

Confidence

There is one element of fishing success that can't be taught or learned. Rather, it must be self-instilled. I'm talking about self-confidence. Often "how to" fishing articles end with a pep talk on the importance of fishing with confidence—that old Positive Mental Attitude. You know it's corny, but somehow it works.

I personally feel so strongly about the need to have faith in your approach and your tackle that I've reversed things and put this topic first. I love fishing even when I don't catch fish. But I love it even more when I do. Often the only difference between an angler who puts fish on the line and one who just wets his line is attitude. So fish with confidence.

Confidence will make you more attentive and more aware. It keeps your mind in gear. But, most importantly, it will encourage you to experiment, to change baits, or lures, or depths, or location until you find fish. This book tells you all you need to know to catch any kind of fish in Southern California. Just add self-confidence. The positive effects of perseverance, confidence and variety of approach can't be over emphasized.

But you say, "How can I fish with confidence if I'm not sure of what I'm doing." And I say, "Learn all you can, and then put what you've learned to work. You might not know it all, but you probably know enough to catch fish and have fun. And isn't that what it's all about?"

When to Fish?

There is no question that the time of year, the time of month and the time of day all impact on fishing success. More so for some species than others. All life moves in cycles. Fish are no different. For example, it's no coincidence that most of California's fishing records were set in the spring months.

March, April, and May are probably the best months to fish. These are the spawning months for most species. Simply stated, here are the best times to fish.

Time of Year. Spring is best all around, followed by fall. Winter is surprisingly good. Summer, for many species is the worst. Yes, I know about summer vacations; the weather is beautiful and fishing seems to be a natural, warm weather sport, but often the fish don't know this. Or maybe they do! However, some fishing is good in summertime, especially if the proper approaches are followed. The table in the next column highlights the best time of year to fish for each species. It's easy to see why fishing if a four season sport in Southern California.

Time of Day. For most types of fish, during most times of the year, there is little doubt that early morning (from first light until 8 a.m.) and late evening (the 2 to 3 hours before dark) are the best times of day to catch fish. These are the times of day when fish are active and feeding. For some situations night-time is also good. For example, bass fishing after dark on warm summer nights, using noisy, dark surface plugs (in shallow water) can be good. Also, summertime catfishing can be good after 9 p.m. and during the two hours before daybreak.

Time of Month (The Tides). Some would say that the phases of the moon have a great deal to do with fishing success, in any environment. This may or may not be true. But, there is no doubt that tides do impact fishing success in shallower tidal waters like bays. Surf, rock and pier anglers know how tide movements effect fishing. In tidal waters, it's always best to fish on days when there is a big change between high and low tide. Waters move faster, bait and bait fish get moved around, so game fish feed more actively.

The height of the tide varies according to the positions of the sun and moon in relation to the earth. These influences are illustrated below. The best fishing is during spring tide periods. Fish the hours before, through and after a high tide change for peak action.

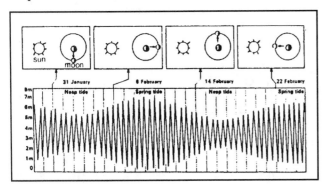

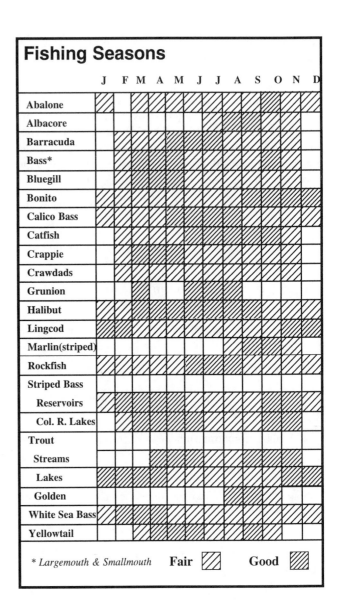

More on the Moon. There is a school of fishing thought that says that the position of the moon (or some say the moon and the sun), on a daily basis, has an effect on the feeding and activity level of fish. These peak activity periods coincide with the moon's strongest gravitational pull which occurs twice each day when the moon is directly above or below a particular point on earth. When the moon is above, it's a major period, and when it's below, it's a minor period according to the theory. These activity periods are published in California outdoor newspapers and in magazines. Or a guide can be purchased to calculate major and minor activity periods each day. If nothing else, it's fun to see if the activity periods coincide with one's own fishing experience.

Where to Fish

This book has tons of "where to fish" information in it. But there are three generalizations about "where to fish" that apply so universally, that they are worthy of special attention.

Fish on the Bottom! To catch many varieties of Southern California fish you've got to fish on or near the bottom. This is true for the following fish:

Bass (even in deep water they're usually near structure)	
Catfish	**Rock Cod**
Halibut	**Striped Bass** (in shallow water)
Lingcod	**Trout** (most often)

Steam trout will rise up for food, but then retreat to the bottom. Trout near shore in lakes are on the bottom. I'd like to emphasize the truism, "fish on the bottom," with this analogy. Most creatures that live on land, actually live on the bottom of a vast sea of atmosphere. This atmosphere is about 100,000 feet deep, yet most creatures live right on the bottom of the atmosphere. Of course, people and all fur bearing animals live on the bottom, but so do most birds and insects. Birds and insects spend most of their time in and around the ground, plants and trees that are part of the atmosphere's bottom structure. Well, the same is true of most fish. Water is their air. And the bottom of the water provides food, shelter and security.

Several popular SoCal saltwater game fish including albacore, barracuda, bonito and marlin are taken in open water (not near the bottom).

Fish at the Right Water Temperature. In big Southern California lakes and reservoirs, the key factor in finding fish during the summer months is water temperature. Lakes stratify into three distinct layers with the coming of summer and stay that way until fall. The middle layer of water, called the thermocline, has a large concentration of dissolved oxygen, bait fish and therefore, trout, salmon and even bass. The thermocline, which provides the right temperature for trout and salmon metabolism, is down from 10 to 80 feet, depending on season and lake characteristics.

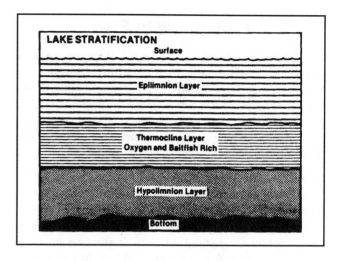

Gauges for measuring water temperature at various depths are available for as little as $5-10. Below is a chart showing the temperatures where you are likely to find fish.

Species	Optimum Temp.	Temp. Range
Trout **(brown and rainbow)**	55-60 °F	44-75 °F
Bass, striped	70-72	60-78
Bass, largemouth	70-72	60-73
Bass, smallmouth	64-66	-
Panfish	-	-
Catfish	-	75-80
Albacore	64	-
Yellowtail	65	-

Fish Don't Like Direct Light. This is one reason why fishing drops off when the morning sun hits a lake. But there are things you can do. For instance, if you're catching fish in a lake early in the day, try deeper down as the light increases. Or, if you're fishing a trout stream, work the shady side. This also applies to lake shores.

Teaching Kids How to Fish

My father died when I was a teenager. But many times he shared his love of fishing with me. In the front of this book I've told a very personal fishing story. It was about how my youngest son came to know and love his grandfather's old lures and tackle box. This story was special to me, but not unique. Fishing brings families together. Teach your children how to fish. Do it for them and for yourself.

Kids and fishing just seem to be made for each other. It's hard to find a youngster that won't jump at the chance to "go fishin'." A good starting age is 3 to 7 years old. And we're not just talking about boys going fishing with their fathers, or older brothers. Over a third of U.S. fishing licenses are sold to women. So a lot of girls learned to fish along the way, and the fathers and mothers are teaching their daughters how to fish in record numbers. One caution: It is not easy, but children can be "turned off" to fishing if parents don't follow some simple guidelines.

Know the Basics. Many parents, who aren't experienced anglers, find out the basics by going fishing with friends who are veteran anglers. And don't be proud. Ask questions. And fish for the same species in the same type of waters, where you are planning on taking your youngster. A fishing guide is another alternative. He or she can teach both parents and youngsters at the same time. They are listed in phone books and they advertise in outdoor publications. Be sure to ask for references, and explain what you expect to achieve on the trip.

Equipment. Youngsters fishing tackle should be easy to operate, light weight, "kid-sized" and somewhat durable. Most experts recommend a spincast reel. These are closed-faced reels that cast and retrieve easily and don't backlash (or tangle the line). One hint: These reels need a little tension on the line to retrieve properly. This is usually of no concern while retrieving in water where a lure or sinker provides the tension. But for "driveway" practice casts and retrieves in store isles, the line right in front of the reel opening should be lightly squeezed between the index finger and thumb of the non-cranking hand. This provides the needed tension so that the line pick-up mechanism in the reel can function. Damage can result if this simple practice is not followed.

Older children, say 9-11 years old, may want to start with an open-faced spinning reel. These are the kind used by most adults. Ask the dealer to explain how to operate them. Match the spincast reel with a short pistol grip rod. Often this combination can be purchased as a package for as little as $10-20. A good rod length is 3 1/2 to 4 feet. Most reels have line already on them. 8-10 pound test line is the best.

A good, well-fitting life jacket is highly recommended for shore, pier or boat fishing. Some kids might put up a fuss, but it's an easy battle to win, and you might just be preventing an unnecessary tragedy.

Practice. And I don't mean practice at the lake or stream. Practice at home, before going fishing. Concentrate on casting and retrieving. Practice plugs are available at tackle stores, or use a small lead sinker. Kneeling behind and slightly above the youngster might be useful on the first attempts. Pick out a target and make a game out of trying to land near it. If you're going to be bait fishing it might also be a good idea to "rig-up" at home. Then when you get to the water, anxious kids can start fishing right away. For kids, I like to use a small snap swivel as the first item at the end of the line. This allows quick change of lures, and easy replacement of lost bait rigs that have been pre-tied and stored in small sandwich bags.

Where to Go. Go close to home. Long drives are just too much for the nervous systems of little anglers. Choose a place where fish are abundant and easy to catch. The size of the fish is secondary. Good possibilities in the Los Angeles area are the fish-for-pay lakes like Anaheim, Santa Ana River Lakes and Irvine. These are well stocked and employees at the lake will provide up-to-date tips and hot spots. Ocean piers are also a good possibility. Call first to assess the bite.

In other parts of the Southland, check for public information on recent trout plants. Recent plants' locales are usually hot spots. Finally, shore anglers need an open shoreline. The only way to keep kids from casting into trees is to have no trees within 100 yards.

Attitude. Simply stated, don't get upset when things go wrong. And they will go wrong. Just try to solve each problem as it comes along, and provide tons of encouragement. And, by all means, when a little guy or gal gets a fish on, don't grab the rod and land it yourself. This advice seems stupid, but in the excitement of the moment many well-meaning parents do this very thing. Let the child try bringing in the fish alone. Give calm advice, based on instructions you communicated earlier (maybe on the ride to the fishing grounds). After a few lost fish, fate will intervene and a fish will be landed. The laughing and cheers will be worth your commitment to patience. And your little one will be very proud.

Final Thoughts. Instill positive values in your children. For example, release undersized fish (a camera will capture the thrill of even a teeny first fish), and follow other fishing regulations. Don't litter. Don't trespass. Buy a fishing license for yourself. Kids under 16 don't need one. One last piece of advice—bring lots of favorite foods and beverages. Little anglers get very hungry.

Casting (also see page 32)

Casting is an integral part of most fishing activities. This is true whether you bait fish with a sliding sinker rig for trout in a lake, or live bait fish for striper on a party boat. And it's also true that better, more accurate casts catch more fish.

Casting with spinning or spincast equipment is quite straightforward, but accurate casting takes some practice. Freshwater or saltwater conventional reel rigs are more difficult to master because of backlash, but good equipment and practice will pay off here too. Novice anglers should read up on the subject at the library and observe more experienced casters whenever possible. Excellent fishing videos are also available for rent or sale, especially at larger tackle dealers.

Fly casting is different. In spinning or bait casting the weight that is cast is concentrated in the lure or bait. And it is the weight that pulls line off the reel. But in fly casting, the offering is virtually weightless, and it is the fly line that is the weight. Fly casting is probably the most difficult casting skill to develop. A good book on the subject is *Fly Fishing From the Beginning*. There are also excellent fly casting videos. Rent them at local tackle shops.

Playing and Landing

A variety of fishing techniques are needed to entice a fish to bite or strike. Once this is accomplished, whether you've got a bass or yellowtail on the other end of your line, there is a certain commonality in playing a larger fish. Here are the elements:

1. Pull the rod up and back forcefully to set the hook. Don't be tentative. Hold the reel handle firmly, so no line is given. After setting, adjust the drag, if necessary.

2. Hold the rod tip up when playing a fish. The rod butt can be held against the stomach area. Lower the rod tip and reel in simultaneously. Stop reeling and pump the rod upwards to move the fish in. Then, reel in again on the down stroke. This rod "pumping" allows you to reel in when tension on the line and terminal tackle is not at its maximum.

3. Never give a fish slack. If it charges, reel in fast. Try to guide fish away from your boat with rod tip high. But if the fish does get under your boat, put the rod tip down into the water to prevent line abrasion or twisting around the outdrive.

4. If your fish runs, let him go against the reel drag. That's what it's for. Then slowly bring him back by reeling in, or if necessary, using the pumping technique. Never reel in when the fish is running against the drag—it twists the line.

5. Keep the rod tip high while landing. This allows the rod to act as a shock absorber and prevents the chance of slack line. Net the fish from below and in front.

Catch and Release

There is a growing awareness among anglers that the fish resource is limited. And some anglers now feel that the ultimate fishing experience is not to "take a limit" but to catch and release as many fish as possible. Of course, no one should keep more fish than they can use, or keep a fish that they don't enjoy eating.

Obviously, catch and release is a personal decision. It's also a practice that can be and should be exercised on a selective basis. Sometimes a fish shouldn't be released; for example, a badly hooked, bleeding fish, or a small rockfish that has been brought up from 50 fathoms, and is dead on arrival. For some reason, I personally don't like to take fish that are about to spawn. I know this is somewhat irrational since it's absolutely true that no matter when you take a fish in its life cycle, you're forever preventing that fish from spawning. But I guess I just feel that when a fish has made it through all the hurdles and survived all the predators and all the hazards, that is has a right to spawn without me interfering. On the other hand, I don't mind taking fish that are in abundant supply or even those that are planted regularly.

When you do want to release fish, there are several things you can do to improve the chances for the fish:

1. Use barbless hooks (or flatten down barbs with pliers) and avoid fishing with bait, if possible. If you do use bait, don't use a sliding sinker rig. Hooks with sliding sinker rigs are often very deep.

2. Time is of the essence. Play and release fish as rapidly as possible. A fish played gently for too long may be too exhausted to recover.

3. Keep the fish in the water as much as possible. A fish out of water is suffocating and, in addition, is twice as heavy. He may seriously injure himself if allowed to flop on the beach or rocks. Even a few inches of water under a thrashing fish acts as a protective cushion.

4. Gentleness in handling is essential. Keep your fingers out of the gills. Do not squeeze small fish . . . they can easily be held by the lower lip. Nets may be helpful provided the mesh does not become entangled in the gills. Hooks and lines catching in nets may delay release, so keep the net in the water.

5. Unhooking. Remove the hook as rapidly as possible with long-nose pliers. If the fish is deeply hooked, cut the leader and leave the hook in. Be quick but gentle — do not roughly tear out hooks. Small fish are particularly susceptible to the shock of a torn-out hook.

6. Reviving. Some fish, especially after a long struggle, may lose consciousness and float belly up. Always hold the fish in the water, heading upstream. Propel it back and forth, pumping water through its gills. When it revives, begins to struggle and can swim normally, let it go to survive and challenge another fisherman.

Fishing Photography

It is no coincidence that this section on Fishing Photography follows the Catch and Release discussion. You see, photography provides a wonderful way to have your fish and release it too. Actually there are several ways to use photography to "keep" fish and release them at the same time. Beyond this, photos are a great way to capture all kinds of fishing memories, even for catches headed for the frying pan.

Skin mounting of trophy fish is now being replaced, by many sportsmen, with acrylic mounts. These plastic mounts are extremely attractive and require that the angler provide good color photos to the taxidermist. A good side view and another looking down along the back are necessary. Measure the fish's length, its girth at the gills, the dorsal fin and the wrist ahead of the tail. Also measure the breadth of the spread out tail. Keep the fish in the water as much as possible while snapping photos and using the tape measure.

If you're not planning on mounting the fish, different photo guidelines are in order. That's because the photo itself becomes the end of the story. Fishing magazines publish a wide array of the best fishing photography. Browse through some of these and pick out the ones that appeal to you. Now, work at developing your ability to see things the way the camera lens sees things. Soon you'll be taking snaps that far surpass the full-length shot of the angler posing with his fish.

Fishing Guides

There are many fine fishing guides in Southern California. Most are specialists and operate in a fairly narrow geographical area, for example, largemouths in the San Diego area or trout in the eastern Sierras. Guides are listed in phone books and they advertise in outdoor publications. Charges can range from $100 to $200 per angler per day. Most guides require two anglers per boat.

Earlier it was suggested that use of a skilled guide was one good approach to teaching children how to fish. Well, it's great for adults too. It allows the angler to learn firsthand about new waters, unfamiliar techniques (e.g. trolling) or an untried species (e.g. marlin).

Telephone prospective guides in the evening. They're out on the water in the daytime. Ask specific questions about charges and what's provided. Often the fee includes boat, tackle, bait and a box lunch. Communicate clearly your purpose in making the trip. Is it for a trophy fish or for knowledge about a specific technique? Ask the guide for two or three references. Be on time the day of your guided trip. Guides are under a great deal of pressure to produce. And they know it will be easier to catch fish earlier in the day.

Hook, Line, Knots and Swivels

Fishing rigs have two ends—the angler's end and the fish's end. On the angler's end you've got rods, reels, clothing, electronics, nets, etc. On the fish's end you've got hooks, line, knots and maybe swivels and lures. Much more money is invested on the angler's end, but when you get a fish on, success often depends on the "loose change" items on the fish's end and how well they've been assembled.

Hooks. An often neglected item is the fishing hook. First, it's important to keep them sharp. Inexpensive little sharpeners are made just for this purpose. Both bait hooks and lure hooks get abused, in use, and in tackle boxes, so do sharpen them regularly.

The designation system used in fishing hook sizing can be confusing for those who don't deal with it regularly. Large hooks (1/10 and up) increase in size as the number increase. (So a 4/0 is a larger hook than a 2/0). Small hooks (1 and down) decrease in size as the number increases. (So a 6 is a larger hook than a 10).

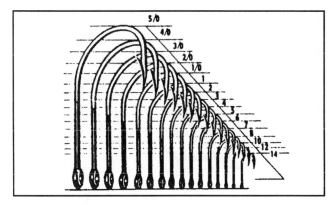

A leading hook manufacturer (Eagle Claw) makes the following hook size recommendations:

Panfish	Bluegill	8 down to 12
	Crappie	4
Bass	Smallmouth	3/0 down to 4
	Largemouth	8/0 down to 4
	Striped	3/0 up to 10/0
Catfish	up to 5# 4 down to 12	
	large	4 up to 8/0
Trout	Rainbow 5 down to 14	
	Brown	5 down to 14
	Steelhead	2 up to 6/0

Sometimes hooks get caught in people rather than in fish. Another leading hook manufacturer (Mustad) provides two hook removal techniques (see diagram). Following removal, allow the wound to be bled freely for a couple of minutes. Then wash thoroughly, clean with alcohol and bandage. Check to see if your tetanus shots are up-to-date. The tips provided apply to routine hook removal only. For serious impalement, see physician immediately.

Finally, a note on terminology: Hooks are sold snelled or unsnelled. A snelled hook has a factory-applied leader attached to it. Unsnelled hooks are bare. Most anglers find snelled hooks to be more convenient for most uses.

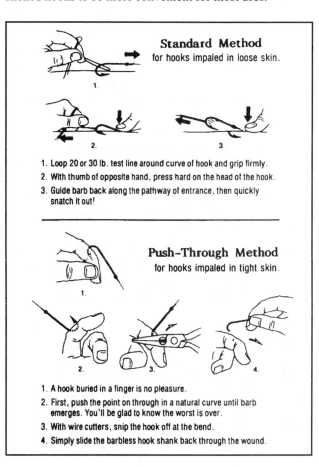

Standard Method
for hooks impaled in loose skin.

1. Loop 20 or 30 lb. test line around curve of hook and grip firmly.
2. With thumb of opposite hand, press hard on the head of the hook.
3. Guide barb back along the pathway of entrance, then quickly snatch it out!

Push-Through Method
for hooks impaled in tight skin.

1. A hook buried in a finger is no pleasure.
2. First, push the point on through in a natural curve until barb emerges. You'll be glad to know the worst is over.
3. With wire cutters, snip the hook off at the bend.
4. Simply slide the barbless hook shank back through the wound.

Fishing Line. Good quality fishing line is a wise investment. And many anglers replace the line on all their reels at the beginning of each fishing season. Monofilament is appropriate for most fishing, and consider the fluorescent feature. It helps immensely in seeing where your bait and line are. Many anglers are now using the new "super lines" made of Spectra or Kevlar fibers. They are either braided or have bundles of small fibers fused under heat into a solid line. Spiderwire Fusion and Berkley Fireline are two examples of popular fused super lines. While these lines are more expensive than nylon monofilament, they also last much longer and are far stronger for their diameter than nylon. They also cast very nicely on both casting and spinning equipment. The only drawback is that tradition knots often slip. The one exception is the Palomar knot (see illustration on following page).

Regardless of what type of line you use, don't use line that is heavier than conditions require. Heavy line impedes the movement of trolled or retrieved lures and it is easier for fish to see.

Many strong fish have snapped good line and escaped because the reel drag was set too tight. After the line absorbs the impact of the strike, the drag must permit the fish to take line off the reel as it makes a run, yet be tight enough to slow it down and eventually tire it out. A good rule is to set the drag at no more than half the pound/test of the line. Remember that the breaking action increases as the spool empties. When fishing deep or in heavy currents, set the drag to about a third of the line's pound/test. To set the drag, attach the line to a reliable spring scale, apply tension and check the pounds of force required to pull it off the reel. Then adjust the drag control to give the desired value. With some experience, a "feel" for proper drag setting is developed, and then it can be set without use of a scale.

Among the things we can do without, along stream banks, lake shores or at the bottom of bays are beverage cans, plastic six-pack holders and monofilament fishing line. Nylon monofilament degrades slowly so the tangle of line stripped off a reel will remain where it's dropped for years. This creates an eyesore, a nuisance to foul the fishing area, and most telling, a lethal hazard for birds and other wildlife. Birds and other animals suffer and die each day because they have been snarled in carelessly discarded monofilament. Let's put an end to this! Discard old line properly. And go a step further—pick up the discarded line that yesterday's air-head angler dropped on the bank.

Knots. A good fishing knot is one that stays tied and one that doesn't weaken the line too much. There are many knots that fit these criteria, but most veteran anglers use only one or two basic knots. The best overall knot is probably the improved clinch knot. It can be used to tie hooks to leaders, swivels to line, etc. There are two versions:

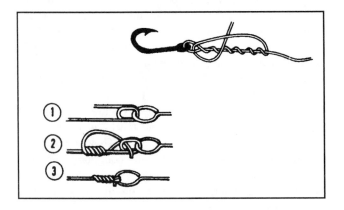

The other popular knot is the Palomar knot. It is especially useful for super lines, but it is also popular for use among saltwater anglers. Here is how it is tied:

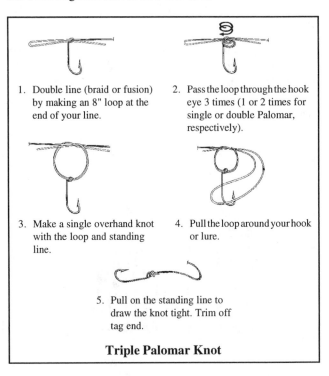

1. Double line (braid or fusion) by making an 8" loop at the end of your line.

2. Pass the loop through the hook eye 3 times (1 or 2 times for single or double Palomar, respectively).

3. Make a single overhand knot with the loop and standing line.

4. Pull the loop around your hook or lure.

5. Pull on the standing line to draw the knot tight. Trim off tag end.

Triple Palomar Knot

Swivels. Swivels are available in a number of shapes and sizes. Their primary purpose is to prevent line twist. Some models have eyes on both ends, while others, called snap swivels, feature a locking device on one end. It is very handy for quickly changing lures. However, the action of some finely tuned lures, like premium brand imitation minnow type lures, may be inhibited by using a snap swivel. Tie these lures

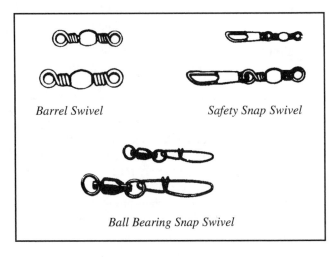

Barrel Swivel   *Safety Snap Swivel*

Ball Bearing Snap Swivel

directly to the line. One tip: Even the highest quality swivels are very inexpensive. Cheap foreign swivels often fall apart, and sometimes don't swivel. So buy good quality.

Fish Attractants and Artificial Baits

There is little doubt that fish have a highly developed sense of smell. Salmon return to their place of origin to spawn by following the faint smell that is unique to each waterway. Attractant and bait manufacturers have done a great deal of experimenting to isolate compounds that attract fish to strike. And there is a growing number of these products on the market. They come in liquid, moldable, formed and even "slime" consistency. Anecdotal evidence among anglers suggest that some of these products, especially the newer ones, are effective in some situations. Liquids and slimes can be sprayed on lures or natural baits. Moldables are packed into or on lures or hooks. It's generally agreed that scented offerings are most effective in slower presentation modes. This gives the scent a chance to be spread in the water. It's always fun to experiment with fish attractants. Put some on one bait or lure and not on another, and see what happens.

Downriggers

More and more anglers in Southern California are using downriggers, in both freshwater and saltwater. Billfish, trout, stripers and sharks are among the game fish being targeted. Often these fish, and others, are down deep. Traditionally, trolling planes, leadcore line and keel sinkers have been used to troll offerings down where the fish are lurking. Often heavy line, stout rods and large reels are required. The advantage of the downrigger is that it enables the angler to regulate fishing depth while allowing the fish to be fought using relatively light gear.

A downrigger is essentially a winch with a heavy (usually 6 to 10 pounds) weight attached to a cable. The cable allows

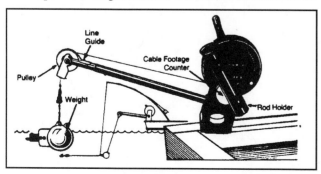

the weight to be raised or lowered to the desired fishing depth. The line holding the bait or lure is attached to the downrigger weight using a spring loaded release clip. When a fish hits, the line is released from the weight allowing the fish to be fought on unencumbered tackle.

Downriggers, like the rest of your tackle, should be tailored to the kind of fishing you expect to do. For offshore saltwater fishing you'll want a heavy-duty model made exclusively of non-corrosive materials. For most freshwater fishing from smaller craft, you'll want to choose something lighter and more convenient.

Fishing Electronics

There was a time, not too long ago, when fishing electronics meant just a fish finder, either with a paper graph output or a flasher output. But now fish locating electronics means a whole lot more. First, fish finders have been available with paper graph, video, LCD (liquid crystal diode) and flasher outputs. Today, LCDs dominate the market. Beyond profiling the slope of the bottom and identifying bait fish schools and individual game fish, some units offer boat speed and surface water temperature read out, split screens, dual frequency operations, integral Loran C, etc. Recently, I was in the market to replace my fish finder with some of this current technology—the options and alternatives were mind boggling! I almost drove my wife crazy by pouring over catalogs and asking questions of salespeople. It took me several months to finally make a choice!

Beyond fish finders, there are other fishing electronics worth considering. A VHF marine radio is essential on the ocean and the bays, and not a bad idea on large inland waters. Loran C and Global Positioning Systems (GPS) instruments are great for returning to favorite fishing grounds, and for helping find your way home in the fog. Some largemouth bass anglers also use pH guides and Color-C-Lectors to improve their success.

Rods and Reels

In the "How to Catch . . . " chapter of this book, detailed catching instructions are provided for each Southern California game fish. There are 24 of them in all. Rod and reel recommendations are made in each section. Not only are the most desirable rod and reel combinations noted, but also alternatives that often work just as well. Happily, you don't need 24 rod and reel sets to enjoy all the fishing experiences in this book.

Often, one rod and reel is useful in several types of fishing. For example, a lightweight spinning outfit can be used to troll or cast for average striper (6-10 pounds). This same light spinning outfit can be used for trout (both lake and stream), bass casting and panfishing. In fact, an angler doesn't even need a fly rod and reel to fly fish, but don't tell avid fly anglers this. A casting bobber on spinning equipment will deliver a fly. See Catching Trout (in Streams). And talking about stream trout fishing, one hot item now is the mini-spinning outfit—a 5 foot rod and tiny reel. It's fun to use, but spinners can also usually be delivered effectively using a 7 foot rod and normal sized reel filled with a 4 pound test line.

Saltwater equipment is usually more specialized. There are light (12-15 pound test line) and medium (20-25 pound test line) live bait rod and reel outfits. And then there are rods for jigging that are designed for 20-50 pound test line. Bottom fishing and surf casting equipment are also quite distinct. Try to purchase equipment that best suits the type of fishing you do most often. For many anglers, a light or medium weight saltwater spinning outfit is a good choice. But make sure it has a strong, smooth drag mechanism and the capacity to hold 200 yards of 10-20 pound test line.

Fortunately, rods and reels of good quality (not gold-plated, but good quality) are not that expensive. But, before considering a specialized rod and reel, first consider using what you've got on hand. Look at what others are using when you get to the water. I'm always surprised at the variety. Besides, the fish doesn't know what's on the other end of the line. Good line, tied well, a decent drag and know-how will land most fish.

Maps

First, let me emphasize that none of the maps included in this book (or in any fishing book, for that matter) are to be used for navigational purposes. Their only intent is to indicate where the fish can be found. Navigational maps for coastal and bay waters are available at marine and boating stores. These are published by the National Oceanic and Atmospheric Administration (U.S. Department of Commerce).

There are other good maps that are especially useful to anglers:

U.S. Forest Service Maps—especially useful in determining which land is publicly owned, and to locate access to public waters.

U.S. Geological Survey—good for detailed topographical features, and for locating out-of-the-way fishing spots.

U.S. Bureau of Land Management—for streams and lakes in this agency's jurisdiction.

Park Scenic Maps—both federal and state parks publish maps that can be quite helpful.

Fishing Spot Location—this book lists Loran coordinates of over 2,000 saltwater fishing locales off Southern California.

Topographical Maps— these are very useful for underwater lake terrain and mountain topography.

Fishing . . . SoCal Style

Fishing in Southern California is much like a sumptuous smorgasbord. And what's so wonderful is that there are so many ways to participate in this feast. Some of the most popular and productive options are profiled in this chapter. It starts out with a collection of Pacific Ocean techniques. Then there's a selection of freshwater techniques, from night fishing and fly fishing to ice fishing. Finally, there's a potpourri of unrelated, but key topics.

Party Boat Fishing

Well over a half million anglers enjoy ocean fishing on a party or sport fishing boat each year in Southern California. To say the least, this is a popular and relatively inexpensive way to pursue saltwater fish.

Most party boats take reservations from individuals and operate on a daily schedule. Charter boats are also available for group rental. Party boat anglers range from regulars who go out every week to vacationers from Peoria who have never even seen the ocean, let alone fished it. One appeal to newcomers is that no equipment or prior knowledge is needed. Rod and reels can be rented (for about $3 to 5 a day). Burlap sacks used to hold the catch are sold for less than a dollar. Bait is included in the price of the trip, and fish filleting services are available on board or dockside at a modest cost. And there are plenty of helpful people around to explain the best way to catch fish. Observing those who are most successful help the newcomers with the finer points.

Party boats are large, safe, well-equipped fishing machines. They have galleys, washrooms, lounges, and other amenities. But no matter what the season and the shore weather, it's best to bring along warm clothing. It gets cool out on the water. Dress in layers. Then you can build up or strip down depending on conditions.

Spring and summer trips most often concentrate on the exciting live bait bite for calico bass, barracuda, bonito and yellowtail. Late summer and early fall trips are scheduled for yellowfin tuna and albacore in some years. Winter runs focus on bottom fishing for rockfish. The techniques used for all these fish are described in the "How to Catch . . ." chapter of this book.

It's always best to make a reservation in advance. There are several types of trips including half-day (either morning or afternoon), three-quarter day and full-day. Call for specifics. Many anglers bring along their own rod, reel, hooks, jigs and so on. Most boats prohibit ice chests, and no alcoholic beverages may be brought on board. Beer is available in most galleys.

Costs of trips vary, of course, but are quite reasonable. For example, a half-day trip is less than $20.00. All party boats are equipped with a live bait tank and chumming (attracting sport fish to the boat by tossing scoops of bait fish into the water) is a big feature of most fishing trips. While baiting your hook, be sure to select a good, lively fish from the bait tank. The most active bait usually get the strike. And don't hesitate to change bait often. Some skippers suggest changing bait as often as every 30 seconds. Live bait fishing is done for bass, barracuda, bonito, yellowtail and yellowfin (after a school is found by trolling). Live bait rods have a sensitive tip and stiff butt. About 20-pound monofilament on a conventional (level-wind is a little easier to handle) or heavy-duty spinning reel completes the live bait rig.

On an anchored boat, anglers often prefer a stern (aft) fishing position. To make it fair to all anglers, many skippers rotate anglers on a pre-announced schedule. But some anglers catch fish more regularly than others, no matter what position they are in. These are the people to watch and to learn from.

Where to Fish. Party or sport fishing boats operate out of over a dozen locations (or landings) along the Southern California coast. Specific operators are listed in the telephone book. Here are the landings from north to south: Morro Bay, Avila Beach, Goleta, Santa Barbara, Ventura, Oxnard, Port Hueneme, Malibu, Santa Monica, Redondo Beach, San Pedro, Long Beach, Seal Beach, Newport Harbor, Dana Harbor, Oceanside, Mission Bay, San Diego.

Surf Fishing

I always think of William Conrad, casting into the surf at sunset on a beautiful beach, when I think of surf fishing. He started his outdoor program on television with this scene, year after year. And why not? Surf fishing is man and nature at its best. It's just you, the roaring breakers, sea birds and salt spray . . . and hopefully the fish.

For those who demand more than sea birds and salt spray, there are practical reasons why so many people enjoy surf fishing:

- There are miles and miles of accessible beaches to fish.

- It can be done year around.

- The necessary equipment is inexpensive.

- Bait is often free.

- Fish can be caught without a great deal of skill.

Fishing Techniques. Some of the best surf fishing spots are listed later in this section. But exactly where on a beach to fish is important. It's best, if possible, to scout a beach at low tide. Steeply sloping beach areas are best. Look for holes and channels where the surf is not breaking. When the tide floods in, these become the feeding grounds for fish. The rising tide up to high tide, and an hour or two after, are usually the best times to fish.

Southern California anglers catch a good variety of fish, including California halibut, spotfin and yellowfin croaker, California corbina, barred surfperch and walleye surfperch. The basic approach for taking all these fish is the same. Cast out a rig consisting of a 2 to 6 ounce pyramid sinker at the end of a rodholder and wait for the bite. If nothing happens in a few minutes, slowly move the rig in about 3 to 5 feet and try this new location. Some novices are tempted to run back from the beach, especially when a large fish is hooked. This is not a good idea. Instead, reel the fish in steadily and move back only near shore. Time your retrieve with the surf so the momentum of a breaker will skid the fish up on the sand. Run and grab him under a gill cover and quickly move back to higher ground.

Tackle and Equipment. As mentioned earlier, tackle and equipment requirements are quite minimal. All you need are the following:

Rod: 10-12 foot surf spinning rod with two-handed grip.

Reel: Saltwater spinning reels are most popular. It should hold 200-250 yards of 15 to 20 pound monofilament line.

Other: Pyramid sinker (assorted 2 to 6 ounce—use the smallest that tide and wave conditions will allow), surf leaders (available at most tackle counters), hooks (#2, #6), sand spike rodholder, and a big pail (for bait and your catch).

Bait and Rigging. The basic rig is straightforward.

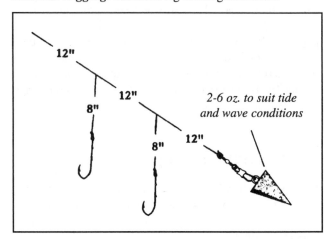

The hook size depends on the fish:

Fish	Typical Catch (pounds)	Hook Size
California halibut	4-8	#2
Spotfin croaker	3-6	#2
California corbina	3-4	#2
Barred surfperch	1	#6
Walleye surfperch	1/4	#6

Most anglers prefer frozen anchovies when fishing for halibut. Some surf anglers like to slowly and continuously retrieve through holes and slopes one of the two rigs shown in the Halibut section. Perch, both barred and walleye, are suckers for blood worms and sand crabs. Blood worms are natives of Maine and are available from bait shops. Soft-shelled sand crabs and another free bait, mussels, are gathered by anglers themselves. Hook the sand crab up through the tail end with the hook tip barely showing. Hook the mussel through the tough gristle-like edge. Croaker also hit blood worms, sand crabs and mussels, as do corbina. If possible, it's probably best to be prepared to toss out several of these baits and let the fish decide. Cut pieces of frozen squid is another good alternative. These strips stay on the hook very well.

Where to Fish. Actually any accessible surf has the potential of being a good surf fishing location. But some locations are more attractive and have developed a reputation as productive fishing stretches. Working south along the coast, here are some of the best:

San Luis Obispo County: Hearst Memorial and Pismo State Beaches (both for perch and jacksmelt).

Santa Barbara County: Jalama Beach County Park (perch), Gaviota State Park (halibut in spring and summer), El Capitan State Beach (perch), Carpenteria State Beach (perch).

Ventura County: San Buenaventura and Point Mugu State Beach (both for perch, halibut and croakers).

Santa Monica Bay Area: Zuma Beach County Park (perch, halibut, croakers), Dockweiler State Beach, Manhattan State Beach, Hermosa Beach, Redondo Beach (all offer perch, corbina and some halibut).

Orange County: Bolsa Chica and Huntington State Beaches and Balboa Peninsula beaches (perch and corbina).

San Diego County: San Onofre State Beach (croaker); Carlsbad State Beach (corbina and croaker); Leucadia, Torrey Pines and La Jolla State Beaches (corbina); Silver Strand State Beach (corbina, croaker).

Artificial Reef Fishing

Ever heard of thigmotropism? I didn't think so. And I willingly admit that I hadn't heard the word either. But fishing experts tell me that thigmotropism refers to the tendency of fish to orient close to solid objects. Historically some of the best Southern California ocean fishing grounds have been the inner and outer banks. These are natural formations that offer excellent fishing opportunities. Unfortunately, many of the banks are 10, 20, 50 or even 100 miles offshore, reachable only by party boats or large private boats.

Over the years the California Department of Fish and Game has been experimenting with and developing a series of artificial reefs along the Southern California coast. These have proven to be excellent fishing locales for near-shore saltwater anglers. Most of the reefs are less than a mile offshore, and some are even within casting distance of the local piers. Roughly, these reefs are located in about 40 to 120 feet of water, and cover areas up to 35 acres. Small boat anglers can tap into sand bass, kelp bass, surfperch, sheepshead, croakers, sargo, sculpin and halibut.

In 1989 the Department of Fish and Game published an excellent artificial reef guide. It covers 25-plus reefs from Atascadero to Mission Bay. This 73-page guide, entitled *A Guide to the Artificial Reefs of Southern California*, pinpoints reef location (loran coordinates and bearings), acreage, water depth and primary fish species. It is available from the Department of Fish and Game offices for about $5.00. Pick up a copy, and then you can take advantage of thigmotropism.

Kelp Fishing

Long before humans were building artificial reef habitat in the near-shore waters off Southern California, nature was growing massive underwater forests that are great fish attractants. These kelp beds provide food and shelter for an amazing array of game fish, including calico bass, barracuda, bonito, a variety of rockfish, white sea bass and yellowtail.

Kelp forests range all along the Southern California coast. There are also major kelp fishing grounds at Catalina Island, San Clemente Island, and at the Channel Islands off Santa Barbara. See the "Pacific Ocean Fishing" chapter in this book for lots of information on specific kelp beds. Many of these areas are highlighted on this chapter's maps.

Two more notes on kelp fishing: sometimes kelp beds are not visible on the surface because of current, tides and swells. Therefore, closer observations is sometimes required to spot promising kelp bed fishing grounds. And finally, don't overlook floating kelp paddies. These drifting tangles of kelp often provide cover for bonito, yellowtail, or even yellowfin.

Pier Fishing

Pier fishing is a special way to fish the Pacific Ocean. Often there is a fellowship and spirit among these anglers that you don't find in other situations. Maybe that's because a number of people share the same experience and the same piece of ocean. Or maybe it's just because there are so many regulars.

Southern California offers some of the best saltwater pier fishing you'll find anywhere. And there are lots of choices with piers ranging from Santa Barbara all the way down to the Mexican border. Almost all are public and free. And there are added bonuses: No fishing license is needed on public piers, most piers offer night fishing, and it's almost impossible to get seasick on a fishing pier.

Pier and barge anglers do quite well depending on season, locale and conditions. Among the species caught are halibut, croaker, rockfish, mackerel, surfperch, bonito and yellowtail. Often the fish caught are quite large.

Techniques, Tackle and Equipment. Fishing techniques vary depending on the species being sought. Many times anglers cast out a baited rig (like a surf fishing rig) and wait for a bite. Fishing straight down from the rod tip is also popular. Perch which frequent the pilings are taken this way. Halibut anglers know that they must keep their offerings moving, so they cast out a halibut rig or jig and slowly retrieve it through likely spots like depressions. Bonito and some other species can be caught using a bobber and hooked anchovy.

A good rule is to use live bait whenever possible. Many piers have a bait shop, or there is one nearby. Soft artificials and silver spoons are also good bets.

Any type of rod and reel made has been used by pier anglers, but since we're talking good-sized fish, tackle should be hefty enough for the fish being sought. A common mistake is to use overly heavy equipment.

For good-sized fish (like bonito, yellowtail or halibut), use a heavy freshwater or light-medium saltwater rod (6 to 8 feet) and a reel capable of holding at least 100 yards of 10 to 25 pound line that has a decent drag system (either spinning or conventional). Popular baits include anchovies, squid, clams, pile worms, blood worms.

Other things you'll need are a big pail (for your catch), a long piece of clothesline, and a crab net. The net is used to raise up good-sized fish from the water line to the pier level. Have a fellow angler operate the net and be sure the fish is tired out before netting and raising it.

Timing is all important to successful pier fishing. Since we can't take the pier to the fish, we've got to go to the pier when the fish are there. And most fish are not there most of the time. They come and go, often in as little as several days or several weeks. This is where local, timely information is essential. Keep in frequent telephone contact with local bait shops. When fish are there, go after them.

At many piers, tide movements can also affect the bite. A large swing in tides (a large difference between high and low tide) marks a good day to fish. Another good time is just before, during and after high tide. A morning incoming tide can be good, but this isn't always the case. Some days the fish are just there and biting no matter what, especially if the bait fish are near the pier.

One fun way to get to know more about techniques that work at a particular pier is to stroll out and observe for an hour or two. You'll see all ages and types of people enjoying pier fishing. And don't hesitate to strike up a conversation or two, especially with anglers who look like regulars. A hint—look for people with more equipment and skill. Many anglers are happy to talk. It's part of the whole scene. Slip in the questions that come to mind between their fish stories.

There are a number of fishing piers along the Southland coast. A list is included here and there is additional information in the "Pacific Ocean Fishing" chapter of this book. Piers offer good facilities including benches, bait (some have live bait), beverages and food, washrooms, fish cleaning tables, etc.

Southland Fishing Pier Locations	
Goleta Point	San Pedro
Santa Barbara	Belmont Shore
Port Hueneme	Seal Beach
Point Mugu	Huntington Beach
Paradise Cove	Newport Beach (2)
Malibu	South Laguna
Santa Monica	San Clemente
Venice	Oceanside
El Segundo	La Jolla
Redondo Beach	San Diego Bay
Hermosa Beach	Imperial Beach
King Harbor	

Goleta Pier is just north of Santa Barbara. From Hwy. 101, take the UC-Santa Barbara exit to Sandspot Road and you're there. This public pier offers lots of calicos and sand bass, various perch and some halibut. Both this pier and *Sterns Wharf* in downtown Santa Barbara are lit for nighttime action. Fishing is usually better at Goleta, but there is less wind at Sterns.

Pt. Hueneme near Oxnard is a good perch, bonito, halibut and shark (thresher and sand) pier. Crabbing is also good.

Malibu Pier is at 23,000 Pacific Coast Hwy. in Malibu. It is private and a fee is charged. But Malibu is also one of the hottest halibut piers. Late March and April are usually the best times. Malibu anglers also reel in mackerel, bonito, tomcod, perch and corbina.

The *Redondo Beach Pier* is at the foot of Torrence Boulevard. This free pier offers a variety of perch, tomcod, mackerel and halibut. Jigs, mussels, anchovies and sand crabs are the most popular baits.

Hermosa Pier is on the Los Angeles waterfront. Take Aviation St. to Pacific Coast Hwy. Turn on Pier Ave. to the pier. Perch and halibut are two prime attractions.

Seal Beach Pier is located at the foot of Main Street in the city of Seal Beach off the Pacific Coast Hwy. Nighttime anglers do well on sharks and bat rays. Daytime action includes a little bit of everything.

South Laguna and San Clemente Piers produce lots of spotfin croakers and corbina. Bonito runs also attract local pier fans.

Shelter Island Municipal Pier at Shelter Island in San Diego Bay is a prime night fishing bet for shovelnose sharks and bat rays. Daylight produces halibut, calico and sand bass, mackerel and croaker.

Imperial Beach Pier is about five miles north of Tijuana off Interstate 5. The take here includes halibut, calico and sand bass, opaleye, croaker and corbina, bonito, barracuda and small yellowtail. This recently reconstructed pier now extends 1,500 feet out into the Pacific. To get there, exit off I-5 or 805 at Palm Ave (Hwy. 75), go west three miles to Seacoast Dr., and then south to Evergreen.

Barges. Unfortunately there aren't as many fishing barges as there once was. A fishing barge is a giant fishing platform anchored permanently over a good fishing area, like a reef or underwater canyon. In a lot of respects, it's like an anchored party boat. And the fishing techniques are the same as described in the "How to Catch . . . " chapter of this book. For example, bottom rockfishing from a barge is the same as from a party boat. And barges are nice because they are less likely to cause seasickness.

The barges still operating in the Southland are unique and special. They are safe, have bait and snack shops, and their shore boats operate on a regular schedule. Depending on the season, barge anglers can catch barracuda, yellowtail, calico bass, sand bass, rockfish, as well as inshore species. Southland fishing barges are at Redondo Beach, Seal Beach, Belmont Pier and Santa Monica Pier.

Rock, Jetty and Breakwater Fishing

There are some things rock anglers know before they even begin fishing. They know they'll catch some fish. They know they'll get wet sooner or later. And they know the experience at the margins of land and sea will be special. But there are some things they don't know. For instance, they don't know what kinds of fish they will catch, or how many hooks, sinkers, jigs and fish they will lose because of snags and hang-ups on the rocks. Fortunately the best bait is free, sinkers and hooks are cheap, and a dry change of clothing just takes some forethought. So the good side of rockfishing surely outweighs the bad.

But a word of caution is necessary. People die every year walking along slippery, moss-covered ocean front rocks and cliffs. So please exercise caution, and wear shoes that provide good traction.

Fishing Techniques. Rockfishing is one of the first ways man took food from the sea. But today, rock anglers work both natural rock formations as well as jetties and breakwaters.

Rockfish (over a dozen varieties), calico bass, sand bass, cabezon, opaleye and croaker are just some of the fish that are caught. It's not unusual to catch a half dozen varieties on one outing. And the nice thing is that only one basic approach is needed.

Most say that rockfishing is at its best on an incoming morning tide. Anglers sometimes like to arrive before sunrise to gather mussels (for bait) and scout the rock formations before the water covers them over. Fishing is often good up to one hour past high tide. By the way, calico bass, a delicious and highly prized catch, often only bite in the first hour of daylight.

Good spots to fish include deep slots or passageways between rocks and pockets where there is some wave action and surging. Quiet water is usually not productive. Another tip—you usually don't need to cast long distances to find fish. The best spot is often right below where you are standing. The fish you're after have moved in with the tide to feed in and about the rocks. Sometimes anglers drop a jig straight down in water 5 or 10 feet deep.

Another key to successful rockfishing is to keep moving. Try a good looking spot for only a short time, and then move to another. If the fish are there, they'll hit right away. Speaking of hits . . . fish in this habitat are aggressive eaters. They hit hard and then shoot for cover; therefore, set the hook immediately and don't give any line. Keep the fish moving in slowly and steadily. Abrupt yanks can tear out the hook.

Landing a hooked fish is often a challenge. Smaller ones can be lifted out of the water. If you're lucky, there will be a good miniature bay or shallow where you can guide your catch. Another good approach is to use a surge of water to bring the fish up on a flat that will be aground when the water recedes.

Casting is the basic technique used in rockfishing. A baited hook or jig is cast out to a likely spot and then retrieved. The slowest possible retrieve is usually best. Keep the line taut on the retrieve, always being alert for bites and snags. Maneuvering or speeding up a retrieve for a brief moment will often prevent a snag. If the pool is open, allow the offering to settle a little before retrieving. If you're fortunate enough to be fishing straight down, yo-yo your offering up and down. In some situations, a bobber can be used to help catch fish. Put it about 2 feet above the hook. Now you can bait fish in spots where a sinking rig would result in snags. Kelp-covered areas are one possibility.

Tackle and Equipment. Most anglers use light tackle. A 6 to 7 foot medium spinning outfit loaded with 10 to 15 pound test line is popular. Bait casting equipment is also used. Heavier rods and reels are used by some. Accurate casts are a must, so use equipment that allows you to accomplish this.

A backpack is good for carrying hooks, sinkers, bobbers, pliers, knife, towel, snacks and maybe a second pair of tennis or jogging shoes. A gunny sack is fine for holding your catch. Keep it wet and in the shade, when possible. Some anglers use tide pools, safely above the swells, as a good spot to put fish, once on a stringer.

Bait, Lures and Rigging. The most popular rockfishing bait is probably mussels. Pry them off the rocks and open them with a knife. Here's how: Locate the water intake hole. Insert the point of your knife there and cut around to the other side. Once cut, it opens up easily. Now use the knife to cut out the strong portion in the middle along with the adjoining more delicate portion. Thread the hook through the tougher section and you're set to fish. Don't forget to check your bait frequently.

Other baits that work include cut pieces of frozen squid and anchovy. Surprisingly, moss is a good bait for opaleye and blue runners (half-moon), but mussels also work. Anglers

twist the moss into a rope and then weave it onto the hook until it's secure.

Rigging for rockfishing is best when kept simple. This prevents lots of snags. Most anglers use a single hook, often tied directly to the main line. Weight is provided by a sinker up about a foot above the hook. Split shot, rubber core sinkers or clinch-on sinkers are all used. An egg-shaped sliding sinker put on the line before the hook is tied on is also a workable rig. The cardinal rule for all of these is to use as little weight as possible. Use just enough to make the cast. Then your offering will settle slower, a slower retrieve will be possible, and less snags and hang-ups will result.

Bait holder hook in the #1 to #6 size range are best. The bigger hooks (like #1) are best for cabezon, rockfish and calico bass. Small hooks (like #6) are good for fish like opaleyes. Speaking of hooks, they're the cause of most hang-ups. It often helps to use a pliers to turn in the tip of the hook (toward the shank) a little ways.

If you're willing to take the risk of losing more expensive offerings, leadhead jigs are very effective rockfishing lures. Jigs like Scampi, Clouts, and Scrounger are popular, and often deadly on calico bass, for example. Twin tail and curly tail models are both good.

Where to Fish. There are many good places to fish rocks and jetties. Dozens are described in the "Pacific Ocean Fishing" chapter of this book. Here's another list of good places:

LOS ANGELES COUNTY

Leo Carillo State Beach
Escondido Beach
Corral Beach State Park
Santa Monica State Park
Ballona Lagoon, Venice
Marina Del Rey (No. & So. Jetties)
Ballona Creek (So. Jetty)
Kings Harbor Breakwater & Jetty (Redondo Beach)
Palos Verdes Estates
Pt. Vicente County Park
Abalone Cove County Park
Royal Palms State Beach
Pt. Fermin Park
San Pedro Breakwater
Long Beach Basin Breakwater
Mouth of LA River
Alamitos Bay West Jetty

ORANGE COUNTY

San Gabriel River (So. Jetty)
Newport Bay (No. & So. Jetty)
Corona Del Mar State Beach
Laguna Beach
Aliso Beach
Niguel Park
Dana Pt. Harbor Breakwater
South Dana Pt. Harbor Jetty

SAN DIEGO COUNTY

South Oceanside Harbor Jetty
San Luis Rey River Jetty
Goldfish Pt. South
La Jolla Hermosa Park
Palisades Park
Pt. Medanos Jetty
Sunset Cliffs
Pt. Loma Naval Reservation
Cabrillo National Monument

Night Fishing

Nighttime is the right time to fish in Southern California. Yes, I know there is a common perception that night fishing is illegal in California. And, it is in some waters and for salmon and trout in some districts and waters. But legal night fishing has much to offer. First, and most important, fishing is probably better in most waters and for most species than at any other time. In lakes, large fish move up to feed in shallow water losing much of their caution. In fresh and salt water, pier lighting attracts bait fish and pursuing game fish. Additionally, night fishing offers a level of tranquility and solitude not often available in the daylight.

Nighttime fishing locales should be scouted in the daylight. After dark or before dawn boat anglers should move at slow speeds and always use running lights. Shore anglers, in most spots, need lanterns and flashlights. Surface fishing techniques work well for trout, largemouth bass, and stripers, even in the heat of summer. Cast surface plugs for trophy-sized bass. Troll plugs for trout and stripers. Often the best nights are on or around full moons. Be sure to check with a current copy of *California Sport Fishing Regulations* before planning your nighttime angling outing.

Fly Fishing

Fly fishing to most people means mountain stream trout fishing. But fly fishing in Southern California can and does mean much more. Fly anglers pursue SoCal trout, panfish, black bass, striper, as well as saltwater species. But anglers considering getting into fly fishing should weigh the pluses and minuses. Fly fishing is an active sport. It involves wading, continuous casting and working the water. A good deal of walking to good spots and wading on slippery rock is required. On the plus side, the scenery is often breathtaking. But fly fishing tackle and gear is generally more expensive than spinning equipment, and fly anglers have more of it. Fly anglers tend to lose more hooked fish than bait or lure anglers because the single small hook that is used is almost always set in the lip area. But this makes the catch and release process much easier for the angler and the fish. Maybe the most important consideration is that fly fishing probably requires more practice and knowledge than most other kinds of angling—for some this is a plus, for others a minus.

Artificial lure fishing of any kind involves the deft presentation of a man-made product that simulates food items in the fish's normal diet. In fly fishing, adult insects, immature insects, crustaceans and forage fish are simulated by various "flies." Dry flies emulate adult insects; wet flies suggest drowned adult insects. Nymphs depict immature aquatic insects, while streamers are designed to simulate bait fish, water worms or leeches. Casting skills need to be developed to get the "fly" at or near the ideal fishing location, and good retrieval techniques are essential to impart the most enticing and natural action to the fly as it is moved through the strike zone.

Tackle selection is critical for good results. Unbalanced equipment can make life miserable. Here are some guidelines.

Fish	Rod	Line	Reel Spool
	(length, ft.)	(weight)	(diam., in.)
Trout	7 - 9	5, 6, 7	3 - 3 $\frac{1}{2}$
Panfish	(same as trout)		
Bass	8 - 9	7, 8	3 $\frac{1}{2}$
Lt. Saltwater	9 - 9 $\frac{1}{2}$	9, 10	4
Hvy. Saltwater	9	11, 12	4

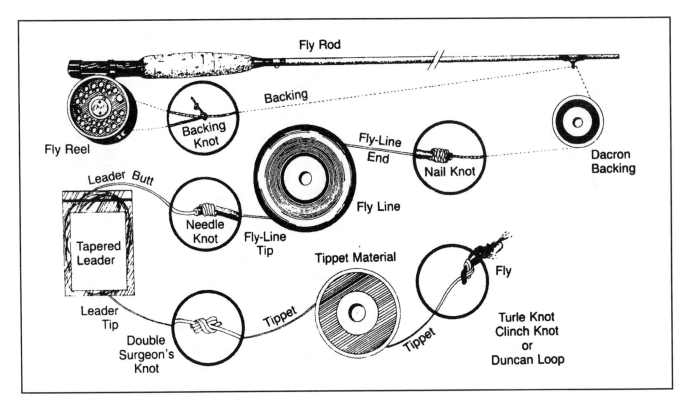

Casting classes often provide balanced outfits that give a beginner a taste for proper setups. Matched outfits (including rod, line and reel) are also marketed by several companies.

There are literally thousands of flies on the market. Here are categories for each game fish.

Fish	Dry Flies	Wet Flies	Nymph Flies	Streamer Flies
Rainbow Trout	X	X	X	X
Brown Trout	X	X	X	X
Brook Trout			X	X
Panfish	X	X		
Smallmouth Bass			X	X
Largemouth Bass	X		X	X
Striped Bass				X

Fly fishing skills are easy to learn because of the numerous clubs, classes and seminars that are readily available. There are dozens of fly fishing clubs in California, many of which offer reasonably priced instruction at various skill levels. Fly fishing shops provide instruction on casting, fly tying and fishing techniques. Several leading tackle manufacturers and magazines also offer fly fishing schools. There are even some excellent video tapes available for rent or sale.

For more information on fly fishing see the Trout (in Streams) section of the "How to Catch . . . " chapter.

Light and Ultralight Fishing

There is a growing movement in California towards the use of lighter fishing tackle, lighter line and smaller, more subtle baits. And it's taking place across the fishing spectrums from mountain trouting to saltwater bottom fishing. Reasons for this trend are numerous. Many anglers consider fishing with lighter tackle to be more of a challenge and more exciting. Others feel it's more sporting in this period of increased pressure on fishing resources. Some anglers are using more ultralight tackle and techniques because it produces more hook-ups. That's because small offerings match the fishes' feeding habits more closely and simply because the fish can't see the light line.

For all these reasons the march to lighter tackle is on. Here are some examples. 1) Largemouth bass anglers are finding that bucketmouths, who are used to eating 2 to 3 inch crawdads and shad, are more likely to strike artificial offerings in this same size range. Ultralight bass tackle matched with 2-6 pound monofilament line is used to deliver these plugs and soft baits. 2) Traditional freshwater largemouth bass tackle is being used in the Pacific Ocean for rockfish, kelp fishing and so on. 3) Striper anglers are using medium-weight trout outfits. 4) Trout anglers are using 2-4 pound monofilament teamed with 5 to 5 1/2 foot graphic spinning rods. 5) More saltwater trollers are using light tackle matched with downriggers.

But there is a down side to lighter fishing tackle. Obviously, when you hook a lunker, it's more likely to break off. Ultralighters will respond, "Therein lies the challenge and excitement." And they have a point. For example, in December 1996, Kevin Saum of Anaheim finessed a 20.1-pound rainbow trout to shore with two-pound test line at the Santa Ana River Lakes in Orange County, shattering the old lake record of 18.8-pounds by over a pound and potentially setting a line class world record for that pound test line. But just a few days later Frank Murata of Norwalk caught a 23.1-pound rainbow to break the Santa Ana River Lakes record yet again—and he also did it with two-pound test. Most anglers have never caught a fish—any kind of fish—that size on any tackle. For more information on the trend towards lighter fishing tackle and line see the "How to Catch . . ." chapter of this book.

Float Tubing (also see page 173)

Here is another trend in SoCal angling. For those not familiar, a float tube is a refined "inner tube." The angler "sits" in the center of the tube on a built-in crotch affair. Waders are good in colder water. Small foot-mounted swim fins are used to move around in the water. These single-person belly boats are marvelous for shallow-water pond and lake fishing. Anglers can silently maneuver along shore while spin or fly casting for trout, bass or panfish. The solitude and closeness to the water, birds and fish make float tubing a unique and very pleasant fishing experience. It's also very productive—just ask a float tuber. One caution: An offshore wind is the enemy of the float tuber. Some belly boaters even use a 100-200 yard rope tethered to shore to make sure they don't get blown too far out into a big lake. Pack-in anglers find float tubes to be a great asset on small, back-country lakes.

Pack-in Fishing

The Sierra Nevada Mountains and the other Southern California mountain ranges cover lots of territory. Most of it is accessible by car, pick-up, or 4-wheel drive. But there are some great fishing spots that can only be reached on foot or on horseback. These high mountain lakes and streams combine good-to-excellent trouting with breath-taking scenery. The Department of Fish & Game plants back-county waters with goldens, brookies, browns and rainbows. They've been doing this since the early 1900's since many waters were without natural trout and cannot support reproduction. Much planting utilizes aerial drops of fingerlings. In these cold waters where food is often minimal it takes about 2 years for plants to reach catchable size. So don't expect to catch trophy-sized fish. Pan-sized is the rule.

Pack in a good quality ultralight spinning outfit or lightweight fly rod. Spinning enthusiasts are well served with a 5 1/2-6 foot ultralight rod rigged with 1 or 2 pound line. Cast shiny spinners and spoons like Panther Martin and Kastmaster. Crystal clear water and pan-sized quarry make 1 pound line a good choice. Bait anglers also do well, as do flies cast with a casting bubble.

Fly anglers use 8 1/2-9 foot pack rods, about a WF6F line, 9 foot leader and 4x to 7x tippet. Mosquitoes, Royal Wulffs, Renegads, Muddlers and Zug Bug all work. Some pack-in tips: Backpacking is not the only way to go. There are numerous packing services available. Most use horses, but llamas are coming into vogue. A good way to find these services is through local Chambers of Commerce. Outdoor shows, mostly held in the spring, are also good. Wilderness permits may be required for overnight trips. They are free and can be obtained from Forest Service Offices. There is an entire chapter on the topic of "Wilderness Troutin'" in Marketscope's book, *Trout Fishing in California*.

Ice Fishing

Ice fishing is not the big deal in California that it is in the upper midwest part of the country. But it is a refreshing (no joke intended) change of pace, and often quite productive. Some of the more popular lakes for ice fishing include Sabrina (out of Bishop), The June Lake Loop, Mammoth Lakes and the Virginia Lakes. Ice fishing, however, can only be done during the open season for trout. In the Eastern Sierra that means you can't fish before the last Saturday in April each year when the season opens.

You'll need an ice auger or pick to make a hole in the ice. A sieved ladle or ice spoon is then used to clear the water of floating ice crystals. Use a short rod (it keeps you closer to the hole for good control) and 6 to 10 pound monofilament. Also, you'll need some split shot sinkers, number 6 or 8 baitholder hooks, or number 10 to 12 salmon egg hooks. Some trout lures like Mini Jigs and Hopkins Spoons are good too.

Where to fish? Near dams or at stream inlets are often good. Yesterday's partially frozen-over hole is also worth a try— they're usually easy to re-open. Some anglers bring along portable fish finders to locate fish through the ice.

Lower lures to the bottom and then jig them in a 2 to 3 foot zone above the bottom. Raise the lure up 2 to 3 feet from the bottom and then release it so it flutters back down. Split shots are placed about 1-1 1/2 feet above the hook for bait fishing. Nightcrawlers, salmon eggs or cheese are jigged in the same manner, just off the bottom. Warm clothing is a must, especially footwear and gloves.

Drinking Water

It's probably not a good idea to drink untreated stream or lake water, even in the high country. The intestinal parasite *giardia lamblia* may be present in any surface water. It causes a very unpleasant disease called giardiases that is not unlike Montezuma's Revenge. Anglers should either carry water or treat local water. Boiling is one way. One minute of boiling is needed at low altitudes and 5 to 10 minutes at high altitudes. Filtering using small, portable pumps also works, if you have the right equipment. You need a filter pore size of 3 microns or smaller. Ask for advice from knowledgeable store personnel. Finally, chemical treatment may also be used. But only iodine treatments are widely recommended for wilderness water purification. Follow the instructions that come with these products.

Seasickness

And now for another unpleasant topic. Seasickness ruins many a boat fishing trip each year, on both the high seas and inland lakes. It also takes its toll on fellow anglers. For example, party boats at times return to port to put ashore one seasick customer, consuming several hours of fishing time for all the other patrons.

Cures for seasickness are possible. But probably the best course is prevention. And prevention starts on shore before the fishing trip begins. Medications are available that greatly reduce the possibility of seasickness. It is thought that they prevent motion sickness by inhibiting the flow of nerve impulses to the brain. Two categories are marketed: antihistamines and scopolamine. Both are effective but they have different side effects and dosages. Most people find the recently available scopolamine patches to be the best bet. These patches, used behind the ear, slowly release minute quantities of the drug at a steady rate over a period of three days. Apply the patch the night before your trip. Once aboard, there are a few more things to do, especially if you begin to feel a little bit queasy: Keep your eyes on the horizon or on any stationary object such as the shoreline or the horizon itself; if and when possible sit near the center of the boat where there is less motion—but don't go below or in a closed cabin.

Licensing and Regulations

Fishing regulations in California are simple and straightforward, but they are also detailed and specific. A Fish and Game Commission publication, *California Sport Fishing Regulations*, is available free at any location where fishing licenses are sold. This is a fact-filled, well-organized brochure that has all you need to know about current regulations. Read it over and know the rules. I'm always bothered when I see a young child on a family camping trip unknowingly violating regulations that are designed to protect the young fish. Parents should be aware of the regulations and supervise their children. Fishing licenses are sold at most places where fishing tackle or bait are sold. They are required for anglers age 16 and older.

Anglers are also reminded that since 1994 we are required to wear our fishing license. It must be displayed above the waist. Most anglers are using clear plastic holders that pin to their shirt or hat.

Organizations and Publications

Some of the most active fishing organizations and some of the best publications for up-to-date Southern California fishing information are as follows:

Western Outdoor News
3197-E Airport Loop Dr.
Costa Mesa, CA 92626
(714) 546-4370

Fishing and Hunting News
Southern California Ed.
511 Eastlake Ave. E
Seattle, WA 98109
(206) 624-2738

United Anglers of California
5200 Huntington Ave. #300
Richmond, CA 94804
(510) 525-3974

California Angling Records

Athletes always say "records are made to be broken." Maybe that's still true of fishing records too. Sixty-five percent (or 17 out of 26) of the records listed below were set in the 1970s and 1980s. Eight were set since January 1980!

Species	Weight (lb-oz)	Where Caught	Date
Barracuda	15-15	San Onofre	Aug 57
Bass			
Calico	14-7	San Clemente I.	Jul 58
Largemouth	22-0	Lake Castaic	Mar 90
Sand	11-7	Pt. Dume	Jul 93
White Sea	77-4	San Diego	Apr 50
Bluegill	3-10	Lower Otay Res.	May 92
Bonito	22-3	Malibu Cove	Jul 78
Catfish			
Blue	59-4	Irvine Lake	Jun 87
Channel	82-2	Lower Otay Res.	Apr 96
Flathead	60-0	Colorado River	Mar 92
Corvina	36-8	Salton Sea	May 80
Crappie			
Black	4-1	New Hogan Lake	Mar 75
White	4-8	Clear Lake	Apr 71
Halibut (California)	53-8	Santa Rosa I.	May 75
Lingcod	53	Tinidad	1969
Rockfish (cabezon)	23-4	Los Angeles	Apr 85
Sargo	4-1	Salton Sea	1972
Striped Bass	67-8	San Luis (O'Neill)	May 92
Trout			
Brook	9-12	Silver Lake	Sep 32
Brown	26-8	Upper Twin Lake	May 87
Golden	9-8	Virginia Lake	Aug 52
Rainbow	27-4	Smith River	Dec 76
Tuna			
Albacore	88-8	Santa Cruz	Oct 97*
Bluefin	71-4	San Diego	Sep 72
Yellowfin	218	San Diego	Sep 70
Yellowtail	62	La Jolla	Jun 53

*This is also a world record.

Recently, the California Department of Fish and Game in its publication, *Outdoor California*, described how to apply for a state fishing record, should you land a whopper. The following description is by Curt Taucher.

"Applying for a State Record: Have you ever dreamed of setting a new record for fish caught by California anglers? These tips will help you protect your record-size catch from any chance of not being included in the record books.

To ensure a legal *catch*, be sure you are the only person to handle your line, tackle or the fish during the time after you've hooked the fish and are reeling it in. Disqualification of your fish could occur if others are involved with landing your prize, with the exception of help in netting or gaffing the fish.

After you land the fish, save the first 10-20 feet of line above the hook or lure for later testing. If necessary, wrap the line around a creel or small tackle box for preservation.

The next very important step is to take the suspected record fish to a place with a certified scale (legal for trade), as soon after the fish leaves the water as possible. The fish will lose moisture and weight rapidly. Do not gut, decapitate, de-fin or scale the fish. Weigh the fish once, and measure total length, tail fork length and the circumference, with two disinterested witnesses in attendance. Be sure to get their complete names and addresses.

It would be best at this time to have color photos taken as a matter of record. Lay the fish on either side and place a yardstick, ruler or some other measuring device (if possible) just below the fish. Be sure the photo is taken close-up, with all the color and outstanding features clearly displayed.

The next vital step in preserving record status is to have the fish's species properly documented by a professional fishery biologist (or person involved with fisheries) or a taxonomist (a person who studies species of wildlife as a profession). Again, be sure to document the name, address and employer of the person identifying your catch, along with the determination of species.

During all the legwork documenting your record, it is advisable to keep the fish as cold, or frozen, as possible. Do not mutilate the fish in any way until you're sure that your record is secure and DOCUMENTED— in other words, keep it in the freezer until properly notified by the record-keeping authorities!

For stat records applications on salt or freshwater fish, contact any Department of Fish and Game office for the proper forms. Of course, at anytime the DFG is more than willing to help you document your record-size fish."

CASTING BASICS

SPINCASTING

Use two hands to cast with spincasting equipment:

1

Grasp rod's pistol grip with one hand. **If you're right-handed,** turn rod sideways so the reel handle points straight up; **if you're left-handed,** point the reel handle straight down. Put other hand in front of reel, and hold the line lightly between thumb and forefinger. Push reel's thumb button down and hold it down.

2

Face target area with body turned at slight angle—about a quarter turn. Arm holding rod handle should be closest to target. Aim rod tip toward the target—about level with your eyes.

3

Swiftly and smoothly, bend your casting arm at the elbow, raising your casting forearm until your hands reach eye level. When the rod is almost straight up, it will be bent back by the weight of the practice plug. As rod bends, move both forearms forward at once with just a slight wrist movement.

4

When rod reaches eye level, **release** the thumb button and let the line travel freely through the fingers of your line hand.

5

As the plug nears the target, **slow** it gradually by applying pressure to the line with your hand.

If the lure landed close in front of you, you released the spincast reel's thumb button too late. If the lure went more or less straight up, you released the button too soon.

SPINNING

To cast using spinning tackle, follow these steps:

1.

Grasp the rod's handle, placing the reel "stem" between your second and third fingers. Place your thumb on top of the handle and extend your forefinger to touch the spool cover. With other hand, rotate reel spool until line roller is directly beneath your extended forefinger. Pick up line in front of roller with forefinger and open, or cock, the reel's bail with your other hand. (Note: Some new reels have a lever so you can grasp the line and open the bail in one motion.)

2

Face the target area with body turned at slight angle—about a quarter turn. The arm holding the rod handle should be closest to the target. Aim the rod tip toward the target at about eye level.

3

Swiftly and smoothly, using just one motion, bend your casting arm at the elbow and raise your casting forearm so your hand is almost at eye level.

4

When the rod is almost vertical, it will be bent by the weight of the practice plug. As the rod bends, move your forearm forward with a slight wrist movement.

When the rod reaches eye level, straighten your forefinger to release the line. As the plug nears the target, slow it gradually by touching the line coming off the reel with your forefinger.

5

When the plug is over the target, stop it by touching the top edge of the reel's spool with your forefinger.

If the lure landed close in front of you, your forefinger released the line too late. If the plug went more or less straight up, you released your forefinger too soon.

Don't be discouraged if your first casts don't go as planned. In casting—no matter what kind of fishing tackle you use—timing is critical for long, accurate casts, and you will improve with practice.

How to Catch . . .

Many fishing books are jam packed with interesting, colorful information. But they have one glaring shortcoming. They never answer the question "how." Our purpose in the next 24 sections is to remedy this problem. So if you want to know "how to catch . . . " just look in the appropriate section. The explanations are simple, straightforward, complete and understandable. The following fish are discussed in alphabetical order for easy reference:

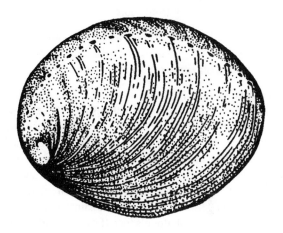

How to Catch. . . Abalone

An abalone is a rock-clinging, single-shelled creature that inhabits shoreline waters (especially where there are concentrations of rocks and kelp) all along the coast and islands of California. It has a large, fleshy foot and sensory projections on its underside. Most all seaside gift shop browsers have seen an eye-catching display of abalone shells. And those who have ordered it on restaurant menus know how delicious it is. But it's possible for anyone with some insight and a little luck to enjoy catching, preparing and eating abalone.

Fishing Techniques

There are three basic techniques for taking abalone:

1. **Rock Picking**—searching the rocky shore on foot.

2. **Free Diving**—diving near shore with a snorkel only (no aqualung).

3. **Scuba Diving**—diving with an aqualung.

North of Yankee Point (at Monterey) only rock picking and free diving are allowed. But all three approaches are allowed and practiced in Southern California waters. It is only fair to say that scuba divers are probably the most successful.

Rock pickers operate at low tides—preferably a minus low tide and a calm ocean. They start about an hour before the low tide and quit before the incoming tide threatens a soaking or being stranded away from shore.

The basic technique is to comb an area looking for abalone attached to rocks. Often it is best to feel under water in crevices and cracks that other rock pickers have missed.

Free divers operate in the water. The wise ones in pairs take turns diving down to rocky bottoms in 5-30 feet of water. Abalone are pried off the rocks with a metal bar. Since this can fatally injure an abalone, it is best to be sure the abalone is of legal size before prying it off. Rock pickers must also make this judgment. To pry the abalone off the rock and avoid injuring it, slip the bar under the abalone. Then lift the handle end up, pushing the tip of the bar against the rock. This prevents injury to the abalone's foot. If it is undersize, hold the abalone back on the spot where it was taken until it grabs hold itself.

Free diving lessons are available at selected locations along the coast. No one should attempt to free dive without proper instruction. Some tips: Dive only on an outgoing tide. Incoming tides create rips that can carry you out to sea. Make sure you are familiar with the weight belt release and the dive area. And dive with an experienced partner.

Scuba divers love abalone hunting, but investing the necessary time and money to learn to scuba dive just to catch abalone isn't worth it to most people—but exploring the undersea world with scuba equipment is a joy itself. Plus, scuba divers not only seek out abalone, but many also spear fish for lingcod, rockfish, halibut, etc. Since scuba divers have more time to judge the size of their quarry before removing it from the rocks, they should be extra careful not to disturb undersized abalone. Remember, everything looks bigger under water than it really is.

Tackle and Equipment

The equipment needed for rock picking and free diving are an abalone iron (of legal dimension), a fixed caliper measuring gauge, a state fishing license, a catch bag (or at least a gunnysack), neoprene boots, neoprene gloves and an inflatable buoyancy vest. In addition, for free diving, you'll need a wet suit, hood, snorkel, mask, fins, knife (for escaping from kelp) and a weight belt.

Where to Fish

Probably the most consistent producer of abalone are the Southern California islands. Excellent spots include San Miguel, Santa Rosa and Santa Cruz in the Channel Islands chain. These are such good abalone hunting territories that party boats take divers out from such places as Camarilo, Oxnard and Ventura. Catalina Island is another good prospect. Along the coast itself, abalone can be found from Pt. Conception all the way south to San Diego. But the best areas are probably north of Santa Barbara and north of Palos Verdes Pt. towards Los Angeles. There are closed areas along the coast, so check current regulations. Check with dive shops for specific locales.

Cleaning and Cooking

Cleaning abalone is different from most other seafood, but it is not actually difficult. Insert the abalone iron between the meat and the shell at the pointed end of the abalone. Now pop out the meat. Next, trim away the flanged edges and all the intestines. A pot scrubber can then be used to rub off the black skin. Scrape off the suction cups with a knife. Now it's time to tenderize the meat. Before slicing pound it with a big mallet. Then slice it 1/8 to 1/4 inch thick. Use the mallet again for a final tenderizing. The end of a bottle may also be used. Some anglers suggest leaving the cleaned abalone in the refrigerator for a day or two before slicing and pounding to allow the muscle to relax, making it more tender and easier to handle.

Most people feel that the only way to prepare abalone is quick pan frying. Tenderized steaks are usually floured, or dipped in egg and sauteed over high heat for less than one minute on a side. Fry only enough to heat clear through and slightly brown.

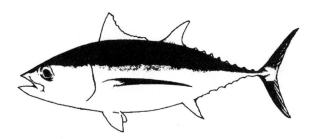

How to Catch . . . Albacore and Yellowfin

Yellowfin tuna and albacore are the targets of commercial fishing boats several hundred miles off the shore. These commercial boats stay out until their freezers are full. Fortunately, there are times each year when yellowfin come close enough to shore (30 to 100 miles) so that sport fishermen can get in on the fun. Albacore also can show up and provide excellent fishing, especially out of the more northerly landings around Morro Bay.

Both of these fish migrate continually throughout their lives, crossing the Pacific Ocean warmer waters than the albacore. It's usually about June or July when the first schools of smaller fish appear around San Diego as they move north. Good fishing can be sporadic early in the season, but as more schools move into the region, it can become fast and furious. The hot fishing can extend clear into November, but usually cools down by mid-October.

There are years when the yellowfin get as close as 10 or 12 miles from shore and as far north as the Catalina Channel. These are the only times most sport anglers consider fishing for these great gamefish from their own boats. At other times, it's probably best to venture out on a well-equipped, fast, large, party boat especially rigged for tuna. Typically the boats leave in the wee hours of the morning (from 11 p.m. to 2 a.m.) and are back in port the following evening. Cost ranges from $120 to $175 for these one-day trips. Increasingly, because fish often show further from port, 1 1/2-day and two-day trips are becoming more popular. They cost from $225 to $275.

Fishing Techniques

Trolling is the most popular technique for taking albacore and yellowfin. But before we get into trolling specifics, a word about where to troll. After all, it's a big ocean! First, albacore congregate and feed in warmer water. Most experts look for water in the 63-65°F range with 60°F being the minimum. The second good fish finder is bird activity. Birds actively pursuing bait fish means that albacore may be doing the same thing from down below the forage fish swarm. When birds are spotted, run the boat through the edge of the activity, not through the center. No need to chance scattering the bait fish and feeding albacore.

Albacore trolling is characterized by the following:

1. Trolling close to the boat. (The theory goes that to the albacore, the wake looks like a bait fish feeding frenzy.) Put the lure right in the white water wake of the boat about 50 to 70 feet behind the stern.

2. Fairly rapid boat speed (perhaps 7-10 knots) to move along the feathered or rubber-skirted jig at a good pace.

3. Party boat captains usually troll in square grids of about 20 minutes per leg until fish are located. A zig-zag pattern is also a good approach.

The other method of albacore fishing is used on party boats and some private boats after a school of fish is located by trolling. The boat is stopped and scoops of bait fish (usually anchovies) are tossed into the water to raise the albacore up to the surface. This technique is called chumming. Fishermen drift live bait near the surface. Since albacore move in schools, it's always a good idea for even private boats to try drift fishing after a trolling hook-up is landed. Frozen anchovies often work even without chumming. Drift, facing the wind, so that the rig is not under the boat. Casting out a Salas or similar jig can also work.

Tackle and Equipment

Albacore and yellowfin are big, fast, open-ocean sport fish. They are one of the most sought after game fish in California ocean waters. A good fish averages 15-30 pounds with some ranging up to 40 pounds or more. Essential equipment includes the following:

1. Large, iced, fish storage box (or cooler, or plastic trash container) and a good-sized gaff.

2. A 6-6 1/2 foot medium to heavy trolling rod with roller tip and a 4/0 to 6/0 sized reel filled with at least 300 yards of 50-80 pound monofilament line. This heavy equipment is needed to quickly land the first fish so that chumming and drift fishing can begin before the school disappears.

3. For drift fishing, a light to medium action, fast-tapered, 7 foot rod mated to a conventional reel capable of holding 300 yards of 15-30 pound test line is suggested.

Lure and Bait

The most productive albacore jigs:

Description —Chrome-plated or abalone-pearl head and a natural feather or vinyl skirt.

Colors—Dark colors (like black, purple, green and yellow) during darker periods. Light colors (like red and white, red and yellow) in bright periods.

Size—4-10 ounces.

The preferred bait is live anchovies. The best are 3-4 inches long, green backed (they seem friskier), with no scale loss or other signs of deterioration. For surface fishing, hook the anchovy through a gill cover. For deeper action, nose hook the

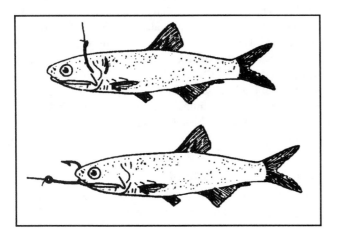

anchovies and use a 1 or 2 ounce rubber-core sinker about 30 inches up the line. Use the sharpest hooks money can buy. Lazer Sharp Eagle Claw hooks in #2, #4 and #6 are a good choice.

When and Where to Fish: Albacore

It varies. Albacore have been completely absent some years off San Diego and very abundant other years. Normally, early season catches off San Diego would come at the Dumping Grounds and 60-Mile Banks in June. The San Clemente Islands, 43-Fathom Banks and the Channel Islands are usually the next to heat up. By September-October, the fishing extends up to Morro Bay. This region has been more productive than San Diego—and it typically produces bigger fish. See the "Pacific Ocean Fishing" chapter of this book for more specifics.

Yellowfin Tuna

Yellowfin tuna are usually caught on Baja trips. But in recent years, terrific runs of these fish have developed off the San Diego area. This is most likely to happen in summer and fall off the Coronado Islands, the 43-Fathom Banks and the 60-Mile Bank. Yellowfins are caught with the same approach used on albacore. Trolling works. Chumming brings them to the boat. But Yellowfin don't like water cooler than 72 degrees.

Bluefin Tuna

In the good old days of Southern California, tuna fishing for the bluefin was king. Two hundred pounders were not that uncommon. Mostly due to the onslaught of commercial seiners, sport-caught bluefins now average 10 to 25 pounds. These are taken from late May through the summer near Catalina Island and Coronado Island. The best approach is drift fishing live, spunky anchovies. Veteran anglers use 12-15 pound line, about a #8 hook, and a long (about 7 1/2 to 8 foot rod) to cast the offering away from the boat. Bluefin, even of modest size, are fierce fighters.

Cleaning and Cooking

Albacore is most often steaked. Make sure the dark flesh is removed from each piece. Like salmon, albacore has a relatively high fat content. Also like salmon, the most popular way to prepare it is barbecuing. The smoke seems to add to the flavor. Poached albacore tastes like canned tuna, but even better. Poached albacore may be stored in the refrigerator for several days or frozen for a short time. Sauteing albacore is also popular. These strong tasting fish work well in recipes with spicy or tomato-based sauces.

How to Catch . . . Barracuda

Barracuda are torpedo shaped, hard hitting, and have a lethal set of teeth. The average keeper fish is now probably in the 3-5 pound range.

These fish frequent the offshore islands and close-in kelp beds and bays, making them accessible to party boats, private fishing boats, skiff anglers, and at times, pier anglers.

Barracuda, as large as 8 to 12 pounds, were once commonplace from Pt. Conception south to the Cedros Islands area of Mexico. But overfishing, both sport and commercial, took its toll. Fortunately, a 28-inch minimum size limit, imposed in 1971, has helped restore this fishery. Be careful to check current regulations.

Fishing Techniques

Barracuda are most commonly located by watching for sea birds working over schools of forage fish, like anchovies. The barracuda drive up the forage fish to a feeding frenzy. Anglers have two choices when this occurs: Either troll a feather or metal jig in this area, or just drift and cast to the breaking fish. After the first fish is caught, a few handfuls of live anchovies thrown into the water (this is called chumming) will bring them near the boat.

If the barracuda are near the surface, a gill-hooked live anchovy is in order. It should be offered without a sinker (called fly lining) or, if necessary, use a small rubber core sinker about a foot above the hook. Let the fish run with the anchovy for a few seconds before setting the hook. Unlike game fish such as bonito and related members of the tuna family, barracuda do not immediately gulp down bait on the initial take. Similar to billfish and not unlike wahoo, they will take the bait, swim off with it, chew on it to turn it around, and then swallow it. Barracuda don't require a stiff hook set—simply come back sharply with the rod. Nose hooking the bait,

up through the lower lip and the nose, is called for when the barracuda are deeper. Also use a small sinker. Move the bait slowly and be ready to flip the reel into free spool, or open the bail, to give the fish time to take the bait before setting the hook.

Tackle and Equipment

When using live bait, barracuda fishing is most fun on light tackle—the same that is commonly used for large trout or bass. Ten- to 12-pound monofilament is more than adequate for most fish. Some anglers even like to use fly fishing equipment. When jig fishing, somewhat heavier tackle and about 20-pound line is recommended. The Penn Jigmaster 500 is a typical reel choice. Other things you'll need include needlenose pliers to remove the hooks (and avoid the sharp teeth) and a big rag to wipe your hands. Barracuda are slimy creatures.

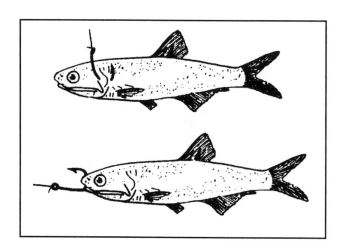

Bait and Lures

Live anchovies are the bait of choice and account for most of the catch. Use about a #4-#6 hook tied directly to your main line. Gill hook (slip the hook under the bone behind the gill cover) for surface fishing and nose hook for deeper fishing.

Barracuda are often suckers for both jigs and feathers, although feathers are not used as much as they once were. Jigs have a built-in action, whereas feathers require the angler to provide the proper action. The category of jigs called candy-bar shaped (e.g. Salsa, Sea Strike, Tady) are most popular in all white, blue and white, and green and white. The light weight size is most commonly used. Use a slow to moderate swimming action. The most common mistake is to work the jig too fast.

When and Where to Fish

Good action can begin as early as February and March in places like Santa Monica Bay (try "Venice Reef," the drop-off outside El Segundo and the kelp beds off Rocky Point). March and April are often good months near the Coronado Islands and La Jolla Kelp. Oceanside, Dana Point, Huntington Beach Flats, Horseshoe Kelp, and Catalina Island are all productive in the May-June peak season. There can also be good fishing right through early fall. Also, see the "Ocean Fishing" chapter of this book.

Cleaning and Cooking

Barracuda is most often filleted. These moderate fat content fillets are good grilled or broiled. Barracuda is very tasty when served with a full-flavored sauce.

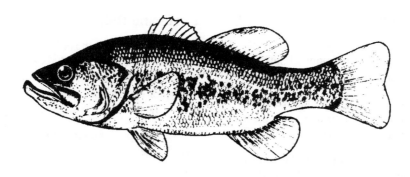

How to Catch . . . Largemouth Bass

Largemouth bass are the most widely distributed and most pursued black bass. They inhabit many of the reservoirs and lakes in Southern California. The other black bass, the smallmouth, is found in only a few Southern California waters like Lake Cachuma, Lake San Antonio and Lake Nacimiento. Smallmouth prefer cooler water than largemouth, and are much smaller fish (a three-pound smallmouth is almost a trophy).

There are two types of largemouth bass that are plentiful in Southern California. The first to be brought to California (no black bass are native) was the northern-strain largemouth, introduced before the turn of the century. It flourished and was the backbone of Southern California bass fishing until about 30 years ago. Around 1960, the Florida-strain largemouth bass was planted in some Southern California lakes. This was done because the Florida-strain grows faster (and thus bigger), spawn earlier, and is considered more difficult to catch than the northern strains.

Now the northern-strain, Florida-strain and hybridized populations are found in Southern California lakes. Experts say that it is almost impossible to tell the strains of a caught fish since the young can exhibit the features of either parent strain. But you can tell by lake records. For example, the former California largemouth bass record, set in 1980 in Lake Casitas, was 21 pounds, 3 1/2 ounces. That's a Florida-strain fish! Lakes that are northern-strain largemouth waters usually have lake records in the 12-pound range. That's still quite a bass, and there's consolation in knowing that northern-strain fish come to the hook more readily.

Monster bass are still being taken in Southern California. For example, Bob Crupi caught a 22.01 pound largemouth on a live crawdad at Lake Casitas in the spring of 1990. This fish was only four ounces short of the world record.

If you want to know more about California bass fishing than is presented here, see *Bass Fishing in California* (Marketscope Books, 1990).

Fishing Techniques

Bass fishing is best during the spring and fall. But ironically, probably most people fish for bass in the warm summer months. Why not? Family vacations fit best when kids are out of school. And the weather is comfortable "out on the lake." Don't get me wrong. Bass are caught in the summer, but it takes more effort since the fish are usually down deeper.

The basic technique used in bass fishing is casting and retrieving a plug, spoon, spinnerbait, jig, plastic worm or live bait. Of course, the retrieve approach must match the lure. All types of casting equipment can and is used including bait casting, spinning, spin casting and fly casting. More on this in the Tackle and Equipment section.

Successful bass fishing centers around the answer to three questions: Where to cast? How to cast? What to cast? Here are some guidelines:

- Bass are almost always on or near the bottom, or near underwater cover like a fallen tree. The "bottom" could be near shore in 2 feet of water, or it might be in 40 feet of water on the slope of a sunken island.

- Largemouth prefer to be near structures, whether it be a rocky fall-off, a sunken log, a weed bed, standing timber, a rocky point, etc.

- Largemouth bass prefer a water temperature of about 70°F. This means that in the spring and fall bass are likely to be nearer shore, in shallow "seventyish" water. When the surface temperature is well above 70°F, bass hold out deeper, but do make feeding forays into shallower water, primarily at night.

- At an unfamiliar lake, seek information about "good spots" from other anglers, bait shops, marinas, etc.

- If you (or someone else) catch a bass at a particular spot, and the lake temperature conditions don't change, the spot will probably produce more bass.

- Cast your offering so it lands or is retrieved near structures. For example, put it next to a pile of boulders that are partially submerged, or place it right by a fallen tree. Retrieve parallel to submerged log, not across it. Try inlets where streams flow into lakes.

- Retrieve slowly. Seventy to eighty percent of the time a slow retrieve is best. But if it's not working, don't hesitate to try a rapid retrieve. A combination may also be in order—for example, a few quick turns of the reel handle just after the offering lands (to get the bass's attention) followed by a slow retrieve.

- Retrieve everything, except surface plugs, near or on the bottom. Since the bass are on the bottom, you've got to put your offering on the bottom. After all, we live and eat on the "bottom" of the atmosphere, so doesn't it seem natural for some fish (particularly bass) to live and eat on the bottom of their "atmosphere."

- With plastic worms and jigs "feel" the bottom during your retrieve. No doubt this practice will result in some lost rigs, but it will also result in more bass. Using snagless, or near snagless offerings as described later, will minimize loss.

- Cast quietly. In fact, fish quietly. Minimize engine noise, oar lock noise, "scraping tackle box along the floor of the boat" noise, and so on. Bass fishing is akin to stalking.

- Catchable-sized bass feed mostly on smaller fish (like shad, minnows, bluegill, etc.), crawdads and worms. This means that offerings that are successful look and act like swimming fish, moving crawdads or worms.

- At times, bass strike out of a reflex action. Sometimes they attack an offering the instant it hits the water. At these times, you could be casting anything and it would work.

- Many professional bass anglers feel that bigger bass come on bigger bait.

Lures and Bait

Many an otherwise sane person is driven absolutely crazy by the immense selection of bass plugs, jigs, spoons, spinnerbaits, plastic worms, etc. And professional bass-tournament fishermen seem to own at least one of everything, based on the size of the tackle boxes in their boats!

Don't despair. You don't need one of everything to take bass. Largemouth bass offerings fall into seven categories:

- Crankbaits
- Surface Plugs
- Spinnerbaits
- Spoon Jigs
- Jigs
- Plastic Worms
- Live Bait

It's probably a good idea for a serious bass angler to have a sampling of the basic offerings in each category, but that isn't even necessary. For example, some bass fishing experts say that one or two types account for more bass than all the others combined. These two are plastic worms and spinnerbaits.

Crankbaits

Crankbaits are a broad category of lures, mostly plugs, that get their name because the reeling speed determines how much the lure dives, vibrates and wobbles. Most of these lures have plastic, fish-shaped bodies. They also have a plastic lip, the size, shape and angle of which imparts action to the reeled

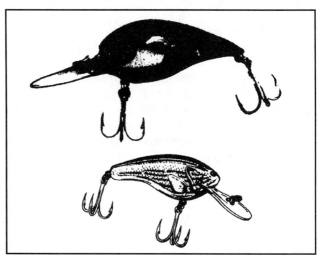

lure. Many have two sets of treble hooks which provide a good chance to hook a striking bass. But this also increases the chance of snags, so crankbaits are best used in open water. Crankbaits work, to one degree or another, almost all year long at sloping points, along shorelines, in shallow flats, etc.

Crankbaits either float at rest, sink slowly or sink rapidly. The most common way to fish this lure is to first jig it for a moment before beginning the return. Then reel fast to get the lure to the bottom. Now slow down enough to either drag the lure along the sloping bottom or bump it along, or return steadily right over the bottom. Crankbaits are designed to be fished parallel to the shoreline so you can keep the lure near the bass, and at the prescribed depth for the longest time.

Popular bass crankbaits include Bomber Model A's, Rapala Fat Rap and Storm Wiggle Wart. Shad and crawdad styles are popular.

Surface Plugs (and Stickbaits)

Surface plugs are top-water lures that simulate a sick or injured bait fish, frog or other creature. They float both when still and when retrieved. Most surface plugs have an action designed into them using blunt ends, propellers, dished-faces, etc. The proper retrieve for most of these is slow, erratic and stop-and-go. But before retrieving many anglers will just let it sit in the target area for up to a minute or two, just twitching it, to send out vibrations and small ripples around it. Popular surface plugs include Rip-N-Minnow, Chug Bug and Devil's Horses.

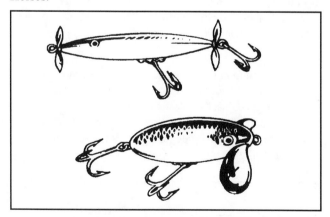

There is another class of surface plugs called stickbaits that are unique because they don't have any action built into them. Probably the most famous of these is the Zara Spook. The action needed to make a stickbait work must come from the skill of the angler. This takes several hours of practice to develop. Articles and bass books can be found at your local library to show you how to do it. The reading and the practice may be worth it because stickbaits have one profound advantage over other surface plugs. They can be kept in the target area longer because very little forward motion is required to give them the action needed. A stickbait in skilled hands may catch more fish than other surface plugs. The prime season for surface plugs is in the springtime spawning season when bass are in shallow water, especially in early mornings and late evenings. They are also good in summertime in shallow water after dark.

Spinnerbaits

Spinnerbaits are one of the most productive of all bass catching lures and are simple to cast and retrieve. They are good all year, especially in water up to 10 feet deep. Use them along brushy structures, in flooded trees or fallen trees. Most spinnerbait designs are semi-weedless so hang-ups are not a constant concern. Veteran anglers vary the return to change depth and action, but in most cases, the slower the retrieve the better.

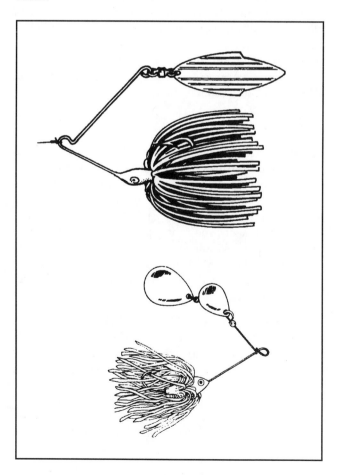

Here are some tips. The best all around colors are probably white or chartreuse (yellowish). Spinnerbaits can be hopped along the bottom like a jig. In this style of fishing, blades that flutter freely on the downfall bring strikes. The size of spinnerbaits should approximate the length of the bait fish in the area. Skirts can be trimmed to accomplish this.

The best tip of all: Add a plastic worm or pork rind on the hook of the spinnerbait. It produces more strikes from bigger bass. Probably because it keeps the lure up in the water, even with a slower retrieve.

Spoons

Jigging a spoon is a little-practiced largemouth technique that is easy and effective. It's a great method to take bass from late autumn through early spring. That's when largemouths seek warm water down deep in Southern California reservoirs. It can also work in midsummer when bass go deep to find water cooler than surface temperatures.

A wobbling spoon is dropped down over the side of the boat and then raised up and fluttered down at whatever depth the bass are at. The more flutter the better on the down drift. Work the jig in about a 3-5 foot, up and down range. Hopkin's 75 and Haddock Structure Spoons in about the one-half to three-quarter ounce range are about right. Fish can be taken in depths between 30-60 ft. with this approach.

Jigs

Jigging, typically with a skirted lead-head jig, is somewhat more complicated than spoon jigging, but it is a very productive technique. The jig is cast out or flipped out (more on this later) and then allowed to drop to the bottom. The most common retrieve is to skip the jig along the bottom in short, sharp jerks. Imagine you're dragging the jig along the bottom from a drifting or steadily trolled boat. That's about how you want your jig to act. Most strikes occur on the initial drop or on the ensuing flutter downs. Garland Spider Jigs and Haddock Kreepy Crawlers are popular.

The most famous jig rig in Southern California bass waters is the "Pig 'n Jig." It's a 3/8 to 1/2 ounce skirted jig (usually dark colored, like brown) with a weedless hook. A pork rind (or plastic trailer) is put on the hook. The rind makes it look more like a crawdad and also slows the rig's descent. When you move the Pig 'n Jig off the bottom, don't just let it drop, let it down and be alert for a take. Keep slack out of your line to feel the strike and watch your line for unnatural movement.

Weedless Jig (with pork rind)

Plastic Worms and Other Soft Plastics

Some people claim that each year more largemouth bass are taken on plastic worms than on all other artificial lures combined. This could well be true. Plastic worms do have several special advantages over other lures:

- They can be fished at all depths of water.
- They have outstanding action at different retrieve speeds.
- Weedless rigging is a snap.
- They're inexpensive so anglers don't mind risking them in heavy cover.

They can be rigged in different ways for different situations. For example, in shallow spring spawning waters they can be fished weightless. They can also be rigged with a dropper or sliding sinker. Three popular rigging styles are shown on the following page.

Plastic worms (from 4-6 inches long) are worked along the bottom much the same as in jigging. Work them slowly and erratically, like a nightcrawler twisting and drifting in the current. Dark colors like purple and brown are most productive. Plastic worms can also be used for vertical jigging, like spooning.

In addition to plastic worms, there are other types of soft plastics that are becoming more and more popular. Some of these are rigged, just like plastic worms. A typical example of this is the soft plastic lizard rig shown below. In this illustration, the bullet weight is pegged up the line using a broken-off piece of toothpick.

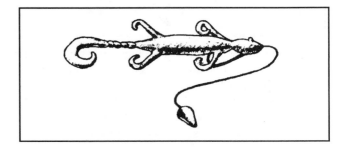

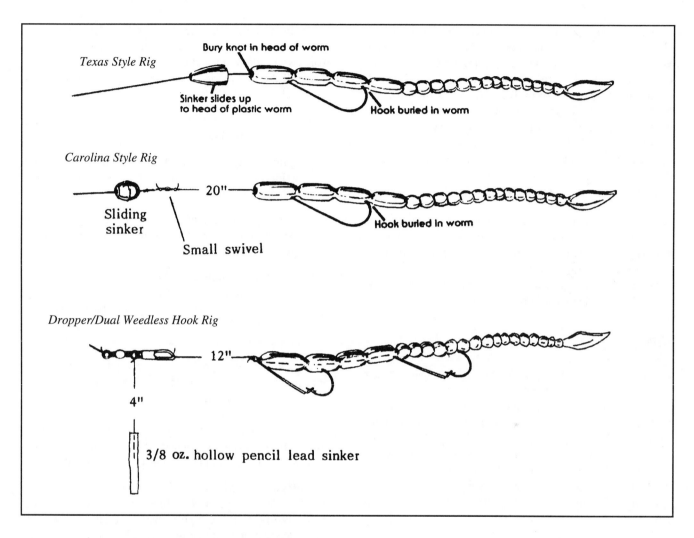

Texas Style Rig

Bury knot in head of worm

Sinker slides up
to head of plastic worm

Hook buried in worm

Carolina Style Rig

20"

Sliding
sinker

Small swivel

Hook buried in worm

Dropper/Dual Weedless Hook Rig

12"

4"

3/8 oz. hollow pencil lead sinker

Probably more common are the class of soft plastic that are rigged on weighted hooks called p-heads and darters. These are miniature jig heads in the 1/16 to 1/8 ounce range. Anglers attach things like 2-4 inch soft plastic curl-tail worms on split-tail grubs. Even more popular and productive are the soft plastic tube baits like the Fat Gitzit.

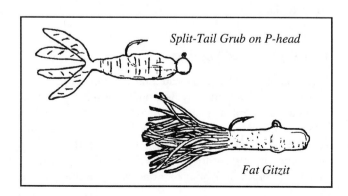

Split-Tail Grub on P-head

Fat Gitzit

Live Bait

Live bait bass fishing isn't all that common anymore. That's strange, in a way, because live bait was the only way bass were caught before plugs, spinnerbaits and all the other artificials came along. For instance, I have several live frog harnesses in my collectibles. It holds the little guy in a swimming posture and would be great for casting and retrieving a frog without putting a hook through it. I've never even thought of using it.

But other live bait are a different matter, especially live crawdads. These critters are the way to go if you want to catch a really big bass. Here's one way to rig them:

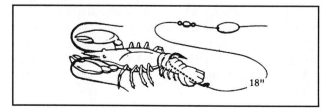

18"

Some anglers prefer to just put some split shot up the line about a foot or two from the hook. Others use no sinker at all. Use a #6, 8 or 10 bait hook, depending on the size of the crawdad. When you see a twitch, that is the largemouth picking up the crawdad. As the fish moves off with the bait, the belly will come out of your line. Let the bass run a few feet and then set the hook hard. Don't allow any slack in your line when playing the bass. Fish rocky points, drop-offs and ledges. Spring is the best time to catch the lunkers on live crawdads.

Casting and Flipping

Accuracy is the measure of a good cast. Consistently accurate bass casters will hook more fish. Besides the traditional overhand cast, often a sidearm or even an underhand cast is called for to reach the target (when casting under an overhanging branch, for example) and to gently put the offering on the water. The three keys to accurate casting are practice, practice and practice.

Flipping (or Flippin') is a specialized casting technique. It's used to delicately put a jig or plastic worm on the water, especially near or in heavy cover. Springtime shallow water bassing is the prime flipping time. In elementary terms, the standing angler strips line off the reel, much like a fly angler, as the offering swings from the rod tip like a pendulum. On a forward swing the jig is flipped out and gently "put" on the water. Accuracy is critical as is an almost ripple-free landing. Weedless offerings are a rule. And in order to fight the bass in close and keep it out of cover, heavy equipment is used. A specialized flipping rod (about 7 feet) is matched with 15-25 pound test line.

Tackle and Equipment

Today, many bass anglers use what is known in the trade as a bass boat. These boats were popularized in bass tournaments. They are about 16-20 feet long, with pedestal seats, large outboard motors, an electric trolling motor (used for maneuvering, not trolling), several depth finders, a fish box, a flashy sparkling finish, and on and on . . .

Bass boats are fun and functional, but the good news is that you don't need one to catch your share of bass. The bad news is that successful bass fishing probably does require some kind of boat that can be maneuvered along an irregular shoreline. Many kinds of boats will do: an inflatable, a canoe, a dingy, a row boat, an aluminum boat, or a small stern-drive cruiser. Shore fishing for bass is also possible. And some lakes like Lower Otay have good shore bass angling. But at most lakes, covering a number of promising structures on foot is difficult.

To find promising bass territory during all seasons, you'd best be equipped with maps of the lake, a thermometer that works well under water and an electronic fish finder. A flasher type will do, but a graph recorder or liquid crystal style is preferred.

Now for the tackle itself. Here, there is a great deal of latitude. The possibilities include the following:

- Spinning equipment—6 to 7 foot, light to medium action spinning rod, open-faced reel with 8 to 12 pound monofilament line.

- Spin casting equipment—5 to 6 foot pistol-grip, light to medium rod, closed-faced spinning reel with 8 to 12 pound monofilament line.

- Bait casting equipment—5 to 6 foot pistol-grip, light to medium rod (can be used with spin casting reel), bait casting reel (some have magnetic anti-backlash mechanisms) with level-wind feature, star drag and 8 to 12 pound monofilament line.

What lures to use with these rods and reels? Beginners and once-in-awhile anglers should probably have a good selection of spinnerbaits, crankbaits and a surface plug or two. These are the easiest to retrieve with good action, and they catch a lot of fish. A few wobbly spoons for spoon jigging in deep water are also handy. More experienced anglers wouldn't be without a good selection of plastic worms and lead-head jigs.

Professional bass anglers often put scent formulas on all their lures. Berkley has a whole line of scented products, from Power Worms to Power Spinnerbaits, and all are scented to attract bass. It adds attracting odors and covers up human odors. Next to vibration, bass probably respond most to odor. This is an inexpensive way to improve your chances. Tests indicate that the color of one's lure is also important in producing strikes, depending upon water clarity. There's an electronic instrument called a Color-C-Lector on the market that tells anglers which color offerings to use at a given depth in a particular water clarity. Results have been promising. It's worth looking into.

Ultralight Bass Angling

Want to put more hook-ups and more excitement into your bass fishing? Here's the way: Use ultralight spinning tackle, 2-4 pound monofilament and "forage-sized" lures. With this setup, you're sure to get more strikes because the bass can't see the line, and your offerings duplicate the size of bucketmouths' regular food—threadfin shad and crawdads. And the sheer joy of fighting bass on this light tackle can't be beat. You'll want a rod in the 5'6" to 5'9" range with a fast taper (i.e. a rod that bends under a load only in the upper third of its length). The solid backbone provides good hook setting in the hard mouth structure of the black bass. Match this with an ultralight spinning reel. Note that front drag systems, though less convenient than rear drag models, offer more drag surface over which to dissipate heat and distribute pressure. Use high quality line.

A wide variety of baits are available. There are ultralight crankbaits from companies like Cordell, Rebel and Heddon. Small spoons (about 1/8 ounce) like Kastmaster and Krocodile are good. Another good bet is soft plastics. Small plastic worms, 2-inch feather-like reapers, tube baits like Fat Git Zit and little curl-tail grubs are all excellent bass takers. Some rigs are best on a 1/16-1/8 ounce p-head jig hook, while others are best on a Texas-style rig. Replace the sliding sinker with a small split shot about 18 inches up the line. Even tournament bass anglers are finding that ultralight bassing can give them that competitive edge.

Cleaning and Cooking

Bass can be scaled, gutted and beheaded, but many prefer to fillet them. This is the easiest way to remove the scales and skin. Any muddy flavor is in the skin. Bass is mild and flaky. It can be cooked in a variety of ways including sauteing, broiling, poaching, baking and frying. But in any method of preparation, remove the skin before cooking.

Of course, tournament bass anglers release all caught fish by utilizing a live-well in their boats. More recreational bass anglers should probably follow the catch and release ethic. And nobody should keep more bass than they can properly use.

Where to Fish

The top largemouth lakes in Southern California are highlighted in the "Freshwater Fishing" chapters of this book. But don't overlook farm ponds, irrigation ditches and sloughs near home.

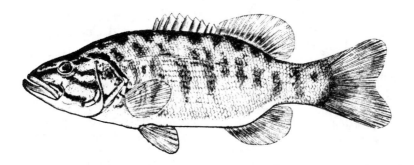

How to Catch . . . Smallmouth Bass

Smallmouth bass are plentiful in some Southern California reservoirs. According to the best historical information, they were planted in the Napa River and Alameda Creek in 1874. Following this introduction to California waters, smallmouths were soon released in many other streams and rivers. They flourished. The addition of dams on these free-flowing waterways restricted the movement of smallmouths, but did not inhibit their successful adaptation. In fact, as canyon-type reservoirs aged, they favored the smallmouth over the largemouth. Smallmouths prefer open, rocky shoreline areas and clear water, which is just what's left after the brush, trees and other organic matter decomposed in a newly flooded reservoir.

The California record smallmouth was caught in 1979 at Trinity Lake in Northern California. It weighed 9 lb 1 oz. This is monster size for a smallmouth. Anything over 4 pounds is bragging size. Many smallmouth anglers insist that they're better fighters, pound for pound, than largemouths. And for those who prefer stream fishing for trout, smallmouth provide another flowing-water fishing alternative. The smallmouth, or "bronzeback," is easily identified by its brownish, almost bronze cast, with vertical dark bars. And in contrast with the largemouth, the upper jaw does not extend beyond the eye, and the dorsal fin has a very shallow notch.

Fishing Techniques

The approaches used for smallmouth fishing have much in common with largemouth angling, but there are critically important differences. It's these differences that this section highlights.

Tackle. Most smallmouth bass anglers scale down their line and lures to match the smaller size of the bronzeback. 6 and 8 pound test monofilament is typical, but largemouth rods and reels are used with several exceptions. For example, fly rodding for smallmouth in rivers and streams with popping bugs and streamers is great sport. And some anglers use ultralight spinning equipment.

Habitat. Lake smallmouth are most often found over rocky points, over submerged gravel bars and near sharp bank drop-offs. Coves and waters with stumps showing just above the water can also produce in lakes. Smallmouths prefer water that is somewhat cooler (mid 60's) than largemouths, so they spawn deeper (8 to 15 feet) and sooner than largemouths in the same waters.

Bait and Lures

Baits are proportionally more productive for smallmouth than for largemouth. Department of Fish and Game creel census checks show that minnows are the best overall bait for smallmouths. Anglers often fish them with a small split shot about a foot above the bait hook, using a bobber. Other productive baits include crawdads, nightcrawlers, hellgrammites and crickets. One caution: Crickets are not allowed in some lakes. But the whole array of artificials also produce smallmouths. Cast surface lures early and late in the day. Work plastic worms and jigs along the bottom and use crankbaits, spinners and spinnerbaits at different speeds and depths next to cover. Shad and minnow imitations are good crankbaits. The Git Zit, a small plastic tube bait on a lead-head jig, is a very effective smallmouth lure.

When and Where to Fish

Southern California lakes are known for their outstanding largemouth fishing. But surprisingly, there are some fine places to chase smallmouths in the southern half of the Golden State. Some of the top producers include Lopez, Cachuma, Nacimiento, Piru, Pyramid, San Antonio and Pine Flat.

Cleaning and Cooking

For information on the cleaning and cooking of smallmouth, see the Largemouth Bass section.

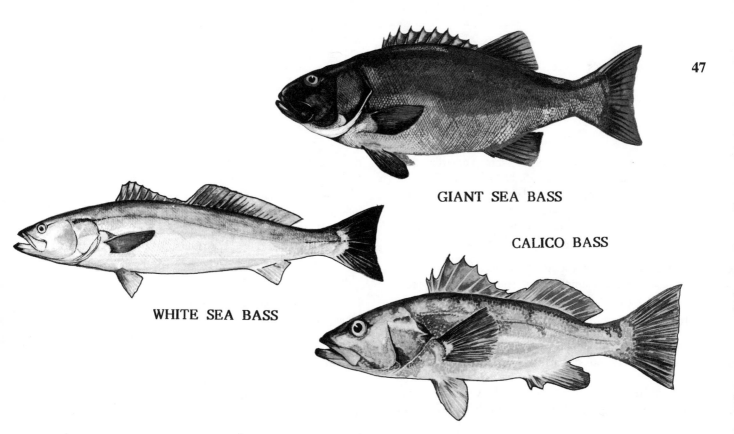

GIANT SEA BASS

CALICO BASS

WHITE SEA BASS

How to Catch . . . Saltwater Bass

Both Northern and Southern California have outstanding largemouth bass fishing. And NorCal anglers, in addition, have a good number of freshwater locales for another bass species—the smallmouth bass. Not to be outdone, SoCal anglers take pride in their "other bass" which aren't in the lakes in rivers, but in the Pacific Ocean. Furthermore, they're not just one species, but four separate and distinct species. And wouldn't you know, one of them (the white sea bass) is not even a true bass.

So SoCal anglers have marvelous opportunities to catch big bass in the largest pond in the world. Let's look at the techniques and tips to catch these big fish.

Calico and Sand Bass

Calico and sand bass combined represent the largest sport catch of ocean-going surface game fish in Southern California. This may be true because there are so many successful ways and places to catch these voracious feeders. Shore, private boat, and party boat anglers all share in the fun.

Calico are considered one of the best eating fish in local waters. They are found over reefs, around rocks, jetties and breakwaters, in kelp beds and off islands like Catalina. Calico bass are most often caught in the 2-4 pound range, but a few reach 12 pounds or more—these are the bulls.

Sand bass are closely related to calico bass. They are often found in schools on sand flats and along breakwaters. These

guys are almost as good eating as calico bass, and are caught in about the same size range.

Fishing Techniques, Lures and Bait. Calico bass in kelp beds go for both bait and lures. Favorite baits include squid, anchovies and mackerel. They will strike Clouts, Scampi and Haddock Structure spoons. When fishing breakwaters, put a small sliding sinker on your line and then tie on a 2/0 to 4/0 sized bait hook. Load it up with a piece of squid, and pull it along and around the rocks and kelp.

Chumming (live anchovies thrown overboard) works great for attracting larger bass in kelp beds. And, when available, the best bait for calico and sand bass is live squid. Frozen squid also works. A sliding sinker above a 2/0 - 4/0 hook or a comparable-sized leadhead hook jig is the best way to rig squid. Set the hook as soon as a sharp hit is felt. See the Yellowtail section of this book for a diagram of the squid rig. Calico and sand bass also go wild over the twister-tail type plastic leadhead jigs. However, sand bass are less likely to take lures than calico bass.

Tackle and Equipment. You don't need heavy tackle for these fish. On party boats, where anchovies are chummed and used as bait, skippers recommend a #500 reel, 10-20 pound test line, and a 6-7 foot saltwater rod with a fairly light tip. You'll want to cast or flip your offering over to the kelp line. For breakwater or bay fishing, a heavy freshwater bass outfit with about 10-15 pound line is fine, as is a light saltwater outfit.

When and Where to Fish. Many good spots, both from shore and boat, are discussed in the "Pacific Ocean Fishing" chapter of this book. Early morning and late evening are the best fishing times. Calico and sand bass will hit all year long, but often peak fishing takes place in the May to July period. Action is often hottest in 40 to 100 feet of water.

Cleaning and Cooking. These fish are almost always filleted. They make delicious eating, no matter how they are prepared.

White Sea Bass

The white sea bass is a highly prized sport fish in Southern California waters, not because of its fighting ability, but because it is outstanding on the table. Unfortunately, its numbers and size have declined over the years. There are season, size and limit regulations on this fish, so be aware of current regulations.

White sea bass are not actually bass, but members of the croaker family, along with corvina and white croaker (or kingfish). They can be caught in Southern California waters almost any month of the year, but February through June are probably the best months. The average catch is in the 10-25 pound range, but lunkers exceeding 60 pounds are also caught.

Fishing Techniques. White sea bass respond best to live squid. Sandy bottom areas are usually most productive, and these bass are generally taken nearer to the bottom than to the surface. Most often, a single hook (2/0 to 4/0) tied directly to 25-40 pound test line is the rig of choice. A small rubber core sinker or sliding sinker rig is put ahead of the hook to help take the squid down. The rig is illustrated in the Yellowtail section of this book.

Gently (hooks in squid's tails can tear out) toss the baited hook into the wtaer and give line off the spool as it sinks. The bass often take it on the way down. If not, use a hesitating retrieve on the way up. When the squid is taken, give about 3-5 feet of line (if you're on the way up, you must release the spool) before setting the hook.

Other white sea bass baits that are good, when available, are sardines and green mackerel. Or if the bass are really hitting, they will take vertically worked jigs. White colors and candy-bar styles are best.

When and Where to Fish, Tackle and Equipment. Often the prime time to take white seas bass is at night during the spring when the squid are mating. But many white sea bass are caught in daylight hours. A heavy, conventional, saltwater rod and reel is used for white sea bass. They don't fight long, but do put up a tenacious, deep battle, and at times, use the kelp to get tangled and escape.

Some of the best places are the Coronado Islands (in winter), Catalina Island, Santa Cruz Island, off Carpenteria, and Rocky Point near Redondo Beach. But white sea bass are taken all year along the Southland coast, some in bays and shallow inland waters. See the "Pacific Ocean Fishing" chapter of this book.

Cleaning and Cooking. White sea bass are filleted or the bigger fish steaked. The preparation method of choice will result in a delicious meal.

Giant Sea Bass

Because of a precipitous decline in both size and numbers, there has been a moratorium on the taking of a giant sea bass in California since 1983. And the ban seems to be helping. Party boats are reporting catching and releasing more and more juvenile giant sea bass while in the process of fishing for other species.

Giant sea bass often reach weights of several hundred pounds—but his takes years and years. They don't even reach sexual maturity until they are 12-15 years old, about 40 inches long, and 60 pounds in weight. Anglers know when they catch a silver gray fish with black spots weighing 80 or 90 pounds, that it's a giant sea bass which must be released.

But problems arise with juvenile giant sea bass. Juveniles are perch-like in appearance, have radically different coloration from adults, but are big enough (averaging about 10 pounds and 24 inches) to be "keepers" in the eyes of many uninformed anglers who often mistake them for other species.

Because of the long life cycle of the giant sea bass, the moratorium on landing them may last for years. Therefore, know how to identify them and how to release them. Juvenile giant sea bass are brick or sandy red with white and black spots along their sides. Often giant sea bass are hooked in a deep rocky environment so they arrive at the surface with their swim bloders inflated. Here's how to release them:

Releasing Giant Sea Bass

Regardless of the size of the fish, the technique is the same. Pick a spot on the side of the fish under the tip of the pectoral fin when the fin is laying against the fish's side. Remove a scale with the point of the needle and insert the needle through the exposed skin and body wall. When the needle has penetrated the gas bladder, the air will rush out the other end. Compress the side of the fish until the sides appear normal or concave. Withdraw the needle and return the fish to the water. The fish will probably swim rapidly to the bottom, but if it doesn't, a few prods with a blunt instrument should sent it on its way. No vital organs are harmed using this method, and the chance of infection is slight if the needle is cleaned between uses. Unhooking the fish is often more harmful than using this technique, so always remember, if a fish is hooked deeply or in the gill area, it is best to cut the leader and release the fish with the hook in place.

How to Catch . . . Bluegill (and Redear Sunfish)

Bluegills are the most abundant panfish in California waters. They're in virtually all warm water lakes in Southern California. They were introduced into California in 1908 from Illinois. These fish are fun to catch and are very enjoyable eating. And in many locations they are abundant, so there is no need to feel guilty about taking them. They reproduce with great success, and heavy populations can crowd out large sport fish and stunt bluegills' growth. Bluegill angling is easy and relaxing fishing. And it is especially enjoyable for youngsters. Give them a rod and reel, a can of worms and a little dock, and they're set for hours of fun and adventure.

Redear Sunfish

Redear sunfish are California's bigger and better, modern day bluegill. Let me explain. When nature shaped the landscape of California, warm water lake and stream habitats, and the fishes that occupied them, were limited. Only the Sacramento perch, tule perch and a number of minnow and sucker species were found in warmer sections of streams and the few permanent lakes that existed prior to 1870. But during the decades that followed, large scale reservoir construction greatly expanded warm water lake habitat. Many species (black bass, catfish, crappie, bluegill) were stocked and flourished in these artificial, warm water lakes.

Redear sunfish are native to waters in the southern United States, Rio Grande and Mississippi rivers. But they were observed in the lower Colorado River, in Southern California, in 1940. They've since been stocked in Southern California lakes and reservoirs because they outperform the old standby bluegill. While not as plentiful as bluegills, which they resemble and with which they often hybridize, redear are highly regarded by SoCal anglers because they usually grow faster and larger then bluegills. The listed California record redear is 3 pounds 7 ounces! Fish in the 1/2 to 3/4 pound range are not uncommon. They can be distinguished from other panfish by their bright orange-red margin on the tip of each gill cover, a more slender body than the bluegill, and a typical greenish color blending to pale yellow on the lower body and abdomen.

Florida Bluegill

The first Florida-strain bluegill came to California by accident with a shipment of Florida-strain bass. Like their southern largemouth cousins, the Florida bluegill also exhibit many of the same traits—namely they grow to larger sizes than their northern cousins. The Florida's were first introduced into San Diego County waters and promptly produced a state record at Lower Otay Reservoir at 3 lbs, 10 oz.

Recognizing their potential, the DFG has continued to plant the bluegill into other waters in the southern part of the state, and where it was once uncommon to see bluegill over 3/4-pound, fish that size are now common. Many lakes—Perris, Otay, and San Vicente are just some examples—now produce a lot of fish over 2 pounds each year and 3 pounders are caught annually.

Finding Fish in a Lake

Fishing habitat and techniques for bluegill and redear sunfish are much alike. So in the remainder of this section, the word bluegill will be used to refer to both bluegill and redear, except where a distinction is made for redear sunfish.

The easiest time to find bluegills is when they spawn in shallow water in the spring (March-May). They'll be in 2 to 10 feet of water over sand or gravel bottoms. Be careful not to spook them if the water is clear. In summer bluegills behave like bass, moving to submerged channels, under docks, over bars, to weed beds or drop-offs. It's at these times that it may be necessary to fish 10-40 feet down. A drifting, rowed or trolled boat with baits suspended at various depths can often find them. Bluegills are always in schools, so when you find one, you've found a bunch. Any type of fishing tackle (spinning, spin casting, bait casting, cane pole) is fine.

Bait Fishing

This is probably the most popular approach, especially for kids. Some of the best baits are red worms, mealworms, crickets, chunks of nightcrawlers and small grasshoppers. Commercial dough-type baits also work. A bobber is most often used to keep the bait off the bottom and to signal a bite. From shore you can use a bobber rig as illustrated below.

From a boat or dock you can use the same bobber rig, or take the bobber off and fish straight below the pole or rod tip.

Still fishing, or bait fishing for bluegills, might be somewhat of a misnomer. Most experts agree that a slight movement of your bait is desirable. With any rig, flick the rod tip frequently to move your bait. Another principle is to change depths if action is slow. Frequently, large bluegills are down deeper than most bobber anglers suspect.

Fly Fishing, Casting Bobbers, Etc.

Fly casting for bluegills is enjoyable and productive. A medium action, 7 1/2 to 8 1/2 foot rod is suggested, but any will do. A wide variety of offerings will produce depending on the lake, the time of year and the time of day:

- Panfish poppers—swim them slowly along in a stop-and-go fashion
- Rubber or plastic-legged spiders
- Mosquitos, Ants, Wooly Worms, Black Gnats (#10,12)
- Bucktail streamers (size 8)
- Nymphs (black, gray, olive, brown, etc.)
- Indiana spinners (#2 blades, #8 hook)

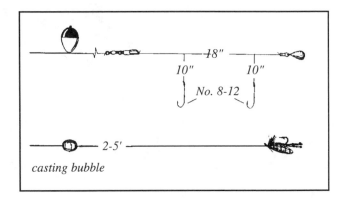

casting bubble

A casting bobber is a small bobber, usually made of clear plastic, that is attached to monofilament line. Because of its weight, (some allow you to let in water to make it even heavier) it allows anglers to cast poppers, flies, etc., using spinning, spin casting or bait casting equipment. So you can enjoy "fly fishing" without having to use a fly rod and reel.

Another category of offering that works great are soft plastic grubs and small jigs. Jig heads (micro jigs) in the 1/16 to 1/32 ounce size are about right. For more details, see the Crappie section.

Where to Fish

Bluegills can be found in just about any waters holding bass or other warm water species. (See the "Freshwater Fishing" chapters.) Redears and big Florida-strain bluegills abound in many of the San Diego area lakes. Ask around and you may happily find that these mega-bluegills have established a colony in your local lake.

Cleaning and Cooking

Since bluegills are small most people clean them in the traditional way. Scale them by rubbing a knife or scaling tool from the tail of the fish towards the head. Next, cut open the belly, starting from the anus, and remove the guts. Finally, cut off the head. Rinse them off and they're ready for the pan. An alternative is to fillet them, especially for bigger sunfish. This yields small fillets and eliminates skin and bones in the cooked fish. See instructions on filleting in the Fish Cleaning chapter. Sauteing the whole fish or individual fillets is most popular. See the Crappie section for an excellent recipe.

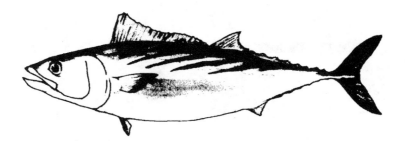

How to Catch . . . Bonito

Bonito are one of the finest sport fishing opportunities for inshore ocean anglers. They are caught from breakwaters, piers, small skiffs, private boats and party boats. Bonito can range in size from a pound or two up to 12 pounds. The average catch is about 2 or 3 pounds. And some say that for their size, bonito are the best fighting fish caught in Southern California ocean waters. Bonito, which are related to the bluefin tuna, fight just as hard as many tuna.

Fishing Techniques

The first order is to find the fish. Shore anglers should keep up on local reports of fishing activity. Party boat anglers count on the skipper to take them to the right spot, and on the deck hand who attracts fish with generous helpings of live anchovies tossed overboard. This approach, called chumming, is also practiced by private boat anglers. Bird activity can also be a tip-off of bonito feeding action near the surface. Boaters sometimes also use a "Bonito Splasher." Dragging it through the water trailing a feather jig on a leader, causes a surface commotion that hungry bonito can't resist. After the feather jig-hooked fish is landed, chumming, live bait fishing, or lure casting can begin for the rest of the school.

The vast majority of bonito are caught on collar-hooked (slipping the hook under the bone behind the gill cover) live anchovies. This applies to shore anglers, private boat anglers and party boat anglers. But cast lures are also used successfully. When large schools of bonito are migrating offshore, trolling is a good method for taking them. Trollers use 20-30 pound test line on live bait outfits. Most successful lures are small albacore feathers (from 4-6 inches) and chrome-headed bonito feathers. All white, all black, and blue or red mixed with white are good. Troll the lure close to the boat (like albacore trolling) at about 5 to 8 knots.

Tackle and Equipment

Heavy freshwater or light saltwater tackle is the way to go for bonito angling. For example, some anglers use a largemouth bass rod with 10-pound test line and an adjustable drag reel. An average fish will put up an exciting 10-minute fight on this equipment. Fly rodders also get in on the bonito action. Whatever tacke you use, make sure it holds adequate line for the bonito's long surface runs. One hundred yards of line is a minimum.

Bait and Lures

Live anchovies are the bait of choice. Collar hook them (see Barracuda section of this book) and don't use any sinker, if possible. A #2 to #6 hook is tied directly to the main line. If you need to go deeper, nose hook the anchovy and use a small rubber core sinker. Small (1/4 to 3/8 ounce) feather jigs, spoons, plugs and spinners (like Rooster Tails) often work when cast. Noisy largemouth bass surface plugs are also a good bet. Bonito like commotion. Sometimes onshore bonito are near the bottom. Try 1/4-ounce chrome Kastmasters or small white curl-tail plastic grubs on 1/4 ounce jig heads to hook your share.

Where to Fish

One place where bonito congregate year around in Southern California is King Harbor in Redondo Beach. They like the warm water flowing out of the Southern California Edison power plant. Besides water inflows, bonito are also found along kelp beds and at the islands. Also see the "Pacific Ocean Fishing" chapter of this book for more boat locations and shore locations.

Cleaning and Cooking

Bonito are usually filleted although they can be steaked. Be sure to remove all the dark lateral meat and the skin. Many anglers are not that excited about the taste of bonito, but it is good smoked or barbecued. Fresh bonito should be bled when caught and eaten that same day, unless it's headed for the smoker. Bonito are bled by cutting the fleshy portion under the head where the gill covers come together. Some suggest that bonito make fine garden fertilizer. But if you're not going to eat it, why not release it.

WHITE CATFISH

CHANNEL CATFISH

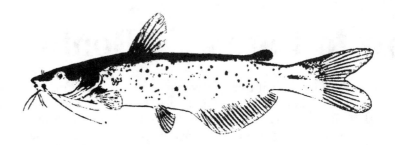

How to Catch . . . Catfish

Catfish are widespread and abundant in Southern California lakes, rivers, sloughs, canals and farm ponds. Despite their unappetizing appearance and somewhat negative image, catfish are very good eating. (Catfish are not as difficult to clean as one might suspect, either.) The delicious meals provided by catfish are attested to by the existence of hundreds of catfish farms, primarily in the Southeastern U.S. where these fish are raised and sold to restaurants and food stores. They get large too. California state records for blue and channel catfish are in the 50-80 pound range.

Fishing Techniques

Catfishing means still fishing. And catfish means warm weather fishing since these critters like warm water and are most active when lakes, ponds and rivers warm up in the late spring, summer and early fall. Boats are not needed for catfishing. Simply find a spot on shore where you have enough room to cast out your weighted rig. Let it sink to the bottom. Snug up the line. And wait for the prowling whiskerfish to find your offering. A bank, dock or pier where you can sit on a comfortable chair makes things perfect.

The best catfishing and the largest catfish (they can weigh 5, 10, 20 pounds or more) are often caught after dark. From dark to midnight and the several hours before sunup are particularly good. Early evening can also be good. But many catfish, including big ones, are caught on lazy summer after-noons. Bring several baits along. If one doesn't produce, try something else. Often, this single maneuver can make all the difference. In daylight hours, concentrate on shady spots.

Tackle and Equipment

Any rod and reel combination that can cast out a rig with a 1/2-6 oz. sinker will do just fine. These include specialized bass fishing tackle, light to medium spinning equipment and surf casting equipment. In some situations, you'll probably be better off with a longer rod (7-8 feet), so longer casts are possible. Use at least 10 pound test. But heavier line such as 15-20 pound test is no problem.

Bait and Rigging

Catfish will eat almost anything, and they feed by both sight and by smell. Their smell sensors are on their whiskers. In fact, some catfish baits are often referred to as stink baits because, at times, it seems that catfish prefer smelly offerings such as beef liver, coagulated blood, chicken entrails, etc.

In Southern California some of the most successful baits are less repulsive. These include fresh clams (keep them on ice, pry them open with a knife, thread hook through hard outer edges), nightcrawlers, anchovies, red worms, sardine chunks and chicken livers. Mackerel pieces, however, are by far the most common bait.

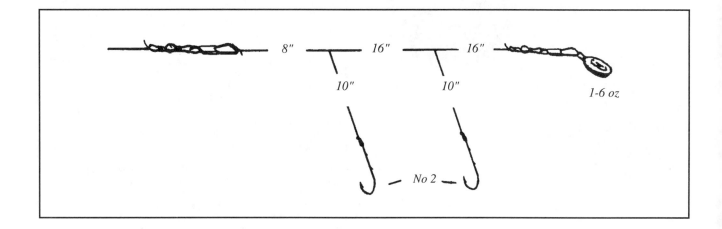

The conventional catfish rig is shown on the next page. A popular alternative is the sliding sinker rig. (For a specific description, see the Striped Bass section.) Some anglers use a treble hook which helps hold on the bait. Use enough weight to get the casting distance you want and to hold the rig on the bottom if there is a current. Some anglers prefer a dipsey sinker. It has a flat metal rim around the edge which makes it flutter up on a quick retrieve, so it's less likely to get caught in rock crevices and roots.

Where to Fish

Some of the best spots are in the lakes and reservoirs described later on in this book. Irvine Lake (which holds the state record for both the channel catfish) and Santa Anna River Lakes in Orange County are both top producers. The largest flathead catfish are taken in the lower Colorado River and the Imperial Valley canals (e.g. All American Canal) and require 30 to 50 pound test line and gear.

In San Diego County, Henshaw, Cuyamaca, Sutherland, El Capitan, Morena, Santee, Otay, Hodges and Wohlford are fine catfish producers. Then add Poway, Dixon, and Jennings as San Diego lakes with nightfishing programs. Further north some good bets include Isabella, Cachuma, Casitas, Pine Flat and Buena Vista.

Cleaning and Cooking

The first step in catfish cleaning is skin removal. To skin a catfish, cut through the skin all around the fish just below the gill cover. Then using a pliers, pull the skin down the fish while holding the fish's gills. Be careful not to be poked by the sharp pectoral and dorsal fin spines. Some people nip these off with wire cutters. For larger fish it is suggested that the fish be nailed (through the head) to a tree trunk or fence post using an adequately sized spike. The skinned catfish can then be filleted or steaked. (See the Fish Cleaning chapter for more details.) Catfish meat is flaky, mild and has a moist texture. It is good sauteed, fried or poached.

Catfish cut into 1/2-inch cubes, dipped in beer batter and deep fried in hot grease is hard to beat. All varieties of catfish are tasty, but channels, taken out of cool, moving water or deep, clear lakes are rated as tops for eating.

Reburying Pismo Clams*

One problem caused by large numbers of small clams at a beach is that a clammer must dig through hundreds of clams to find a limit of 10 clams over 4-1/2 inches. Often, some of these small clams are left unburied. Clams left exposed on the beach can overheat and die, or be eaten by gulls, or be smashed by vehicles where cars are allowed on the beach.

To increase survival of small clams left behind and to ensure the conservation of this resource, California sport fishing regulations require that undersized clams be reburied in the area from which they were dug.

Pismo clams have very thick shells to withstand pounding surf on sandy beaches. Their shells are thickest at the hinge and they are normally found with their "backs" (hinge) toward the incoming surf. Also, a clam has a top and bottom end. The top, which is the end closest to the brown bump (hinge ligament), is where siphons bring in and expel sea water for feeding and respiration.

It is important to bury a clam with the top and brown bump up so the siphons can reach the surface of the sand and with the hinge towards the ocean. The clams should be buried in a hole or pushed into the wet sand until covered. Following these simple steps will help ensure survival and conservation of Pismo clams.

How to Catch . . . Clams and Mussels

I know that clams aren't fish and that they are gathered rather than caught on a hook and line. But clamming is a whole lot of fun, and clams are very good eating. Therefore, we decided to include a section on Southern California clamming, even if it rubs purists the wrong way.

There are three major types of clams and clam gathering opportunities. Each is done in a different habitat, and each requires a different approach and equipment.

Littleneck Clams

Pacific littleneck clams (or cockles) inhabit intertidal, rocky, cobble areas, especially near stream mouths and under boulders. Their shells are circular in shape and defined by many fine radiating and circular lines. The exterior of the shell is usually tan or cream, but some may be dark gray. The interior is white.

Look for a beach that is covered with stones and rocks. The best time to go is when the tide is very low, about a minus 1.0 or so. Stay away from sandy areas. Look for empty shells—a tip-off that a colony may be nearby. Once you hit a good spot, a limit may be found in a small intertidal area. Some clammers move boulders with crowbars to get at littlenecks. Sometimes keen-eyed clammers can spot the narrow clam siphons, cream-colored with black tips.

You'll need digging tools like bars, trowels, or rakes (usually with a short handle). A homemade measuring device to return underside clams is also required. Be sure to also bring a clam basket and gloves. Most littlenecks are only about 3-4 inches below the rock and sand mix. Minimum size is 1 1/2 inches (big ones are 3 inches) and the limit is 50. Any soft-shell clam, regardless of size and condition, must be retained and counted in the limit.

Pismo Clams

Pismo clams are big and solid, sometimes growing over 7 inches. Their shape is roughly triangular, and coloration ranges from tan to chalky gray, sometimes with darker radiating lines. Their siphon is light colored. Pismo clams can be found all the way up to Half Moon Bay in Monterey County, but are scarce above Pt. Conception because of the foraging of sea otters.

Again, the best gathering conditions are at a minus low tide. Wade out as far as you can with a pitchfork or rake in hand. Jab the pitchfork into the sand until you feel something hard. Then with your free hand, reach down, with the fork still in position, and dig out the clam. Measure it, and then put it in your pan, gather-bag, or return it. When using a rake, apply downward pressure and hold onto the clam until you can dig it up with your free hand. Offshore sand bars are always prime spots to search. Clammers wear all kinds of outfits, from wet suits, to jeans and sweaters, to hip waders.

Skin divers also dive for pismo clams at high tide. Look for them in 10 to 20 feet of water. Shallower water is too turbulent.

There are clam preserves in San Luis Obispo County in the Pismo Beach area. There are also size limits, bag limits, and seasons in some counties.

Mussels

Mussels live on exposed rocky shorelines and on manmade structures like jetties or islands. Blue or bay mussels have a shiny blue shell and grow to about 3 inches. They are found worldwide and are a popular food in Europe. The California mussel is narrower and coarser than the blue and can grow up to 7 inches. There are circular rings and ribs on the shell's surface which is almost black at the edges. Mussel hunters should wear boots with non-skid soles. A pocketknife is sufficient to pry off the mussels. They store well in a gunnysack. The current limit is 10 pounds including the shells.

Mussels are usually quarantined from May through October when they concentrate deadly toxins in their bodies.

Cleaning and Cooking

One caution: never put clams in a galvanized bucket. An electrolyte action may be set up, ruining the clams.

The best way to get sand out of clams is to keep them in saltwater for one or two days. Change the water several times during this period. Don't use fresh water. Clams are shucked (opened) with a clam knife or a dull and rigid paring knife. Force the knife between the shells, being careful not to mutilate the meat. Once open, the connecting muscles can be separated from the shell. Another way to clean clams is to freeze them. When they thaw they'll gape open and the sand can be quickly rinsed out. Cockles are a favorite for eating. Many people steam them and then dip them in butter sauce (perhaps seasoned with garlic). Overcooking of any clam should be avoided to prevent toughness.

Mussels are generally steamed open when recipes call for shucked mussels, but they may also be cooked in the shell. They are a good substitute in recipes that call for cooked clams or oysters.

Special: Pismo Clams Rebound*

It was 6 p.m. and growing dark on a cold January evening at Pismo Beach when five marine biologists from the Department of Fish and Game's Morro Bay field laboratory retrieved and loaded up their clam digging gear.

They had just completed digging one of nine trenches to count and measure Pismo clams in the Pismo Beach-Oceano Beach area. The information is used to estimate the success of Pismo clam spawning on the beaches and to determine how much the clams have grown in the last previous year.

In this trench, the biologists found 692 clams, ranging in size from 3/4 inch to just over 4-1/2 inches, the minimum legal size for Pismo clams south of the San Luis Obispo-Monterey County line. The biologists found only one legal-sized clam in the 280-feet by 6-inch trench dug from the upper beach down to the water. But this clam was one of the first legal-size Pismo clams the biologists had seen in this area in many years.

Just five years earlier, in 1986, there were only seven clams in this same trench and the largest was 3-1/4 inches. By 1988, the trench yielded 228 clams ranging from 5/8 inch to 3-1/2 inches.

The changing numbers of Pismo clams in the Pismo Beach-Oceano Beach area over the last 10 years is the result of a complex of interactions involving Pismo clams, sea otters, sport clammers and oceanic conditions.

The Pismo and Oceano beaches have been world-renowned for sport clamming. The City of Pismo Beach calls itself the "Clam Capital of the World" and for many years this was true. For decades, clammers crowded the beaches during minus tides and took home limits of 10 clams for chowder and other clam dishes.

In 1979, however, the California population of sea otters extended its range into the Pismo Beach area and began foraging on Pismo clams. The number of clams available for the sport clam digger rapidly declined.

Department biologists studied the otters foraging on clams. One otter ate 40 clams in two hours. Sea otters do not have a thick layer of insulating fat like other marine mammals. Instead, other adaptations, such as thick fur and a large daily food intake, allow them to live in cold ocean water. A sea otter may consume up to 25 percent of its weight in food each day. Collectively, otters foraging along Pismo Beach ate thousands of clams daily, some as small as two inches.

By June 1981, it was difficult to find Pismo clams of any size anywhere along the Pismo Beach coast, and it was rare to find sport clammers trying to find any. The decline in clams along the beaches followed the movement of foraging sea otters from north to south along the beaches. And, the decline in clam numbers occurred at all beaches, whether or not they were open to sport clammers.

As the otters continued to forage on the clams, the clam population declined to a point where it became difficult for otters to find clams. The otters then shifted their foraging activities to more readily available prey items, such as crabs.

Seven trenches were dug during the winter of 1985-1986 in the Pismo Beach area and only 36 clams were found. Department biologists have been digging clam trenches at Pismo Beach since 1925 and had never noted such a dramatic drop in number of clams. They were concerned the Pismo clam population would never recover to a point where it could support a recreational fishery.

But the winter of 1986 brought with it oceanic conditions exceptionally favorable for Pismo clam spawning and larval survival, and the Pismo clam population began to rebound at Pismo Beach. The favorable conditions occurred again in 1987 and in 1988. The combination of reduced foraging on Pismo clams by sea otters and three years of excellent spawning and survival resulted in the tremendous clams densities the biologists saw during their survey in January 1991.

Millions of clams are again on the Pismo-Oceano Beaches, surviving and growing. The sport clam fishery has revived and hundreds of clammers are on the beaches on days of low tides trying to get their limit of 10 clams. Clams too small to be kept are growing about one inch per year.

Clams that settled into the sand in 1986 are now over 4 inches, the 1987 clams are 3-4 inches, and the 1988 clams are 2-3 inches. Over the next couple of years, many of these clams could be harvested as they reach the 4-1/2 inch size limit.

Marine biologists continue studying the clams and are watching both the clammer success rate and the activities of the otters. The otter population has continued to grow, but it has not expanded its range much since the early 1980s. Department biologists are watching sea otters in the area to document numbers and foraging habits.

Their observations of sea otter feeding habits in late 1991 indicate sea otters are increasing their foraging activity on Pismo clams over levels noted in the last few years.

Biologists performing the annual clam studies have documented evidence of some clam spawning and survival since 1988, but small clams are not being found in the abundance seen from 1986 to 1988. Reports indicate that clam populations may go for as long as 20 years without episodes of extremely successful spawning and survival. It is possible that it will be years before favorable oceanic conditions produce another great "set" of Pismo clams at Pismo Beach.

If sea otters resume heavy foraging on the clams, there may be fewer clams reaching legal size in the upcoming years. This would result in fewer clams available for sport clammers and the number of clammers could again decline as it did 10 years ago.

Department biologists will continue counting and measuring clams, monitoring clammer success, and observing foraging activity of sea otters to follow the future abundance of Pismo clams.

---

* by Sandy Owen, *Outdoor California*, July-August 1992

BLACK CRAPPIE

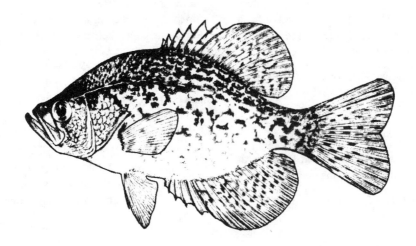

How to Catch . . . Crappie

Crappies (pronounced krop'-i) are the king of the panfish. Both black crappies and white crappies can grow quite large (state records: black crappie—4 pounds 1 ounce; white crappie—4 pounds 8 ounces), but most crappies average a pound or even less. A two-pounder is bragging size. Crappies provide fun and relaxed fishing on light tackle and are excellent eating.

Black crappies are the most widespread of the two types and do the best in clearer water. Adult crappies are fish eaters, so they need an abundant supply of forage, like shad, to do well. Surprising to some, crappies also need a good deal of fishing pressure, otherwise they overpopulate their lake and all are stunted. So enjoy catching and eating crappies, it's good for the fish and good for the angler.

Finding Crappies in a Lake

The key to successful crappie fishing is finding them. These are school fish that cluster in different parts of a lake depending on season, water temperature, reproductive cycles, underwater contours, etc.

Crappies are easiest to find and catch when they move into shallow water to spawn. This happens when the water temperature reaches about 60-65°F. March, April and May are the likely months. These fish like heavy cover to accompany the shallow water. Look for water 3-8 feet deep with sunken trees, tule beds, cattails, lily pads and undercut rocky banks. This is much like the cover used by largemouth bass. Shore anglers do well in spring, as the fish move in close.

In summer and winter crappies are harder to find, so stringers get skimpier or are empty. But they are still there and eating. Here are some ways to find them. Look in deeper water. They're usually down in 10-20 foot water or deeper. Crappies like underwater islands and stream beds, ledges, etc. Often they are in deeper water just adjacent to where they were in the spring. One good way to find them is to troll a jig or minnow across likely spots with lines of various depths. Mark the spot and depth when you get a hit. Troll slowly with oars or electric motor, or drift. Electronic fish finders will also do the job.

In the fall, crappies are not quite as deep as in the summer (8-16 feet). And early and late in the day, crappies, like bass, move into shallower water to feed. So even in the summer, the first angler on the lake, or the last to call it a day, may fill a stringer with crappies in shallow water.

Jig Fishing

This is by far the most popular method of taking crappies all year long. A word of caution before getting into the technique of this approach: It's easy to spook schools of crappies (especially in shallow water), so fish quietly and keep a low profile. And don't, for example, slide an anchor or tackle box along the bottom of your boat. Approach likely spots slowly and carefully.

Crappie jigs, or mini-jigs, are in the 1/32 to 1/8 ounce size range. Most are little lead-head jigs with a bright colored feather covering the hook end. Eyes are often painted on the head end. Some like Sassy Shad Jigs have rubber bodies that imitate swimming shad.

Tie these jigs directly on about a 4, or even a 2 pound test line. Light line gives the jig better action. Short, accurate casts are called for from boat or shore. But since you'll be casting into cover, expect snags and expect to lose some jigs. Allow the jig to sink to the desired depth, and then retrieve either smoothly and slowly, or impart a twitching action with the rod tip.

A small, clear casting bobber can be added up the line from the jig if it's too light to cast the desired distance. The bobber will also prevent the jig from going deeper than it is set below the bobber. See the Bluegill section for illustration of a casting bobber. Boat anglers, when directly over a school of crappie, can drop a jig straight down and then twitch it around.

Crappie jigs come in many colors. Here are some guidelines. Light colors, like white, work well on clear days in clear water. Yellow is better on overcast days and at dawn and dusk. In off-colored water try dark colors like brown and blacks. Experiment with different styles and colors. These jigs are inexpensive. Sometimes color doesn't even seem to matter.

Bait Fishing

Crappies love minnows, so if you prefer live minnow fishing, this is the way to go, but be sure minnows are a legal bait where you are fishing. Bait can be fished from shore, dock or boat. Most anglers use a bobber. A typical rig is shown below.

Minnows are best hooked up through both lips.

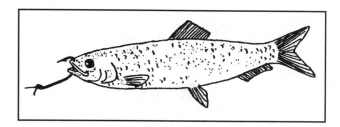

Most experts agree that a slight movement of your bait is desirable. Flick the rod tip frequently to move your bait. Another basic principle is to change depths if the action is slow.

Frequently, larger crappies are deeper down than most bobber anglers suspect. These anglers use a sliding bobber rig to get their bait deeper while still being able to cast and retrieve the crappie to back near the rod tip. The main line slides through the slip bobber. This rig can be reeled in all the way until the bobber is up against the swivel. That's because the rubber band bobber-stop is small enough to pass smoothly through the rod line guides. After casting out, the sinker will pull the rig through the bobber until the rubber band bobber-

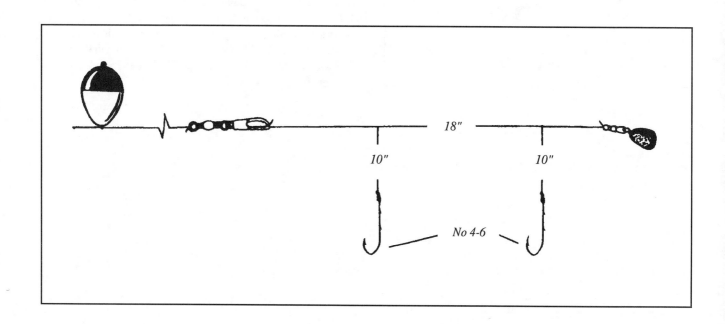

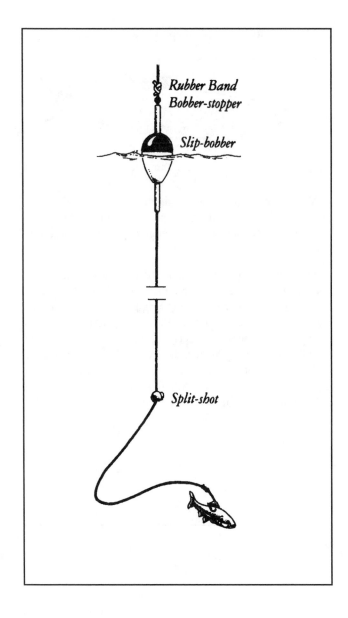

Rubber Band
Bobber-stopper

Slip-bobber

Split-shot

stop gets to the bobber. By changing the location of the bobber-stop on the line, you can change fishing depth.

Tackle and Equipment

Just about any light freshwater tackle will do such as light spinning, spin casting, bamboo poles and long fly rods. Actually, the lighter the tackle the better, since it will help cast out the light jigs and baits. Ultralight spinning tackle is popular. The only other thing you'll need is a stringer or a collapsible fish basket.

Where to Fish

Crappies are found in abundant supply in many Southern California lakes. Some of the lakes that are known for fine crappie fishing are Henshaw, Isabella, Silverwood, Casitas and El Capitan. See details on these and other fine crappie lakes in the "Freshwater Fishing" chapters.

Cleaning and Cooking

Many people clean crappie in the traditional way. Scale them by rubbing a knife or scaling tool from the tail of the fish to the head. Cut open the belly and remove the guts. Finally, cut off the head. Rinse them off and they're ready for the pan.

An alternative for good-sized fish is to fillet them. This yields a little less meat, but filleting eliminates skin and bone in the cooked fish. See instructions on filleting in the "Fish Cleaning" chapter. Sauteing the whole fish or individual fillets is most popular. Dip them into sifted flour and sprinkle with salt, pepper, parsley and lemon flakes (if desired). Melt butter in a hot skillet, toss in the fish and turn until golden brown. Another delicious method is to batter and deep-fry pieces cut from fillets.

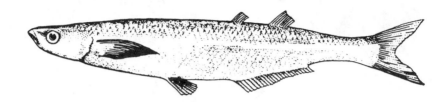

How to Catch . . . Grunion

Grunion catching, or watching other people catch grunion, or watching other people try to catch grunion, or all three, is a special treat that all anglers and their families should experience at least once in their lifetimes.

Grunion catching is done on the beaches in Southern California. You see, these fish spawn by the light of the moon, not in the water, but right on the beach. Why should we be so surprised? Some people do the same thing. In fact, maybe the grunion learned it from us!

Grunion spawn only 3 or 4 nights after the highest tide associated with a full moon, or new moon, in the spring and summer. A run lasts from one to three hours. Females bury themselves in the sand up to their pectoral fins before dispeling their eggs which are eagerly fertilized by males surrounding them. Both males and females then return to the sea. Falling tides cover over the eggs. They incubate for about two weeks and then hatch after being exposed by ensuing rising tides. These newborn little grunion then swim into the sea. Isn't nature marvelous?

Fishing Techniques

Full-size grunion are about 5 to 6 inches long. The first sign of a run occurs when a smattering of male grunion show up on a beach. If all looks right (anglers should stay back and be quiet at this point) hoards of male and female grunion will soon follow. This in turn prompts grunion seekers to run onto the beach with pail and flashlights. They pick them up as best as they can using their bare hands. It's best to grab the front half of the fish to prevent them from wiggling away.

It's hard not to get a lot of fish during a good run. But don't take more than you can eat, or freeze, for future eating. They're also good bait.

Tackle and Equipment

Follow all of the Department of Fish and Game regulations. No tackle or equipment can be used to catch grunion—only bare hands. No bucket scooping either—it's illegal. Bring a flashlight to see the grunion and a bucket to hold them.

When to Fish

Forecasts are made to predict summer grunion runs. In some areas these are broadcast or printed in local papers and most tide books have run dates listed. Ocean-oriented bait and tackle stores can be helpful. Most of the predicted runs are around midnight.

Where to Fish

The best beaches are gently sloping and have fine sand. If there are crowds of people on the beach (not spawning, but watching for grunion), move to the end of the beach (grunion don't like people to watch). Some of the top Southern California beaches for grunion are as follows:

Santa Barbara	Huntington
Santa Monica	Newport
Venice	Corona Del Mar
Hermosa	La Jolla
Cabrillo	Mission Beach
Long Beach	Coronado Strand
Malibu	Catalina Island

Cleaning and Cooking

Behead, gut and wash before cooking. On these tiny fish, this is easily done with a scissors. A popular way to prepare these little guys is to roll them in a mixture of cornmeal, flour, salt and pepper. Then fry briefly in hot oil, or pan fry them in butter.

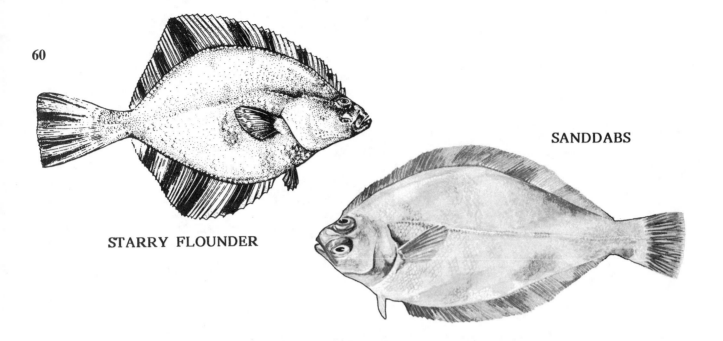

STARRY FLOUNDER

SANDDABS

How to Catch . . . Flounder and Sanddabs

Here are two great saltwater species that don't get the attention they deserve. Both of these junior-sized members of the flatfish family are lots of fun to catch, and rank among the best eating of all Southern California sport fish. The flounder caught in Southern California, both commercially and by sport anglers, is the starry flounder. It is sometimes sold in fish markets as sole. The pan-sided sanddab, served in some of the finest fish restaurants, is not available at most fish markets.

Catching Starry Flounder

Each winter thousands of starry flounder migrate from Pacific Ocean waters (at a depth of as much as 900 feet) into bays, lagoons, and to some extent even into the fresh water of coastal runs, where they then spawn. Fishing is usually good from mid-December through March with a peak in February. The average catch is 1 to 3 pounds and 12 to 18 inches in length. But 6 to 7 pounders about 2 feet long are caught. Starry flounder are dark brown on the top side, white on the bottom side, and have a very distinctive checkerboard orange and black alternating color pattern on both the upper and lower fin lines.

San Diego Bay, Mission Bay, Newport Bay, San Pedro Bay, Santa Monica Bay, San Luis Obispo Bay and Morrow Bay are all good prospects.

Fish shallow water with sandy or mud bottoms. One key to success is to seek out areas around the bays where fresh water runs in. River inlets, sloughs, creeks or even storm drains are all likely spots.

Any freshwater or light saltwater tackle and line will do. Tie or snap on a surf rig as shown in the Surf Fishing section of Chapter 2. Two #6 baitholder hooks and a 1 to 2 ounce pyramid sinker are about right. Sliding sinker rigs also work. Top baits for starry flounder are pile worms, blood worms, mussels, and shrimp. Bring along several different baits and experiment. Best fishing is before, during and after a substantial high tide (5 feet or so). Remember to keep your rig on the bottom—that's where flatfish feed.

Catching Sanddabs

Some seasoned fish eaters consider sanddabs the best tasting of all ocean fish—including salmon, halibut and albacore tuna. These little guys are commonly caught commercially, and served in many fine restaurants. But not many sport anglers pursue them, perhaps because they're small, only about 6 to 12 inches long. Although sanddab inhabit water that is from 30 to 1800 feet deep, they are most abundant at depths of 120 to 300 feet. As their name suggests, they live on sandy bottoms.

Some rockfish anglers, who work canyon drop-offs, will "stop off" at about 20 fathoms to catch a mess of sanddabs on their way back to the harbor, if time and weather permits. Live bait anglers who are getting "skunked" also switch over to sanddabs at times. A good spot in Long Beach is out about 9 miles, outside the oil islands.

Off the coast of Southern California if the depth is correct (120-250 feet) and the bottom suitable, it is extremely difficult to keep sanddabs off the hook. Rock cod rigs work. Surf rigs work. Use cut pieces of squid, pile worms, or shrimp for bait. In years when ocean waters are warmer than usual, sanddabs are also plentiful in coastal bays.

Cleaning and Cooking

Starry flounder are usually large enough to fillet. Remember there are 4 fillets on flatfish. Use a sharp, flexible fillet knife. See the five steps in the diagram at the right.

Starry flounder have a delicate, but distinctive flavor and nice texture. You can use them in any sole recipe. Skinless fillets are suitable for sauteing, poaching or broiling (if on the longer side).

Sanddabs are very easy to clean. The shape of their body is such that you can remove their head and their intestinal cavity in one cut taken diagonally over the head and the top of the pectoral fin. No need to scale or skin them. Just rinse them in cold running water after cutting. This fish is sweet, nut-like and moist. It's great charcoal grilled or pan fried. Breaded dabs pan fry quickly in about 2 minutes per side. They can be easily de-boned at the table, just like pan-sized trout or sunfish. Insert a butter knife or fork (or two) beneath the upper fillet and lift it off. The skeleton is now exposed on top of the bottom fillet. Just lift these bones off in one piece and you have a second de-boned fillet.

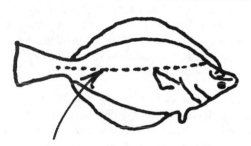

1. Make vertical cut down lateral line.

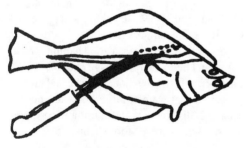

2. With angled blade, shave off flesh.

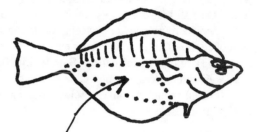

3. Shave off fillet from stomach side of fish.

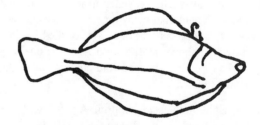

4. Repeat steps 1,2,3 on fish's light side.

5. Skin fillets by holding the edge of skin and shaving off the flesh.

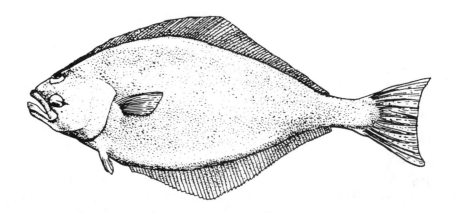

How to Catch . . . Halibut

Growing up in the Midwest as we did, halibut was one of the few store-bought fish that our family enjoyed. As a boy, I didn't know where halibut came from (except from the ocean), what they looked like (that they have both eyes on the same side of their head), or how to catch them. But the firm, flaky white meat was sure a treat on our table. Everybody in Southern California is lucky to live so close to some fine halibut fishing grounds.

California halibut is a flatfish and can range in size up to 50-75 pounds. The typical keeper is from 10 to 20 pounds. The minimum legal fish of 22" will weigh about 3 to 4 pounds. Adult halibut move into shallower water in the late spring and summer to spawn. Young fish swim upright, but during their first year, one eye migrates to the other side of the head and they begin to swim in a horizontal position. Also, the side with the two eyes (the top) turns dark, or sand-colored, while the bottom side turns light.

Halibut live right on the sandy bottom. A ruffling of fins and tail kicks up a cloud of sand that settles back on the fish, hiding it from both its predators and its prey. Only its two eyes are noticeable above the sand. They don't look for food—they wait in hiding for it to come to them. Therefore, successful anglers, in one way or another, keep their offering moving along sandy bottoms.

Fishing Techniques

California halibut fishing is primarily shallow water fishing. Because of this situation, it is possible to catch halibut from piers, by surf fishing on beaches, or from a boat. In all these cases, the basic idea is the same—get your offering down on the sandy bottom and keep it moving.

Cast out, let your offering sink to the bottom, and then retrieve. Move along the pier, putting special attention on casts just at the surf line.

Surf anglers have much more latitude. They can move along the beach, but can't reach as far out as pier casters. For specifics on pier and surf fishing for halibut, see the Pier Fishing and Surf Fishing sections in the "Fishing . . . SoCal Style" chapter of this book.

Fishing for halibut from a boat can be done by either trolling or drift fishing. Drift fishing here means to fish with bait from a boat drifting over productive areas. This is the dominant method for taking halibut in Southern California waters.

Waters of bays like Santa Monica and San Diego are popular halibut grounds. Most action takes place in depths of 6 to 60 feet. Some anglers seek out bottoms that are a combination rocky-sandy area, a good habitat for forage fish. In bays like San Diego, drifts across a channel are a good bet. Fishing is often best the few hours before and after high tide. In the protected bay waters, large boats are not necessary. Bass boats, tri-hull, ski boats and aluminum cartoppers are all used successfully, as are 40-foot yachts.

When drifting, lower your baited rig until you feel bottom. Let out some line (maybe 30 yards) to begin the drift. Then either set the drag just enough to prevent more line from going out, or release the bail or spool and hold the line between your fingers. When a halibut picks up the bait, most anglers give it line immediately. Some count to 20 or 30 before setting the hook! Others give the halibut "time to eat" before setting the hook. There is much controversy on "when to set the hook" when halibut fishing. Whatever you do, don't set the hook too hard. Many halibut are lip hooked. It's best to error on the gentle side.

Tackle and Equipment

Either spinning or conventional reels can be used for drift fishing. Since there is little or no casting involved, a conventional reel with a spool release and star-drag won't give backlash headaches. A medium to heavy spinning reel that will hold 150-200 yards of 10-12 pound test line is a good alternative. Use a rod of 6 to 7 feet with a sensitive tip. You'll also need a gaff, a large landing net, and a fish billy. A sharp blow midway down the body is recommended. Use a needlenose pliers to remove the hooks, and watch out for the sharp teeth

The most popular bait is live anchovies. These and other bait are nose hooked. Speaking of other baits, there is a group of them. These are usually referred to as brown baits which include tomcod, kingfish, herring and smelt. More and more anglers are finding success with these offerings. Some are bigger and tougher than anchovies.

Two types of rigs (shown below) and two types of hooks are used by halibut anglers. One rig uses a dropper for the sinker and the other uses a sliding sinker. Some prefer a treble hook (#8 or #10) while others prefer a single hook (#4 or #6). Either hook can be used with either rig.

Where to Fish

Santa Monica Bay and San Diego Bay are well known halibut grounds. For other boat spots and shore fishing opportunities, see the "Pacific Ocean Fishing" chapter.

Cleaning and Cooking

Smaller halibut can be filleted. Larger ones are steaked. Even when filleting, the tail section can be steaked. When filleting, first make a vertical cut (the fish is laying flat) along the lateral line down to the spine. This allows you to "lift off" two manageable-sized fillets from each side of the fish. Halibut is dense, mild, somewhat sweet, and low in fat. Popular cooking methods include broiling, barbecuing, poaching, frying and baking. The fillets can be sauteed.

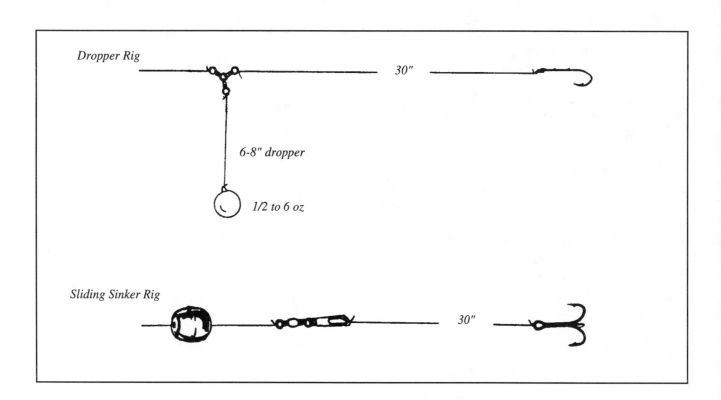

Dropper Rig

30"

6-8" dropper

1/2 to 6 oz

Sliding Sinker Rig

30"

How to Catch . . . Lingcod

Guess what? Lingcod are not cod. Lingcod are actually a greenling and are rockfish. But they are much larger and put up a tougher fight than other rockfish. Lings can reach upwards of 5 feet long and weigh up to 70 pounds. Average catches in Southern California are in the 10-15 pound range. Lingcod have an elongated bodies and very large mouths. They come in mottled browns, blues and turquoises.

Fishing Techniques

Lingcod can be caught at any time of the year. And many are caught by rockfish anglers, particularly while fishing in deep water (300-600 feet). In fact, at times a large ling will strike a small rockfish that has just been hooked. Veteran anglers gaff the ling before he lets go.

Experienced lingcod pursuers, however, choose to fish in the fall and winter. November to February are good. In these months the surface bite for other sport fish is off, the seas are often calm, and the ling are sometimes in shallower water. Lingcod fishing, like rockfishing, is bottom drift fishing. It is done over rocks or reefs. Once the rig has been lowered to the bottom it should be jigged up and down. Try to stay off the bottom to prevent snags.

Tackle and Equipment

You'll need a gaff (lings will tear up a landing net), a fish billy (to subdue this fish that has sharp teeth and fins), and a needlenose pliers (to take out the hook). The tackle you'll need is the same as needed for deep-water rockfishing:

- Medium heavy to heavy roller-tipped, 6-7 foot rod
- A 6/0 or 4/0 ocean reel
- 30-50 pound monofilament line

Lures and Bait

The most commonly used lures for lingcod are chrome hex bars, Tady Salsa and Straggler jigs, as well as Scampi and Salty Dog type lures. The appropriate lures range from 4 to 16 ounces, depending on ocean conditions and the lings' preferences. Some fishermen remove the strong treble hook that comes on this lure, and replace it with light wire treble hooks. When hung up in the rocks, the light hook bends and gives before the line breaks, thus saving the expensive (about $5.00) lures.

Many lingcod fishermen prefer bait fishing. The best bait is whole fish. Good choice include sanddabs, rockfish or squid. Some anglers cut the dorsal fin off rockfish and use it as bait. They say it makes the bait more appetizing. It's best if the bait is alive, or at least freshly caught. Seven to ten inches is a good size. Use a two-hook rig like the one shown below. The end hook goes through the bait fish's upper lip (or through both lips) and the other hook goes into the side of the fish near the tail.

Where to Fish

Some of the best spots are San Miguel Island, Santa Barbara Island and along the coast in the Avila Beach-Morro Bay-San Simeon region at Pt. Purisima, Pt. Buchon and Pt. Lopez. See the "Pacific Ocean Fishing" chapter of this book.

Cleaning and Cooking

Lingcod are most often filleted. Larger ones can be streaked.

Lingcod fillets or steaks are lean and mild tasting. Lingcod meat (depending on the age of the fish where it is caught) is often green, but turns white upon cooking. Thick fillets or steaks can be barbecued or broiled. They are also suitable for poaching or frying. Thinner fillets can be sauteed. Lingcod is rather dense, so it takes somewhat longer to cook.

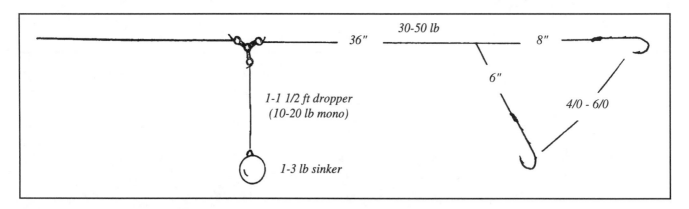

30-50 lb · 36" · 8" · 1-1 1/2 ft dropper (10-20 lb mono) · 1-3 lb sinker · 6" · 4/0 - 6/0

How to Catch . . . Marlin (Striped)

Striped marlin are one of the truly exotic sport fish available in the Pacific off Southern California. They are spectacular, strong, big fish. Some caught in local waters exceed 200 pounds. And they often make spectacular leaps when hooked.

Striped marlin, at times, make their first appearance in Southern California waters as early as July. But the best fishing months are usually September and October. Some striped marlin can still be around in November or even early December. In Baja, they are available year-round.

Striped marlin are not generally considered good eating fish (although there is a big commercial market in Japan), but they do make spectacular trophies. Most anglers catch these fish for the sport of it, and release them to be caught again some other day.

Fishing Techniques

Striped marlin are sometimes seen before they are hooked. They seem to live most of their lives near the surface and jump spontaneously. When sighted they are often swimming lazily at the surface with their dorsal fin and upper half of their tail fin sticking up out of the water. Anglers who sneak up on these schools of "sleeping" fish often get a strike by casting live Spanish or green mackerel or sardines.

But most striped marlin are caught by trolling, especially those that are sighted nearby or suddenly surface to hit a lure. Set the boat speed at about 7 or 8 knots and place your lure 50 to 75 feet behind the boat. When a hook-up occurs it's a good idea to use the boat to help set the hook in the marlin's tough mouth (even with the sharpest of hooks). Accelerate the boat for a short burst and let the fish take line against a snugged-down reel drag.

Tackle and Equipment

Some party boats will incidentally hook up with a striped marlin when trolling for albacore, but they generally do not actively pursue marlin. This fact, plus the fact that striped marlin are true blue-water fish, means that anglers need an open ocean boat to pursue marlin (or a friend or relative who has one). But a 45-foot sport fisher with fighting chair is not necessary. Many local fish are caught from boats in the 20-plus foot range.

A heavy trolling rod with roller tip and a 4/0 to 6/0 sized reel with 30-40 pound test monofilament line is also a must. Outriggers are also helpful, but not necessary. You don't even need a live bait tank since about two-thirds of SoCal marlin are taken by trolling artificial lures. Stand up fighting gear (i.e. rod belt, kidney harness, etc.) is fine for the typical SoCal marlin of 100-200 pounds.

Lures

The most popular striped marlin trolling lures go by such names as Clones, Koneheads, etc.

Size:	about 10-12 in. with size 7/0 to 10/0 hook
Color:	very bright psychedelic colors
Description:	clear plastic head with multi-colored skirt trailer
Leader:	10 ft. of 150-lb. monofilament with two hooks inside the skirt. Use a high quality ball bearing swivel to attach the leader.

Where to Fish

The best Southern California area is a strip of water which ranges from the east end of Santa Catalina Island, offshore to about San Clemente Island, and south in the direction of Los Coronados Islands, to the Mexican boundary.

SALMON GROUPER

How to Catch . . . Rockfish

Rockfish, often called rock cod, are a group of about 50 different bottom dwellers. They congregate around bottom structures like reefs and canyons all along the Southern California coast. Rockfish are fun to catch and among the best eating fish found in our ocean. Some of the most common rockfish names are salmon grouper, vermillion, olive, chili pepper and cow cod. In general, rockfish are bass-like in appearance with a compact body and large mouth. These bottom and kelp bed dwellers run up to 10 pounds or more, but the average catch is 1 to 4 pounds.

Fishing Techniques

Rockfishing for most anglers means drift fishing from a boat. It can be done as close as 1/2 mile from shore to as far out as 25 miles or more over offshore reef and bank areas. The technique is quite simple. With the use of an electronic fish finder, locate the boat over a rocky bottom. Often the best location is one where a depth is changing, either on the upslope of a canyon or on the changing slope of a reef. Position the boat so it will drift towards promising territory. Now just lower your rig over the side until you feel the weight hit the bottom. Put the reel into gear and crank up a foot or two. Check for the bottom by lowering your line frequently to avoid drifting into snags or letting your bait move too far from the bottom. Jigging (moving your offering up and down a few feet) is also a good idea. The motion catches the eye of the rockfish.

Sometimes rockfish are also caught alongside kelp beds in the shallows near shore. Again, fish near the bottom and reel in fast to keep the fish from snagging in the kelp.

Traditional Tackle, Equipment, Rigging, Bait and Lures

The heft or weight of the tackle needed for rockfishing depends primarily on the depth of water you're fishing in. See the chart accompanying this section.

At the end of your line fasten a heavy swivel snap. To this, attach a rock cod rig or shrimp fly rig with about 6/0 size hooks. Many anglers prefer the shrimp fly rig since they have feathers that add to the attractiveness of the offering. Shrimp fly rigs can be purchased in most ocean-oriented bait and tackle shops for less than a dollar each. They typically have 3 hooks and a snap swivel at the end to attach the sinker, as shown on the next page.

Component	50-100 Feet	300-400 Feet
Rod:		
length	6-7 feet	6-7 feet
stiffness	med.-med. heavy	med. heavy- heavy
guide	(roller tip helpful)	(roller tip)
Reel:	med. ocean baitcasting	Penn Senator 114 6/0
Line:	25-40 lb. mono	40-80 lb. mono
Sinker:	4 oz. to 1 lb.	1/2 to 2 lb.

The most common bait for rockfishing is cut-up squid pieces. Cut the pieces large enough to cover the hook. Other common baits are pieces of small rockfish or anchovies. At times, fish can be hooked using bare shrimp fly rigs. But bait adds an odor that is often helpful in enticing a bite.

Rockfish are also taken on lures, especially metal jigs and soft plastics. Diamond hex bar jigs and Tady, Salsa and Sea Strike metal yo-yo type jigs are all producers. Jigs in the 4 to 6 ounce range will work in shallow water, or even up to 200 feet of water when the boat drift speed is slow.

Light Tackle Rockfishing

The Southern California trend to lighten fishing tackle is apparent in rockfishing. Depending on wind and current conditions, water depth and rockfish species, anglers are taking fish on freshwater spinning tackle, black bass tackle

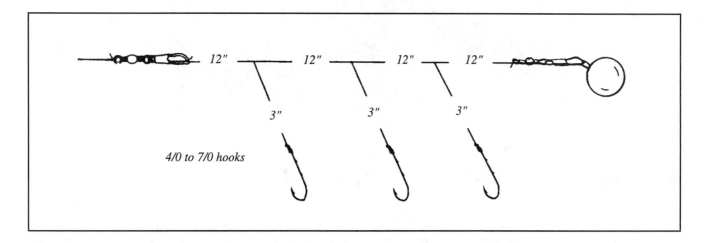

4/0 to 7/0 hooks

and even on ultralight rigs. It makes rockfishing much more challenging and exciting. And it surely beats cranking up a two or three pound weight and several bucketmouth rockfish from a depth of 300 feet or more.

Best light tackle opportunities occur in water that is 30-120 feet in depth. Light wind and current is also desirable because then less weight is needed to take the offering down to the fish. And with less weight, you can use lighter tackle and line. One approach is to use this lighter tackle with a rock cod rig or shrimp fly rig. Casting out one or two ounce jigs in the direction of the drift is also a good approach. If your main line is less than 10 pound test, consider using about a 10 pound, 2 foot leader. If the jig stops sinking, put the reel in gear and set the hook. If there is no hit, retrieve in short, quick hops by pumping the rod tip, or jig it up and down near the bottom. Bucktail jigs and soft plastic lead-head jigs work well. At times, you can fish suspended rockfish in shallow water.

Yellow rockfish are the most likely candidates. It's great fun to cast to these 2 to 5 pound fighters.

Where to Fish

Rockfishing locales all along the Southern California coast and islands are highlighted in the "Pacific Ocean Fishing" chapter.

Cleaning and Cooking

There are almost 50 varieties of rockfish along our coast. Commercially caught rockfish are most often sold in fish markets as snapper. All varieties are almost always filleted. Since most varieties of rockfish have very large heads, the yield of fillets can be as low as 20-30% of fish weight. Rockfish meat is lean, has low fat content and is mild tasting. These fillets lend themselves to the cooking method of choice including sauteing, broiling, poaching, frying or baking.

How to Catch . . . Sculpin

The techniques on catching different types of rockfish is covered in the previous section, but there is one SoCal rockfish that deserves special attention. It's the easy to catch, dangerous to touch, and delicious to eat sculpin.

The sculpin's body is stocky and slightly compressed. The head and mouth are large, as are the pectoral fins. Sculpin are red to brown, with dark blotches and spotting over the body and fins. But most important, the needle-sharp spines protruding from the dorsal, pectoral and anal fins are extremely poisonous.

Some might say, "Well, if they're so poisonous, I just won't fish for them." But it's not that simple—if you fish enough, you're going to catch a sculpin once in awhile. Most are caught near the bottom, but surface anglers also hook sculpin at times. So anglers have two choices: Release the hooked sculpin without touching them, or learn how to handle them so you can enjoy the exceptional fillets. Sculpin rarely exceed three pounds.

Fishing Techniques

Sculpin range from Pt. Arguello (just west of Santa Barbara) all the way down to the tip of Baja. Some are caught over sandy bottoms, but most are hooked over rocky points, submerged rock piles, and stony areas close to kelp. They're taken in water as shallow as 20 feet and as deep as 600 feet or more, but sculpin are most common in water less than 100 feet deep.

A multi-hook bottom fishing rig (see the previous rockfish section for a diagram) is the way to go. Experts recommend long-shanked hooks (like Kirby or Charlisle) because they make hook removal much easier and safer. Pieces of squid, or a piece off the side of a mackerel, bonito, tomcod, smelt, or herring are great baits. Anchovies are also good. Try to pass your hook through the bait twice to secure it better. Sculpin also take slow-moving artificial lures like Scroungers, Scampia and plastic grubs.

If you're pursuing bottom fish like sculpin and are having trouble getting your hook down through suspended perch, mackerel, or small bass, try using a much larger sinker. A swiftly sinking rig has a better chance of getting the bait to the bottom dwellers.

Sculpin Handling

All of the sculpin's heavy fin spines are venomous and can cause an extremely painful wound. A sting from a live fish will produce instantaneous and excruciating pain. This is frequently followed by swelling, nausea, dizziness, and sometimes fainting. Treatment includes squeezing out the venom, immersion in hot water (or coffee), and pouring on meat tenderizer.

Party boat anglers often let the well-trained deck hands get sculpin from hook to gunny sack. A safe do-it-yourself approach is to cut the leader near the hook and let the fish drop in the sack. By the way, if you want to release sculpin, cutting the leader above the hook will drop the fish safely into the sea. The hook will eventually dissolve and most fish will survive.

Sculpin venom loses its toxicity rather rapidly after death. But care should be taken while handling a sack with sculpin in them. Spines seem to always protrude through the sack and can still cause quite a sting. Sculpin spines can be trimmed off caught fish before filleting if you want to play it perfectly safe.

Veteran anglers and deck hands handle a freshly caught sculpin by grabbing its lower jaw between their thumb and the side of their index finger. Holding a fish this way makes hook removal possible. Some anglers also trim the spines at this time.

Cleaning and Cooking

Filleting is the cleaning method of choice. Sculpin fillets are white, fine in texture, and mild in flavor. It is excellent when fried, baked or broiled. Many fish chowder fans say that sculpin is the fish they relish.

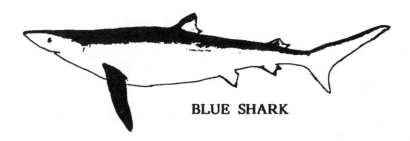

BLUE SHARK

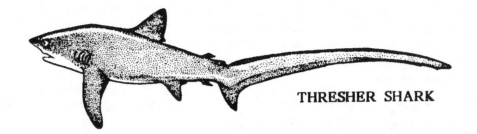

THRESHER SHARK

How to Catch . . . Sharks

Sharks are misrepresented fish. All the media ever talks about are great white sharks. But there are other varieties of shark in Southern California waters. These include thresher, mako and blue shark. What's more, the media never mentions that these sharks are becoming more and more popular among sports anglers—popular to fish for and popular to eat.

The mako shark is the most sought after shark that swims in local waters. It puts up a tremendous aerial battle when hooked and is considered by many just as good on the barbecue as a swordfish steak.

Most sharks caught by sport anglers weigh between 40 and 100 pounds, though blues weigh over 150 pounds, threshers top 200 pounds, and makos over 100 pounds are not all that uncommon. One angler caught a 640 pound mako from a private boat off Redondo Beach in August 1988. The possibility of catching a truly large fish is one reason why shark fishing is becoming more and more popular. Another reason is the reputation sharks have as cold-blooded eating machines.

Sharks are found in local waters all year-round, but most shark fishing takes place from late May through early November. This is when surface water temperatures are warmest and the sharks move inshore in large numbers. During the summer months sharks are not really that hard to find, so first-time anglers have a good shot at some very exciting hook-ups.

Party Boat Fishing

Several years ago when albacore fishing was in a lull, regulars and boat captains began looking for an alternative. Party boats began offering shark trips, and the public responded. Interest has been growing ever since.

It's a big ocean out there and boat captains know it better than most everyone else. Specifically, they know where to fish for sharks on any given day. Most angling is done from a drifting boat that has been positioned upwind and up current of promising waters. Deck hands then lay down a chum line. Anglers cast baited hooks into the oily slick. Most are equipped with a big-game outfit in the 50-pound range. Terminal tackle is simple. Use a 4 or 5 foot-long steel 60-pound test leader and a single #9/0 hook. The hook needs to be extremely sharp. Baits include fresh mackerel, bonito, tomcod or anchovies. Sinkers may be needed depending on the speed of the drift.

Experts suggest letting the shark run with the bait which allows time for him to swallow it. Then engage the reel, point the rod at the fish, and wait for the line to go taught before setting the hook.

Private Boat Fishing

Private boats can also use the drifting and chumming technique. But you need a sizable supply of chum to make it worthwhile. One technique is to chum with a basket full of ground up frozen fish. Anchovies are good and can be caught with a crab net off a wharf. Carcasses from filleted rockfish or other commercial fish are also good. Carcasses are available in quantity from commercial fish processing operations or some fish markets. Call around. You'll be surprised how easy it is to find dead fish or fish carcasses. Frozen fish are easiest to grind. You'll want enough to fill 2 or 3 half gallon milk cartons. Fill these with the processed chum and freeze them solid (2 days or more). A floating panfish basket makes an excellent chum block holder. Once at sea take off the carton, drape the block in the basket and drop the whole thing off the back of the boat on a short rope. A dead drift will lay down an oily, enticing chum slick.

With some luck you'll see sharks cruising behind your boat soon. But, be patient. It may take up to an hour.

If you don't have a sufficient supply of chum, trolling may be the best alternative. Heavy marlin jigs trolled between 3 and 6 knots about 20 to 40 yards behind the boat are proven mako-catching techniques. Large swimming plugs that resemble bait fish (e.g. 10 to 12 inch Rapala Magnum 26) trolled only about 15 to 20 yards back can be deadly. Slow trolling live mackerel also works, especially if surface action is off. Use a downrigger to take the nose-hooked bait down to between 50 and 150 feet. A speed not much over idle is often best.

A final possibility for private boaters is sight fishing. Sharks, especially makos, can be spotted while fishing along the surface. Approach cautiously, and then gently lob a live bait in front of and to the outside of the shark. As the shark turns away from the boat, hopefully it will spot the bait and hit it.

Some of the best shark waters in the Southland are the La Jolla Trench, off Oceanside, off Newport, and Santa Monica Bay.

Safety, Cleaning and Cooking

All sharks can do a great deal of damage to fingers, hands, arms and other body parts that come within their range. And large sharks are extremely dangerous. If you plan on keeping a big shark, it should be killed while still in the water. Experts use a bang stick, available at dive shops, to accomplish this. Make sure the fish's head is under water. Cautious anglers will not bring aboard any shark over 5 feet in length. They tie it off in the water. For smaller sharks, a fresh billy and gaff are recommended. Remain cautious even with small sharks.

Mako and thresher sharks are good eating if bled immediately after landing, but blue sharks are considered poor table fare. Most anglers release all of these graceful fighters. It is easiest by just cutting the wire leader. Bronze hooks will dissolve much faster than stainless steel hook material.

Good eating requires immediate cutting in the tail area to bleed the fish. Smaller specimens are filleted, while the large ones are steaked. Remove the tough skin and any red meat. Soaking in a mild solution of vinegar, lemon juice or milk will remove any ammonia smell or flavor. Shark meat is very firm, mild to moderate in flavor and has very little fat. It can be grilled, broiled, barbecued, deep fried or smoked. Add it to soups, stews or casseroles.

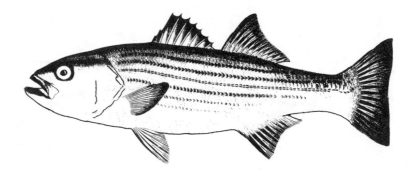

How to Catch . . . Striped Bass

Striped bass represent a marvelous, relatively new freshwater fishing opportunity for Southern California anglers. And they get just about everything one could want in a sport fish:

- Stripers are relatively easy to hook because they are voracious feeders.

- These are tough and spunky fish, so expect a good fight.

- Stripers are big fish. It's quite possible that when you catch your first striper, it will be the biggest fish of your life. Twenty pound fish are common!

- They are excellent table fare.

Striped bass are native to the Atlantic coast. They were first introduced to California, in the San Francisco Bay, in 1879. Striper are naturally anadromous fish, which simply means they breed in fresh water and live much of their lives in salt water. Salmon are the most famous of this class of fish, but are not related to striped bass. Striped bass have flourished in the San Francisco area over the last 100 years, migrating back and forth from the ocean to the freshwater Sacramento and San Joaquin Delta system.

Then starting in the 1960s the Department of Fish and Game experimented with plants of striped bass in landlocked fresh water in Southern California. And guess what? The stripers don't seem to miss their time in the ocean at all. In fact, they're thriving in places like Lake Havasu, Lake Mead, Pyramid Lake, Lake San Antonio and other Southland waters. The Southern California record freshwater striper is in the 60-pound class! By the way, stripers have populated some Southern California lakes by the migration of small fish through the Aquaduct System.

The best fishing technique for catching striped bass depends on many things, including the nature of the waters being fished, the season, etc. In this section, the basics of each of the most successful approaches is covered. If you want to know more about which works best, where and when, refer to the part of this book that deals with lakes and other Southland waters. For example, if you want to know what works at Havasu, look in the Lake Havasu section of this book.

Trolling

Trolling (pulling a lure through the water behind a boat) is one of the most popular techniques. It allows the angler to cover a wide area, if you're not sure where the fish are. Once a striper that hits a trolled line is landed, some anglers shift to one of the other techniques like casting, jigging, or bait fishing. They do this because striper are often in schools; therefore, if you've got one, there are probably others in the vicinity. Of course, trolling through the area where the first hook-up occurred is another option.

Most striper trolling is done by tying the lure directly to the main line, or a snap swivel may be used. Big (5-7 inches) shad or minnow-shaped plugs, like Rebel, Rapala, Bomber, Cordell Redfin and Storm Big Mac, are the choice of most trollers. These lures come in differing depth configurations such as shallow running (4 to 10 feet), deep diving (8 to 10 feet), and extra deep diving (15 to 30 feet). Try several configurations on different rods to locate the right depth.

Once a rig is in the water, check the tip of your rod. It should be twitching constantly. This is the action from your lure. Adjust the boat speed to get this effect. Set the drag on your reel just firm enough to prevent line from being taken out. Set the clicker in the "on" position. A singing clicker means a strike. The forward motion of the lure will usually set the hook. Tighten down slightly on the drag before playing the fish.

Sometimes stripers are down deeper than simple trolled lures can reach. If you're equipped, lead-core line or downriggers can be used to troll at the depth that the stripers are lurking. The same type of lures or Kastmaster or Hopkins-

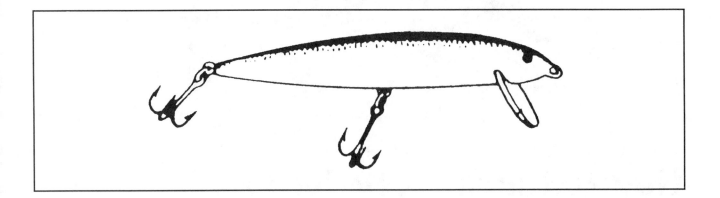

type spoons can be used. More information on deep trolling is in the Trout (Lakes) section of this book.

Electronic Fish Finder

The widespread use of electronic fish finders has provided another way of finding stripers, besides trolling. Paper and LCD depth recorders are great for locating schools of stripers that are over underwater drop-offs and points, or just suspended. Knowledge of the stripers' location and depth make them easier to catch. This is especially true when using bait fishing or jigging techniques. Let's take a look at bait fishing first.

Bait Fishing

Bait fishing can be done from a boat or from shore. Boat anglers usually anchor. A large hook (about 2/0 to 4/0) can be used since stripers are not hook shy. The most common rig used is a small rubber core sinker, with the hook held directly to 12-20 pound line.

Sometimes, especially if lighter line is used, it's possible to eliminate the sinker all together. This allows the bait to free fall and flutter on its way down below the boat. This approach is the same as used on saltwater party boats.

Shore anglers or shallow-water bait anglers are more likely to use a sliding sinker rig. This is much like a trout bait rig, but on a larger scale. When the striper takes the bait, play out 5-10 feet of line. When it hits hard, set the hook. Some anglers prefer a catfish-type rig for striper (see Catfish section of this chapter).

The most popular striped bass bait is probably frozen anchovies. Other baits that are used with success include nightcrawlers, mudsuckers and threadfin shad. Local bait shops will know which are most effective depending on location and season of the year. Live bait fish are hooked just below the dorsal fin, with the hook entering on one side and exiting on the other side of the fish. Or you can hook them through the lips. Once a live bait fish dies, the hook may be put in more securely, often with the leader secured to the tail by a half-hitch knot.

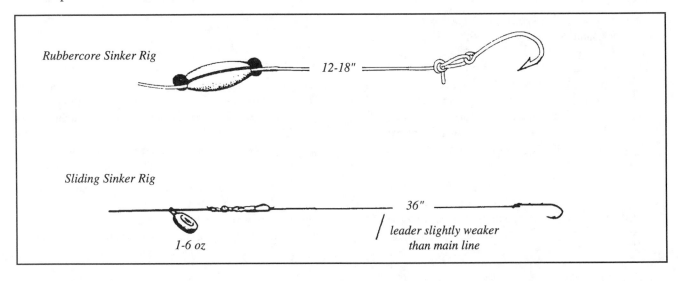

Rubbercore Sinker Rig

12-18"

Sliding Sinker Rig

36"

leader slightly weaker than main line

1-6 oz

Jigging

Once striped bass are located, especially if they're found down deep below a boat, the vertical jigging approach has proven to be dynamite. Here's how it works. Drop a spoon-type lure (tied to the line or attached with a snap swivel) over the side and let it flutter down to the depth where the fish are feeding. If it's not taken instantly, a yo-yo action is used to bring on a strike. When the striper are on the bottom, flick the rod tip to raise the spoon off the bottom, and then let it flutter back down. Strikes seem to occur most often on the fluttering fall. Kastmasters and Hopkins (e.g. a Shorty 75) are popular.

Casting

Sometimes striper anglers are lucky enough or cunning enough to be there when stripers are surface feeding on shad. The tip-off is bird activity and/or a noticeable "boiling" of shad forage fish on the surface. This is one of the occasions when casting is the way to go. First, approach the boil carefully and slowly. And move slowly to within casting range. You don't want to drive the frenzied striper back down. Some of the best casting lures are Pencil Poppers, Zara Spooks, 1/2 ounce Krocodiles or Kastmasters.

Another casting approach that works on stripers, especially when they're feeding in shallow water, is structure casting: casting near dams, rocky shorelines, shore cover, bridge columns, etc. It's the same as largemouth bass casting. The approach is the same and the same types of lures often seem to work.

Tackle and Equipment

Striper fishing can be done with a wide variety of tackle. Light weight black bass tackle can be used. Medium weight spinning equipment, or free spool/star drag conventional reel-light action rods are used for trolling. Light spinning equipment can also be used. Some feel this is the most exciting way to take stripers in the 4-12 pound range. Rods in the 6-7 1/2 foot range are about right. Live bait saltwater equipment is also widely used.

Where to Fish

Many of the best waters are profiled in the "Freshwater Fishing" chapters of this book. Lake Havasu, Lake Mead, Pyramid Lake, San Antonio, Silverwood and Skinner should be included on any list of top locales.

Cleaning and Cooking

Small stripers are usually filleted. Large ones (above say 10 pounds) can be steaked.

Striped bass fillets or steaks are white, mild in flavor, low in fat and especially good eating. Barbecuing, broiling, poaching, baking and frying are all good approaches.

RAINBOW TROUT

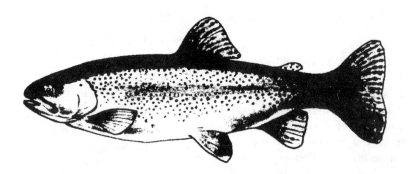

How to Catch . . . Trout (in Streams)

We are blessed by the numerous, fine trout streams in Southern California (these are described in the "Freshwater Fishing" chapters). Stream trout fishing is appealing because it can be the type of experience you personally want it to be. It can be accessible or remote, challenging or relaxing, simple or complicated.

Many people have a stereotype in their minds of the typical trout angler. It includes a fly rod, hip-high waders, a vest decorated with multi-colored flies, a hat with more multi-colored flies, a landing net hanging from the waist, all topped off with a Norman Rockwell-like wicker creel. This, of course, exactly describes some trout fishermen. But, forget this stereotype. Stream trout fishing can be productive and enjoyable, not only for the avid, well-equipped fly fisherman, but for everyone. You don't even need to use a fly rod if you don't want to.

The purpose of this section is to describe, in detail, several of the basic ways to catch stream trout, regardless of the type of fishing you prefer and the type of tackle you have.

There are several different types of trout in Southern California streams. The most common are rainbow. Most of these are planted, but some are wild. Others include the German brown trout, the brook trout and the golden trout.

Marketscope Books publishes the bestseller, *Trout Fishing in California*, for those who want to know more about stream trout fishing.

Some Fundamentals

Stream trout fishing, no matter what equipment is used, focuses on casting a fly, spinner, spoon or bait into a likely place in the stream and then retrieving it in as natural a manner as possible. Other fundamentals:

- Trout always face upstream, watching for food to be delivered to them by the moving water. So your offering should be presented in the same manner—moving from upstream to downstream.

- Trout are very leary and easily spooked. Since they're facing upstream and smelling the water that comes from upstream, always move upstream as you fish. This way you're less likely to be detected. Move quietly and stay out of the line of sight of likely trout hangouts. Keep your shadow off the water. Wear dark clothing. When wading, move slowly and try not to dislodge rocks.

- In the same vane, fish on the shady side of the stream, especially in the hours after sunrise and just before sunset.

- Casts in an upstream direction or up and across the stream are preferred over downstream casts. Down stream casts require a retrieve that is against the current, and therefore unnatural in appearances.

- Trout stay near the bottom of the stream. So your offering must move along near the bottom. The exception to this rule is when dry fly fishing. Dry flies (floating flies) imitate floating insects being carried along by the current. Trout will rise up to take these flies. Dry fly fishing is evening fishing.

- As with most fishing, early morning and evening are best fishing periods. But trout can be caught at any time of the day.

- Keep hooks sharp. Banging rocks and pebbles can dull them quickly.

- If you're not succeeding in whatever approach you're using (flies, spinners, bait), try other offerings until you find the one that works.

- Trout hang out behind boulders that break the current, in deep holes, in slower water near the undercut edge of a stream (especially in shaded areas), and at the head and tail of pools. Concentrate your efforts on these areas.

- When you spot an obviously expert trout angler, watch where he or she casts from, where he or she put the offering and how it is retrieved.

Often the best places to cast from are in the water. Don't let that stop you. Just be careful and carry a wading staff to probe the bottom and improve balance. Waders may or may not be necessary.

Fly Fishing

Flies, both dry (floating) and wet (sinking), are very small and light—too light to cast any distance. In fly fishing this difficulty is overcome by using fly line that has enough weight so *it* can be cast. The fly, connected by a light leader to the end of the fly line, "just goes along for a ride" as the line is played out and finally set on its final trajectory. The purpose of the fly reel is simply to store line that is not being used at the moment, and to retrieve line when necessary.

Fly fishing is an art and a science. Some say it is the ultimate fishing experience. Some people only fly fish. Many entire volumes have been written on fly fishing. In our limited space we cannot compete. But here are some insights that produce fish in Southern California.

Most experts agree that stream trout feed primarily below the surface. In fact, they probably spend 90% or more of their eating time feeding on aquatic life or terrestrial life that does not float (e.g. worms that fall off banks). Sure, if there is a good batch of mayflies, caddis or stoneflies, trout will come up to feed. And this is the time for dry fly fishing. But if trout spend most of their time feeding below the surface, then that's where you should put your fly most of the time.

So trout fly fishing is roughly divided into two categories. The first is dry fly fishing. Dry flies are designed to emulate adult forms of terrestrial and aquatic insects.

- Dry flies must float. Floating solution, tapered leaders and good floating fly line make this possible.

- Present the dry fly beyond the suspected feeding fish and let it float naturally through that feeding area, free on the current.

- Dry fly fishing is an evening affair. The several hours before dark are best. As the truism goes, "match the hatch," dry flies should match nature as closely as possible. To accomplish this, catch a flying insect and

then use a similar fly. A premier SoCal outdoor writer, Rex Gerlach, carries these dry flies: Adams (sizes 18, 16, 14, 12, 10), Royal Wulff (sizes 16, 14, 12, 10), Black Ant (sizes 18, 16, 10), Blue Wing Olive (sizes 18, 16), Blonde Goofus Bug (sizes 16, 14), Elk Hair Caddis (sizes 18, 16, 14), Joe's Hopper (sizes 12, 10, 8), and Bird's Stone Fly (sizes 8, 6, 4).

The second major category of trout fly fishing is wet fly fishing. Wet flies imitate underwater creatures such as the larva or pupae state of aquatic insects, nymphs, grubs, etc. The traditional winged wet flies are meant to suggest drowned adult insects. Streamer wet flies imitate bait fish.

- The whole idea behind successful wet fly fishing is to present the fly and allow the current to sweep it along close to the bottom at the exact same speed as the surrounding currents.

- As the fly drifts back towards you, keep the fly line from becoming too slack, so you can respond promptly should the line pause or stop, indicating a take.

- It is often difficult to detect underwater strikes. It is sometimes helpful to attach a strike indicator (a small, bright-colored float) to your leader and watch closely for any slight hesitation. The strike indicator should be set to correspond with the depth of the water.

- Sometimes two wet flies of various colors are better than a single fly. Use a standard nine foot tapered leader with a dark pattern fly at the tip, and 12 inches up from the tip, use another lighter colored wet fly on a six inch dropper leader.

- There are literally thousands of wet flies. But Rex Gerlach, the expert angler and SoCal outdoor writer, carries these nymphs: Black Rubber Legs (sizes 8, 6, 4, 2), Trueblood's Otter Shrimp (sizes 12, 10, 8), Carey Specials (sizes 10, 8, 6), Dragonfly Nymph (sizes 8, 6), Damselfly Nymph (sizes 12, 10), Bird's Nest (sizes 12,10), Hare's Ear Nymph (sizes 16, 14, 12, 10), Zug Bug (sizes 16, 14, 12, 10).

- Popular streamers (which imitate bait fish) are the matuka (in olive), the marabou streamer and the muddler minnow.

There is a great deal of variety in fly fishing equipment. One can spend hundreds of dollars, or you can buy a rod/reel combination that is quite decent for less than $50. For starters, a 7 1/2 to 8 1/2 foot rod matched with #6 line is good. An automatic reel costs a few dollars more, but makes taking up excessive line so much easier.

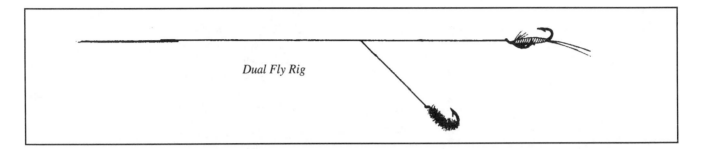

Dual Fly Rig

If you're having trouble handling fly fishing equipment, consider a fly fishing class, watch others do it, read up on the subject in specialized books, and check out some videos.

One last, yet very important point, that applies to both dry and wet fly fishing: Casting skill is not as important to fly fishing success as it often seems. In fact, long, accurate casts are not necessary or desirable on most Southern California mountain trout streams. Long casts just put flies in the branches and waste valuable fishing time. Instead use stealth as you move upstream. And then just flip your fly 10 to 20 feet out to likely territory. Use a short, precise flip of a cast. That's all that is needed in most situations. Flip casting and "dapping" (or just dropping your fly over brush, beyond a boulder or next to an undercut bank) are great when wading up the center of smaller streams. This approach puts emphasis where it should be, on fly fishing, not fly casting.

Spinning

Spin fishing means stream trout fishing using spinning or even spin casting equipment. The most popular setups include light or ultralight spinning tackle. Ultralight tackle is the easiest to handle and probably the most appropriate. It's capable of casting even small offerings with a 4 pound test line to sufficient distances. Here are the fundamentals of stream trout fishing with spinning tackle:

- The most common lures are very small spinners. Since retrieves are with the current (you're still casting up stream), a spinner whose blade rotates freely with little more motion than current speed is more desirable. These spinners imitate swimming bait fish. A popular example of a spinner of this caliber is the Panther Marten #2, 1/16 ounce black-bodied spinner. Gold blades are good for low light or overcast periods, chrome blades are recommended for sunny periods, and copper is good for not-so-clear water. Try several.

- Besides spinners, spoons are also good, like the Kastmaster. Retrieval speed is critical for the success of both spinners and spoons. Test both in quiet pools. Both types put out a vibration that can be sensed in the motion at the tip of the rod. Watch for this and adjust retrieval speed accordingly. Also, frequently change retrieve speed to give the offerings a more natural swimming pattern.

- Spinners and other lures need to be worked near the bottom. Adjust your retrieval speed to achieve this. You'll hang up some lures, but you'll catch more fish.

- Drifting spinners and spoons is also a good approach. Instead of retrieving, drift these little lures (like you would drift bait) in riffles and in fast moving water of the head and tail of pools, etc.

- Some lures are best tied directly to the main line. Others may twist the line if a small snap swivel is not used. Experiment, but if using a swivel, make sure it is in good working order and has a rounded connector at the lure end. This will insure proper action in the water.

Bait Fishing for Trout

Stream trout fishing with bait is the most flexible of all approaches. It's flexible because of the wide choice of baits that produce fish. And it's flexible because it can be done with either fly fishing equipment or spinning equipment. Some devotees even combine the two by using monofilament line on a fly rod and reel. All these possibilities are fine. Here are the fundamentals of trout stream bait fishing:

- Red worms are probably the most popular bait followed by bottled salmon eggs. Cheese and marshmallows are also popular, as are moldable manufactured baits like Berkley Power Bait. Then there is a whole category of natural live baits including crickets, beetles, grubs, larvae and pupae. Some anglers collect bait right out of the stream by using a fine mesh screen to trap bait dislodged by moving large rocks in the stream beds.

- If you're using live bait, it should be alive. So store and transport them carefully and hook them so as not to inflict fatal damage (at least not instant fatal damage).

- A short shank #8 or #10 hook is good. Try to conceal the entire hook into the bait.

- You want the bait to drift along with the current near the bottom of the stream. Unweighted drifting is best. If you need weight to get near the bottom, use as little split shot as possible, about 8-10 inches from the hook.

Since your bait is under water and drifting, it's not all that easy to detect bites. It helps to keep slack out of the line (while still allowing drift) and to set the hook on any sign of hesitation or pause in drift.

Using Casting Bobber for Trout

Purest fly fishermen may cringe at this approach, but here it goes anyway. Some people would like to be able to cast flies or small baits without mastering a fly rod. And some can't afford fly fishing equipment. For this group a casting bobber is the answer.

A casting bobber is a small, clear plastic float that adds enough weight to a fly or a small bait to allow casting with a spinning or spin casting reel and monofilament line. Thread the main line through the bobber and then tie on a swivel to keep it in place. Now add a leader and fly.

Casting bobbers are available in several sizes and configurations. Cast-a-Bubble in sizes FS25 or FS35 are good. Some even allow you to vary weight by allowing water inside the bobber. A bobber about half full of water provides a good casting weight. Most casting bobbers sink when filled with water.

Fish a casting bobber rig just as you would a dry fly. If you use a wet fly or bait, allow enough distance between the bobber and the hook so your offering gets down to near the bottom. In rapidly flowing water, some split shot about 8 inches from the hook may be added. A casting bobber/fly rig can also work in trout lakes in the evening when a hatch is on. Use a slow retrieve and twitch the fly from time to time.

Tackle and Equipment

Besides your choice of rod, reel, line and enticements to put at the end of it, trout anglers need several other items. Essential are both a creel (canvas ones can be purchased for as little as $5.00) or a fishing vest and an inexpensive landing net. A needle-nose pliers or other hook removing device like a hemostat is also essential. Small trout should be released with as little hook damage as possible. In fact, some trout fishermen flatten the barbs on their hooks to facilitate catch and release. Releasing large trout is possibly even more important. It takes large ones to produce small ones.

Optional equipment for trout fishing includes polarized sun glasses, waders and a wading staff. The sun glasses help take the glare off the water and improve underwater visibility. The use of waders depends on air temperature, water temperature, the number of stepping stones in a stream and one's desire to stay dry. Wading staffs (a proper length, light tree limb) are great to help maintain balance.

Cleaning and Cooking

Small trout (pan size) are generally just gutted and gilled (field cleaned). Larger trout are often filleted. Trout is mild, lean and sweet. It is suitable for just about any cooking approach. Sauteing is probably the most popular. The flesh of trout is tender, delicately flavored and can range in color from white to a pinkish we associate with salmon.

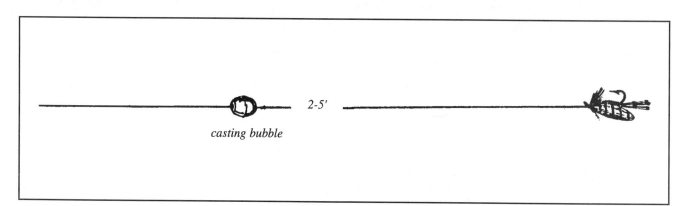

casting bubble   2-5'

California Trout

Rainbow Trout—Native of California, found in nearly all lakes and streams where water temperatures do not exceed 70°F for any length of time. Dark, bluish-green back, black spots on back and tail, red stripe on sides, silvery belly. Spawns on gravel bars in fast, clear water. Most suitable of all trout for artificial propagation and highly regarded as a game fish for its fighting qualities.

Brook—Native of Atlantic coastal area, found in many mountain lakes and spring-fed streams throughout the state. Dark olive, worm-like lines on back and sides, red spots along sides, belly reddish-orange to lemon, lower fins red tipped with white. Unlike other species, it may spawn in shallow areas of lakes having spring seepage.

Brown—A native of Europe, generally the hardest of California inland trouts to catch. Plentiful in many Sierra streams and scattered elsewhere throughout the State. The record fish in California weighed 26 pounds. Dark brown on back with black spots, shading to light brown with red spots on sides. The only trout with both black and red spots on its body.

Golden—State fish of California, the golden trout is native to the high country of the Kern River watershed, and now is found in many lakes and streams in the Sierra from Mt. Whitney north to Alpine County. Medium olive back, shading down the sides to brilliant golden belly and reddish-orange stripes from head to tail, crossed with olive vertical bars. Lower fins golden-orange.

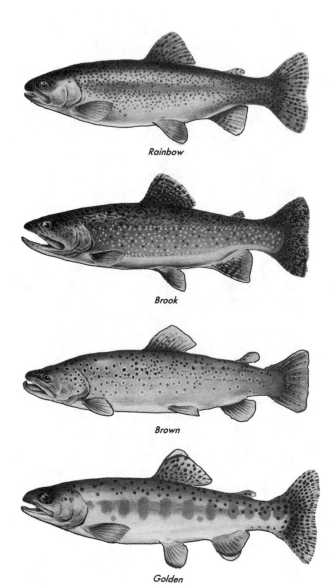

Rainbow

Brook

Brown

Golden

BROWN TROUT

How to Catch...Trout and Salmon (in Lakes)

Fishing for trout in lakes is very different from stream trout fishing. This is true because the lake environment changes the behavior of trout. Stream trout are always facing upstream, confined to shallow waters, on or near the bottom, and near or behind structures like boulders, undercuts, etc. The stream determines the location and habits of trout.

Trout in lakes have different ground rules dictating their lives. Food doesn't necessarily "flow" to them, they must find it. Lake water temperatures vary by season and depth, so trout will change depth to find oxygen rich water of a comfortable temperature for them. At times they may be near the surface, and at other times they may be down 80 feet or more.

Several Southern California trout lakes also had kokanee and/or silver salmon planted in them. Salmon and trout in lakes behave and are caught using the same techniques, lures and bait. Usually, anglers pursuing trout will catch an occasional salmon if they are present.

If you're catching trout in a trout and salmon lake, especially in the summertime, and you'd like some salmon, it sometimes helps to fish a little deeper. Research has shown that rainbow and brown trout favor water temperatures of between 55 and 60°F. But, the same research determined that salmon favor 55°F water, which will be down deeper.

Marketscope Books publishes the bestseller, *Trout Fishing in California*, for those who want to know more about lake trout fishing.

Reading a Lake

The specifics of a lake says a lot about the location of trout, and as many anglers have discovered, you've got to find them before you can catch them. As a matter of fact, catching trout in lakes is quite easy, once they are located. Here are the fundamentals:

- Trout, even in lakes, relate to structures. Trout use structures to shelter themselves from predators and to keep out of direct sun. Depending upon the time of year, overhanging trees, cliff areas, submerged points, coves and submerged river channels are good starting points.

- Trout move to locate food and oxygen. The primary inlet to a lake is always a prime location. It washes in food and cool, oxygen-rich water. In cooler months, shoreline weed beds may also provide insects and bait fish. The windward shoreline is also a good possibility. Drifting food will concentrate here. Finally, newly planted trout usually hang around the planting site for several days or more.

- An electronic fish finder can be an important tool. It not only will locate structure-like underwater islands and submerged drop-offs, but it will also locate schools of bait fish and the trout themselves.

- Trout are found down deeper in lakes in the summer months. Some Southern California lakes stratify (or divide) into three layers during the warming months and can remain in this condition until fall. The top layer is too warm and too low in oxygen for trout and salmon. They concentrate near the top of the second layer, or thermocline. In this layer there is plenty of oxygen and forage fish. This layer may be from 15-50 feet down depending upon lake depth and size. Water temperature will be in the 55-60 degree range. A fish finder, under-water temperature gauge or locals can all help you to determine the proper depth to fish.

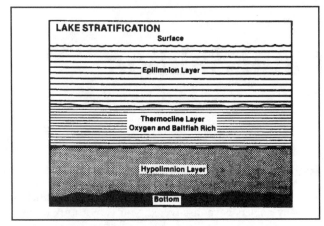

Fishing Techniques

There are three primary methods of catching trout in lakes:

1. **Trolling**—In one form or another, this is probably the most productive method of catching trout in lakes.

2. **Bait Fishing**—A very good method, especially for shore fishing. Can also be done from a boat; for example, at a stream inlet of a lake.

3. **Casting**—Also a very productive shore fishing method. Can also be done from a boat.

It is also possible to catch trout in lakes by fly fishing. But even avid fly fishermen will admit it is difficult. Dry flies will only work, for example, when an insect hatch is taking place. Even then, they may not work because they don't move with the current as they do in streams. Wet flies, streamers, etc. can be used in lakes, and can produce at times if you're either very skillful or very lucky. When there are hungry trout and little angling pressure, remote, high altitude mountain lakes are the best candidates for lake fly fishing success. If you're inter-ested in more information on lake fly fishing, check out several fly fishing books from your local public library, or rent a specialized video.

Trolling for Trout

Trolling is simply pulling an offering at the end of your line through the water using a boat. It can and is done with boats ranging from a canoe, to a rowboat, to an inboard/outboard. There are also several different trolling approaches ranging from trolling a fly on spinning tackle to downrigger trolling. But no matter what depth you're trolling, or what techniques or equipment you're using, these tips will help produce fish:

- Troll slowly. The best trolling is slow trolling. For example, some highly successful trollers use only oar power.

- Change trolling speed often. Every minute or two isn't too frequent. Sometimes it even helps to over speed for just a few seconds and then slow down. This gives added up and down action to the flasher and lure.

- Change depth. If you're not sure of the depth you're trolling at (it can vary depending upon boat speed and amount of line out for all approaches except downrig-ging) or the depth the trout are at, vary depth until you get a strike. Then stick at this depth.

- Troll an "S" pattern. Trolling experts suggest this ap-proach because (1) it covers more territory than straight line trolling, and (2) it causes speed, direction and depth changes to occur in the flasher and lure. These move-ments and resulting vibrations attract trout.

When trout are feeding near a lake's surface (i.e. when surface temperatures are low), light tackle trolling is in order. Just about any light spinning or spin casting rod and reel combo will do. Conventional bait casting tackle is also appro-priate. Use 6 to 10 pound monofilament line depending upon the size of the trout you're expecting to catch and the type of rig you're trolling.

A full-blown trolling rig consists of several components which are listed below in order of placement on the line.

1. Rudder—A blade to prevent line twist. It also has a hole in it where a weight can be attached to take the trolling rig deeper.

2. Flasher—An attractant that imitates a school of bait fish. It's highly visible and also sends out vibrations.

3. Swivel—Useful in preventing line twist.

4. Snubber—A rubber tube ensemble that absorbs the shock of the strike, sometimes helping to prevent the hook from pulling out of the trout's mouth.

5. About 18 inches of monofilament that is often lighter and less visible than the main line.

6. Offering—A spoon, plug, spinner or baited hook. The best choice for each lake and season is detailed in the "Freshwater Fishing" chapters.

The flasher and rudder are usually sold in a packaged unit. Use larger units for murky water or deep trolling. Then you just attach on the snubber, tie on a leader and attach your offering. See the diagram below.

It's not always necessary, or even desirable, to use a complete trolling rig. Sometimes just a minnow plug is the best choice. If line twist is a problem with the offering you're pulling, add a good quality swivel, or even a trolling rudder between two swivels. Flashers, at times, really do help attract trout to strike.

When putting your rig into the water behind the moving boat, pull the line off your reel, in strokes, with your free hand. By counting these "pulls" you can return fairly accurately to a specified depth, or be able to increase or decrease depth.

Deep Trolling

Trout are often down quite deep, especially in warmer weather months. Pulling a trout rig, as described above, at this time will not produce fish. What should you do? Here are several options:

- Use leadcore trolling line on a good-sized conventional reel. Medium Penn freshwater reels with levelwind are popular. With a slow trolling speed, leadcore line sinks at about a 45 angle, so for example, 50 feet of line will produce a 25 foot trolling depth. Most anglers use a full trolling rig (i.e. rudder, flasher, etc.) when leadcore trolling. The flasher helps attract fish in the low visibility light condition of deeper water, and it also adds a weight to the already weighted line.

- Use a downrigger—this is by far the most desirable approach, especially if you need to go down to 30 or 40 feet or more. A downrigger will take your trolling rig down to a known depth (they're equipped with depth counters), and allow you to play and land the fish on light tackle (see illustration below). The trolling rig can be made even lighter by removing the flasher from the trolling rig setup. Instead, attach it to the downrigger weight (see illustration on next page).

- Use a diving plane—a weighted, airfoil device that uses the motion of the boat to dive and take the terminal tackle with it.

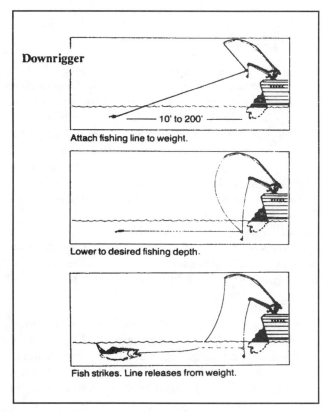

Downrigger

10' to 200'

Attach fishing line to weight.

Lower to desired fishing depth.

Fish strikes. Line releases from weight.

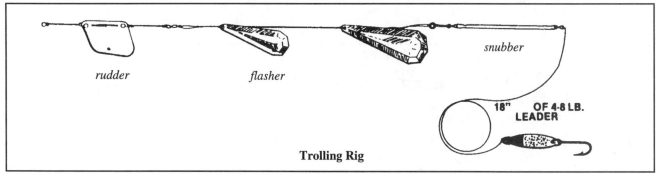

rudder   *flasher*   *snubber*

18" OF 4-8 LB. LEADER

Trolling Rig

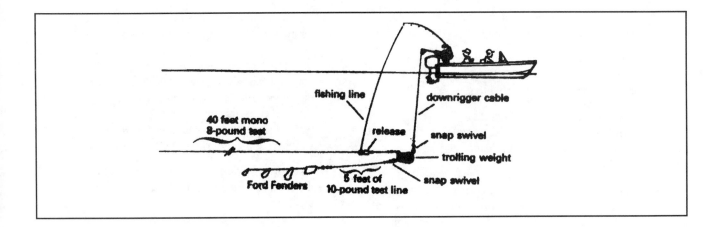

Trolling a Fly

Sometimes trout will rise up in a lake in the evening to feed on insects. The trout will jump right out of the water producing raindrop-like rings on the surface. Summertime from 6 pm until dark is the time to be alert for this show. And here's how to catch your share of these insect-chasing trout. Simply tie a fly onto the end of 4-6 pound monofilament rigged on a spinning rod and reel. Let out about 40 yards of line and slow troll through the feeding activity, usually near shore. An electric trolling motor is ideal. You'll be very pleased with the results. By the way, if you see evening hatch activity on a lake but are without a boat, try this. Tie a small spoon, like a Kastmaster, on your spinning outfit. Then remove the treble hook, put on a 2 1/2 foot leader and tie on a fly. Cast softly into the feeding activity and be ready to set the hook.

Bait Fishing for Trout

Bait fishing can be done from shore or boat. The most common tackle is light spinning equipment. Despite all the variety in trout bait fishing, the most productive technique is probably the sliding sinker rig. It is most often used from shore, but it's also well suited to anchored boat fishing in coves and inlets.

The purpose of the sliding sinker rig is to allow the bait to move freely when a trout picks it up. With a fixed sinker rig, the trout would notice the drag on the offering and drop it.

The process begins by casting out the baited rig to a likely spot. Let it sink all the way to the bottom and then slowly crank in any slack. Now, sit down, get comfortable and open the bail on your spinning reel. Personally, I don't believe in putting a rod down or propping it up on a stick. I believe in holding the rod. Then you can feel the slightest tug on your bait. In fact, I like to have my line in front of the reel go between the thumb and index finger of my non-reeling hand.

When the trout picks up the bait, play off line from the spool so no resistance is felt by the fish. A pause may be detected after the first movement of line. Wait until it starts moving out again (this means the trout has swallowed the bait, literally swallowed the bait). Close the bail and set the hook. You've got yourself a fish.

A wide variety of baits are used such as salmon eggs, cheese, minnows, shad, worms, commercial baits, and crickets. A combination of baits is also popular. Some use a small marshmallow/salmon egg/nightcrawler combination. The egg provides visual attraction and the marshmallow provides

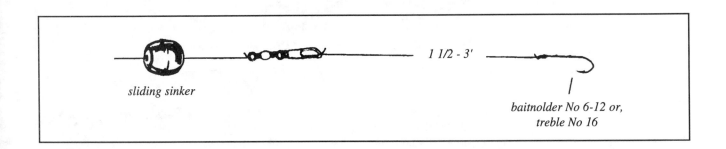

buoyancy, so the whole offering floats slightly off the bottom. Another way to accomplish this buoyant effect using nightcrawlers is to inflate them with air. Crawler inflaters are available to accomplish this task. Many large trout are caught on both combination baits and inflated nightcrawlers.

Bobber fishing can also be quite effective for trout. This is an especially effective method in winter and early spring when lake surface temperatures are cool and trout are often feeding near the surface. Simply tie your hook to the line, put a split shot a foot or so up from the hook, and snap on a bobber up the line. Six feet is a good distance to try first. Cast it out and watch your bobber closely. By the way, up to 3 hooks are allowed on one rod. So two or three hook rigs like crappie rigs can also be good trout getters. With his type of setup you can try several baits at multiple depths.

Sometimes trout are holding at mid-range in a lake, they're too deep for regular bobber fishing, but they're not on the

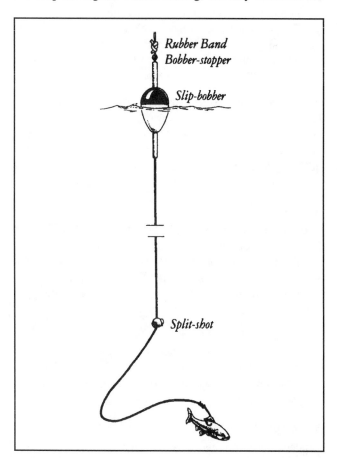

bottom. When this occurs, it's time to pull out the sliding bobber rig. With this rig you can fish at 20, 30 or even 50 feet, while still being able to cast a short rig and retrieve the hooked

trout right up to near the rod tip. This rig allows the split shot weighted bait to pull line through the slip bobber until the bobber stop gets to the bobber. When reeling in, the stop-knot slides through the rod guides so you can bring in line all the way to the split shot. Stop-knots and sliding bobbers are available in packaged kits, or stop-knots can be tied. Some anglers use thread to tie a knot larger than the hole in the bead, while others use a piece of rubberband to tie the stop-knot.

Casting for Trout

Casting for trout is a popular shore option, especially among younger anglers. And it can be effective. The most popular tackle is again light spinning or spin casting.

Lures can be tied directly to the end of the main line or attached with a snap swivel. I prefer the snap swivel. It prevents any line twist and provides a way to change lures easily. Most trout lures imitate small bait fish. Silver and gold colors are good in 1/16 to 1/4 ounce sizes. Some popular trout casting lures are Kastmasters, Roostertails, Phoebes, and Mepps Spinners.

Cast out as far as possible, let the lure settle to the desired retrieve depth, and return at the speed that provides the most natural action. Slower is probably better. And vary the pace of your retrieve. The small bait you're trying to duplicate don't swim as fast, and they don't swim at a steady pace. Sometimes it's best to let the lure sink for some time before starting your retrieve. A problem with this approach is the frequent snags (on sunken branches, etc.) and lost lures. Some anglers minimize this difficulty by replacing the original treble hook with a weedless hook. It's even possible to cast a fly from shore using spinning tackle. See the Trolling A Fly discussion earlier in this section.

Cleaning and Cooking

See the Trout (in Streams) section for cleaning instructions. Smaller trout are best when sauteed or oven-fried, or when baked, either plain or with a light sauce. The larger, whole trout are excellent when baked or poached. Trout is at its best when prepared simply.

How to Catch . . . Trout (Golden)

Are you ready for a completely different kind of fishing experience? Well that's what fishing for our state fish, the golden trout, will provide. Goldens are considered by many to be the most beautiful fish in California, or anywhere, for that matter. They appear almost luminescent when contrasted to the blue and green hues of their high, clean, mountain water habitat.

Goldens were first discovered around the turn of the century in waters of the Kern River system, where they then inhabited about 300 miles of streams. Golden trout are native to no other waters. Later, rainbow trout were planted in tributaries of the Kern River, resulting in widespread hybridization with goldens. Introduction of brown trout also displaced the golden from many of their ancestral streams. By the 1950's these actions combined to squeeze the pure golden trout into about 20% of its original territory.

Fortunately due to man's positive actions, golden trout are much better off today. Six lakes in the Cottonwood Lake System are used to protect golden trout brood stock, and supply hundreds of thousands of eggs to California hatcheries each year. These eggs are taken down from the lakes by pack mules. Now the list of golden trout lakes and streams is 5 pages long (single-spaced, 2 columns per page). Most of these waters are in the Southern Sierra.

But golden trout fishing is not for everyone. You can't park on the shores of golden trout streams or lakes. To catch golden trout and enjoy the magnificent mountain scenery, you must be prepared to backpack or ride a horse to the high country. Many good spots are at an elevation of 8,000 feet or more. Here the air is thin and the effort is great, but the goldens make it all worthwhile.

Where to Fish and What to Take

The California Department of Fish and Game publishes a list entitled, "Where to Find California's Golden Trout." For your convenience, we have included this list at the end of this section. As you can see, there are many opportunities. Interestingly, many spots on the list are high mountain, alpine lakes where the golden trout have been planted. None of these lakes contained trout prior to this, and contrary to popular belief, golden trout never occurred naturally in lakes. Some of the best golden trout angling is in the high country of the Southern and Eastern Sierras. Information on these fine destinations is detailed in the Southern Sierra and the Eastern Sierra Freshwater Fishing chapters. The most popular pack-in stations are along Hwy. 395 in the Eastern Sierras.

Backpack anglers obviously need light gear and equipment like sleeping bags, tents, cooking gear, freeze-dried food, etc. Good hiking boots are also a must. For those interested in horse packing, seek out a guide or outfitter. They advertise in outdoor papers and magazines and are also listed in the local yellow pages for a given area.

Tackle and Lures

Rod and reels that are especially designed for backpacking are the equipment of choice. For example, pack rods come in about four sections of 15 or 16 inches each, and ultralight spinning reels weigh about a half a pound. But most two-piece spinning or fly rods and reels aren't that bulky or heavy, so they will do nicely.

Spin anglers should bring a good assortment of small spinners and wobbling spoons. Red and whites are good colors. Also take some casting bubbles to use with flies. Flyrodders can take a wide selection of favorite dry flies, wet flies and nymphs.

Catching Golden Trout

Golden trout are on-again, off-again biters. This makes catching them as easy as tossing something into the water one day and getting skunked the next day. Maybe this just makes them like any other trout. All of the "How to Catch" information in the previous two sections also applies to golden trout. Of course, only artificial lures with single hooks (except in the mainstream of the Kern River) are allowed in the Golden Trout Wilderness Area. Both fly and spinning gear anglers do well.

The best advice for catching golden trout is to be persistent. Experiment with different offerings. Try something, and then try something else. And when you do catch golden trout, consider releasing many of them. But you'll enjoy the eating with the few you keep. They are delicious. See Trout Cleaning and Cooking section in the "Trout (in Streams)" chapter of this book for specific instructions.

Where to Find California's Golden Trout

FRESNO COUNTY

Bear Creek Drainage

Apollo Lake (Cub Lake)
Bear Creek above Kip Camp;
 S. Fork, E. Fork, W. Fork
Bearpaw Lake
Beartrap Lake
Big Bear Lake
Black Bear Lake
Brown Bear Lake
Claw Lake
Coronet Lake
Den Lake
Flatnote Lake
Hilgard Creek
Italy Lake
Jumble Lake
Little Bear Lake
Lou Beverly Lake
Marie Lake
Medley Lake
Orchid Creek
Orchid Lake
Rose Lake
Rosebud Lake
Sandpiper Lake
Seven Gables Lakes 1,2,3
Sharpnote Lake
Teddybear Lake
Three Island Lake
Toe Lake
Tooth Lake
Ursa Lake
Vee Lake
White Bear Lake

Fish Creek Drainage

Fish Creek, ab. Purple Creek
Franklin Lakes
Glen Lake
Glenette Lake

Grassy Lake
Hoof Lake
Horn Lake
Izaak Walton Lake
Lagoon Lake
Pocket Lake
Purple Creek headwaters
Ram Lake
Shiner Lake
Tully Lake
Virginia Lake

Hooper Creek Drainage

Chamberlain Lake
Gordon Lake
Harvey Lake
Hooper Creek
Hooper Lake
Neil Lake

Kings River, Mid. Fork Drainage

*Amphitheater Lake
Crown Creek, above Crown Basin
Crown Basin Lakes 1,2
*Dougherty Creek
*Dusy Basin Lakes (Upper 4)
*Fallen Moon Lake
*Glacier Lakes, Upper and Lower
*Helen Lake
*Kennedy Creek
*Kennedy Lake, West
*Kings River, Middle Fork hdwtrs
*Kings River, Dusy Branch
*Lost Canyon Creek
*Palisade Creek
*Palisade Lakes 1, 2; Upper 1, 2
*Slide Creek
*Slide Lakes 1, 2, 3

Kings River, N. Fork Drainage

Arctic Lake
Chapel Lake

Ewe Lake
Guest Lake
Island Lake
Little Joe Lake
Midway Lake
Nelson Lake, Upper
Ram Lake
Square Lake
Turf Lakes, Upper and Lower

Kings River, S. Fork Drainage

*Gardiner Creek
Grizzly Creek
*Kings River, S. Fork hdwtrs
Roaring River
*Sixty Lake Basin Lakes (11)

Mono Creek Drainage

Bighorn Lake
Fourth Recess Lake
Golden Lake
Hopkins Creek
Hopkins Lake, Upper
Mills Creek Lakes, Up. & Low.
Mono Creek, above North Fork
Mono Creek, North Fork
Pioneer Basin Creek
Pioneer Basin Lakes 3, 5, 6
Silver Pass Creek
Silver Pass Lake
Snow Lakes, Upper & Lower
Summit Lake

Piute Creek Drainage

Alsace Lake
Aweetasal Lake
Big Chief Lake
Chevaux Lake
Cony Lake
Desolution Lakes, Big & Little
Elba Lake
Forsaken Lake
French Lakes, Big and Little
French Canyon Creek
Goethe Lakes
Golden Trout Lakes, Upper & Lower
Hidden Lakes
Honeymoon Lakes, Upper & Lower
Jawbone Lake
Knob Lake
"L" Lake
LaSalle Lake
Lobe Lakes, Upper & Lower
Lost Lakes
Lovejoy Lake
Marmot Lake
Merriam Lake
Moccasin Lakes, Big & Little
Moon Lake
Muriel Lake
Old Squaw Lake
Paine Lake
Paris Lake

Pemmican Lake
*Pinnacles Cree, East & West
Piute Creek
Puppet Lake
Ramona Lake
Royce Lakes 1, 2, 3, 4, 5
Rust Lake
Spearpoint Lake
Star Lake
Steelhead Lake
Tomahawk Lake
Turret Lake, Lower
Vista Lake
Wampum Lake

San Joaquin River, S. Fork Drainage

Bonita Lake
*Darwin Canyon Creek
*Darwin Canyon Lakes 1, 2, 3
*Davis Lake
*Emerald Lake
*Evolution Creek
*Evolution Lake
*Geothe Basin Lakes 1, 2, 3
*Goddard Creek
Heart Creek
Heart Lake
Jawbone Lake
Lost Lake
*Martha Lake
*McGee Creek
*McGee Lakes 3, 4, 5
Neil Lake
Salley Keyes Lkes, Upper & Lower
San Joaquin River, S. Fork, above
 Piute Creek
*Sapphire Lake
Sheep Lake
*Wanda Lake

INYO COUNTY

Baker Creek Drainage

Hidden Lake

Big Pine Creek Drainage

Finger Lake
Thumb Lake

Bishop Creek Drainage

Treasure Lakes 1, 2, 3, 4, 5, 6

Cottonwood Creek Drainage

Cirque Lake
Cottonwood Creek
Cottonwood Creek, North Fork
Cottonwood Creek, South Fork
1/Cottonwood Lakes 5, 6
Frogpond Lake
High Lake
Long Lake
Lower South Fork Lake

1/ Cottonwood Lakes 1, 2, 3, and 4 are closed to protect golden trout broodstock.
* National Park Waters

Muir Lake

Horton Creek Drainage

Horton Lakes 3, 4

Independence Crk. Drainage

Golden Trout Lake #3

Olancha Creek Drainage

Higgins Lake

Pine Creek Drainage

Golden Lake

Red Mountain Creek Drainage

Red Mountain Lake

Rock Creek Drainage

Dade Lake
Mills Lake

MADERA COUNTY

Granite Creek Drainage

Alpine Lake
Burro Lake
Isberg Lakes; Up., Mid., & Low.
Ward Lake, Upper

King Creek Drainage

Anona Lake

Merced River Drainage

*Adair Lake

San Joaquin River, N. Fork Drainage

Bench Canyon Creek
Bench Canyon Lake
Blue Lake
Iron Lake
Long Creek
Rockbound Lake

San Joaquin River, Mid. Fork Drainage

Agnew Pass Lake
Shadow Creek Drainage
Cabin Lake

MARIPOSA COUNTY

Merced River Drainage

*Boulder Lake
*Fletcher Creek headwaters
*Fletcher Lake
*Townsley Lake
*Vogelsang Lake

MONO COUNTY

Convict Creek Drainage

Bighorn Lake
Edith Lake
Cloverleaf Lake

Gibbs Creek Drainage

Gibbs Creek
Gibbs Lake
Kidney Lake

Hilton Creek Drainage

Stanford Lake

Lee Vining Creek Drainage

Conness Lakes; Low., Mid, & Up.

Mill Creek Drainage

Cascade Lake
Excelsior Lake
Helen Lake
Odell Lake
Potter Lake
Shamrock Lake
Towser Lake

McGee Creek Drainage

Flag Lake
Gold Lake
McGee Lake, Lower

Laurel Creek Drainage

Laurel Lakes
Laurel Creek

Robinson Creek Drainage

Tamarack Lake

Rush Lake Drainage

Alger Lakes 1, 2, 3
Rush Creek, North Fork, above falls

West Walker River Drainage

Anna Lake
Grizzly Lake
Koeing Lake
Latopie Lake
Ski Lake
Tower Canyon Creek
Tower Lake

TULARE COUNTY

Kaweah River, Mid. Fork Drainage

*Kaweah River, Mid. Fork hdwtrs
*Tamarack Lake

Kern River Drainage

*Amphitheater Lake
Beach Creek
*Big Arroyo Creek
Bonita Creek

Chicken Springs Lake
Cold Creek
*Coyote Creek
*Crabtree Creek
*Crabtree Lakes 1, 2, 4
*Diamond Mesa Lks. 1, 2, 3, 4, 5
Durrwood Creek headwaters
*Funston Lake
Golden Trout Creek
*Guyot Creek
*Hitchcock Lakes 2, 6
Johnson lake
*Kern River headwaters
*Laurel Creek
Little Trout Creek
Long Canyon Creek
*Lost Canyon Creek
Nine Mile Creek
Osa Creek headwaters
*Perrin Creek
Red Rock Creek
*Red Spur Creek
*Rock Creek
Rocky Basin Lakes 1, 2, 3, 4
Salmon Creek
*Siberian Pass Creek
*Sky Blue Lake
*Soda Creek
*South America lake
*Tyndall Creek
*Wales Lake
*Wallace Creek
*Wallace Lake
*Whitney Creek
*Willow Creek
*Wright Lake

Kern River, S. Fork Drainage

Brown Meadow Creek
Cow Canyon Creek
Fish Creek headwaters
Jackass Creek headwaters
Kern River, South Fork
  headwaters
Little Trout Creek
Long Stringer Creek
Machine Creek
Manter Creek headwaters
Mulkey Creek
Shaffer Meadow Creek
Snake Creek
Snow Creek
Soda Creek
Strawberry Creek
Taylor Creek headwaters
Tibbetts Creek headwaters
Trout Creek, above Lit. Trout Creek

Kings River, S. Fork Drainage

*Brewer Creek
*Cunningham Creek
*Ferguson Creek
*Guitar Lake
Poison Meadow Lake
*Roaring River headwaters
*Soldier Lakes 1, 2
*South Gard Lake
*Sugarloaf Creek, South and East Forks
*Vidette Creek
*Vidette Lakes 1, 2, 3, 4

Little Kern River Drainage

Clicks Creek
Deadman Creek
Fish Creek
Lion Creek
Little Kern River headwaters
Mountaineer Creek
Pistol Creek
Rifle Creek
Shotgun Creek
Silver Lake
Soda Springs Creek
Tamarack Creek
Wet Meadows Creek
Willow Creek

TUOLUMNE COUNTY
Cherry Creek Drainage

Wilson Meadow Lake

Stanislaus River, Mid. Fork Drainage

Blackhawk Lake
Blue Canyon lake
Iceland Lake
Ridge Lake
Sardella Lake

Tuolumne River, Main Branch Drainage

*Bingamen Lake
*Mary Lake
*Otter Lake, Big
*Tilden Creek headwaters

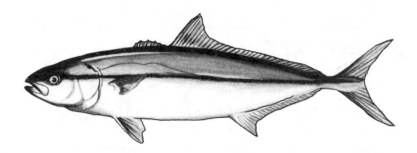

How to Catch . . . Yellowtail

Yellowtail, or "yellows" or "tails" are one of the premier sport fish in Southern California waters. These close relatives of the amberjack have earned this reputation because they are vicious strikers, hard and cunning fighters and more prevalent and accessible than many other fish in Southern California waters. Besides all this, yellowtail is good eating. Some fish are caught from shore, but the bulk are caught from rented skiffs, private boats and party boats. The average yellowtail catch is in the 5-20 pound range, but some exceed 40 pounds.

Yellowtail fishing in Southland waters can begin as early as March, but late spring is usually the peak season. Summer can be good, and then there is usually an upsurge in the fall. Yellowtail like a water temperature of 67 to 69 degrees. Once hooked, yellowtail have the unnerving ability to head for the nearest object that will help them break loose. This could be kelp, rocks, boat propellers or anchor lines. Maximum drag tension short of breaking the line is needed in this instance to prevent the fish from reaching these objects.

Although yellowtail will often take a variety of baits and jigs, at times, they are finicky eaters. It's at these times when sly anglers go down in line and hook size. Live squid, mackerel and anchovies all work for yellowtail, as do several types of jigs. Let's look at each approach.

Live Squid Fishing

Live squid is the "bait of choice" for yellowtail, as well as for white sea bass, large calico bass, rockfish, and large halibut. If an angler has live squid in his or her bait tank, the chances of yellowtail success rises sharply. Squid are seasonal, but when they are available, they are worth going after. In the spring (the squid spawning months) boat anglers sometimes fish for the squid, before fishing for the sport fish.

There are two approaches. At night squid are attracted by light. Bright lights from the boat are shined into the water and when the squid arrive, they are corralled in a net.

Hook and line are necessary to catch squid at times. A 3 to 3 1/2 inch squid jig is used. Two or three jigs are placed about one foot apart and are taken down to the bottom with a 1-6 ounce sinker. The jigs have two sets of bristled metal rings at the bottom. Squid attach themselves to the jigs and are reeled up. A little shaking puts them in the bait tank. Veteran squidders like spots at about the 18 fathom mark. Good squid concentrations are south of Catalina Island, the Channel Islands and the La Jolla Kelp Beds.

Fresh dead or frozen whole squid are also used if live squid aren't available. Squid are hooked through the tail on a single 3/0 to 5/0 hook with a 1-2 ounce sliding sinker riding right at the hook. Lead-head hooks can be substituted for the sliding sinker. No sinker is used if the fish are near enough to the surface to be seen.

There is a technique to hooking squid. It's best to hold the squid so that its head (and sharp beak and tentacles) are in the palm of one hand with its tail stretching out between your thumb and index finger. Now just take the hook in the other hand and run it through the pointed tail as shown on the next page.

Cast the hooked squid out gently and allow it to sink to the bottom, thumbing the spool as line goes out. Strikes often occur on the way down. Give line and count to 6 or 8 before setting the hook. If the squid makes it to the bottom unmolested, retrieve it with a pumping, stop-and-go motion. You'll need to throw the reel out of gear when a hit occurs. Give the yellowtail about 4-5 feet of line and then put the reel back in gear and set the hook. Twenty-five to thirty pound test line is good for live squid angling.

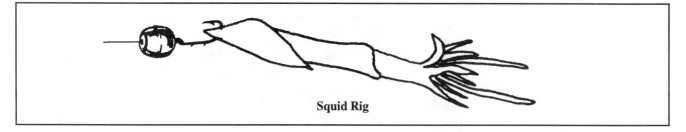

Squid Rig

Live Mackerel Fishing

Both Spanish and greenback mackerel are used. But the smaller Spanish variety is more desirable. They are also good for large calico bass and white sea bass angling. They are sometimes available from bait sellers, and can be caught quite easily on multihook rigs like Lucky Joes or Shrimp fly rigs. At times, it's difficult not to catch a mackerel.

Mackerel are most often fished on a hook tied directly to a 1/0 to 4/0 hook, depending on the size of the bait. Twenty-five to thirty pound test line is recommended. Many anglers prefer to hook the mackerel across the nose. Others prefer to hook them through the anus to make them swim deeper.

Since mackerel have a rather tough head, a stiff rod is helpful in setting the hook. Allow the yellowtail to swallow the large bait before the set.

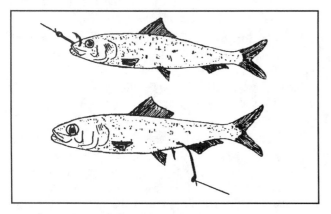

Live Anchovy Fishing

Anchovies are small and more fragile than mackerel and squid. So live anchovy angling requires lighter line to get a good swimming effect in the water. Twenty pound line or even 15 pound line is needed. The problem with this situation is that this light line might not be enough to prevent wise yellowtail from running for the kelp, rocks, or whatever. But if squid or mackerel aren't available and the fish are leery of heavier line, anchovies on 15 pound line is worth the gamble. Hook the anchovies through the nose or gill cover on about a #4 hook. See the Barracuda section of this chapter for illustrations. The number one key when fishing with anchovies is to change your bait frequently. Fresh bait is essential.

Jig Fishing

There are several jig approaches that work, at times, on yellowtail. The most popular is called "yo-yo" jigging. A 4-12 inch "candy-bar" type or C-Strike jig is used on about 40-pound line. Begin by dropping the jig straight down all the way to the bottom. Sharply lift and crank the jig up 4-5 feet. Drop it down and repeat it a time or two. If no strike occurs, retrieve the jig as fast as possible. Party boat captains tell customers to "crank like crazy" all the way up to the surface. Yellowtail that aren't otherwise interested in feeding will often strike a fast-moving jig.

Tackle and Equipment

Most yellowtail anglers use conventional reels. Popular models are the Penn Jigmaster and Newell equivalent size. Spinning reels are not recommended because of the need for relatively heavy line and tough drag systems to keep yellowtail out of obstacles. Rods like the Sabre 660, 665 and 670 are good matches. For live anchovy angling, 15-pound line and something like a Sabre 870 is more appropriate.

Where to Fish

Yellowtail are always on the move, but they do hang out in selected places. Some of the best are rock pinnacles, floating kelp patches or even sunken wrecks. Anchoring near these types of structures rather than drifting is recommended. Birds working the surface are always a tip-off. Good fishing spots are detailed in the "Pacific Ocean Fishing" chapter of this book. The North Island, South Kelp, Middle Ground and Rockpile are good in the Coronados. Southland hot spots include the Channel Islands, reefs near Santa Barbara, kelp at San Pedro, La Jolla and Pt. Loma, Santa Catalina Island and San Clemente Island.

Cleaning and Cooking

Yellowtail are most often filleted, but large ones can be steaked. The fish is moderately fatty and nearly as rich as tuna in flavor and texture. Freshly caught fish is good barbecued, smoked or canned.

Special: SoCal Saltwater Launch Ramps

San Diego Bay

San Diego Bay has four excellent launch ramps. They are located at National City Shelter Island, Glorietta Bay on Coronado, and Chula Vista Marina in the South Bay. All four ramps are free of charge, open 24 hours a day, and offer free parking. The most popular ramp is the one at Shelter Island, due to its close proximity to the harbor entrance. The run to the harbor mouth from Chula Vista is a long one, however, though bay anglers should note there can be some good fishing in the South Bay. Live bait is available at the Everingham Bros. barges located on the right hand side of the channel when headed outside. For more information, call the San Diego Port Authority (619) 686-6340.

Mission Bay

By far the best ramp in Mission Bay is the large, multi-lane ramp located in Dana Marina. The ramp is free of charge and there is a good amount of parking, although it can fill up fast in the summertime. The ramp, the newest in the bay, is good even at a low tide. There are three other ramps in Mission Bay. A steep, sandy and at times slimy ramp is located at Ski Beach and features four lanes. A long, slow-slanting ramp is located at the Information Center in the back corner of the bay, and is often sandy and weedy. Another ramp is located in Sail Bay. Live bait is available year-round from the bait barge near the channel entrance.

Oceanside

Oceanside Harbor has a free launch ramp with two lanes that is open 24 hours a day. The catch here is it costs to park in the adjacent lot. Trailers left in the lot past 8 p.m. incur an additional charge. Holiday weekends can fill the lot quickly, especially since RVs are allowed to park in some areas of the lot. There is a parking alternative, however, as a free lot is located on the other side of the railroad tracks adjacent to Helgren's Sportfishing. This lot rarely fills up. Live bait can be purchased from a receiver close by the launch ramp, and availability has been excellent since the recent owners of the bait operation took over. For more information, phone the Oceanside Harbor Master (760) 966-4580.

Dana Harbor

Open 24 hours a day, the Dana Harbor ramp in Dana Point charges an entry fee at a mechanized gate. This eight-lane ramp can get a lot of boats in the water quickly, but the large parking lot will fill up on weekends or even hot summer days when the yellowtail are biting under the kelp paddies. An additional fee is charged for a permit to keep vehicles and trailers in the lot overnight. Live bait can be purchased at the bait receiver year-round, subject to availability. For more information, phone the Embarcadero at (949) 496-6177.

Newport Beach

There is only one public launch ramp in Newport Harbor, which is located in the Dunes off of Jamboree near Coast Highway. The Dunes was recently renovated, but the one thing that remains the same is the ramp, which can be a little slick on low tides. The ramp is open 24 hours a day. The launch fee is higher on weekends. Available parking will fill up on summer weekends by about 10 or 11 o'clock in the morning, but can be gone even quicker. An eight-lane wash rack is one of the new features. Live bait is available on a seasonable basis, with a receiver moored near the channel entrance during the summer months. For more information, call the Dunes (949) 729-3863.

Huntington Harbour

There are two public launch ramps in Huntington Harbour, one operated by the city and the other by the county. The city ramp is a one laner located at Warner and the Pacific Coast Highway between the Huntington Beach Yacht Club and some condominiums. Launching is free, but you are going to need a fistful of quarters to park in the adjacent lot. The meters give you 20 minutes for each quarter, with a six-hour maximum limit. The lot is closed from midnight to 6 a.m. Yearly parking passes are available from Lifeguard Headquarters, located at 103 Pacific Coast Highway, Huntington Beach. For more information, call (714) 536-5281.

The Sunset ramp is operated by Sunset Aquatic Marina, and is an excellent multi-lane ramp located at the end of Edinger Ave. The ramp offers fairly fast access to the open ocean. The ramp is machine operated. For more information, phone Sunset Aquatic Marina (562) 592-2833 or (714) 846-0179. Live bait is available by running north to the receiver or the bait boat operated by Bill's Bait in the Long Beach/L.A. Harbor.

Long Beach/L.A. Harbor

The Long Beach Harbor Master, (562) 437-0041, operates three launch ramps in Long Beach Harbor. The Second St. ramp located at Second St. and Marina is open 24 hours a day and is the most popular with anglers, offering fairly quick access to the open ocean via Alamitos Bay. This ramp is usually full by 8 a.m. on a warm weekend day. Another ramps is located at the Marine Stadium, but is only open from 8 a.m. to 5 p.m. Both ramps are machine controlled. The City of Los Angeles operates a launch ramp in Cabrillo Beach off of Stephen White Dr. The ramp is currently open 24 hours a day. There is a washdown facility. For more information, phone (310) 548-7738. Boaters operating out of any of the Long Beach/L.A. Harbor launch ramps looking for live bait can obtain it from the receiver in the harbor run by Bill's Bait or at times from the bait boat itself.

Redondo Beach

Redondo Beach Marina in King Harbor doesn't have a launch ramp, but it does have a hoist that is open to the public. Many anglers prefer the hoist, as they don't have to put their trailer into the saltwater. Redondo's location is also an advantage to those who want to fish the Rocky Point area. The hoist operates from 6 a.m. to 6 p.m. on weekends and from 7 a.m. to 5 p.m. on weekdays. Parking can be limited in the summertime. The charge for launching varies as to the size of the boat. These fees cover both putting the boat in the water and taking the boat out. Live bait is available from the receiver operated by Pacific Live Bait. Call Redondo Sportfishing for bait availability and charter information at (310) 372-2111. For more information on the hoist, phone (310) 374-3481.

Marina Del Rey

The launch ramp in Marina del Rey has eight lanes and a large parking area. The launch fee is collected at the entry gate. For more information, contact the Marina del Rey Harbor Patrol, (310) 823-7762. Vehicles and trailers can be parked up to 48 hours. Live bait is available from the receiver at Marina del Rey Sportfishing. Call for availability, (310) 822-3625.

Channel Islands Harbor

The launch ramp at Channel Islands Harbor in Oxnard is free, although there is a day use fee for parking (the machine takes quarters). There is a fair amount of parking, although the lot will fill up on Saturdays and Sundays by 10 or 11 a.m. in the summer. The ramp is located at 3001 S. Victoria, just past Channel Islands Blvd., and consists of three large lanes and one smaller lane. There is no limit on how long you park in the lot. For more information, call harbor patrol at (805) 382-3007. Live bait is sold at the CISCO sportfishing docks. Call (805) 985-8511 for availability.

Ventura Harbor

The six-lane ramp in Ventura Harbor is free of charge and is located on the 1600 block of Anchors Way Dr. There is ample parking for vehicles with trailers, and a few spaces for single cars. There is a one-foot drop-off at the end of the ramp on a minus tide. If a vehicle and trailer are left in the lot overnight, the Ventura Harbor Police ask that you file a float plan with their office, (805) 642-8618.

Santa Barbara

The launch ramp in Santa Barbara Harbor is free, but the parking is not. There is a maximum vehicle length of 20 feet, with no restriction on the trailer length. More information is available on a 24-hour basis at (805) 564-5520 or on VHF 12. Live bait is available from a receiver operated by SEA Landing.

Port San Luis

A hoist is open to the public on Harford Pier, with prices varying depending on the size of the boat for boats from 12 to 32 feet. There is adequate parking. The hoist, which requires two operators, is open from 5 a.m. to 5 p.m. during the week, and from 4 a.m. to 5 p.m. on weekends; call (805) 595-7214. Live bait is sometimes available in the summer months from Patriot Sportfishing at (805) 595-7200.

Morro Bay

There is a free launch ramp in Morro Bay located at the end of the Embarcadero. The ramp is three boats wide and parking can be limited during weekends and holidays. No overnight parking is allowed. Virg's Fish'n will sell live bait to the public during the summer months, when available. For more info, phone (805) 772-1222.

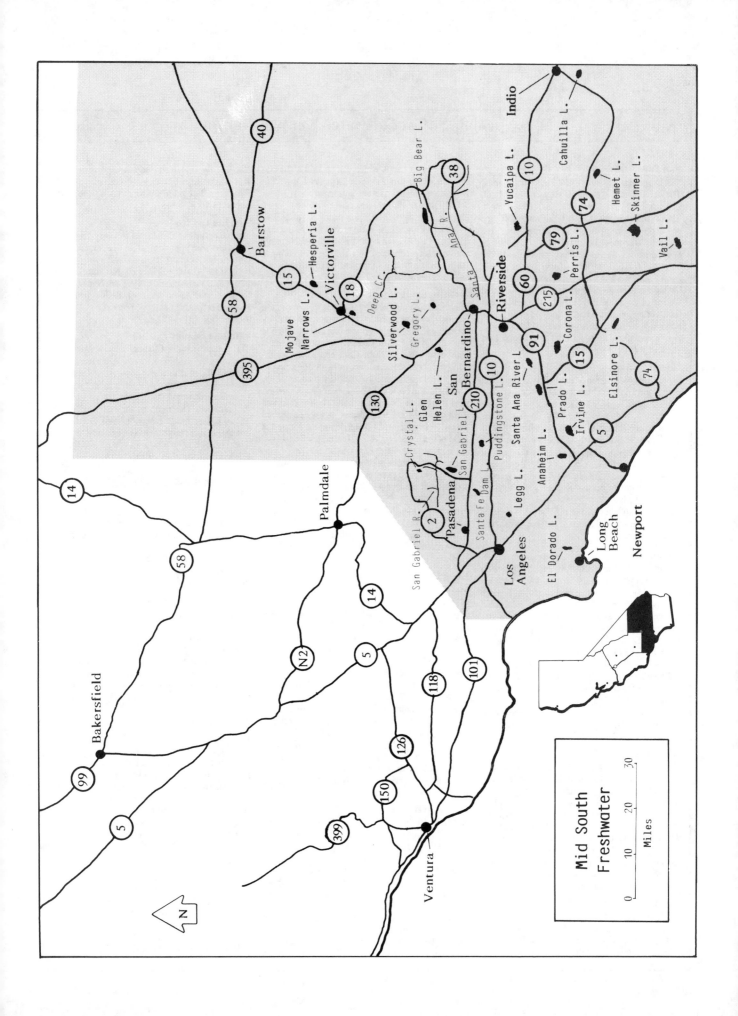

Mid South
Freshwater

Miles

0   10   20   30

Mid-South Freshwater Fishing

This is the first of five freshwater fishing chapters. This chapter as well as the succeeding chapters covers a specific zone of Southern California. These regions are illustrated on the map below.

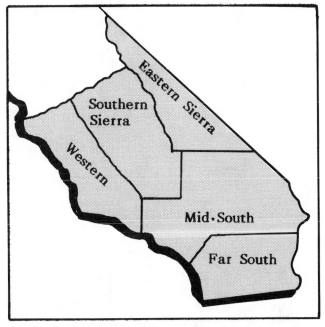

The Mid-South freshwater area encompasses the Los Angeles Metropolitan area, the Angeles and San Bernardino National Forests, Orange County, San Bernardino County and Riverside County. People who don't know Southern California would be amazed by the number and variety of outstanding fishing lakes and even streams that are presented in detail in this chapter. In all, the Mid-South features 15 major fishing lakes (some urban and some out in the country), trout streams in two convenient, yet unspoiled national forests, plus a number of lakes in county park settings.

Almost all Southern anglers like getting away for a weekend or week-long fishing trip to one of the many great fishing areas in Southern California. But it is also nice, at times, to take advantage of the great freshwater fishing opportunities close to home. Look at the map and see how convenient most of the lakes are. They offer great fishing only a short drive from home. They're fantastic for day trips, or even half-day or evening outings. Read up on these lakes, and then plan a "close-to-home" fishing adventure with a friend, or the entire family.

Anaheim Lake (map - p. 92)

Anaheim Lake is a very convenient place to catch better-than-average (and even trophy-sized) catfish in a pleasant urban setting. This 100 acre lake (2 1/2 miles of shoreline; maximum depth of 50 feet) is located several miles north of I-91 (Riverside Freeway). The lake is actually a percolation pond for the Orange County Water District. There is a five-fish limit where fish can weigh between one pound to over 10 pounds. Facilities at Anaheim include a paved launch ramp, large picnic area, cafe, bait and tackle shop, and a paved road encircling the entire lake for easy access. No fishing license is required, but there is a daily, per-person fishing fee at this private lake.

Anaheim Lake is currently only open when Santa Ana River Lakes, a nearby water in Orange County, is closed. Recently, it has only been open during the summer catfish season, but should Santa Ana River Lakes be closed for any reason during the winter, Anaheim would be opened then, and trout would be planted.

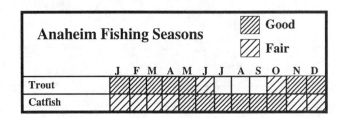

Anaheim Fishing Seasons														Good Fair
	J	F	M	A	M	J	J	A	S	O	N	D	
Trout													
Catfish													

Anaheim Fishing Tips

The number of trout in the lake is kept high enough so it's not difficult to catch your limit. All basic methods can be productive. Bait anglers use a #16 treble hook (baited with a night-crawler/marshmallow combination, inflated nightcrawlers, or Berkley Power Bait) about three feed down from a sliding sinker (1/8 oz.). This can be fished on the bottom or below a bobber, using light line (4 pound or even 2 pound test). When water is cold, a good fishing depth is about 8 feet. Lures seem to work best in the morning hours (from opening time of 7 a.m. to about 10 a.m.). Popular choices include light-colored sonic Roostertails, gold or silver Kastmasters, gold Phoebes and No. 4 Panther Martins. Trollers find good results (around islands and along shore) at about 15 feet down using the same lures as well as Needlefish and Rapalas.

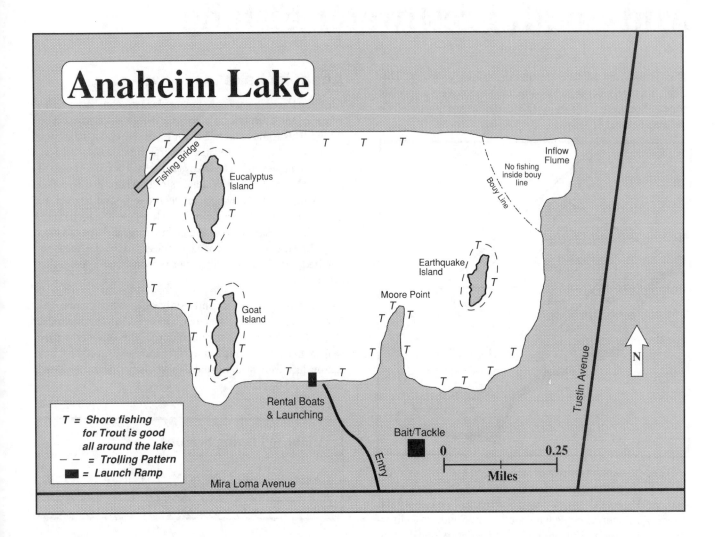

Moore Point is a consistently good trout producer. Another is the Bubble Hole. It is the first cove east of Moore Point and requires a boat to fish it. Early morning and late afternoons generally have a better bite, but trout are taken all day. Anaheim is a great place to take children. They're almost guaranteed a chance to hook fish.

While trout are planted throughout the winter and spring, catfish plants take over in the summertime when the water warms too much for the rainbows. Most anglers use chunks of mackerel, often doused with a scent, fished on 8- to 20-pound test line and a sliding sinker rig. Most of the cats are around 2 pounds, but fish over 20 pounds are caught annually.

Keep any eye on local fishing reports: Anaheim Lake is also sometimes stocked with sturgeon and wipers, a sterile white bass-striped bass hybrid. Both provide great fishing.

Anaheim Lake Facts

Location: A few miles north of I-91 in Anaheim. Take the Tustin Ave. off ramp.

Size: Almost 100 acres with 2 1/4 miles of shoreline and three islands

Species: Varies, call for information

Facilities: Launch ramp, marina, rental boats, cafe, tackle shop at the day-use facilities

Season: Late October to early summer

Information: Contact Santa Ana River Lakes at (714) 854-9193

Big Bear Lake (map - p. 94)

Big Bear Lake is nestled among tall pines at 6,570 feet in the San Bernardino National Forest. It's a big lake—3,000 acres and over seven miles long. Fishing opportunities at this popular resort area, only a two-hour drive from many places in the Los Angeles Basin, include rainbow trout, crappie, bass (both northern largemouth and smallmouth), catfish and panfish (bluegill and pumpkinseed). A wide variety of facilities are available to visitors. There are full-service resort towns, marinas, campgrounds, motels, restaurants, etc. It's no surprise that Big Bear is so popular with both weekenders and vacationers. The excellent lake fishing is detailed below. But when you're in the Big Bear Area, don't overlook the stream trout action. It is covered in the San Bernardino National Forest Stream section of this chapter.

Big Bear Fishing Seasons											Good / Fair
	J	F	M	A	M	J	J	A	S	O	N
Bass	D			▨	▨	▨	▨	▨	▨	▨	▨
Catfish				▨	▨	▨	▨	▨	▨	▨	▨
Panfish				▨	▨	▨	▨	▨	▨	▨	▨
Salmon	▨	▨	▨	▨	▨	▨	▨	▨	▨	▨	▨
Trout	▨	▨	▨	▨	▨	▨	▨	▨	▨	▨	▨

Big Bear Fishing Tips

One key to Big Bear angling success is to be aware of fish migration patterns and then to match tactics to correspond with the current situation. During winter, the trout are primarily in the eastern most shallow sector of the lake. Bait fishing can be excellent at this time and the trout are firm and feisty. Use a sliding sinker rig, 2 to 4 pound test leader and a No. 16 or 18 treble hook. This approach also works all along Big Bear's shoreline in the spring.

As is true in many mountain lakes, trolling is the most productive approach. Spring trolling depths are 5-10 feet in the morning to 10-15 feet in the afternoon. Summer trollers go down 6 to 8 colors of leadcore line or use downriggers. Big Bear trollers use flashers in front of nightcrawlers, Kastmasters, Phoebes and Rapalas. Trollers concentrate on the triangular area between Boulder Bay, Gray's Boat Landing and Papoose Bay. This is the circular trolling pattern shown on the map. Summertime bait anglers can score at the dam from boats. Use a slip bobber rig. Adjust the rig so your offering goes down from 15 to 25 feet. Rainbows in Big Bear generally run about 12 to 14 inches and slightly over a pound. But fish in the 5 to 8 pound range are caught each season.

Big Bear has had a longstanding northern strain largemouth population. The lake record fish is 8 3/4 pounds—not big by Southern California Florida-strain standards, but the light pressure at Big Bear has created a quality fishery. These bass are toughened by the cold water and bulked up by an ample food supply. Big Bear is also an ideal habitat for smallmouths, and following a recent introduction, they are developing nicely.

Bass are active at Big Bear beginning in April, peaking during late May, and then continue to provide steady fishing through early fall. Leadheads, double-bladed spinnerbaits, Rebel deep-runners and plastic worms (in black, purple and brown) all take their share of 2-3 pounders in the spring fishing period before weeds and moss cover up many productive holding areas. Nightcrawlers and live crawdads will also score. Summertime bassers do best late in the day. Use spinnerbaits under docks. At dusk use top-water offerings (Zara Spooks, Hula Poppers) for some exciting action in quiet, wind-protected coves. Fish the holes in heavy weeds or along submerged weed channels. In fall, Big Bear's bass begin to feed heavily. Use shallow-running plugs (due to weed growth), plastic worms near rocks, and leadheads. You'll find these cold-water bass are short and stocky and full of spunk. Locals call them "chunks." The flat and weedy bays at the east end of the lake are favorites for largemouth bass enthusiasts in summer and fall.

Smallmouths take a slightly different approach. They are more prone to rocky structures instead of weed beds. Boulder Bay and Metcalf Bay on the south side of the lake are good. Use anything that resembles a crayfish, either in shape or color. Visiting anglers are encouraged to release all smallmouths to help encourage this fishery.

Panfish are a tradition at Big Bear in the summertime. Weedy coves as well as under docks and other structures are prime haunts for crappie, bluegill and pumpkinseeds—a colorful member of the sunfish family. Larger panfish are in deeper water in the daytime, but smaller ones can be taken all day. Use mini-jigs near the bottom on light line, or hang a hook under a bobber baited with meal worms or red worms.

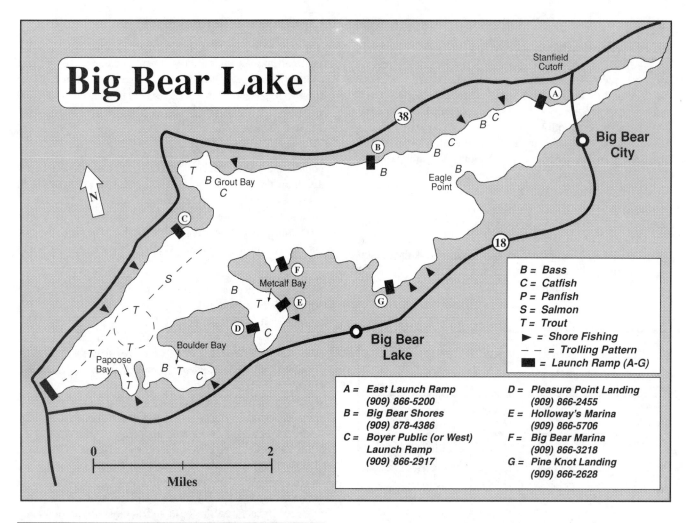

Big Bear Lake Facts

Location: Big Bear is about 90 miles east of Los Angeles via Highway 330 and Highway 18 from San Bernardino. Another route is Highway 38 through Redlands and over Onyx Summit. A third way is to take Highway 18 from the Apple Valley/Victorville area.

Size: 3,000 surface acres, 7 1/2 long x 1 1/2 miles wide with about 22 miles of shoreline. Maximum depth is about 70 feet.

Species: Rainbow trout, silver salmon, largemouth bass, smallmouth bass, crappie, bluegill, channel catfish and pumpkinseed.

Boating: A valid boating permit (available at most marinas) is required.

Facilities: There are numerous resorts, marinas and launch ramps at Big Bear Lake. Contact the Big Bear Chamber of Commerce.

Information: U.S. Forest Service, (909) 866-3437; Big Bear Chamber of Commerce, (909) 866-4607

Lake Cahuilla

Lake Cahuilla, a fine little fishing lake south of Indio, is one of the reservoirs in the Riverside Regional Park System. A special aspect of Cahuilla is that it is actually at the very end of the Coachella Canal, which begins at the Colorado River. This means that Colorado River fish can swim right on into the lake. Consequently, there is more variety and larger fish in Cahuilla than one would normally suspect. Flathead catfish in the 20 pound-plus range are taken, with a few going up to 40 pounds. Another surprise is the possibility of catching a lunker striped bass. Striper over 10 pounds have been hooked. Unofficial reports say the largest Cahuilla striper weighed 26 pounds!

There are also largemouth bass, crappie, bluegill and trout in the winter months. Yes, that's right, trout are planted in this low desert lake from November through April. There is no boat rental on the 135 acres lake, but boats (with electric, oar or sail power) can be beach launched. There are also about 150 campsites (both developed and primitive).

Lake Cahuilla Facts

Location: About 8 miles south of Indio at the intersection of Jefferson and 58th St. and nine miles south of Hwy. 111.

Size: Cahuilla covers 135 surface acres and has 2 1/2 miles of shoreline.

Species: Rainbow trout, largemouth bass, catfish, crappie and bluegill.

Facilities: Swim beach, picnic area, campgrounds, and fishing jetties on the east and west shorelines (handicapped accessibility).

Boating: Electric, oar or sail boats can be shore launched.

Information: Lake Cahuilla County Parks, (760) 564-4712

California Aqueduct

The far south portion of the California Aqueduct provides some surprisingly good fishing action. This section runs from Palmdale in an easterly direction towards Hesperia and then southerly through Lake Silverwood on down to Lake Perris. See the California Aqueduct section of the "Western Freshwater Fishing" chapter for specific information.

Corona Lake (map - p. 97)

Corona Lake is one of the newest of several well-stocked, private, fee-based fishing lakes in Southern California. The others include Irvine, Santa Ana, and Laguna Niguel. For decades Corona was a storage location used by Temescal Water Co. to keep run-off for later use in agriculture. But now it has been reborn as a dedicated all year-round fishing lake stocked with lunker trout and catfish, as well as largemouth bass and crappie. Corona's 86 surface acres of water offer lots of good cover, including stumps and willows. Rental boats are available and are needed to reach some of the good spots, but shore fishing is also excellent because of the aggressive stocking program. The west shore is the ticket for bank anglers. Boaters head for the east shore and the stick-up areas. Trout that exceed 10 pounds and catfish in the 40 pound class are taken with some frequency. The lake is also stocked with wipers—or hybrid striped bass—which are excellent fighters and superb table fare. There is a bait and tackle shop.

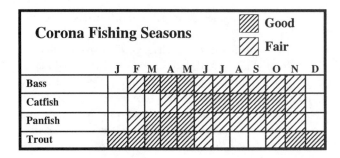

Corona Fishing Seasons	J	F	M	A	M	J	J	A	S	O	N	D
Bass			▨	▨	▨	▨	▨	▨	▨	▨		
Catfish					▨	▨	▨	▨	▨			
Panfish				▨	▨	▨	▨	▨	▨	▨		
Trout	▨	▨	▨	▨						▨	▨	▨

Legend: ▨ Good   ▨ Fair

Corona Fishing Tips

In winter, rainbow trout are the prize at Corona. These fish seem to prefer cheese, inflated nightcrawlers or commercial floating baits rigged on a sliding sinker rig. Remember to move your offering in a few feet every couple of minutes. Hanging bait below a bobber also works. Popular hardware for casters include Mepps and Panther Marten spinners and spoons like Kastmasters. Trolling also works for trouters. The spring months are good for bass. Crankbaits and spinnerbaits tossed from a boat to areas that provide cover are a sure winner. Summer nighttime fishing is offered at Corona (5 p.m. to 11 p.m.) and it is the best time to tie into those large catfish. Anglers work the shallow areas with baits such as mackerel, shrimp and nightcrawlers.

Corona Lake Facts

Location: 9 miles south of the town of Corona off I-15. Take the Indian Truck Trail exit westbound and then turn right 1/4 miles along Temescal Canyon Road.

Size: Corona covers 86 acres.

Species: Rainbow trout (in winter), largemouth bass, catfish, crappie, bluegill and wipers (hybrid stripers).

Facilities: Rental boat, bait and tackle shop

Boating: Private boats over eight feet are allowed with a 5 m.p.h. boat speed limit.

Information: Corona Lake (909) 277-3321

El Dorado Lakes (map - p. 98)

El Dorado Park (450 acres) is the home of four small urban lakes that are great places for youngsters to learn how to fish, and for adults to catch fish close to home. The park is located in southeast Los Angeles County in the northern section of the city of Long Beach. Trout are stocked frequently in the cooler months. Most are in the 9-13 inch range. Catfish typically run about a pound and a half, but 10 pounders are caught each year. Largemouth bass are also taken, mostly in the spring months as are crappie. While there, don't overlook the Nature Center (85 acres), picnic areas, paved trails for bikers and roller skates, the archery center and Vita Course. Paddle boats are rented and can be used for fishing, but most fish are taken from shore.

El Dorado Fishing Seasons		J	F	M	A	M	J	J	A	S	O	N	D
Bass			▨	▨	▨	▨	▨						
Catfish		▨	▨	▨	▨	▨	▨	▨	▨	▨	▨		
Panfish				▨	▨	▨	▨	▨	▨	▨	▨	▨	
Trout		▨	▨	▨	▨						▨	▨	▨

Legend: ▨ Good ▨ Fair

El Dorado Fishing Tips

Trout go for hardware (spinners and spoons) for about two or three days after planting. Fish near the planting sites. After that, switch to bait. Velveta, floating baits, salmon eggs and marshmallows all work at times. The winter trout stocking program begins in about mid-November. Three of the four fishing lakes are planted. These include the two lakes in Area 3 on the north end of Wordlow Road and the largest lake in Area 2 south of Wordlow.

When fishing for bass, crappie and catfish, a good strategy is to look for cover in the water and fish near it. Be sure to stop in at the boat rental office and ask about the current hot spots. Most bass are taken on plastic worms and nightcrawlers. Catfish go for mackerel chunks, commercial catfish baits and nightcrawlers.

El Dorado Lake Facts
Location: In Long Beach; take the Spring Street ramp off I-605 and head one block west.
Size: There are six small lakes in El Dorado. The four fishing lakes, in total, cover about 20 acres.
Species: Trout (in winter), largemouth bass, catfish (planted in summer), crappie and bluegill
Facilities: El Dorado is a fully developed urban park. It offers paddle boat rental, golf course, archery range, picnic area and group camping among other attractions.
Information: El Dorado Park, Long Beach, (562) 570-3100

Lake Elsinore (map - p. 99)

Here is a lake known for its fluctuating largemouth bass, panfish and catfish population, as well as for sailing and waterskiing. It features a number of campgrounds, resorts and marinas and a city park. Boating traffic is very heavy in the summertime so serious anglers often fish Elsinore from November through early spring. The largemouth bass average one to three pounds and are plentiful some years. This may be due to the tremendous cover in Elsinore. Because Elsinore dried up in years past, the lake has propagated submerged trees, brush and stumps. There are the places to work for northern largemouths. Surprisingly, catfishing is also best in heavy cover areas. Lake Elsinore, at 1,600 surface acres, is located about 70 miles southeast of Los Angeles at the town of Elsinore.

Elsinore Fishing Seasons		J	F	M	A	M	J	J	A	S	O	N	D
Bass				▨	▨	▨	▨	▨	▨	▨	▨		
Catfish				▨	▨	▨	▨	▨	▨	▨	▨	▨	
Panfish				▨	▨	▨	▨	▨	▨	▨			

Legend: ▨ Good ▨ Fair

Elsinore Fishing Tips

When bass populations are up, the south shore is probably the most productive locale. Flipping plastic worms and jigs into the cover is a good approach. Plastic worms, four and six inches in brown, black and motor oil, are all winners. Spinnerbaits have accounted for a lot of the larger bass at Elsinore. One-quarter to one-half ounce offerings in white, chartreuse and blue/white are good. Slab-style crankbaits are also favored by some regulars, especially in spring and summer. Catfish can be taken in Elsinore during most months, maybe because the lake is shallow, making the catfish accessible even in winter. Because of the heavy cover, some catfish hunters swear by 20 pound test line and a fairly stiff rod. Chunks of mackerel are the most consistent bait. Some anglers add stink bait solution (like Bowker's). Nightcrawlers are also good. Hook several on a single hook. Bait holder hooks (2/0 to 4/0) are less likely to hang up than treble hooks.

Elsinore bluegills are small but plentiful. Crappie are good-sized but hard to locate. A good approach is to slow troll inside the 5 m.p.h. buoy line with crappie jigs. For a change of pace, consider Elsinore's carp. They are plentiful and seem to favor garlic-flavored bait. A popular spot is the San Jacinto inflow at the lake's east end.

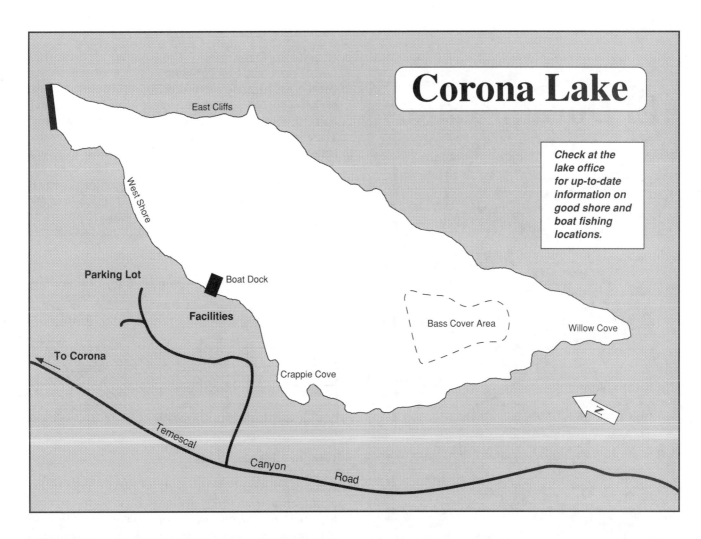

Corona Lake

Check at the lake office for up-to-date information on good shore and boat fishing locations.

East Cliffs

West Shore

Parking Lot

Boat Dock

Facilities

Bass Cover Area

Willow Cove

To Corona

Crappie Cove

Temescal

Canyon Road

N

Lake Elsinore Facts

Location: At the town of Elsinore, about 70 miles southeast of Los Angeles

Size: About 1,600 surface acres

Species: Largemouth bass, channel catfish, crappie, bluegill and carp

Facilities: There are about a half dozen resorts, parks, marinas, and campgrounds on Lake Elsinore, including about eight launch ramps. Specifics on these are available from the local Chamber of Commerce.

Information: Lake Elsinore Chamber of Commerce, (909) 674-2577 then press "0."

Glen Helen Regional Park (map -p. 100)

The two small lakes in Glen Helen Regional Park, situated just 15 miles north of downtown San Bernardino off I-15, offer catfish and bass during the summer and trout during the winter months. It's all shore fishing since boating is not permitted. And don't overlook the all year-long bluegill bite. Plus, there are lots of other activities at this San Bernardino County Parks Department operation including a 350 foot water slide, paddle boats, aqua-cycles, swimming area and snack bar. Glen Helen is open all year. From I-15, take the Sierra off ramp. Turn left and follow the road for one-half mile, then turn right on Devore Road three miles to the entrance. For more information, (909) 887-7540.

Lake Gregory (map - p. 101)

Lake Gregory is a fine mountain (elevation 4,500 feet) fishing lake that is sometimes overshadowed by two much larger and more famous fishing haunts (Big Bear and Silverwood) in the same vicinity. This exceptional trout lake is located in the San Bernardino National Forest approximately 72 miles east of

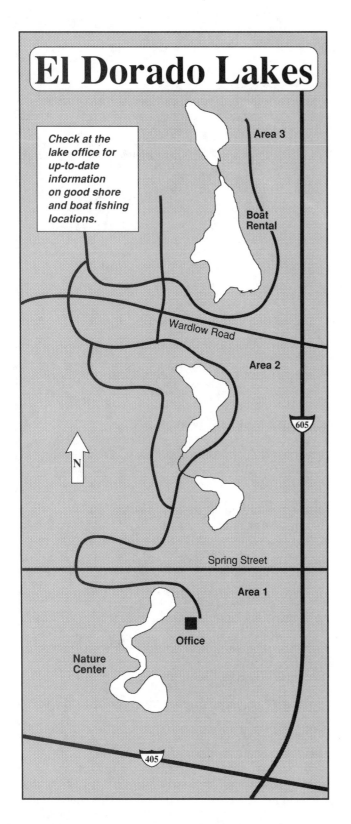

El Dorado Lakes

Check at the lake office for up-to-date information on good shore and boat fishing locations.

Area 3

Boat Rental

Wardlow Road

Area 2

605

N

Spring Street

Area 1

Office

Nature Center

405

Los Angeles and 14 miles north of San Bernardino. Lake Gregory has 4 1/2 miles of shoreline (most of it providing fine bank fishing) and 120 surface acres of water. Private fishing boats are not allowed on the lake, but float tubes are allowed. There is a boat house that rents row boats at a reasonable hourly rate. The boat rental and float tube season here starts the last Saturday in April and extends to the third Sunday in October, but shore anglers can go at it all year long. There is no charge for shore fishing. Bank anglers can fish from one hour before sunrise to one hour after sunset. There is no camping at the lake. Swimming and picnic facilities are provided June through August.

Gregory Fishing Seasons												
	J	F	M	A	M	J	J	A	S	O	N	D
Bass		▨	▨	▨	▨	▨	▨	▨	▨	▨	▨	
Catfish		▨	▨	▨	▨	▨	▨	▨	▨	▨	▨	▨
Panfish		▨	▨	▨	▨	▨	▨	▨	▨	▨	▨	▨
Trout	▨	▨	▨	▨	▨	▨	▨	▨	▨	▨	▨	▨

Legend: ▨ Good   ▨ Fair

Gregory Fishing Tips

Rainbow trout are planted regularly in Lake Gregory. Catches are in the pan size to 1 1/2 pound range. Both boaters and shore anglers do well on trout depending on the whims of fish. All popular baits and lures work well. Two local favorites for still fishing are Velveeta cheese and mini-marshmallows. Rental boat anglers who want to troll can row, or bring along their own trolling motor. Spinners like Panther Martins, Roostertails, flashers trailed by nightcrawlers and small spoons like Needlefish and Kastmasters are effective at Gregory.

Largemouth bass were introduced into Lake Gregory several years ago by the Department of Fish and Game. Their purpose was to add a new fishery and at the same time to use the bass to control the massive population of small crappies. The plan seems to be working. Anglers are catching nice sized bass, and crappie stringers are holding bigger fish. Yellow and white mini-jigs are the most productive route to crappies. Gregory bass, most in the two pound class, are taken on nightcrawlers (some by trout anglers) or on crawdad simulators. Flipping Pig 'n Jigs near the brushy shoreline produces. Crankbaits, in crawdad or silvery like small crappie, are another option. Two good bass areas are east of the Fountains area and in the San Mortiz arm.

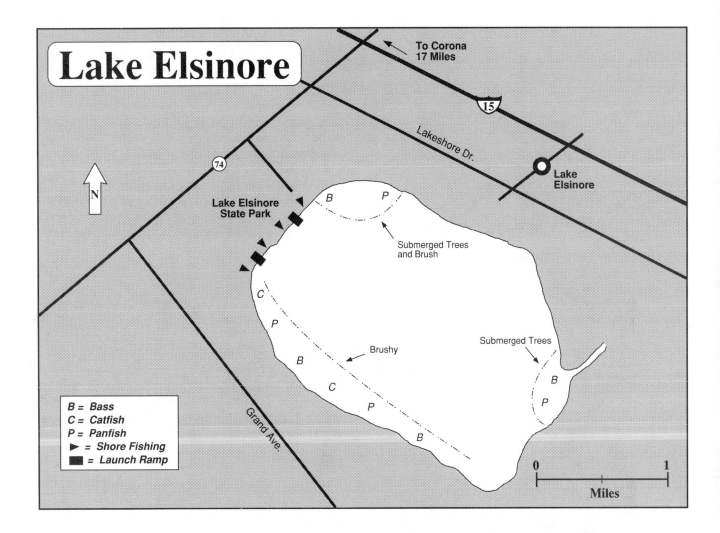

Brown trout are the most recent introduction into Lake Gregory. They were introduced in 1987 to produce trophy fishery and to eat some small and stunted crappie but few have been seen in recent seasons, and they are no longer being stocked. Earlier they were planted in Silverwood, but this stopped working when the marauding stripers of Silverwood took a fancy to the brown trout fingerlings. Browns seldom go for trout bait. One way to go after them is by trolling Rapala or Rebel minnow-type lures in rainbow coloration. In the fall, look for browns to be in the weed beds. See the Crowley Lake section of the "Eastern Sierra Freshwater Fishing" chapter of this book for some added insights.

Catfish are another good fishing option at Gregory. Every year someone catches at least one monster weighing upwards of 20 pounds. Use cut mackerel, nightcrawlers or chicken livers. Two good areas are Catfish Cove and to the east of the Fountains, in the shallows.

Lake Gregory Facts

Location: Gregory is only a 20 minute drive from downtown San Bernardino. Follow Hwy. 18 out of San Bernardino to the Crestline/Lake Gregory turnoff. Then follow the signs.

Size: 120 surface acres

Species: Rainbow and brown trout, largemouth bass, catfish, crappie

Boats: No private boats. Rental boats (oar only) are available.

Facilities: Swimming and water slide, camping in nearby public and Forest Service campgrounds, motels and restaurants in Crestline (one mile from the lake). Lake Gregory is part of the San Bernardino Regional Park System.

Information: Lake Gregory, Crestline, CA, (909) 338-2233

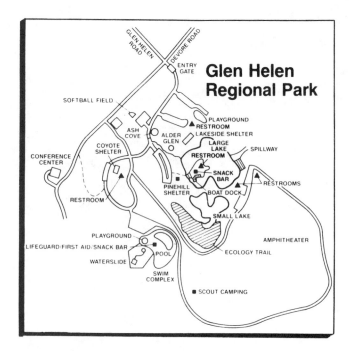

Hemet Lake

Hemet Lake is a pleasant 22-mile drive east into the San Jacinto Mountains from the town of Hemet. This smallish, 420 surface acre lake is located in a mountain meadow at 4,340 feet. It has a reputation for kicking out lots of trout for knowing anglers. Hemet has very clear water, so light leaders are in order. There is also an underrated fishery for northern-strain largemouth bass. Bass in the 6-8 pound range are caught each year, and 2 to 4 pounders are not too uncommon. Again, because of the clear water, light tackle and subtle baits and lures are required. Much of Hemet's shoreline is closed to the public (except for a portion of the northern shore which has free parking and camping facilities), so a boat is required in many angling situations.

Lake Hemet has over 800 campsites, a launch ramp, rental boats and a small store. For more information, contact the Lake Hemet office, (909) 659-2680.

Hesperia Lake

Hesperia Lake is a great option for anglers in the Barstow-Hesperia area who want to do some local trout and catfish catching. This little lake is nestled in a park-like setting that offers a campground, picnic areas and expansive grass lawns. It's just a few miles east of the town of Hesperia in the upper desert. The shoreline is lined with tules in places and there are many trees scattered along the bank. Trout stocking usually

begins in about mid-October. Boats are not allowed so bank fishing is the only option.

Most of the action seems to take place along the eastern shoreline and at the north end. Hesperia is shallow along the southern shore and fishing there is tough. Not that there aren't trout there, but they spook easily in the clear water. Hesperia trout often favor jigs and spoons, over bait. One popular way to go is with a Bullet Jig. Try suspending a 1/32 ounce Bullet Jig in yellow and white three to four feet below a one inch red and white bobber. Cast the rig out and then retrieve it with a very short, gentle stroke, moving it just a little bit a time. Allow it to stop awhile between each move. On breezy days, the wind will push it around for you. Some Hesperia anglers add a meal worm on the jig hook.

Crocodile and similar spoons, especially in the gold and red flame patterns, are also effective. Bait anglers are advised to use 2-4 pound leaders and a No. 18 treble hook. Berkley Power Pait and Velveeta cheese are good options.

When the temperatures in the high desert start breaking the 100-degree mark on a daily basis, the stocking program switches from trout to catfish. Weekly plants of channel cats provide good action for anglers fishing the usual array of baits on the bottom—chicken liver, mackerel pieces or prepared stink baits. Most of the channels are from 1 to 3 pounds, but bigger fish are caught each year.

Hesperia Regional Park, which contains the lake, is five miles from Hesperia on Arrowhead Lake Road. It's open all year. Catfish are planted in the summertime.

For more information, contact the Hesperia Regional Park, (760) 244-5951 or (800) 521-6332.

Irvine Lake (map - p. 102)

Irvine Lake is a private, fish-for-fee lake that has earned a reputation for putting out super-trophy-class trout and catfish. It also boasts excellent largemouth, crappie and bluegill fisheries. The lake records attest to the large fish to be caught: rainbow—20 pounds, 6.5 ounces; largemouth—14 pounds, 7 ounces; catfish—76 pounds, 8 ounces; crappie—4 pounds; bluegill—1 pound, 14 ounces; redear—2 pounds, 6 ounces; sturgeon—28 pounds, 8 ounces. Irvine is a good-sized body of water at over 700 acres. Fish are stocked weekly—trout in the winter months and catfish in the summertime. Irvine offers rental boats, but also provides for launching of private craft. There is a 5 m.p.h. speed limit on the entire lake. Despite the fishing access by boat, most of the fish at Irvine are caught by shore anglers. The lake is open to anglers year round, starting at 6 a.m.

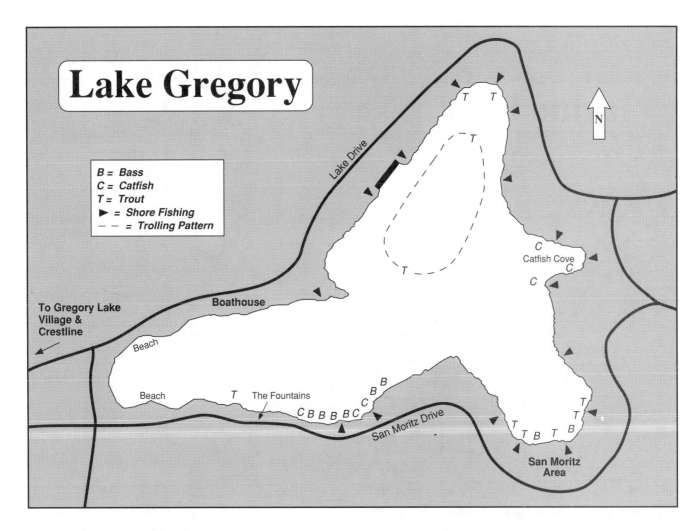

Lake Gregory

B = Bass
C = Catfish
T = Trout
► = Shore Fishing
– – = Trolling Pattern

To Gregory Lake
Village &
Crestline

Boathouse

Beach

Beach

The Fountains

Catfish Cove

San Moritz Drive

San Moritz
Area

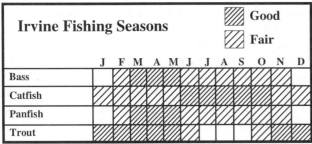

Irvine Fishing Seasons		J	F	M	A	M	J	J	A	S	O	N	D
Bass													
Catfish													
Panfish													
Trout													

Good / Fair

Irvine Fishing Tips

The favorite trout baits at Irvine are probably Berkley Power Bait and inflated nightcrawlers. Other approaches that keep bait up off the bottom, like floating bait and marshmallow combinations, are also good. A sliding sinker rig using about a No. 16 treble hook is fished on the bottom, or below a bobber. Lures, like spinners (Roostertails and Panther Martin) and spoons (Kastmasters and Phoebes) in smaller sizes are most productive in the early hours. These can either be trolled or cast from a boat or shore. Troll along the shoreline but not close enough to interfere with bank anglers. Consistently good bank and boat angling takes place along the entire western shoreline, at the boat docks, in Sierra Cove and at Trout Island. The trout bite is usually best in the early morning hours, but often is steady all day.

Irvine has a tremendous population of natural bait fish including threadfin shad, golden shiners, crawdads, frogs, plus an abundance of other aquatic life. This fact, in conjunction with the stocking program, produces very healthy sized game fish. Catfish are a prime example. Channels and blues come big at Irvine. So big that anglers interested in pursuing them should use appropriate tackle rigged with nothing less than 20 pound test line. Some avid Irvine catfish hunters bring a bucket of ocean pier-caught mackerel for bait. Commercial

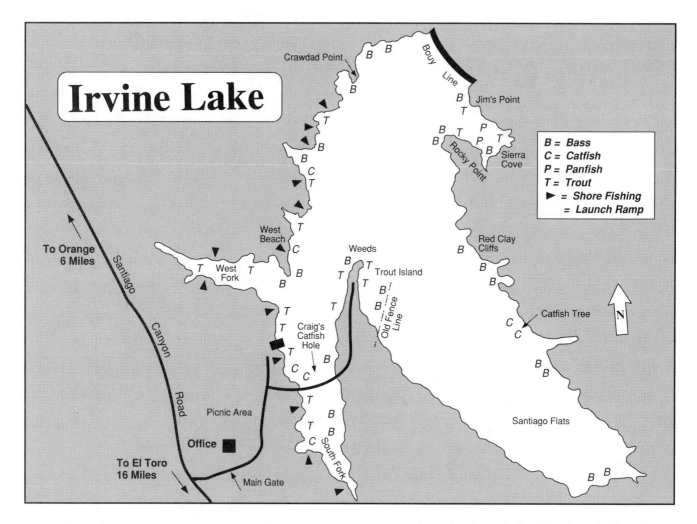

baits and nightcrawlers are also fine options. Adding some liquid catfish scent is a plus. Catfish are caught in shallow water around submerged brush.

Warm summer nights produce some of the best channel catfishing at Irvine. The lake has a 5-11 p.m. fishing session designed for evening catfishing. At sunset the cats begin to gang up in schools of threadfin shad. That's when anglers bait up with chunks of mackerel and cast out an unweighted rig using a 3/0 hook on about 15 pound test line. Feeding cats are located by the sounds of noisy surface feeding. This "fly-line" technique is best done from a cruising boat, but shore anglers using traditional rigs and methods also do very well after dark.

Largemouth bass are overlooked at Irvine. Florida strains have recently been introduced and are growing rapidly on all the forage fish, crawdads and frogs. Bass action peaks in April and May. Irvine features steep rocky cliffs, shallow coves, deep creek channels, submerged high spots, overhanging

trees and flooded timber. During the early spring months, bass take plastic worms and leadhead jigs rigged with pork rinds. When bass are located busting schools of shad, it's time for spinnerbaits and shad-colored crankbaits. Local experts suggest working Irvine shoreline from south to north since breezes are usually blowing down from the foothills, so this direction makes boat-holding on a particular spot easier. Morning anglers should concentrate on the west shore at day break and then move to the shaded east shore around 8 a.m. Reverse this pattern for evening bassing. Some of the most consistent bass hot spots are Rocky Point, Sierra Cove, Red Cliffs, Crawdad Point and the creek channel in Santiago Flats. Nighttime bass fishing is legal at Irvine. The bite can be very good.

Crappie also grow big at Irvine. Look for them in brush piles and around floating docks. Sierra Cove is an especially good spot for 3/4 to 1 1/2 pound slabs. Bluegill are all over the lake in shallow coves.

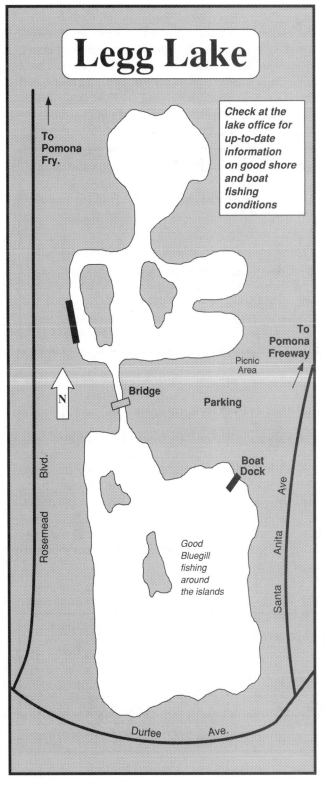

Irvine Lake Facts

Location: In the city of Orange. Take I-55 to the Chapman Ave. East off ramp. Go east on Chapman Ave. three miles to Santiago Canyon Road, turn right and go four miles to Irvine Lake.

Size: About 700 surface acres

Species: Rainbow trout, largemouth bass (northern and Florida), catfish (blue and channel), crappie, bluegill, redear sunfish and sturgeon.

Facilities: Launch ramp, 150 outboard-powered rental boats, tackle store and picnic area

Information: Irvine Lake (714) 649-9111

Legg Lake (map - p. 103)

Legg Lake is a small (77 acres) lake that offers good fishing at a convenient, metropolitan location. It is nestled in Whittier Narrows Recreation Area, near the intersection of the Pomona Freeway (60) and the San Gabriel River Freeway (605). The lake is fished all year-round for warm-water species (bass, catfish, panfish), and it receives stockings of trout in the cooler months. Shore fishing is good all around the lake, but row boats can be rented every day in the summertime, and on weekends in winter. At times there is good action around the lake's islands. In addition to fishing, Whittier Narrows offers hiking, picnicking, shooting and archery ranges, horseback riding, a golf course and tennis courts. It is operated by the Los Angeles County Parks Department.

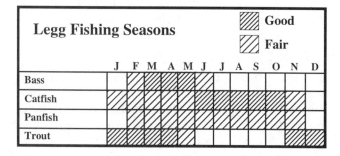

Legg Fishing Tips

If you're at Legg just after a trout plant, try casting and retrieving small spinners or spoons. Mepps, Roostertails and Kastmasters all work. Retrieve them at various speeds and depths to find what is working. Best baits for trout include Velveta cheese, salmon eggs and floating commercial baits. Trout and other fish are often found in holes. So move around until you locate a pocket of deeper water. Catfish go for nightcrawlers, cut pieces of mackerel, cheese balls, commercial stinkbaits and commercial doughbaits. Nightcrawlers are also good for largemouth bass. Hook the worm in and back through the sex collar on a #6 or #8 bronze, long shank, bait holder hook. Crimp a #5 shot about 12 to 18 inches above the worm. Fishing with no shot at all also works. Crawl the worm slowly along the bottom. Strikes may also occur on the drop.

Legg Lake Facts

Location: From Los Angeles take I-60 to the Rosemead exit. Go south on Rosemead and then east on Durfee to the park entrance road.

Size: 77 surface acres

Species: Rainbow trout, largemouth bass, catfish and bluegill

Facilities: Whittier Narrows Recreation Area, a 1,110 acre multi-purpose facility including golf, tennis, horseback riding and athletic fields. Row boats can be rented.

Information: Los Angeles County Parks/ Recreation, (213) 738-2961; Whittier Narrows park ranger, (626) 575-5526.

Mojave Narrows (map - p. 104)

Mojave Narrows Regional Park outside of Victorville provides excellent trout, largemouth bass and catfish angling. There are actually two lakes here. The larger, Horseshoe Lake, is often referred to as Mojave Narrows Lake. It has warm-water species and planted trout (some in the heavyweight category) in the winter months. Pelican Lake, the small body of water, as well as Horseshoe Lake are planted with catfish during the summer months and have a decent population of bass and crappie.

Mojave Fishing Seasons													Good Fair
	J	F	M	A	M	J	J	A	S	O	N	D	
Bass			▨	▨	▨	▨							
Catfish					▨	▨	▨	▨	▨				
Panfish			▨	▨	▨	▨	▨	▨	▨				
Trout	▨	▨	▨								▨	▨	

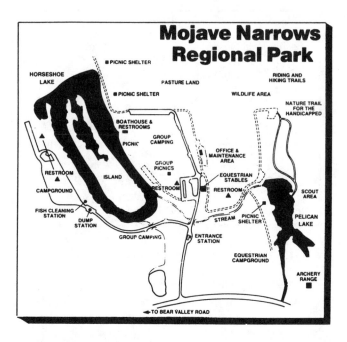

Mojave Fishing Tips

Most trout action at Horseshoe Lake is from shore, although there are rental boats. The southeast and north shorelines are often the best areas. After a trout plant, work the south end first, and then move north if action is slow. The inlet by the boat house at the north end can be excellent if it's running. The western shoreline, by the campground, is shallow and unproductive. Lures often do best the first few days after a plant. Top lures include 3/8 ounce Krocodile Tiger Tail Spinners and pearl Roostertails. Fish them real slow on 2 or 4 pound line. Another local favorite is the Bullet Jig. Fish it as described in the Hesperia Lake section of this chapter.

Light line is also important to bait angling. Baits, including commercial floating bait, Velveeta and inflated nightcrawlers work well at the north end several days after a plant as the trout migrate to this deeper water. Horseshoe Lake is about 20 acres in size. Bass fishing can be excellent there in the spring. A hot spot, which can only be reached by boat, is the center of the island. Work the various tule patches. Largemouths to 16 pounds have been taken. Some say Horseshoe is the best bass lake in San Bernardino County. March is when it really starts getting good. Darker colored (like black or purple) Pig 'n Jigs bring bucketmouths out of the tules. The weeds and tules on the south and north shores are also good. Live crawdads, plastic worms and grubs are also winners.

Horseshoe and Pelican are also good for early spring crappie. Check out the tules in the south end of Horseshoe. Both lakes also hold planted and native catfish, but they're easier to catch in the smaller Pelican. Try the east side first. Use mackerel, crawdads or nightcrawlers. Add some scent to your bait. All areas of Pelican produce catfish, but if your finding it slow, move to the north shore of Horseshoe. Catfish planting begins around April each year.

Mojave Narrows Facts

Location: Between Hesperia and Victorville. Exit I-15 at Bear Valley Road and go east four miles to Ridgecrest Road, and north three miles to the lake.

Size: Mojave Narrows Regional Park covers 840 acres. Horseshoe Lake covers about 20 acres. Pelican Lake is smaller.

Species: Rainbow trout (in Horseshoe), largemouth bass, catfish, crappie, bluegill

Boating: Rental row boats in Horseshoe. Personal trolling motors can be installed.

Facilities: Campgrounds, picnic areas, stables and equestrian campground, native trail and wildlife area.

Information: Park office, (760) 245-2226

Perris Lake (map - p. 107)

Perris Lake is a fully developed recreational area run by the California Department of Parks and Recreation. It is a good-sized lake (2,400 surface acres) that is located 70 miles east of Los Angeles and 80 miles north of San Diego. This is a great place for a family or group outing. Anglers in the party can fish the lake early and late in the day. And swimmers, water skiers, jet skiers and sail boaters can enjoy the water during the warmth of the day. Perris offers anglers rainbow trout, Alabama spotted bass, largemouth bass (Florida strain), catfish and bluegills. There are 100 foot fishing piers and three launch ramps, as well as 450 campsites, picnicking, boat rental, stores, bait and tackle.

Perris Fishing Seasons														Good / Fair
	J	F	M	A	M	J	J	A	S	O	N	D	
Bass		▨	▨	▨	▨	▨	▨	▨	▨	▨	▨		
Catfish			▨	▨	▨	▨	▨	▨	▨	▨	▨		
Panfish			▨	▨	▨	▨	▨	▨	▨	▨			
Trout	▨	▨	▨	▨	▨					▨	▨	▨	

Perris Fishing Tips

Among avid anglers, Lake Perris was best known for its spotted bass population, but its healthy population of Florida-strain largemouths have stolen the limelight in recent years. Two former world record spotted bass (9 pounds, 4 ounces) were pulled from Perris in 1987. Spotted bass seem to favor a little deeper water and rocky shorelines while Perris large-mouths prefer structure and shoreline willows. But the same tactics and lures will catch them both, many times in the same area. There is a 15-inch minimum size on bass, but of the legal bass caught, most average 3 to 5 pounds.

Regular Perris bassers favor either live bait or plastics. Live crawdads are a top choice. Some anglers pull off one claw to stop them from digging into the sand. Mudsuckers are another good bet. Green is the top color in plastics. Grubs, worms or Green Weenies fished 15 to 20 feet deep over rock piles is the way to go except when the bass are in shallow. A favorite worm is the Workin' Girl four incher in "magic green" color. Use a Texas-style rig. Work all plastics very slowly. Floating Rapalas work really well along the dam. When the bass are very deep, it's best to spoon for them. Try a Hopkins spoon and just hop it off the bottom. The face of the dam is a top locale for both spotted bass and largemouths. It stretches for almost 2 1/2 miles so their is lots of room. Most feel the south end is most productive. Another good bass area is off the marina. Note that part of it is restricted. There are also several sunken islands at the east end of the lake that are good bets. Alesandro Island at the north end is also good. The Tire Reef at the south end of Lake Perris is one of the better spots in the entire lake. It's down about 40 to 50 feet deep.

There are two rainbow trout peak fishing seasons at Lake Perris. The first is the normal winter trout season that is supported by regular planting. A second excellent trout bite occurs in the summer months when the fish are in deep water at the dam. Anglers take large (2-3 pound) holdover trout near the buoy line on live shad at these times. During the winter, Perris is stocked with trout about twice a month. But anglers take them from bank or boat with Berkley Power Bait, Zeke's Floating Bait or inflated nightcrawlers, among other offerings. Trolling the lake favorite Needlefish (in brown, nickel or green frog) is another good way to go. Go down three to four colors of leadcore in spring and about eight colors in summer. Good trolling areas are off the swim buoy line, around the 5 m.p.h. markers and at Bernasconi Beach and Perris Beach.

There are bigger bluegills in Lake Perris than just about anyplace else in the entire state. These are Florida-strain fish. They have evolved in warmer eastern lakes and seem to grow all year long. If you get into big bluegills, you can expect to catch a bunch in the 1 to 1 1/2 pound range! One key is to put your offering at the depth where the slabs are hanging out. Try baiting crappie jigs with crickets and then drift the dam buoy line. Set each rod at a different depth. Also try different jig weights. Another approach that works is to fish crickets with a minimum of weight. Flip them over rocks or brush and let them settle down very slowly. The marina area can be fished from boat, but dock fishing is not permitted. Catfishing is best after dark near the dam, and at the east end.

Perris Lake Facts

Location: In Riverside County, east of the city of Riverside, south of I-60, east of I-15 and north of the Ramona Expressway. There are three access points. The south entrance to the Lake Perris State Recreation Area is just off Ramona Expressway; take I-215 to this street and turn east. The park entrance is a little over two miles from the interstate. To reach the north entrance, take Moreno Beach Drive off I-60 and go south to the park. Both of these routes take you into the main part of the park, with parking areas from the dam to the north shore. You can also drive into Bernasconi Beach on the southeast side of the lake, pay the mechanical fee collector, and fish there. You reach this entrance by taking the Ramona Expressway another four miles east past the main park entrance.

Size: About 2,400 surface acres

Species: Spotted bass, largemouth bass, rainbow trout, Florida-strain bluegill, redear sunfish, green sunfish and catfish

Facilities: Lake Perris has a full-service marina, launch ramps, boat rental and fishing piers. The associated State Recreation Area has hundreds of campsites, stores, and much more.

Information: Lake Perris State Recreation Area, (909) 657-0676, Lake Perris Marina (909) 657-2179

---

ming in the lake is permitted. Other on-site activities include an equestrian center and trails, camping, two 18-hole golf courses, and shotgun and airgun shooting ranges. Prado Park is easily reached by exiting I-71 at Euclid Ave. (Rte. 83) and heading north. For more information, (909) 597-4260.

Puddingstone Lake (map - p. 109)

Puddingstone Lake, in the 2,000 acre Bonelli Regional Park, combines fine fishing with a completely developed recreational facility. It is located at the intersection of the San Bernardino Freeway (I-10) and the Orange Freeway (I-210). Puddingstone has 250 surface acres of water and is open to all boating activities. Rainbow trout are stocked in the cooler months (some up to 10 pounds) and the average catch is 12 to 13 inches. Bass are plentiful because of the heavy forage level of threadfin shad. Every year anglers take three or four fish over 10 pounds, and there isn't as much pressure as at the more heralded lakes. Channel catfishing gets going in May with many fish in the five pound range. The lake record is 37 pounds. Facilities at Puddingstone include boat rental, swimming, about 450 campsites, horseback riding and Raging Waters.

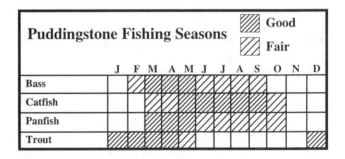

Puddingstone Fishing Seasons														Good — Fair
	J	F	M	A	M	J	J	A	S	O	N	D	
Bass			▨	▨	▨	▨				▨			
Catfish					▨	▨	▨	▨	▨	▨			
Panfish				▨	▨	▨	▨	▨	▨	▨			
Trout	▨	▨	▨	▨							▨	▨	

Prado Park Lake (map - p. 108)

The 80 acre Prado Regional Park and its 56 acre lake are operated by the San Bernardino County Regional Park System. Prado Lake has good angling for bass, catfish, bluegill and wintertime trout. Shore access for anglers is easy, but a boat rental is also available. In addition, anglers can launch their own boat provided it's are under 16 feet and has a rigid hull. But no fuel-burning engines are allowed and no swim-

Puddingstone Fishing Tips

The most consistent trout producer at Puddingstone is floating baits (Power Bait, Zeke's Cheese, marshmallows). Anglers use a size 12 to 16 treble hook, a light leader and several split shot up the line. The sliding sinker rig is another choice. Trolling seems to be the most consistent approach for people out on the water. Trail silver or gold Super Dupers or Kastmasters. Straight monofilament is good in January and

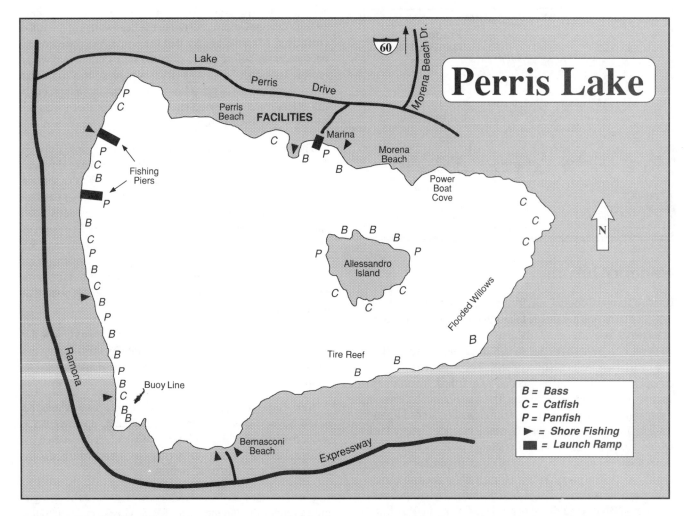

February. Use leadcore line as the water warms up in March and April. Two consistently good shore spots for trout are Sailboat Cove and off the rocks near the dam. Trollers work in the dam area, along the cliffs and off the north shore beach.

Largemouth bass usually start hitting the third or fourth week of February. Puddingstone bass will run an average of about two pounds. Large fish are taken most often during the spring spawn in the shallows. The eastern shore is loaded with good spawning areas as is Sailboat Cove. The canal area is another good producer of spring bass, and don't overlook the rocky area around Picnic Island.

When the largemouth are down deep, the cliffs on the north side of the lake are productive with plastic worms and live crawdads. Deep-water crankbaits like the Rat-L-Trap are winners also. Black or purple plastic worms seem to get Puddingstone bass to respond anytime they're on a bite.

Catfishing heats up in May and stays solid all summer long. A hot spot is the dam area. Channel cats hang out in deep water there. Cut mackerel and nightcrawlers account for most of the catches. In the summertime, the night bite is the most predictable. Off the swim beach is a good bet.

Puddingstone Lake Facts
Location: Between La Verne and Pomona. Take the Via Verde exit from I-210 north, or the Ganesha exit off of I-10 east.
Size: Puddingstone covers 250 acres.
Species: Rainbow trout, largemouth bass, catfish, redear sunfish and some crappie
Facilities: Launch ramp, boat rental, camping, swimming, horseback riding and Raging Waters
Information: Bonelli Park, (909) 599-8411

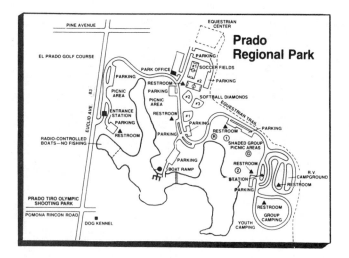

Rancho Jurupa Park

Rancho Jurupa County Park, located just east of Riverside off I-60, contains one manmade lake and several smaller natural ponds that provide good fishing year-round. The natural waters are bordered by dense strands of cattails and tules. Bass and catfish are the main quarry here. The manmade lake has an open shoreline and is planted and fished for trout (in season), catfish and largemouths. The water is much clearer in the manmade lake than in the natural waters, so use lighter leaders. Rancho Jurupa is a beautiful Riverside County Park with open grass verandas and scattered white boulders. No water sports or boats are permitted on any of the lakes. There are 86 campsites, picnic areas, hiking trails and a nature area. You reach the park by taking I-60 to Rubidoux Blvd., go south to Mission Blvd., the left 3/4 of a mile to Crestmore Road, and right 1 1/2 miles to the park. For more information, (909) 684-7032.

San Bernardino National Forest Streams (map - p. 110)

The San Bernardino National Forest hosts some fine trout streams, including the upper reaches of the Santa Ana River, Bear Creek and Deep Creek. Each of these is described in detail in this section.

The Santa Ana River drains much of the southern slopes of the San Bernardino Mountains. This river and its tributaries offer some outstanding trout angling for wild and planted fish up to a foot long, and occasionally longer. But we're not talking about the concrete channel Santa Ana that winds through Orange County, but rather the headwaters of this once great river. It's little known that the Santa Ana once hosted steelhead runs before it was diverted into a municipal water source. The upper Santa Ana River is so narrow in spots that hikers can jump across it as it runs down the mountain, but it still offers some very good stream fishing for those who are willing to put forth a little effort.

The headwaters of the Santa Ana generally flow through the mountains from the vicinity of Big Bear Lake down to Hwy. 30 between Highland and Redlands. If you're serious about fishing here, it's best to get auto club and San Bernardino National Forest maps. There are four basic sections to the Santa Ana. The first, known as the "headwaters," consists of the South Fork and Fish Creek tributaries. They run out of the San Gorgorio Wilderness. These are walk-in streams. You can park where Hwy. 38 crosses the South Fork and fish both streams. These are tiny waters with bright-colored browns that rarely exceed seven inches.

The "Seven Oaks" portion runs for eight miles below the South Fork junction. It is heavily planted by DFG during the summer. And there are also wild browns here averaging 7 to 10 inches.

Next comes the "Gorge" section. It runs from where the paved Seven Oaks Road meets the stream, downward for about four miles. This is wild, rugged country populated by rattlesnakes, but it's also a lovely canyon stream with a healthy number of browns up to 12 inches.

Finally comes the "Lower Canyon." It consists of an eight mile stretch from the junction of Bear Creek on down to the Edison hydroelectric plant on Green Spot Road. This section is dry during low water years, but it quickly fills with water and fish in good rain years. Concentrate at feeder stream inflows.

The map accompanying this section shows Bear Creek, below Big Bear Lake. It is actually a tributary of the Santa Ana River. Bear Creek is a small stream that runs through a narrow canyon. It's entire 8.75 mile length is protected by the state's wild trout program. Be aware of current lures and take limitations. Bear Creek probably has the highest number of trout per mile and number of fish over eight inches in the entire area.

Cold water from deep down in Big Bear Lake feeds Bear Creek all summer long, so healthy trout here are feasting on prolific summer hatches. The two best locations for fishing Bear Creek are the Slide Lake area and where the Glory Ridge

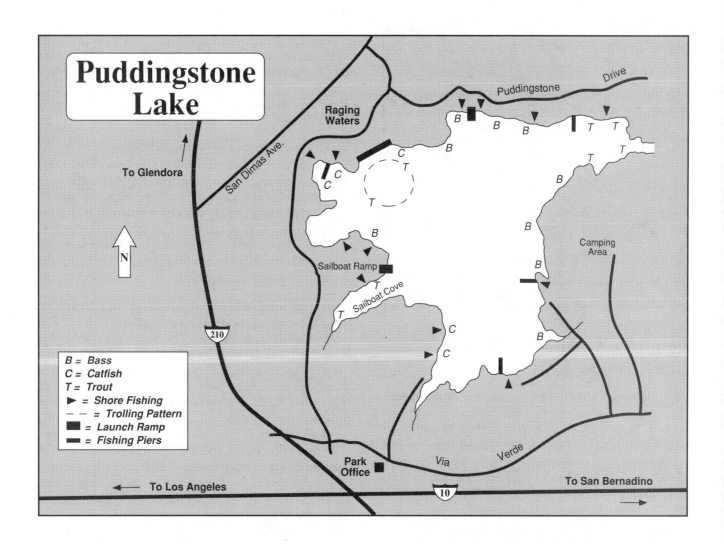

Puddingstone Lake

To Glendora

N

To Glendora

210

Raging Waters

Puddingstone Drive

San Dimas Ave.

Sailboat Ramp

Sailboat Cove

Camping Area

B = Bass
C = Catfish
T = Trout
► = Shore Fishing
– – = Trolling Pattern
■ = Launch Ramp
▬ = Fishing Piers

Park Office

To Los Angeles

Via Verde

10

To San Bernadino

trail meets the stream. Most of the shoreline of Bear Creek is lined with lots of oak and willows. Short casts with light tackle (two or three weight rods for fly anglers) is the ticket to success.

Deep Creek is actually the east fork of the Mojave River. It flows down on the north ridge of the San Bernardino Mountains and is an officially designated wild trout stream. Check current regulations. It produces the largest stream fish (browns to 24 inches), but the bulk of the population is rainbows. The Pacific Coast Trail follows the whole length of Deep Creek so getting across to different sections is easy. And good hiking shoes are required for the climbs down to the water. Be watchful for the rattlesnakes and the skinny dippers.

They (the naked people, not the snakes) are attracted to the stream's huge, deep pools. Fortunately they usually leave before the evening surface bite begins.

Deep Creek is known for pool after pool of crystal clear water. Experts say that Renegades and Woolly Worms are best for browns, while Royal Coachman are food for rainbows. Larger flies take larger fish. No. 10 through 14 are worth a try. If you can't interest bigger ones, slip down to No. 18 or even No. 22 for smaller fish. There are no overnight facilities in the Deep Creek area so save enough energy to climb back to your car. A detailed map of Deep Creek is available from the U.S. Forest Service, Arrowhead Ranger Station, Rim Forest, CA 92378. You can call at (909) 337-2444.

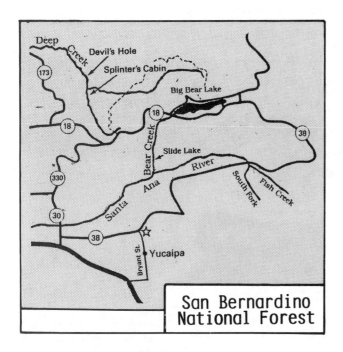

San Gabriel Wilderness Area Streams (map - p. 111)

The San Gabriel Wilderness Area is located in the Angeles National Forest directly north of the Los Angeles metropolitan area. The primary access route is by Hwy. 39 north out of Azusa. This road parallels the San Gabriel River canyon, which eventually spreads out into West, North and East Forks. It's this drainage that provides some excellent close-to-home mountain trout angling for Southern Californians (only about 30 miles north of downtown Los Angeles).

The premier trout water in the San Gabriel Wilderness area is the West Fork of the San Gabriel River. This is a wild trout catch and release stream. The wild rainbow trout runs up to 14 inches, but their worth can't be measured in size. The West Fork provides a look back at what Southern California was like before wetlands were drained, streams damed, and steelhead runs destroyed. Wild trout dancing at the end of your line in this picturesque stream setting makes it hard to believe that there is smog and traffic just down the mountain side.

Although a service road runs along the designated wild trout section of this stream (it leads to Cogswell Reservoir), no vehicles are allowed to use it. Some anglers take advantage of this right-of-way by pedaling bicycles from place to place

along the stream. The wild trout waters begin at Bear Creek and run over five miles. Below that is plant water.

The West Fork is a very good fishing spot in the spring and fall. Summer anglers are advised to fish early and late in the day. Good flies to try include a dark Parachute (about size 18), Caddis (size 18 and 20), Royal Coachman (size 14), Mosquitos, Red Ants and Royal Wulffs. Average fish are not big here—probably about 8 to 10 inches.

All of the wild trout section of the West Fork offers good fishing, but perhaps there are more fish in the upper end where water is cooler and habitat better. Some anglers like the water around the old cabin, about three miles in the no-kill stretch. Early in the season sunken patterns drifted through deep pools and riffles are the best. The West Fork has prolific mayflies, caddis and midge hatches that intensify as the water warms. In summer the water is low and very clear, so use light, long leaders and a delicate presentation.

The San Gabriel Wilderness area has more to offer anglers, besides the West Fork. There is also the North Fork and East Fork of the San Gabriel River. The North Fork is accessible from Rte. 39 along its entire length, whereas the East Fork requires use of a hiking trail that parallels it. These waters are heavily planted and heavily fished. Most anglers use salmon eggs and nightcrawlers, but flies are also popular. Then there is Bear Creek, a tributary of the West Fork. Bear Creek runs north off the West Fork right into the San Gabriel Wilderness. Fishing can be quite good, but the terrain is difficult. A backpacking permit is required. A final possibility for trout anglers is Crystal Lake. It is a tiny (7 acre) trout water off Rte. 39 along the North Fork. Since you can drive right up to it, it is heavily fished. It offers planted rainbow, as well as some bass and catfish.

As you can see on the accompanying map, there are four reservoirs in the San Gabriel Wilderness Area. The three largest, Cogsell, San Gabriel and Morris, may or may not be open to fishing, depending on current regulations, but they could be fine trout opportunities. But San Dimas is open. It's a lower elevation, 35 acre lake that is regularly stocked with channel catfish. So after you've got your limit of trout, or tire of releasing fish in the West Fork, hop in your car and get some catfish at San Dimas. It's reached from San Dimas Canyon Road out of Glendora. The best catfishing is at the north and south end of the lake, along the eastern shoreline. By the way, when conditions permit, trout are also planted at San Dimas.

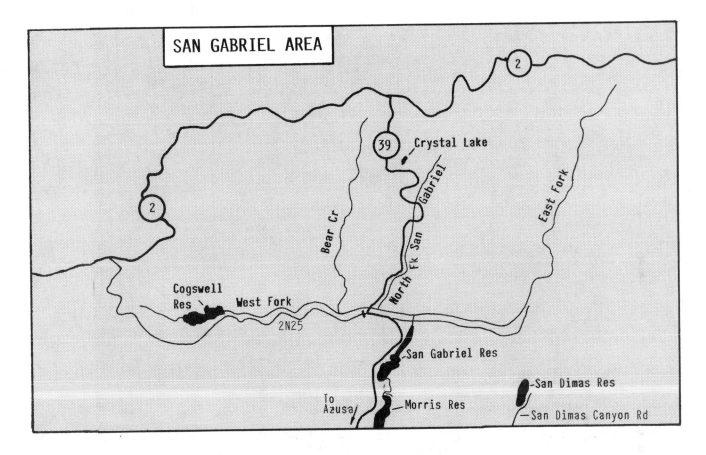

A map of the San Gabriel Wilderness Area is available from most U.S. Forest Service offices in the Mt. Baldy Ranger District, 110 N. Wabash Ave., Glendora, CA 91740. There are a number of campgrounds in the San Gabriel River area. For information call the main office of the Angeles National Forest in Arcadia at (626) 574-5200.

Santa Ana River Lakes (map - p. 112)

For anglers who want to catch rainbow trout and catfish right near home, including some lunkers, this could be the place.* Santa Ana River Lakes are located in the City of Anaheim, just north of Hwy. 91 (Riverside Freeway). This facility is made up of three small lakes: Trout Lake (87 acres), Catfish Lake (10 acres), and Chris Lake (6 acres). Fish are stocked weekly— trout in the winter months, catfish in the summertime, and wipers on occasion. Rental boats are available and private boats can be launched in Trout Lake. But shore angling is very popular at Santa Ana River Lakes. The lakes are open to anglers from 6 a.m. to 4 p.m. and from 5 p.m. to 11 p.m., seven days a week, all year long. There is a moderate, per-person fishing fee at this private lake.

Santa Ana Fishing Tips

Trout over 10 pounds are planted at Santa Ana River Lakes. The lake record is over 20 pounds! And there are many single-digit fish. Some trout hot spots for shore anglers include the Pump House, the north shore and the boat dock area of Trout Lake, also by the spillway areas at Chris' Pond and Catfish Lake. Both bank and boat anglers use sliding sinker rigs for the lunkers. Winning baits include Velveeta, salmon eggs, marsh-mallows, nightcrawlers and Zeke's Floating Cheese Baits. But Berkley Power Bait (in pink or yellow) has been the bait

Santa Ana Fishing Seasons				Good / Fair

	J	F	M	A	M	J	J	A	S	O	N	D
Catfish					▨	▨	▨	▨	▨	▨		
Trout		▨	▨	▨	▨						▨	▨

Santa Ana has produced the largest rainbows ever caught in Southern California. In 1996, the lake record fell 3 times around Christmas, standing at 23.1 pounds as this edition went to press—and sure to get bigger.

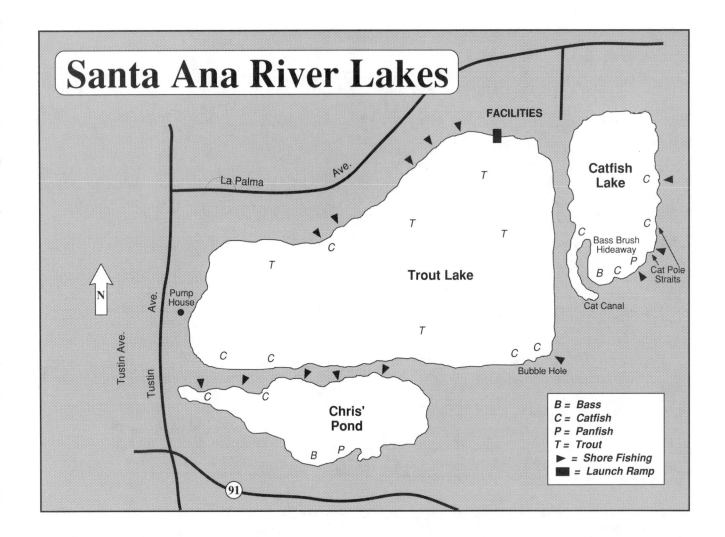

of choice recently. Bring along several choices and then switch if necessary. Most fish are shy, so go to a light leader (two pound test) on your sliding sinker rig and use No. 16 or 18 treble hooks. Set the drag fairly lightly. Then if you hook a big fish, just let it peel off line and work it back slowly.

Lures are also effective at the lakes, particularly early in the morning and late in the afternoon. Roostertails, Kastmasters, Mepps Spinners, and Rapala-type plugs are all popular. Anglers also get good results with Bullet Jigs and Crappie John Finger Jigs. Fish them below a small bobber and use enough leader so that the jig is just off the bottom.

Catfish plants (channel mostly) run from May to October. Terminal tackle that works is a sliding sinker rig using a one-half to three-quarter ounce sinker, about 8 pound leader and a No. 2 to No. 4 hook. Commercial stink baits and cut mackerel often produce. The best bass and panfish areas are the south shores of the two smaller lakes. The brushy area in Catfish Lake is a good bet.

Santa Ana River Lake Facts
Location: In the City of Anaheim, just north of I-91. Take Tustin Ave. north to La Palma Ave.
Size: There are three lakes (Trout Lake—87 acres, Catfish Lake—10 acres, Chris' Pond--6 acres)
Species: Rainbow trout, catfish, plus some largemouth bass and panfish
Facilities: Launch ramp, boat rental, store and picnic area
Information: Santa Ana River Lakes, Anaheim, (714) 632-7851

Santa Fe Dam Lake (map - p. 114)

Santa Fe Dam Lake offers good fishing right in the heart of metropolitan Los Angeles. This 70 acre lake and surrounding 830 acre park is located about 20 miles east of downtown Los Angeles. But many people drive right by and don't see it. That's because of the five mile long Santa Fe Dam stretching along the southern boundary of the park. It is part of the San

Gabriel River flood control project. The park itself is quite pleasant (biking, picnicking, wildlife area) and fishing is popular year-round. Trout are planted from early November until May. Most are half-pounders, but some top a pound. Bass fishing (most just under the 12 inch minimum) and panfishing are good in the spring to early summer. Catfish are planted regularly during the warmer months with the average catch about three pounds.

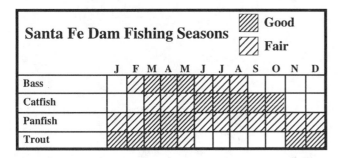

Santa Fe Dam Fishing Seasons												Good Fair	
	J	F	M	A	M	J	J	A	S	O	N	D
Bass			▨	▨	▨	▨	▨	▨				
Catfish				▨	▨	▨	▨	▨	▨			
Panfish		▨	▨	▨	▨	▨	▨	▨	▨	▨		
Trout	▨	▨	▨								▨	▨

Santa Fe Dam Fishing Tips

Bait angling for trout, probably the most productive approach, focuses on Velveta cheese, Zeke's Floating Cheese Bait, marshmallows, salmon eggs and nightcrawlers. Be prepared to change off if the bite is slow. Some anglers hang bait under a float while others use a sliding sinker rig. Mepps spinners, Panther Martins and Roostertails are best for cast and retrieve. Catfishing hot spots include the west end of the lake, out off the boat rental area, at Coot Point and around the fishing pier at the south end of the lake.

In the heat of the summer, catfishing is often best in the deeper parts of the lake. That's when some shore anglers use surf rods so they can reach the deeper water in the middle of the lake. Chunks of mackerel are the top offering, but night-crawlers and chicken livers also produce.

Bass anglers should hit the shallows at the west end and around the eastern island early and late it the day. On overcast days, these spots produce all day long. White and chartreuse spinnerbaits with willow-leaf blades are a top producer. Top-water lures such as gold or black Rapalas can also be good early in the morning. Purple or motor-oil four inch flip-tail plastic worms are a local favorite for working the deeper channels of Santa Fe. As summer sets in, a good approach is to work the water over weeds with buzzbaits, spinnerbaits, or your favorite top-water lures.

Shore anglers can fish almost the entire perimeter of Santa Fe. The only exceptions are the launching and swimming areas. The south and east sides of the lake are bordered by lawns, parking lots and day-use facilities. Native vegetation is featured in the Natural Wildlife Management Area that encompasses the north and west shores.

Most Santa Fe crappie run between 8 and 12 inches. Crappie jigs or mini-jigs worked along the shoreline is the way to get them. Meal worms or pieces of nightcrawler tipping the jig hook may make the difference. There are also plenty of bluegill.

Santa Fe Dam Lake Facts
Location: Just north of Arrow Hwy. in Irwindale. Take I-605 to the Arrow Hwy. exit and then go east to the lake entrance. Or, take I-210 to Irwindale Ave., go south to Azusa Canyon Rd. and then turn west to the lake entrance.
Size: The 70 acre lake is surrounding by an 830 acre park. Maximum depth is 15 feet.
Species: Rainbow trout, catfish, largemouth bass, crappie and bluegill
Boating: Only electric-powered or oar-powered boats are allowed.
Facilities: The Santa Fe Dam Recreation Area is operated by the Los Angeles County Department of Parks and Recreation. There is a launch ramp, boat rental, bait shop, group campground, nature walks, etc.
Information: Santa Fe Dam Lake, Irwindale, (626) 334-1065

Silverwood Lake (map - p. 115)

Silverwood Lake, in the Silverwood Lake State Recreation Area, is one of several reservoirs along the California Aqueduct that is known for its striped bass fishing. In fact, Silverwood is known for producing some of the largest land-locked stripers, a number in excess of 40 pounds. The lake record is 48-8 caught in 1993. But Silverwood is an all-around fishery. Before stripers migrated in via the aqueduct, Silverwood was known for its trophy trout. And on top of this, Silverwood is considered by many as one of the top largemouth bass producers in Southern California. Catfishing, especially at night, is also very good. Silverwood has a surface area of just under 1,000 acres and a shoreline of 13 miles. It is located 85 miles east of Los Angeles and about 30 miles north of San Bernardino on the edge of the high Mojave Desert. Silverwood Lake offers full recreational facilities. Water skiing is permitted on portions of the lake.

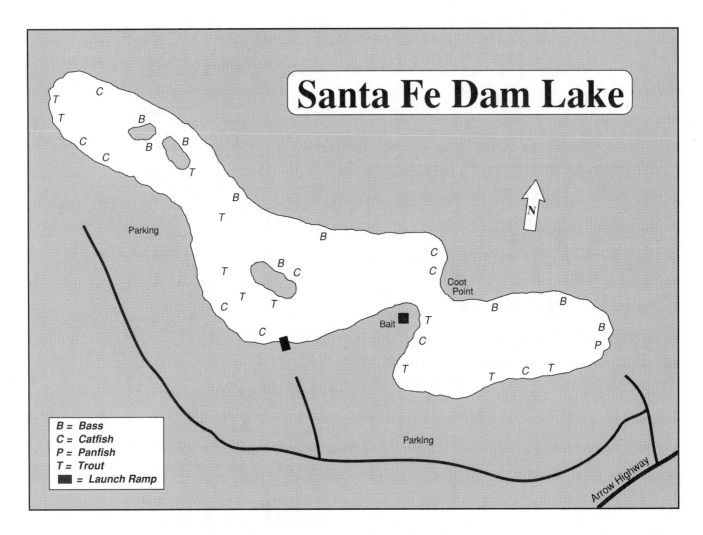

Santa Fe Dam Lake

B = Bass
C = Catfish
P = Panfish
T = Trout
■ = Launch Ramp

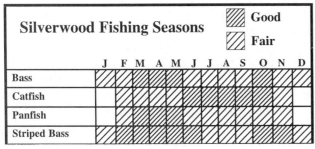

Silverwood Fishing Seasons													
	J	F	M	A	M	J	J	A	S	O	N	D
Bass													
Catfish													
Panfish													
Striped Bass													

Good

Fair

Silverwood Fishing Tips

A primary reason that stripers grow so large is that Silverwood is a fertile reservoir. Two streams come into it in addition to the aqueduct water. The West Fork of the Mojave River forms Cleghorn Canyon, and the East Fork of the West Fork creates Miller Canyon. Both of these canyons are major fishing areas for crappie, trout and largemouth bass as well as striper. A hot spot at Silverwood is where the water from the aqueduct comes into the lake. Stripers lie in wait in the aqueduct water intake hoping to feast on small entrained fish. Anglers work the white water behind the buoy line. Since long casts are needed for this type of "buoy line" angling, the regulars use surf casting tackle to get trout and small striper imitation lures into good holding areas. Long rods are also useful for night-time striper angling from shore. No boating is allowed at night, but this is when some of the biggest striper are on the prowl. Miller Canyon, and sometimes Cleghorn Canyon, are hot spots for nighttime striper action. Early and late are tradition-ally the best time for striper. Sometimes late evening or two or three in the morning is the best time.

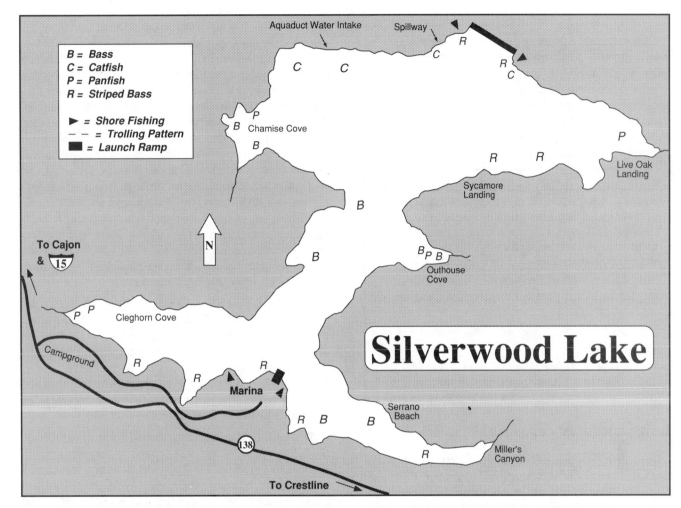

The park gate is closed at night so striper hunters either camp in the park or park along roads outside the park and walk in to night fish. Broken-back Bombers and J-Plugs are two popular nighttime offerings. Daytime striper anglers position their boats at the above-mentioned buoy line and cast to white water or they deep troll. A 3 oz. Kastmaster in chrome is a popular offering. Bait angling from shore is another option, and it can be done with trout gear and 10-15 pound test line. Many bait anglers use a sliding sinker rig with a 3 foot leader, about a 1/0 bait holder hook and a whole anchovy. Finally, it's always a good idea to keep your eyes peeled for shad to boil up on the surface. Cautiously casting shad imitations into these striper feeding frenzies can produce fish.

Here's a seasonal rundown on Silverwood stripers. Number one, after a trout plant is always good. The buoy line action is most popular from early April through June. By the middle of June, the spillway action tapers off as the stripers scatter all over the lake feeding on huge schools of shad. From early summer through early November, the surface action for

stripers can be excellent, especially early or late in the day. After the early-morning surface action, the fish move deeper and cruise the edges of drop-offs and schools. Drift fishing frozen anchovies from a boat, or bait fishing from shore, take fish in the summer through fall daytime action. An electronic fish finder is extremely helpful for drifting boat anglers. Deep trolling with leadcore or downriggers is another approach. It is in the late fall and winter though that trolling gets the biggest play for stripers. Points and shelves adjacent to deep water are usually the most productive spots. A slow troll is best. As a general trolling rule, use small lures to represent shad when the water is at its coldest in the winter and large lures when the water is warmer.

One overlooked opportunity at Silverwood is the largemouth bass fishing in winter. The near consistent water flow seems to keep Silverwood productive when other reservoirs are shut down. Two and three pound bucketmouths are typical at these times. Working spinnerbaits and grubs in the rocky areas is an all-seasons largemouth producer.

Channel cats at Silverwood can bite all over the lake, but two consistently good areas are Miller's Canyon and by the spillway. Chicken livers are good, as are mackerel. Silverwood is known for its large crappies. At times they run between 1 and 2 pounds. Bullet Jigs in smoke or red and white are a top crappie taker. A perennial hot spot is on both sides of the dam. Fish shallow early and late in the day and down about 15 feet in the daytime.

Silverwood Lake Facts

Location: Silverwood Lake State Recreation Area is located on the north side of the San Bernardino mountain range near the town of Hesperia. From the Los Angeles area take I-15 north through Cajon Pass. Exit at Hwy. 138 and follow it 11 miles to the park entrance.

Size: Just under 1,000 acres with 13 miles of shoreline

Species: Rainbow trout, striped bass, largemouth bass, catfish, crappie, bluegill

Facilities: Launch ramp, boat rental, hiking trails and developed campsites

Information: Silverwood Lake State Park office, (760) 389-2303; Silverwood Lake Marina, (760) 389-2299

Lake Skinner (map - p. 117)

Lake Skinner, in a picturesque setting at 1,500 elevation, is a fine fishing lake. And it is surrounded by the very nice 6,000 acre Lake Skinner Park. It is located about 90 miles southeast of Los Angeles and about 70 miles northeast of San Diego. The lake is owned by the Metropolitan Water District and leased to the Riverside Parks Department. This is a dedicated fishing lake with no bodily contact with the water and a 10 m.p.h. speed limit on the water. Skinner is 1,200 surface acres with about 14 miles of irregular shoreline. Fishing is a year-round activity with rainbow trout, largemouth bass (northern-strain), stripers, catfish and panfish.

Skinner Fishing Seasons — Good / Fair

	J	F	M	A	M	J	J	A	S	O	N	D
Bass												
Catfish												
Panfish												
Trout												

Skinner Fishing Tips

Trout are probably the most popular fishery at Lake Skinner. Rainbows are planted almost weekly, alternately by the Department of Fish and Game, or by the Riverside Parks Depart-

ment. This planting extends from October to May. In colder months, shore anglers do well with bait and lures in the south arm. Trollers also do well, both in cool months and when the water temperature increases. The average Skinner trout runs from 3/4 to 1 1/2 pounds, but 2-3 pounders are not uncommon. Bait anglers favor Power Bait, nightcrawlers, Zeke's Floating Bait, salmon eggs and marshmallows. Two or four pound test leaders are about right. Some of the most productive lures at Skinner are Roostertails and Panther Martins for casting, and Needlefish and Kastmasters for trolling. Trout anglers, both bait and lure, do best early in the morning or just before dusk. Still fishing is a predominate method of trout taking at Skinner, but most anglers do it from a boat. Shore fishing is less productive. The prime Skinner trout area is at the lake inlet, reachable only by boat. But there are good shore fishing spots in coves and points near both launch ramps.

Striped bass have become a major fishery at Skinner in the past few years with excellent action on fish from 3 to 5 lbs, and fish in the 20-pound class are caught regularly throughout the year. Large, trout-like plugs get the most play for the bigger fish with lures like the new A.C. Plug—a very hot item here. But the fish are also taken by bait anglers on live shad and frozen anchovies. The best places to fish for stripers are in the deep water by the dam and at the aqueduct inlet.

The peak bass season runs from March through May. Skinner does not have many large bass, but they are plentiful. Average fish run from 1 to 2 pounds. However, bass up to 5 or 10 pounds are caught each year. Live nightcrawlers and plastic worms as well as spinnerbaits get consistently good results in the spring. Bassers work any of the many coves at the east end. The tules in the cove at launch ramp No. 1 are also good. The inlet area and the corresponding south shore produce bass. Plastic worms are the way to go for fall bass. Finally, don't overlook Skinner's crappies. They range from 1 to 2 pounds. March and April are prime months.

Lake Skinner Facts

Location: Lake Skinner is located near the town of Winchester in southwestern Riverside County. Anglers from the Los Angeles area should take Hwy. 91 east to Hwy. 15 south to the Rancho California Road. Anglers coming from San Diego should take Hwy. 15 north to the Rancho California Road.

Size: 1,200 surface acres with 14 miles of shoreline

Species: Rainbow trout, largemouth bass, catfish, crappie, bluegill

Facilities: 200 campsites, 2 launch ramps, a half-acre swimming lake and beach, picnic area, boat rentals and store. Facilities are very well maintained.

Information: Lake Skinner, (909) 926-1541; Lake Skinner Marina, (909) 926-1505

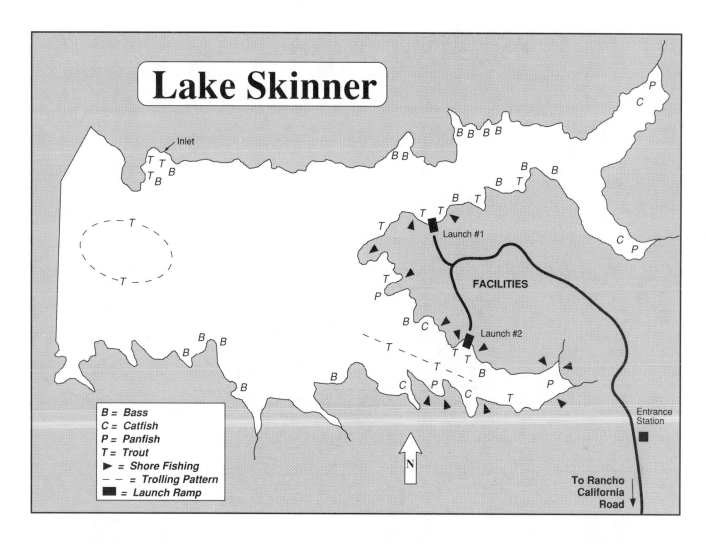

Lake Skinner

Legend:
B = Bass
C = Catfish
P = Panfish
T = Trout
► = Shore Fishing
– – = Trolling Pattern
■ = Launch Ramp

Vail Lake* (map - p. 118)

Vail has recently developed a well-deserved reputation as a premier lake for magnum-sized Florida-strain largemouth bass. This 800 acre Riverside County lake is stealing some of the thunder of the famed San Diego City bass lakes. Vail's largest bass in the 15 pound class, and a surprising number of fish over 10 pounds are coming out. The average fish is 1-3 pounds. Vail is privately owned and is open daily, all year, sunrise to sunset. Trout are planted from November through April, and the lake also offers good-sized catfish, crappie and bluegill. The trout plants give the bruiser bass something more to feed on (besides threadfin shad), and combined with the excellent bass habitat and cover, this makes Vail a bass angler's delight. Vail is at about 1,500 feet elevation in the Cleveland National Forest.

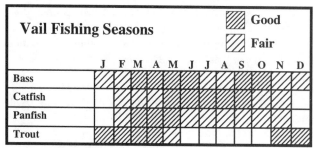

Vail Fishing Seasons														⬚ Good ⬚ Fair
	J	F	M	A	M	J	J	A	S	O	N	D
Bass												
Catfish												
Panfish												
Trout												

Vail Fishing Tips

Bass habitat at Vail includes brush, hardwood trees, rocky areas, channels, ridges and flats. In spring, Bayou is the first to get going. This is followed by Hunter's Cove and the north shore. Later, the south side gets going as does the flatter

*Vail Lake, once open to the public, is currently closed. It is only open to anglers who are willing to pay a hefty annual membership fee. The 800-acre lake has a tremendous largemouth bass fishery, and it was well-known for its crappie and catfish. The Department of Fish and Game was considering the purchase of the property around Vail Lake for an ecological reserve, but there was no news on this proposal at press time.

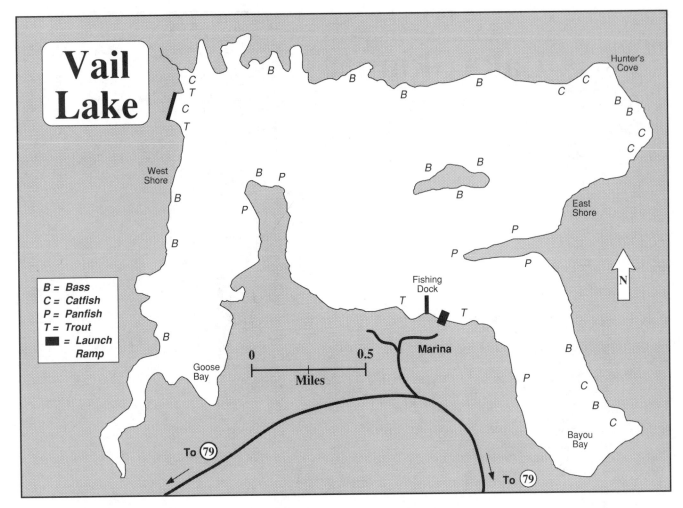

portions of Goose Bay. Spawning begins as early as February and continues through April. Since the lake is open daily (unlike the San Diego lakes), it's best to fish Vail during the week when less anglers are on the water. Things can get quite hectic on weekends when the lake is hot.

Typical Vail spring largemouth (2 to 5 pounders) go for plastic worms, Pig 'n Jigs (in black, brown or green) and spinnerbaits (try chartreuse). Bayou Bay has a series of cuts and banks at the mouth that is good flipping water. Farther back in this arm, brush, tree lines and other cover produces the largest fish. The north shore is dominated by brushy coves with a clay or gravel bottom. Fish these coves and corresponding points with spinnerbaits or plastic worms, depending on water temperature.

By the middle of May, the post-spawn period is established. Early morning anglers score big bass on Zara Spooks and Willowleaf spinnerbaits. Crankbaits are a real producer in early summer. Fat Raps and Shad Raps bring strikers along brush lines in the back of bays and along steeper walls and points. Also try the face of the dam.

Crappie run big at Vail Lake. The average fish is about 1 pound. Mini-jigs fished around trees and brush is often productive from late winter to early summer. Try a variety of colors. Most anglers use boats at Vail. There isn't that many good shore locales. Hunter's Cove turns out heavy stringers of channel catfish.

Vail Lake Facts

Location: 10 miles east of I-15 on Hwy. 79 near Rancho California.

Size: 800 surface acres at capacity

Species: Largemouth bass, rainbow trout, channel catfish, crappie, bluegill

Facilities: Vail is a day-use facility. It has a small store, rental boats and one launch ramp.

Yucaipa Park Lake

Yucaipa Regional Park encompasses three nice fishing lakes totalling 60 acres. All three lakes are stocked with trout in the winter months. When the water warms up enough, usually in May, trout planting halts and catfish stocking begins. Although fishing can be productive in each lake, Lake Three is often the best trout producer. In all lakes, fish spinners and spoons just after a trout plant, and bait when rainbows have moved into deeper water or a rain brings up color in the water. Although bass fishing isn't nearly as good as, for example, Mojave Narrows, it's worth a try if the trout aren't cooperating in the springtime. Boating is limited to rental paddle boats. There is swimming inside a sheltered lagoon at Lake Two. Other attractions include a 350 foot water slide and campgrounds. This San Bernardino County Regional Park is located at the town of Yucaipa. Take the I-10 exit at Yucaipa Ave., go east to Oak Glen Road and then turn left into the park. For more information, (909) 790-3127.

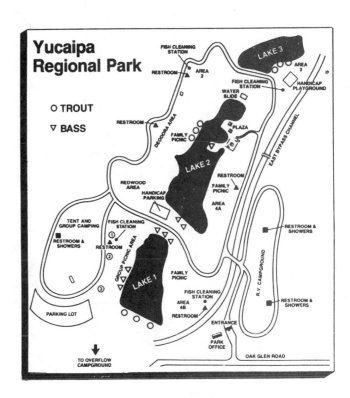

Special: Laguna Niguel Lake

Laguna Niguel Lake provides anglers an opportunity to fish in the heart of southern Orange County. The lake is stocked at least six times a year and boasts a variety of game fish, including trout, bluegill, and bass, as well as catfish and carp. The lake is open daily from 6:00 a.m. to sunset.

A state fishing license is not required to fish at Laguna Niguel Lake, but fishing permits are required. Permits are available at the Concession Building for: Adults—$12; Seniors—10; Juniors—16 yrs and younger—$8.

Laguna Niguel Lake is a "catch and keep" lake. Anglers may use their permits for a five-fish total limit on trout, bluegill, catfish, and carp. Laguna Niguel Lake also prides itself in maintaining a quality catch & release largemouth bass fishery. Resident bass reach sizes in excess of 13 pounds. All bass are a catch & release species.

Due to the steep banks along the lake, there are many prime fishing areas at Laguna Niguel Lake. Many prefer to fish towards the dam, where fishing docks are provided. Shoreline fishing is easily accessible with a variety of fishing structures located all around the lake. The lake itself is quite picturesque, with trees surrounding the lake and

adjoining park, and a bird sanctuary on the lake's island. Shaded picnic areas are also available.

For fishermen who prefer to get right out there with the fish, Laguna Niguel Lake offers boat rentals. With a boat, an angler can fish near the islands in the center of the lake, another favorite spot for the fish to gather.

Laguna Niguel Lake is located inside of Laguna Niguel Regional Park, an Orange County Public Park located in Laguna Niguel, California. Laguna Niguel Lake can be reached by taking I-5 south through Lake Forest (past where the San Diego 405 freeway merges) to the La Paz Road exit. Go south on La Paz Road, until just past Aliso Creek Road; the park is on the right. There is a $2 entry fee.

Laguna Niguel Recreation, Inc. is a private corporation that, under contract to Orange County, operates Laguna Niguel Lake, located in Laguna Niguel Regional Park.

For 24-hour information you can call Laguna Niguel Lake at (949) 362-2955.

For further information, call (949) 362-3885 (Concession Building) or (949) 489-9960 (Direct Office). (949) 489-9915 FAX.

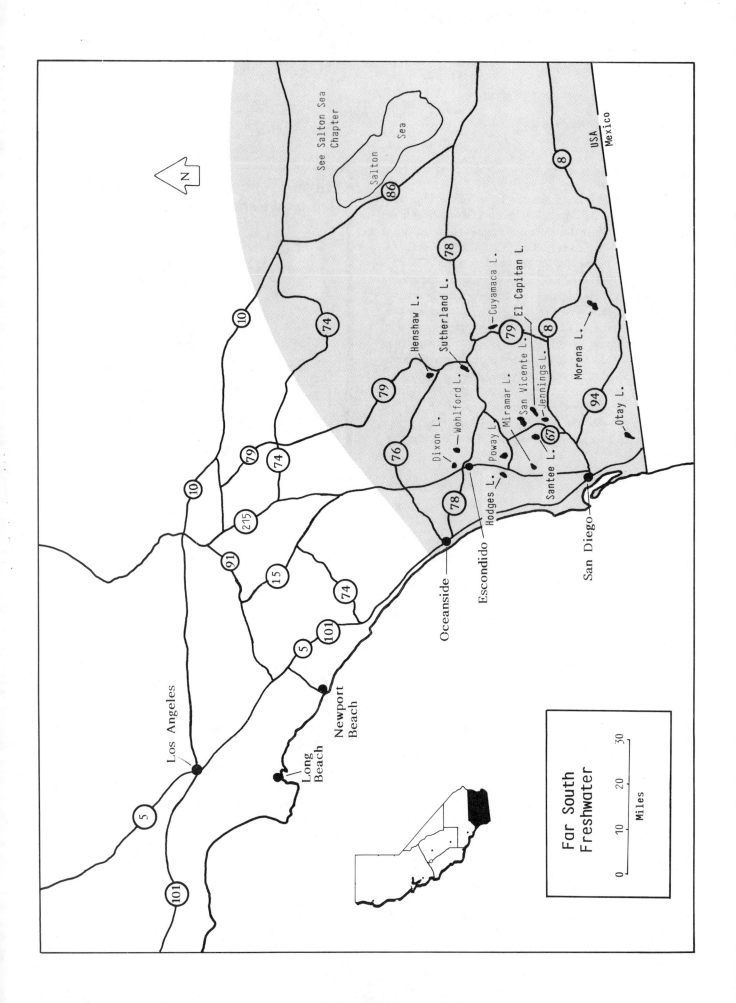

N

See Salton Sea
Chapter

Salton
Sea

86

USA
Mexico

8

78

Henshaw L.
Sutherland L.
Cuyamaca L.
El Capitan L.
79
8
Morena L.

10

74

79

76

Dixon L.
Wohlford L.
Miramar L.
San Vicente L.
Jennings L.
94
Otay L.

79

74

Poway L.
Hodges L.
67
Santee L.

10

215

78

91

Escondido

San Diego

15

74

Oceanside

101

5

Los Angeles

Newport
Beach

Long
Beach

5

101

Far South
Freshwater

0   10   20   30
Miles

Far South Freshwater Fishing

The Far South freshwater fishing area boasts an amazing collection of fishing lakes. Of course, the San Diego area is most famous for its Florida-strain largemouth bass lakes. These lakes, most notably Hodges, Otay, El Capitan and San Vicente, have produced many fish that approach the state and world records. And bucketmouths in the 5 to 10 pound class are common. But most of the Far South lakes are also prime waters for large catfish. Cats are planted in significant numbers in some of these. A list of the best whiskerfish waters would include Jennings, San Vicente, Wohlford, Dixon and Santee.

The uninformed, thinking of the mild climate and great warm-water fishing in the Far South, would not suspect that trout fishing is also outstanding. But it is. And the best of lakes, with high quality planting programs and fine-catch rates, in no particular order must include: Miramar, Poway, Dixon, Wohlford, Jennings, Santee and Cuyamaca.

A good percentage of the lakes in the Far South are day-use facilities. And that's fine, because most are within easy driving distance for hundreds of thousands of anglers. But a variety of campgrounds are available at some lakes. So pick your favorite species, read up on the excellent possibilities, and then go fishing!

Barrett Lake (see page 239)

(see page 239)

Lake Cuyamaca (map - p. 122)

(map - p. 122)

Going to Lake Cuyamaca is like going to the Sierras, except the drive is so much shorter—it's only one hour from San Diego and three hours from Los Angeles. Cuyamaca, situated at 4,600 feet elevation, is a high mountain, alpine lake encircled by pine and oak trees. The water is very clear and cold, and it's planted with rainbows on an aggressive, year-round schedule. In total, almost 60,000 fish are planted, some going up to five pounds. Limits are quite common. The lake itself lies in a broad mountain meadow of the Cleveland National Forest and is surrounded on three sides by Cuyamaca Rancho State Park. Nearby attractions include hiking, horseback riding, camping and nature trails. Although rainbows are the main bill of fair, Cuyamaca also has largemouth bass, catfish, crappie and bluegill.

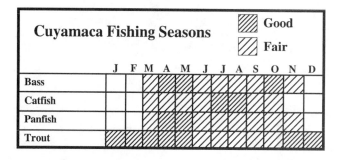

Cuyamaca Fishing Seasons		J	F	M	A	M	J	J	A	S	O	N	D
Bass				▨	▨	▨	▨	▨	▨	▨	▨		
Catfish						▨	▨	▨	▨	▨	▨		
Panfish					▨	▨	▨	▨	▨	▨	▨	▨	
Trout		▨	▨	▨	▨	▨	▨	▨	▨	▨	▨	▨	▨

Legend: ▨ Good ▨ Fair

Cuyamaca Fishing Tips

Trout anglers do well from shore, rental boats and private boats. Although some maps show Cuyamaca to be quite large, the underwater portion (to the west of the dike and spillway) is only about 110 acres. This means that all the good spots on the lake are readily accessible. There is a 10 m.p.h. boat speed limit and no water skiing. The main trout hot spots are down the main channel of the lake from the dike to the dam, around the rock jetty north of the launch ramp and from the launch ramp on down to the fishing float.

Trout anglers do well with nightcrawlers, marshmallows, Power Bait, red salmon eggs and floating corn (Zeke's). Trolling is best between the dam and the dike using Super Dupers, Kastmasters and Roostertails (orange is good). Troll deep in the summer months. A favorite trout casting lure is the Vibrax Roostertail in 1/8 ounce sizes, but bass-type crankbaits (like the Shad Rap) have scored some lunkers. Use light leaders (2-4 pound) because of the clarity of the water and, when bait fishing, float your offering up off the weed-covered bottom. Inflated nightcrawlers are a local favorite. In-line spinners and wobbling spoons are deadly in the spring. Minnow-shaped Rapala and Rebel plugs are tops for mid-lake trolling.

On weekdays float tubes are permitted. Anglers use these with spin or fly tackle to take both rainbows and largemouths. Fly angling can be excellent.

Bass at Cuyamaca are Florida-strain. The lake record is 13 lbs., 12 oz., but typical catches go from 1 to 4 pounds. The clear water demands light tackle and a delicate presentation. But there is some heavy weed growth, especially at the south end,

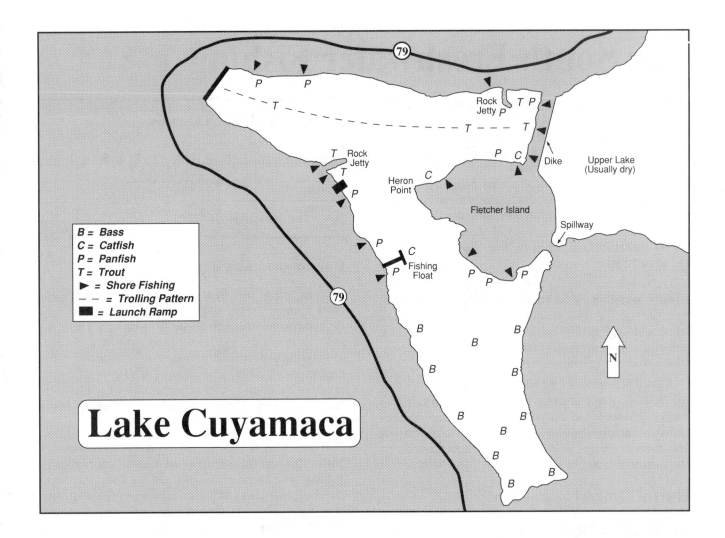

Lake Cuyamaca

B = **Bass**
C = **Catfish**
P = **Panfish**
T = **Trout**
► = **Shore Fishing**
– – = **Trolling Pattern**
■ = **Launch Ramp**

so move up in line strength. Early morning and late evening top-water action in the summer when weed production is peaking can be great. But worms and other soft plastics are the most consistent producers.

Catfish (most in the 1 1/2 to 2 pound range) are often near the pump house at the east end. A favorite bait is mackerel. Crappie up to two pounds are caught at Cuyamaca. Use crappie jigs in yellow and white, or in clear-sparkle, smoke or green and white. Crappie fishing turns on in the spring when the water temperature goes above 59 degrees. Both boat and shore anglers do well in shaded areas, like the fishing floats, and anywhere there are rocks such as the jetties or the points on the island. Bluegill go for meal worms, red worms, and crickets.

Cuyamaca Lake Facts

Location: From Los Angeles take I-15 to Temecula, then turn south on Hwy. 79. It's about a 160 mile drive. Cuyamaca is about 51 miles northeast of San Diego. Take I-8 east and then north on Hwy. 79.

Size: 110 surface acres of water

Season: Year-round

Species: Rainbow trout, largemouth bass, crappie, bluegill, catfish

Boating: 10 m.p.h. speed limit, 18 foot maximum length

Facilities: Boat rental, R.V. camping, launch ramp, restaurant and store. Tent camping at nearby state park.

Information: Lake Cuyamaca, (760) 765-0515; Cuyamaca Rancho State Park, (760) 765-0755

Dixon Lake (map - p. 124)

Here is a well-stocked fishing lake in the San Diego area that also offers good camping facilities. Dixon Lake is operated by the City of Escondido. It's located about 30 miles from San Diego. Dixon has two miles of shoreline surrounding its 70 acres of water. At an elevation of 1,000 feet, this primary warm-water fishery offers fine trout fishing in the cooler winter months. Trout are planted heavily and frequently from late October through spring. Another attractive feature of this lake is the opportunity it provides for shore fishing. Counting the boat docks there are four fishing piers. There are several pleasant picnic areas and a store.

Dixon Fishing Seasons — Key: Good (dark hatch), Fair (light hatch)

	J	F	M	A	M	J	J	A	S	O	N	D
Bass		G	G	G	G			F	F			
Catfish			F	F	F	G	G	G	G	F		
Panfish			F	F	F	F	G	G	G	F		
Trout	G	G	G	G	F						F	G

Dixon Fishing Tips

If you hit Dixon just after a trout plant, start out by trying spinners or spoons. Roostertails (in green, brown and yellow) and Kastmasters are winners. For larger trout (the lake record is just over 12 pounds), Mepps Cyclops and Sonic Roostertails are productive. These work from both shore and boat. Spinners are a good bet for big trout early in the day. Bait anglers use Power Bait, salmon eggs, nightcrawlers and floating cheese baits. Sometimes only Velveeta seems to work.

Most people fish Dixon from the banks. Access and fishing are excellent at Trout Cove, Boat Dock Cove and Whisker Bay, as well as at the fishing piers. Rental boat anglers work Trout Cove, Catfish Cove, along the buoy line in the Bass Point area and in Jack Creek Cove. Bait is probably the top producer at Dixon. Most anglers rig up with a size 18 treble hook and a 24 inch, 2 pound test leader in a sliding sinker format.

Trout dominate the winter fishing scene, but diligent anglers can also take channel cats and largemouths in the cooler months. A good winter catfish haunt is at the buoy line.

Once trout stocking ends in May, channel cats are put in throughout the summer. The average catch is about three pounds, but they go up to 20 pounds. Top producers include cut mackerel, anchovies, chicken livers, and nightcrawlers.

The top largemouth area is from the south end of the log boom on up to the dock. Plastic worms rigged Texas-style and plastic grubs will score. Bait fishing for bass is popular at Dixon. Shiners and crawdads both work, but are not sold at the lake. Tackle stores in Escondido (Bob's or Fisherman's Headquarters) are a good source.

Dixon Lake Facts
Location: The lake is just north of the city of Escondido. Take the El Norte off ramp from I-15 east to La Honda Drive, then turn left on La Honda to the lake.
Size: Dixon covers 70 acres, with two miles of shoreline. It's located in the 527 acre Dixon Lake Recreation Area.
Species: Rainbow trout, largemouth bass, channel catfish, crappie, bluegill
Boating: Only rental boats are permitted.
Facilities: Campground, picnic areas, store, boat rental
Information: Dixon Lake Ranger Station, (760) 741-4680; Camping Reservations, (760) 741-3328

El Capitan Lake (map - p. 125)

El Capitan Lake is a very fine dedicated fishing lake, located about 30 miles east and north of San Diego. It is primarily a day-use facility, but camping is available nearby. At maximum capacity, El Capitan Lake is about 1,110 acres, and has about 15 miles of shoreline. This canyon-style lake has a bushy shoreline at the north end that is one area that attracts the attention of bass anglers. Besides bass, El Capitan offers crappie and catfish. Crappie fishing is among the best in the San Diego area. El Capitan is open to anglers from about April through the late fall, on Thursdays, Saturdays and Sundays. The boating speed limit is 10 m.p.h. and there is no swimming or body contact with the water.

El Capitan Fishing Seasons — Key: Good (dark hatch), Fair (light hatch)

	J	F	M	A	M	J	J	A	S	O	N	D
Bass				F	G	G	G	G	F	F		
Catfish					F	G	G	G	G	F		
Panfish				F	G	G	G	G	F	F		

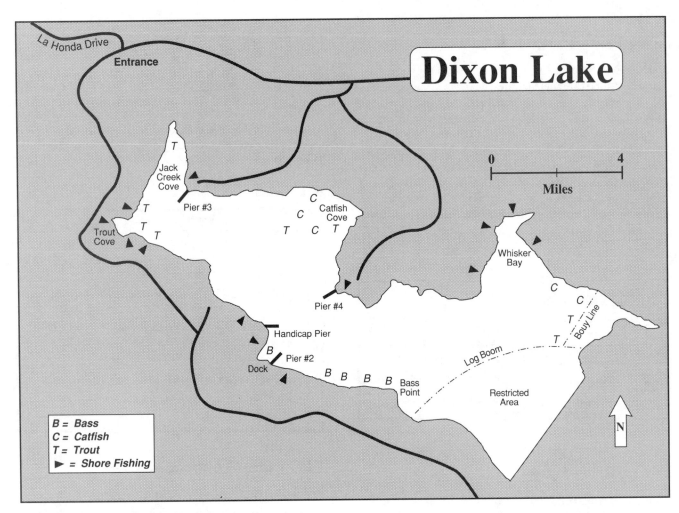

El Capitan Fishing Tips

Most bass caught at El Capitan are in the 1 to 3 pound range, but some much larger fish are caught. Work the ledges, drop-offs and bushy areas. Live crawdads are a good bet here. Plastic worms and jigs also are local favorites. A number of Florida-strain largemouths topping the 10 pound mark are taken from El Capitan each season.

But surprisingly, this smallish lake is a hot bed for avid crappie anglers. El Caps "slab" black crappie run up to 3 pounds, and stringers can average 2 pounds per fish! In most lakes, crappie are found around underwater weeds, sub-merged trees and rocky structure. But at El Capitan, during most of the season, crappie are found suspended at depths ranging from 5 to 20 feet, near little or no underwater structure. Two exceptions are during spawning and during very-high water times when they are around half-submerged trees. At all times, the crappie at El Capitan are concentrated in the northernmost part of the lake foraging on schools of threadfin shad.

A most common way to take large crappie is to still fish for them. But at El Capitan, a better way is to troll small jigs on plastic grubs at a very slow speed. Anglers use electric trolling motors or lake breezes to move the boat along. Lures are tied to 2 pound test monofilament spooled on an ultralight spinning outfit. Popular jigs include Scroungers, mini-jigs and Bass Buster Beetles in sizes 1/32 to 1/8 ounce. Good colors include white, red and yellow. Some crappie hunters put a meal worm on the jig hook to add scent. Slow troll the middle of the lake channel around the "D" buoy at the upper end of the lake until a school is found. Live shiner minnows are another alternative that works from a moving boat. Remember, crappie have delicate mouths, so set the hook gingerly. Usually a flick of the wrist is all it takes. Hooked slabs should be played carefully with a light drag and brought in with a landing net.

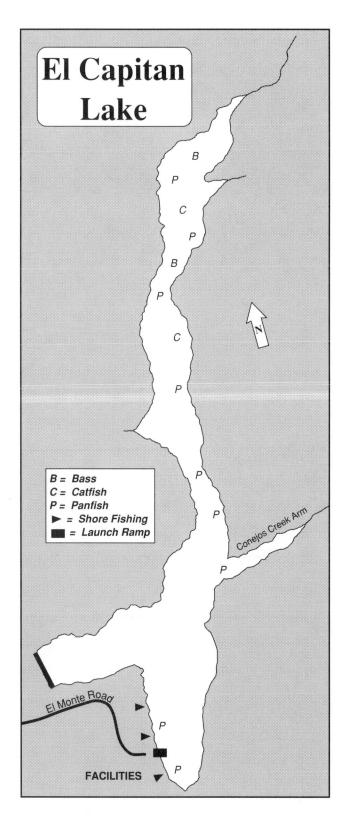

El Capitan Lake

B = Bass
C = Catfish
P = Panfish
► = Shore Fishing
■ = Launch Ramp

Conejos Creek Arm

El Monte Road

FACILITIES

El Capitan Lake Facts

Location: El Capitan is located seven miles east of Lakeside on Lake Jennings Road. From I-8 take the Lake Jennings Road exit. From Hwy. 67 in Lakeside, Mapleview Road turns into Lake Jennings Road.

Size: 1,100 surface acres

Species: Largemouth bass, crappie, catfish (channel and blue), bluegill

Season: April through September on Thursday, Saturday and Sunday

Facilities: Launch ramp, store, boat rental, picnic tables

Information: El Capitan Lake, (619) 668-2060; Current fishing information, (619) 465-3474

Henshaw Lake (map - p. 126)

Besides being an almost world famous fishing lake, Henshaw has other attributes. Unlike many lakes in the greater San Diego area, it is open all year-round, offers fishing every day of the week and has on-site camping facilities. This 1,100 acre body of water is located on the southern slope of Polomar Mountain at 2,700 feet above sea level. Henshaw offers crappie, catfish, bluegill, and a few largemouth bass. Henshaw has the space and shoreline to be a much larger lake. At the 1,100 acre level, Henshaw has approximately five miles of shoreline. There is a 10 m.p.h. speed limit on the water. A pool is available for swimming. Also, there are over 500 campsites, grocery store, snack bar, restaurant, bait and tackle shop, laundromat and hot showers. What more could an angler want?

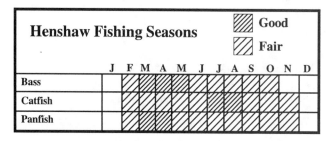

Henshaw Fishing Seasons														
		J	F	M	A	M	J	J	A	S	O	N	D
Bass														
Catfish														
Panfish														

Good / Fair

Henshaw Fishing Tips

Lake Henshaw is known for its outstanding crappie fishing. While the size of the fish seems to fluctuate from season to season, most years there is very good fishing for crappie weighing from 1/2 to 1 pound and some fish up to 3 pounds are caught nearly each year. Most anglers catch these crappie

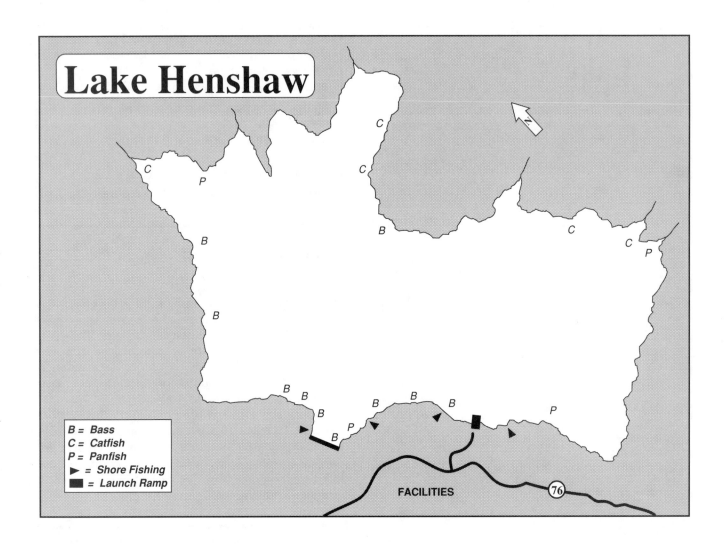

Lake Henshaw

B = Bass
C = Catfish
P = Panfish
► = Shore Fishing
■ = Launch Ramp

FACILITIES

76

by drifting from Monkey Island (which is usually not an island at all) toward the dam with small jigs, often tipped with Berkley Power Bait or meal worms.

Catfish are also very popular with anglers here and fish to 10 pounds are caught each year. Most are taken on small chunks of mackerel in the deeper water near Monkey Island or the dam, but anchovies, chicken liver, and nightcrawlers are also popular bait.

While there is very little structure in the lake, there are a few largemouth bass caught each year. While the lake record is a whopping 13 lbs., 6 oz., the few bass caught now are small, usually less than 1 1/2 pounds.

Lake Henshaw Facts

Location: Henshaw is about 60 miles northeast of San Diego, just east of Hwy. 76.

Size: It's average size is about 1,110 surface acres.

Species: Largemouth bass, catfish, crappie, bluegill, trout in higher water years

Season: Open all year

Facilities: Camping, store, restaurant, laundromat, launch ramp, boat rental

Information: Lake Henshaw Resort, (760) 782-3501

Lake Hodges (map - p. 128)

Lake Hodges is famous for its lunker Florida-strain large-mouth bass. Because of this reputation, it is the most fished of all the San Diego City lakes. And surprisingly, the lake is holding up well, producing fine catches of bass for most anglers. Hodges, about 1,110 surface acres, is located just south of Escondido on I-15. It also offers excellent catfish, crappie and bluegill angling. Lake Hodges has outstanding cover and structures for bass. There are downed trees along grass banks, rocky points and drop-offs as well as plenty of shoreline cover like tules for spring flippin'. Because this is a shallow lake (mean depth of 20 feet), it allows warm-water fish to utilize most of the lake. Hodges is open from about March through November on Wednesdays, Thursdays and weekends.

Hodges Fishing Seasons												Good Fair
	J	F	M	A	M	J	J	A	S	O	N	D
Bass			▨	▨	▨	▨	▨	▨	▨	▨		
Catfish			▨	▨	▨	▨	▨	▨	▨	▨		
Panfish			▨	▨	▨	▨	▨	▨	▨	▨		

Hodges Fishing Tips

Hodges is such that one can do just about any type of bassing, from flippin', to spinnerbaits, to plastic worms, to surface plugs, to live bait. And they all work at times. Flippin' in the tules is popular in the spring months. Use Pig 'n Jigs and plastic worms on the Del Dios shoreline, in the narrows and along the north shore. In low water years or later in the year, anglers need to be focused on bottom contours and work drop-offs, points and mouths of coves and deep structure. Shad-type crankbaits are hard to beat at Hodges. A local favorite is the Fat Rap No. 5 in shad or crawdad pattern. A good crankbait area is the cove north of the launch ramp. Single willow blade spinnerbaits (with chartreuse, white or blue skirts) are also good. A top-producing plastic worm is the six-inch straight-tail by Western Plastics in cinnamon with black flake or sparkle cinnamon with neon blue, black and purple. Motor oil color worms are good in off-color water. For top-water action, which typically starts in mid or late May, use Rapala No. 7 or 9 floaters (in a shad pattern), plus Buzz Baits, Zara Spooks and Rebel Pop-R's.

Live baits take lots of "hawgs" at Hodges, and shiners are definitely the live bait of choice. Fish them right into the tules in early spring. Later, drift them off points.

Float tubes are now permitted at Hodges (and other San Diego City lakes). You must meet visibility requirements and stay in protected areas. But that's where you want to be anyway. Concentrate in back waters where boats can't reach. One other point about Hodges—it's big bass attract big crowds so expect to line up at the launch ramp. And once you position your boat on a likely looking area, it may be advantageous to stay there for some time. Leave, and that place may be taken by someone else. And, you may have trouble finding a better location. Fish do move around, so slow spots can improve with time.

Catfishing heats up in the summertime. Use cut mackerel, bonito, frozen anchovies or nightcrawlers. Hodges' bluegill are large, running up to 3/4 of a pound or more. Best action is in late spring and summer. Dunk meal or red worms in the tule areas. Crappie are another possibility. Good locations include the Hwy. 15 bridge pilings and among the large trees near the shoreline leading to the bridge. Use mini-jigs or small live shiners.

Lake Hodges Facts

Location: To reach Lake Hodges, travel five miles south of Escondido on I-15 to Via Rancho Parkway. Head west to Lake Drive, then turn south to the lake.

Size: Lake Hodges covers about 1,200 acres.

Species: Florida-strain largemouth bass, catfish, crappie, bluegill

Season: Early March through late fall

Facilities: Boat rental, docks, multi-lane launching ramp, concession-tackle store

Information: Lake Hodges, (619) 489-1930; Current fishing information, (619) 465-3474

Lake Jennings (map - p. 130)

Lake Jennings is an excellent little trout lake that also offers good angling for largemouth bass, channel and blue catfish, crappie and bluegill. Plus there is camping for RV's, tents and walk-in primitives. The schedule is worth noting. Camping is on a year-round basis, and campers can fish from shore all year. But day-use fishing and boat rental runs from

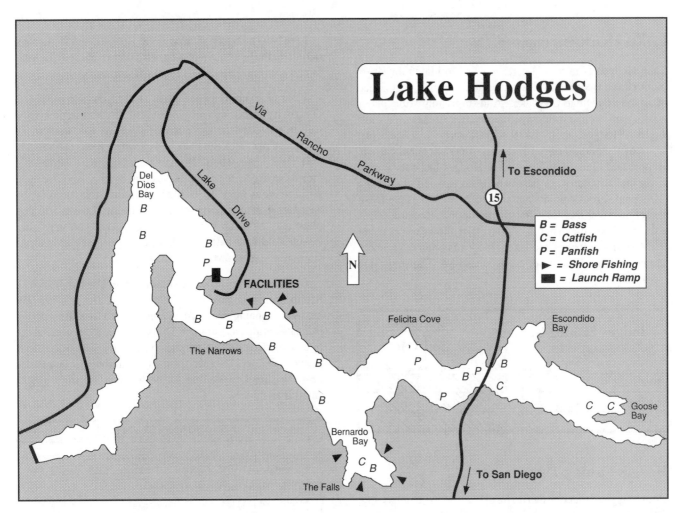

October through May, on Fridays, Saturdays and Sundays. Opening time is 5:30 a.m. The lake remains open until midnight in the summertime for catfishing. There is no water skiing, sailing or swimming, and the lake has a 10 m.p.h. speed limit. During the winter trout season, Jennings is planted weekly, including some big fish. The lake is 145 surface acres and has about four miles of fairly steep shoreline. Lake elevation is about 700 feet.

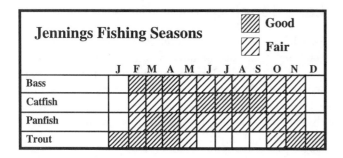

Jennings Fishing Seasons	J	F	M	A	M	J	J	A	S	O	N	D
Bass			▨	▨	▨	▨	▨	▨	▨	▨		
Catfish			▨	▨	▨	▨	▨	▨	▨	▨	▨	
Panfish			▨	▨	▨	▨	▨	▨	▨	▨		
Trout	▨	▨	▨	▨	▨					▨	▨	▨

Good / Fair

Jennings Fishing Tips

Although many trout caught at Jennings are in the 2-3 pound class, they are hook-shy. So many anglers use a very light leader when bait fishing. Two or three pound test leader is just about right. Make sure your reel drag is set properly, or you'll lose some of the larger fish. Smaller hooks are also in order. Try a size 20 treble. Recently, a hot bait has been Berkeley Power Bait. Form it around the hook. Other offerings that score include salmon eggs and nightcrawlers. Slowly retrieved lures like Kastmasters and Roostertails also work, and seem, at times, to produce larger fish than bait does. Winter trolling also works—if you keep it slow. Troll a nightcrawler behind several split shots, or a spoon or spinner. Keep the split shots back about three feet.

Largemouths are taken most consistently in Half Moon Cove, Eagle Cove, and along the shoreline from the fishing float on up to Hermit Cove. Bass go for plastic worms and live crawdads. Find structure, like rock piles and tules, and work it thoroughly. Bass weighing in the mid-teens have been taken.

Jennings is an excellent catfish lake. In season, it is planted regularly with cats averaging 2-3 pounds, including some monsters. Bank fishing is good, but make long casts into deeper water. Often a hot spot is around Sentry Point. Cut mackerel is the top bait, but other common offerings also score.

Lake Jennings Facts
Location: 20 miles northeast of San Diego off I-8, near Lakeside off Lake Jennings Park Road
Size: Jennings covers 145 acres and has about four miles of shoreline.
Species: Rainbow trout, largemouth bass, catfish, crappie, bluegill
Restrictions: No water skiing, sailing or swimming
Facilities: Campground (RV, tent, walk-in), launch ramp, fishing float, boat rental, store. Nearby Lakeside has restaurants and motels.
Information: Lake Jennings, (619) 596-3860; San Diego County Parks, (858) 565-3600

Lake Miramar (map - p. 131)

Miramar, one of the "chain" of San Diego City lakes has several special features. An important one to many anglers is that this day-use facility is open for fishing all year long. Another is that, although there are warm-water fish here, trout can be taken most of the time. Miramar, a smallish reservoir at 162 surface acres, is in the hills south of Poway, near Mira Mesa. It is open for fishing on Saturday, Sunday, Monday and Tuesday of each week. Miramar is a clear-water reservoir so bass don't prosper as they do in sister lakes like Hodges. But some Florida-strains do grow to major proportions. The lake record is 20 lbs., 15 oz. An average stringer of five bass will weigh about 7-8 pounds.

Miramar Fishing Seasons		Good — Fair											
	J	F	M	A	M	J	J	A	S	O	N	D
Bass		▨	▨	▨	▨	▨	▨	▨	▨	▨		
Catfish		▨	▨	▨	▨	▨	▨	▨	▨	▨		
Panfish		▨	▨	▨	▨	▨	▨	▨	▨	▨		
Trout	▨	▨	▨	▨	▨					▨	▨	▨

Miramar Fishing Tips

Miramar is stocked with over 30,000 trout annually. In winter, bank anglers using bait do just about as well as boat anglers. There are four fishing floats (two wheelchair accessible) that give shore anglers access to deeper water. Best baits are Power Bait, Zeke's Sierra Gold and inflated nightcrawlers. Other good possibilities are salmon eggs, kernel corn, Velveeta and marshmallows. There is a lot of weed growth on the bottom, so baits need to float up. For example, a piece of marshmallow is good to float up a section of nightcrawlers. Miramar cool weather boat anglers are advised to troll. Roostertails, Kastmasters or a chunk of nightcrawlers in front of a Ford Fender flasher is a good way to go. No added weight is needed.

Late spring to early summer trout anglers need a boat to score. Although trout planting has stopped, there are big, beautiful holdover trout feeding down deep as the lake stratifies. Anglers get down with leadcore line. Fish finders help locate the thermocline and the trout. Needlefish are the most popular deep-trolling lure.

Miramar is bordered by a thick ring of tules, and this is where the bass hang out. Because of this, most bassers find success by flipping plastic worms or tossing shiners. Crankbaits and spinnerbaits are far less successful. Channel cats are not much pursued at Miramar, but those who put in the effort are usually quite pleased with the results. There are also some big bluegill and redear in the lake—fish up to 3 pounds are caught each year.

Miramar Lake Facts
Location: From I-15 take Mira Mesa Blvd. east to Scripps Lake Blvd. Then go south and east to the lake.
Size: Miramar covers 162 acres and has four miles of shoreline. It sits at an elevation of 714 feet.
Species: Rainbow trout, Florida-strain largemouth bass, channel catfish, bluegill, redear sunfish
Season: All year except for part of October. Open Saturday, Sunday, Monday and Tuesday.
Facilities: Boat rental, launch ramp, store, picnic area
Information: Lake Miramar, (619) 668-2060; Current fishing information, (619) 465-3474

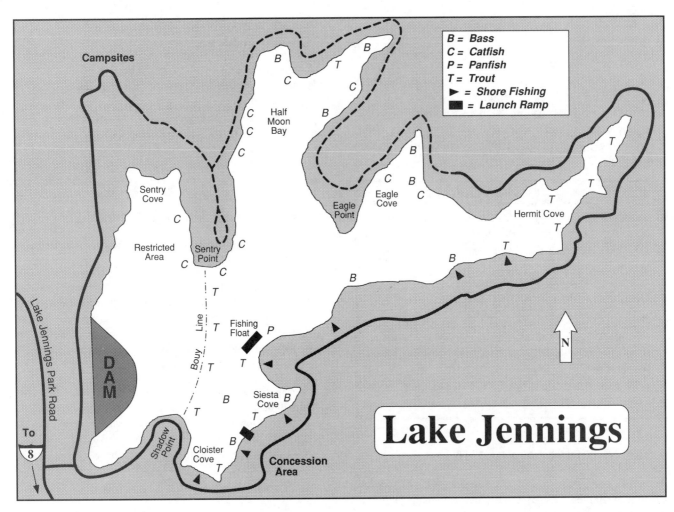

Morena Lake (map - p. 132)

Morena Lake is a fine fishing lake located in San Diego County, but it's not part of the famed San Diego Lakes system. Rather, it's administered by the County Parks Department. Morena is primarily a warm-water fishery (bass, catfish, panfish), but rainbows are planted in the winter (usually starting in January) and offer good action. This is a deep lake (almost 100 feet in some spots), so there are holdover trout that get quite large. Morena is also an outstanding late spring to summer largemouth bass lake. And then there are some of the largest bluegill in the southern half of the state. They are taken to 1 1/2 pounds, especially in the spring. There are 86 developed campsites, boat rental, hiking and a small bait shop at the lake. Restaurants and tackle are available in Morena Village within walking distance. Lake Morena has 1,500 acres of water, but no water skiing, sailing or swimming is allowed. Lake elevation is 3,000 feet at this Cleveland National Forest location of granite foothills and oak trees.

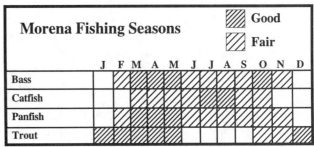

Morena Fishing Seasons												
	J	F	M	A	M	J	J	A	S	O	N	D
Bass			▨	▨	▨	▨	▨	▨	▨	▨		
Catfish			▨	▨	▨	▨	▨	▨	▨	▨		
Panfish			▨	▨	▨	▨	▨	▨	▨	▨		
Trout	▨	▨	▨	▨	▨					▨	▨	▨

Good = ▨ Fair = ▨

Morena Fishing Tips

Lake Morena gets a lot less pressure than some of the other San Diego County bass lakes. This is partly true because of its remoteness, and also because it was known for years as a lake full of smallish fish—most under 12 inches. But Morena's bass population is "growing up" (the majority are in the 1 1/2 to 2 pound range, some are in the 3 to 7 pound class, and a few are even bigger) and the word is getting around. Morena bass are cooperative.

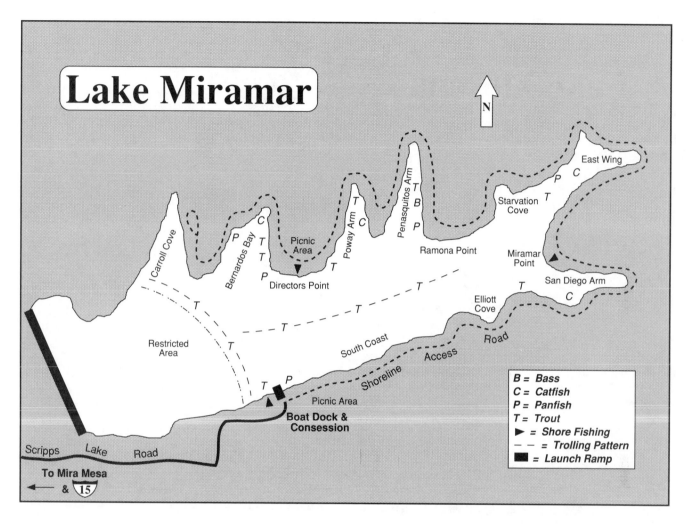

Lake Miramar

B = Bass
C = Catfish
P = Panfish
T = Trout
▶ = Shore Fishing
– – = Trolling Pattern
■ = Launch Ramp

Morena is one of the best structure lakes in the area. It has trees, brush, rocks and thick weed beds, so anglers can use a variety of skills and tactics. One that works very well for lunkers over 10 pounds is drifting jumbo live shiners. Most anglers hook shiners through both lips and "fly-line" them, or just drift with the midmorning breezes. One good spot for the technique is the northernmost point of Goat Island. Bass are in the beds there in 10 to 15 feet of water. Most local experts suggest that the larger shiners you use, the large bass you'll hook.

Another prime Morena technique is plastic worm fishing. Use a 6 to 8 inch curl-tail in black, fire-motor oil, cinnamon-blue, or purple. Rig them Texas-style. Split shot salt-and-pepper grubs are also good at Morena. Work both worms and other plastics as slowly as possible.

Surface action usually starts in earnest at Morena in May. But a surface bite can develop any time the water warms and

the wind is down. Zara Spooks and Shad Rap No. 5 are both good. A perennial surface hot spot is the entire shoreline of Goat Island.

The improved bass action at Morena has overshadowed the outstanding bluegill fishing. Most bluegill run from 1/2 to 3/4 of a pound, but 1 pound-plus guys are not unusual. The lake record is 2 lbs. 4 oz. Some spots to try include the shallow area behind Goat Island, the rocky outcropping near the old launch ramp and the brushy area towards the dam. Most bluegill are hooked on a piece of meal worm or red worm. Fly anglers use small poppers, streamers and nymphs. Catfishing can be good in the main channels and inlet areas.

Fly anglers and float tubers do well with bass and bluegill. Access to good fly fishing coves does not require a boat. The 26 miles of shoreline are accessible in about nine locations via well-kept Forest Service roads. Tubers can get into brush pockets that boaters avoid and shore anglers can't reach.

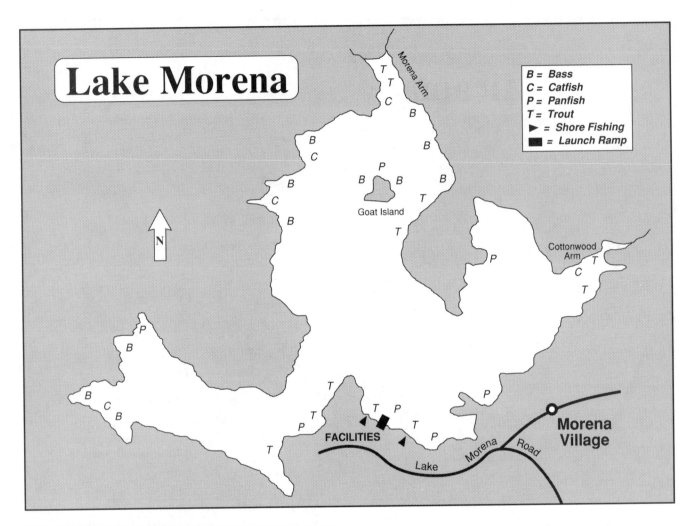

Lake Morena

B = Bass
C = Catfish
P = Panfish
T = Trout
► = Shore Fishing
■ = Launch Ramp

Morena Arm

Goat Island

Cottonwood Arm

N

FACILITIES

Lake Morena Road

Morena Village

Morena Lake Facts

Location: Morena is located in the eastern half of San Diego County, about 1 1/2 hours east of the city of San Diego. Take I-8 east from San Diego to Buckman Springs Road. Turn right and go four miles to Lake Morena Road. Finally, turn right to the lake.

Size: This 80-year-old reservoir has a surface area of about 1,500 acres with 26 miles of shoreline.

Species: Largemouth bass (both northern and Florida), rainbow trout (plant in colder months), catfish, crappie and bluegill

Facilities: Developed campsites, launch ramp, boat rental, hiking trails and bait shop. Groceries, restaurants, etc. are available in Morena Village within walking distance.

Information: San Diego County Parks, (858) 565-3600; Current fishing information, (619) 478-5473. The Morena Resource Guide map can be purchased for a small amount at the Ranger Station near the launching facility.

Otay Lake (Lower)* (map - p. 133)

Lower Otay Lake is one of the San Diego City lakes that is known for its great Florida-strain largemouth bass fishing. Anglers there catch large bass in good numbers. The average bass caught is just under three pounds, and the lake record is 18 lbs., 12 oz. Each fishing season, which runs from February to mid-October, anglers catch over 15,000 bass. Other fine features of Otay include good bass shore fishing along the west shore and at North Point.

Lower Otay Lake, with 1,100 surface acres of water and 13 miles of shoreline, is located in the vicinity of Chula Vista, about 20 miles from downtown San Diego and two miles from the Mexican border. Otay is open for fishing on Wednesday, Saturday and Sunday, from sunrise to sunset. Besides bass, Otay has good populations of healthy-sized catfish, hefty crappie and bluegill.

Upper Otay is also open to shore and float tube anglers on a catch-and-release basis for bass, while you can keep bluegill and catfish.

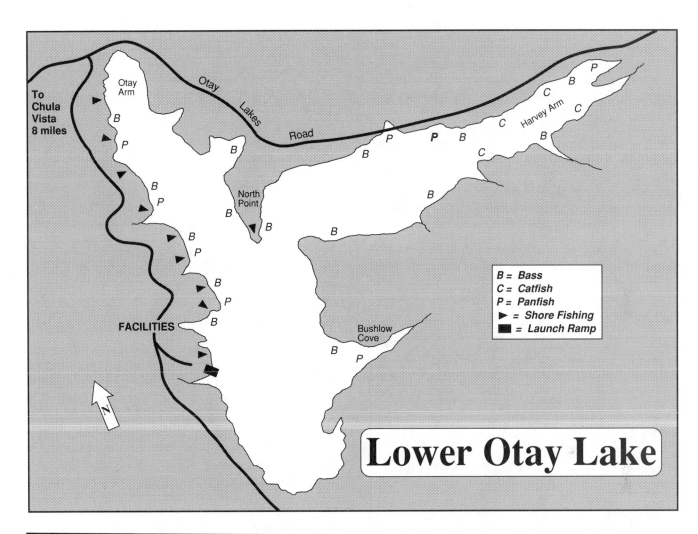

Lower Otay Lake

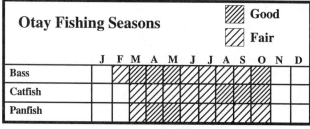

Otay Fishing Seasons														
	J	F	M	A	M	J	J	A	S	O	N	D		
Bass														
Catfish														
Panfish														

Good
Fair

Otay Fishing Tips

As the fishing season opens many Otay anglers concentrate on live bait (crawdads and shiners) bass fishing in hopes of landing a trophy-sized, or lake-record fish. Early season bassers also work plastic worms and Pig 'n Jigs in brown shades. As the fish move into shallow water at dawn and dusk in the warm months, top-water lures like Rapalas, Rebels and Zara Spooks work well. Flippin' plastic worms and other offerings into the tules is also popular. Live shad, caught in

the lake, are fished here for bass. Shore bass anglers have best results with live crawdads or shiners and plastic worms.

Otay has a lot of classic structure, including submerged trees, sunken brush, well-formed rock piles, jutting points, submerged stream channels and tules. The end of both the Harvey and Otay arms sport flooded trees—great places to use plastic worms and grubs.

Reaper-type worms and grubs are great at Otay. Some anglers split shot them while others prefer to fish grubs on small dart-heads. Western plastic worms in 4 or 6 inches (cinnamon-blue or cinnamon-black) are also local favorites.

At times during the season, Otay produces more bass per angler than any other lake in Southern California. So this is a great place for novices to hone their skills, or for experienced anglers to take younger bassers. In recent years, Otay has produced fewer really big bass than in years past, but it boasts a tremendous quantity of 1-8 pounders.

Almost everyone at Otay is choosing bucketmouths, but there is another bruiser species waiting for anglers. It's the lunker catfish out in the Harvey arm. An angler recently took 10 catfish with a total stringer weight of 112 pounds and a maximum fish of 13 lbs., 8 oz.! Another had a stringer of 8 fish weighing almost 74 pounds with a 10 pounder being the largest! The state record blue catfish is an 82.1-pound fish caught and released in 1996 here. Fresh or frozen mackerel are the baits of choice. Load up large hooks (3/0 or 4/0) with this bait and try adding some commercially prepared catfish scent. Use a sliding sinker rig with as small a piece of lead as possible.

Florida-strain crappie have recently been introduced at Otay and they seem to be doing well. They get large like their fellow Floridian bucketmouths. The flooded creeks in both arms offer excellent locations for crappie action under the right conditions.

Otay Lake Facts

Location: Otay is about 20 miles from downtown San Diego. To get to the lake take the "L" Street (Telegraph Canyon) turnoff, east off I-5 or I-805 to Wueste Road. Turn right to the lake.

Size: Otay covers 1,100 acres and has 13 miles of shoreline. Lake elevation is 492 feet.

Species: Florida-strain largemouth bass, catfish, crappie, bluegill

Season: February to mid-October on Wednesdays, Saturdays and Sundays.

Facilities: Launch ramp, boat rental, store

Information: Lower Otay Lake, (619) 688-2060; Current fishing information, (619) 465-3474

Lake Poway (map - p. 135)

Lake Poway, run by the City of Poway, is a little lake (just 60 acres) with big fishing opportunities. It is located three miles east of I-15 and northeast of the city. Shore fishing is very productive here. Private boats are not allowed, but boats (both row and electrically powered) are available for rent. Poway is stocked regularly with both pan-sized and larger rainbow trout and catfish. The lake record fish are impressive: trout—13 lbs., 1 oz., Florida-strain largemouth bass—17 lbs., 8 oz., catfish—28 lbs., 3 oz. Speaking of catfish, Lake Poway allows night fishing until midnight during the peak summer catfishing season. And unlike some other lakes, there is no

extra charge over and above the modest daytime fee. At the lake there are bait and tackle shops, a snack bar, horseback and hiking trails, picnic areas, a ball field and playground area. Poway is open Wednesdays through Sundays all year long. A Poway trout fishing instruction handout is available at lake office.

Poway Fishing Seasons													
	J	F	M	A	M	J	J	A	S	O	N	D
Bass			▨	▨	▨	▨	▨	▨	▨	▨		
Catfish			▨	▨	▨	▨	▨	▨	▨	▨		
Panfish			▨	▨	▨	▨	▨	▨	▨	▨		
Trout	▨	▨	▨	▨	▨					▨	▨	▨

Good ▨ / Fair ▨

Poway Fishing Tips

Trout fishing begins in earnest in late October or November with a large planting, including a fair share of lunkers. About 1,200 pounds are added each week until June. Nightcrawlers are probably the best bet, for both trolling and still fishing. Crawlers are inflated by shore anglers who also use corn, cheese, or Berkley Power Bait. Use a two pound test leader, a 1/8 or 1/4 ounce sliding egg sinker and a size 14 or 16 treble hook. The light leader is critical because of the lake's ultra clear water. Another popular way to bait fish at Poway is with a casting bubble. Fill the small, clear bubble with water rigged on a 2 or 3 pound leader. Bait up with a salmon egg or nightcrawler and cast it out. It will slowly sink to the bottom. Retrieve it slowly if you haven't gotten a bite on the drop. There are trout all the way around the lake, so shore anglers have lots of choices. But some of the perennial hot spots are from the shore to the left of the fishing float, all the way along the shore from the boat docks to Half Moon Bay, in Boulder Bay, and between Bucktail Bay and Hidden Bay.

Trollers use light leaders (3 to 4 feet of 2-4 pound test) and just a split shot in front of their nightcrawlers in the colder months. The favorite trolling lures are Super Dupers and gold Countdown Rapalas. Local experts suggest a slow troll. Poway's rental boats have five-speed trolling motors. The best choices are either speed one or two.

Poway anglers concentrate on trout in the winter, bluegill and bass in the spring, and channel catfish in the summer. The top catfishing area is on the east side of the lake. Try near the logs or in front of the dam. A good place to catch bluegill is from the fishing float. Mini-jigs tipped with bits of nightcrawler are a local favorite.

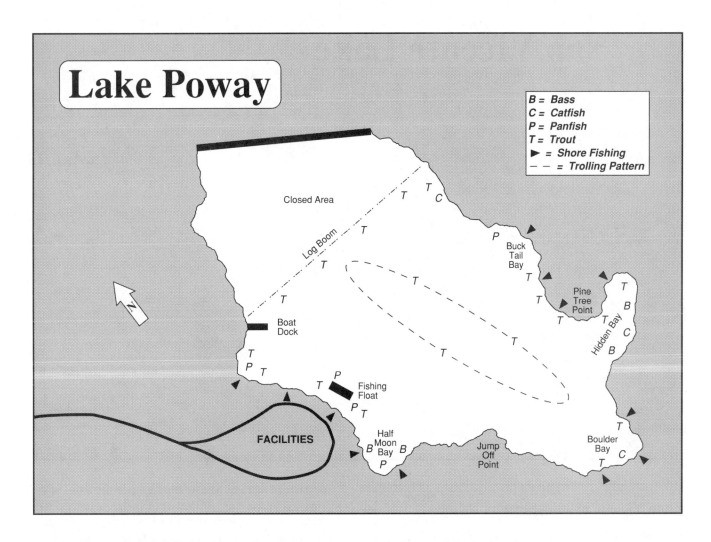

Shiners and nightcrawlers are popular bait for bass at Poway. Lures that imitate shad are also good, as are plastic worms. Many of the bass caught are in the 1-4 pound range.

Poway Lake Facts

Location: Poway is located northeast of the city of Poway, three miles east of I-15. Use the Rancho Bernardo Road exit.

Size: 60 acres

Species: Rainbow trout, bass, channel catfish, bluegill

Facilities: Rental boats, fishing float, horseshoes, volleyball, nature trail

Boating: Private boats are not allowed.

Information: Lake Poway, (858) 679-5465

San Vicente Lake (map - p. 136)

San Vicente Lake is one of the six lakes in the San Diego area that is owned by the city of San Diego and operated as a fishing lake as well as a reservoir. San Vicente (about 1,100 surface acres) and the much smaller Lake Miramar (about 160 acres) are the two that function primarily as trout fisheries. But San Vicente Lake is more than a trout fishery. There are Florida-strain largemouth bass (lake record—18 lbs., 12 oz.), catfish (lake record—57 lbs., 11 oz.), crappie and bluegill. San Vicente Lake is open for fishing from November through May on Thursdays, Saturdays and Sundays and from June through October on Thursdays (only for private boats and shore anglers).

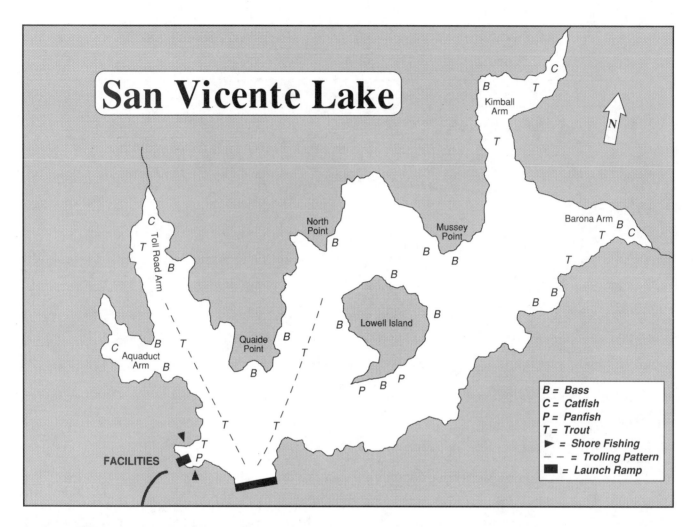

San Vicente Lake

San Vicente Fishing Seasons		J	F	M	A	M	J	J	A	S	O	N	D
Bass													
Catfish													
Panfish													
Trout													

Good — Fair

San Vicente Fishing Tips

San Vicente is fed by aqueduct waters from northern California and supplemented by Colorado River water, so it is less vulnerable to low-participation problems than some other Southland reservoirs. When the three day per week fishing season begins in October, San Vicente has been stocked with trout. But in mild years, the bass bite is also still pretty good. Anglers can expect some fine top-water action at the back of arms including Barona, Toll Road and Aqueduct. Plastic worms, grubs and reapers should also produce bass.

In the cold months, best trouting is up in the arms, at the marina and by the dam. At inlets, both bait anglers and lure casters do well. A sliding sinker rig is always good for trout and floating bait like marshmallow combinations and inflated nightcrawlers produce. The water is ultra clear, so use light, long leaders. Spring is good for both largemouths and rainbows. Artificial lures and live bait both produce bass at this time. But probably the top choice is live shiners and live crawdads. Traditional spring hot spots are the Toll Road, Barona, and Kimball arms and around Lowell Island.

Late spring, summer and early fall trout chasers turn to deep trolling. Holdover rainbows can get quite large in this reservoir that has a maximum depth of 150 feet when full. Flashers and bikini-pattern Needlefish are a favorite combination. Flashers and nightcrawlers also produce. Much of the warmer weather trolling success is between the marina and the dam.

Catfish is a big draw at San Vicente. Every year someone catches a blue catfish in the 35-plus pound range. But channel cats are the most plentiful. They run from 6-8 pounds. Use cut mackerel. Most catfishing is done from a boat since much of the shoreline is steep. Top spots are the Toll Road, Kimball and Barona arms. Crappie are elusive at San Vicente. Try the gap between Lowell Island and the south shore.

```
┌─────────────────────────────────────────────────┐
│            San Vicente Lake Facts               │
├─────────────────────────────────────────────────┤
│ Location: Off Hwy. 67 in Lakeside. Take Vigilante Road │
│ coming from Poway, or Morena Road from El Cajon. │
│                                                  │
│ Size: 1,100 acres with 14 miles of shoreline.   │
│                                                  │
│ Species: Largemouth bass, rainbow trout, blue and channel │
│ catfish, bluegill and crappie                    │
│                                                  │
│ Facilities: Boat rental, launch ramp, concession store, picnic │
│ area                                             │
│                                                  │
│ Season and Boating: Fishing from November through May │
│ on Thursdays, Saturdays and Sundays; fishing from June │
│ through October on Thursdays (only for private boats and │
│ shore anglers).                                  │
│ There is also a summer water skiing schedule.    │
│                                                  │
│ Information: San Vicente Lake, (619) 668-2060; Current │
│ fishing information, (619) 465-3474              │
└─────────────────────────────────────────────────┘
```

Lake Sutherland (map - p. 138)

Lake Sutherland is another in the "chain" of San Diego City fishing lakes. Sutherland is a warm-water fishery that offers largemouth bass (Florida-strain), catfish and bluegill angling from March to late fall, on Thursdays through Sundays. This is a day-use facility that is nestled in the rolling hills seven miles northeast of Ramona, 138 miles southeast of Los Angeles, and 45 miles northeast of San Diego. Lake Sutherland covers about 550 acres when filled to capacity. There is a 10 m.p.h. speed limit on the lake. The nearest camping facility is about five miles west of Ramona on Hwy. 67. Facilities at the lake include a store, boat launching, a picnic area and boat rental. As is true at all San Diego City lakes, there is a modest daily fishing fee.

Sutherland Fishing Seasons			J	F	M	A	M	J	J	A	S	O	N	D
	Good / Fair													
Bass					▨	▨	▨	▨	▨	▨	▨	▨		
Catfish						▨	▨	▨	▨	▨	▨	▨		
Panfish					▨	▨				▨	▨			

Sutherland Fishing Tips

Sutherland is not as famous a Florida-strain largemouth bass fishery as several of the other San Diego City lakes. But because of this, it's probably less crowded and less hectic. Anglers here consistently catch stringers of bass in the 2-4 pound range. And Sutherland does produce its share of fish over five pounds. The current lake record is 15 lbs., 8 oz. The north shore is a favorite spot for bassers. It actually extends from east of the dam (there is a restricted area in front of the dam) up into the Mesa Grande Arm. Plastic worms and Pig 'n Jigs work good along the rocky outcroppings. Usually an annual surface bite begins at Sutherland along the west shore in March or April. Rapalas, poppers and prop-plugs take them.

The variety of structure in Sutherland also makes spinner-baits and crankbaits effective offerings at various times during the season. Some of the bare banks on both the east and west shores are particularly adapted by lightline enthusiasts, with split shotted plastic worms a favorite offering. Shiners are always a top bass taker at Sutherland. Catfishing is most productive in the Santa Ysabel arm using cut mackerel.

```
┌─────────────────────────────────────────────────┐
│               Lake Sutherland Facts             │
├─────────────────────────────────────────────────┤
│ Location: Seven miles northeast of Ramona via Hwy. 78 and │
│ Sutherland Dam Road                              │
│                                                  │
│ Size: 550 surface acres with 11 miles of shoreline. Lake │
│ elevation is 2,100 feet.                         │
│                                                  │
│ Species: Florida-strain largemouth bass, catfish and bluegill │
│                                                  │
│ Season: Late March to late fall on Fridays, Saturdays and │
│ Sundays                                          │
│                                                  │
│ Information: Lake Sutherland, (619) 668-2060; fishing info │
│ (619) 465-3474                                   │
└─────────────────────────────────────────────────┘
```

Santee Lakes (map - p. 139)

Santee Lakes are a great year-round fishing spot and family activities center that is locate only 15 minutes from San Diego. The seven small lakes, located in Santee Lakes Regional park, are situated in a narrow valley. Trout, including a number of lunkers, are planted in two of the lakes in the winter months, and all of the lakes offer catfish (some planted in the summer), largemouth bass and bluegill. Other attractions include campgrounds (some at lakeside), horseshoe

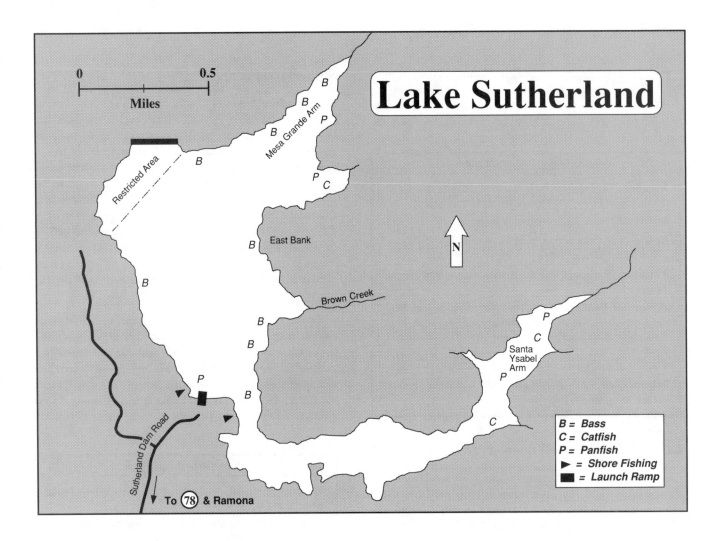

pits, volleyball, row and pedal boats, and a swimming pool (for campers).

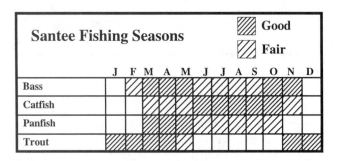

Santee Fishing Seasons	J	F	M	A	M	J	J	A	S	O	N	D
Bass		Fair	Good	Good	Good	Good	Good	Good	Good	Good	Fair	
Catfish				Fair	Good	Good	Good	Good	Good	Good	Fair	
Panfish			Fair	Good	Good	Good	Good	Good	Good	Fair		
Trout	Fair	Good	Good	Good	Fair					Fair	Good	Good

Legend: Good, Fair

Santee Fishing Tips

Lakes No. 3 and 4 are planted with trout from the first week in November through the end of April. Planting, which includes many multi-pounders, averages about once a week. Of course, the hottest fishing is the day of the plant. All the fishing is from shore in all the lakes since boats are not permitted. Lake No. 3 has a fishing pier and it can get pretty crowded. The best spots along the shorelines are shown on the accompanying map. The lake's record, a 12 lb., 5 oz. giant, was taken from Lake No. 4, but large trout are more consistently taken from Lake No. 3. Lakes No. 3 and 4 also have catfish, largemouths, and bluegill.

Here is a rundown on the other lakes. Lake No. 1 is open to fishing only briefly during the year, usually February or March, but at this time, it produces large catfish and bass. Lake No. 2 is the most popular for catfish anglers. Cats are planted here that range from 2 to 10 pounds. The lakes' record fish came out of No. 2—it weighed 25 lbs., 12 oz.

Bass anglers concentrate a lot of attention on Lake No. 5. It has an abundance of cover at the north end. Four to eight pounders are not unusual. Walk the shoreline and work the small islands that parallel the bank. Plastic worms and Bassmaster-type lures are solid producers. Lake No. 6 has bass and catfish, but it is best known for its spring bluegill bite. The floating docks are a popular spot. Lake No. 7 is a consistent producer of catfish and bass.

Lakes 1 through 5 are open to all anglers who pay the modest park entrance fee. Lakes 6 and 7 are reserved for campers.

Santee Lakes Facts
Location: In the rolling hills just west of the town of Santee
Size: There are seven small lakes.
Species: Rainbow trout, largemouth bass, catfish, bluegill
Boating: No boating is allowed on Lakes 2 through 7. Canoes and pedal boats are for rent on Lake No. 1.
Facilities: General store, laundromat, campground, playground, fishing lakes
Information: Santee Lakes Regional Park, (619) 448-2482

Lake Wohlford (map - p. 140)

Lake Wohlford is a fine, small fishing lake located a short distance (about six miles) northwest of Escondido. It's about 120 miles from Los Angeles and about 40 miles from San Diego, off I-15. The City of Escondido owns the reservoir and it is maintained in conjunction with the Escondido Mutual Water Company. This is a lake that is convenient to the urban area, yet still offers a get-away-from-it-all atmosphere. Lake Wohlford opens each year sometime during December (call for exact date) and remains open for fishing until October or so. There is a launch ramp and a boat speed limit of 5 m.p.h. But many anglers fish from shore here. There is good access all around the lake and the shoreline is pretty much unobstructed. Rainbow trout are the quarry early in the season (they are planted weekly). But Wohlford also offers very good-sized largemouth bass (lake record is 19 lbs., 12 oz.), catfish and panfish. There is one (Oakvale Lodge) private campground right near the lake.

Wohlford Fishing Seasons														
		J	F	M	A	M	J	J	A	S	O	N	D
Bass														
Catfish														
Panfish														
Trout														

Good — Fair

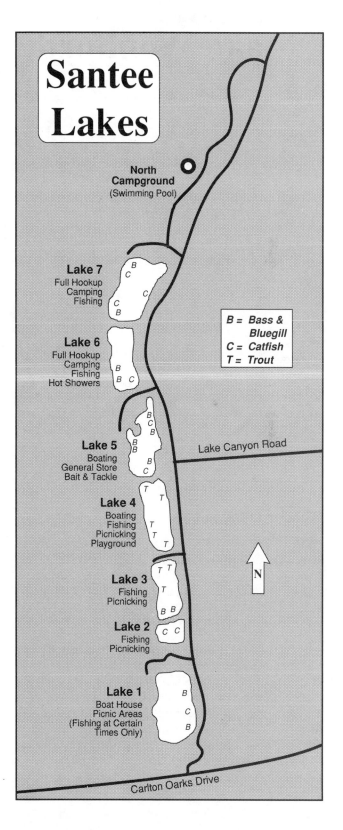

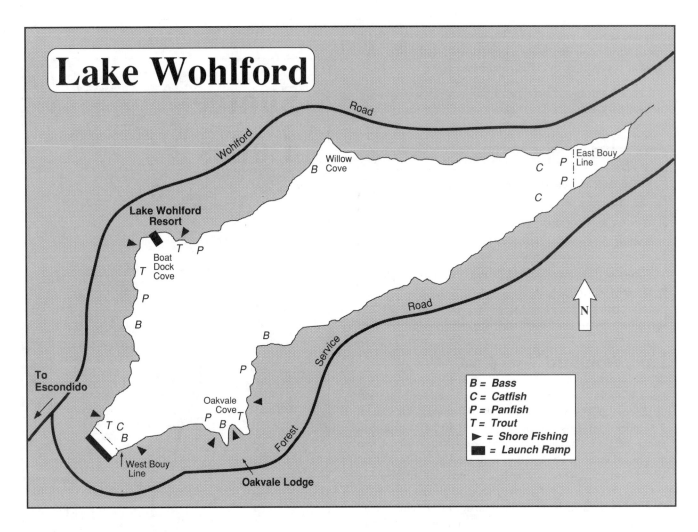

Wohlford Fishing Tips

Fishing begins at Wohlford in December when trout are the main quarry. But some anglers will pursue early season largemouths by jigging deep-water structure. And bucketmouths in the 16 pound range have taken nightcrawlers aimed at trout as early as January. Trouters should use light leaders because of the clear water.

Rainbow trout plants extend from December through early summer. A good spot for shore anglers is in the vicinity of the launch ramp and dock. Two other prime areas are the small bay opposite the launch ramp and near the dam along the barrel line. All of the popular methods of taking trout work well at Lake Wohlford. Bait anglers are encouraged to use a sliding sinker rig and to keep hands or eyes on the rod or line to detect pick-ups. It's also always advisable to float the offering up off the bottom. Inflate nightcrawlers, or add a small marshmallow to cheese or salmon egg baits. Floating cheese and marshmallow baits are available commercially.

At less than 200 acres, Wohlford is like a farm pond compared to some other San Diego area lakes. But it ranks right up among them as a bass producer. Wohlford bass will average 1 1/2 to 3 pounds, but 6 to 7 pounders are not unusual. March is generally the month when the bass action is best, but the bite holds up until Wohlford closes after Labor Day. Oak and willow trees line the waters gently sloping shoreline. Plus there are lots of rock outcroppings. Anglers should concentrate on shaded areas on sunny days. Early morning action is best on the eastern shoreline, and late afternoons are best on the western shoreline. Crankbaits in crawdad or shad patterns are consistent producers. Midday bassers do well by working plastic worms on rocky structures along the shoreline in 8 to 12 feet of water. Consistent good spots are Oakvale cove and the south shore rock pile. And bass chasers don't need a boat at Wohlford. It's a great lake for walking along and casting. Bait is popular for bass. Live crawdads and shiners are best. Shiners are dip-netted out of the lake and hooked through the lip. Two to three inch crawdads are the best size.

Channel catfish in the 3 to 5 pound range are taken at Wohlford from March through Labor Day, with most action coming later in the season. Early season action comes at the buoy lines and out in the middle of the lake along the old river channel. Summertime cats are up in the shallows. A variety of baits will work, but cut mackerel is tops.

The crappie bite is off and on throughout the fishing season. In spring, look for them in shallow water and coves, especially Willow Cove, Oakvale Cove, the southeast shoreline, the rocks east of the boat dock and the east end of the reservoir. When these guys, in the 1 to 1 1/4 pound range, are hitting just about any approach will work. Summertime

anglers drift for schools of crappie out in the main lake which can reach 80 feet of water.

Lake Wohlford Facts

Location: Wohlford is six miles from downtown Escondido. From Escondido take Valley Parkway east for two miles and turn off on Lake Wohlford Road to the lake.

Size: Wohlford covers about 200 acres and is about 1 1/2 miles long. Lake elevation is about 1,500 feet above sea level.

Species: Rainbow trout, largemouth bass, channel catfish, crappie, bluegill

Season: Early January through Labor Day

Boating: 5 m.p.h. speed limit, 18 feet length limit

Facilities: Boat rental, launch ramp (unpaved), camping, and store at Oakvale Lodge (760) 749-2895

Information: Ranger Station, (760) 738-4346

Special: Imperial Valley Canals

Most SoCal anglers are totally unaware of the fact that there are almost 3,000 miles of fish-filled canals meandering through the 500,000 acres of farm lands of the Imperial Valley between the Salton Sea and the Mexican border. But the locals, in towns like Imperial, El Centro, Brawley and Calexico, as well as the winter-visiting seniors have been enjoying this fishing feast for a long time. Irrigation canals host an abundance of largemouth bass (up to 8-10 pounds), lunker channel catfish and bluegills, along with some striped bass and flathead catfish.

The main canals are the East Highland which run north-south along the east side of the fields, the Central Main Canal which winds through the center of the valley, the West Side Main Canal on the west and the All-American Canal on the Mexican border. Canals vary in size from the 120-foot wide, 10-foot deep All-American, to lateral canals of about 20 feet wide, on down to ditches you can almost hop across.

Most of the largemouth bass are caught by local anglers in the hotter months—July and August are prime—and evening fishing is popular. But knowing anglers take bucketmouths year-round. During any season, the canals

that have lots of moss and grass growth are best. Plastic worms and plastic crawdads seem to produce better than live bait in the summer. There is a good top-water evening bite with buzzbaits, spinnerbaits and plugs with propellers. Local experts suggest slow-moving crankbaits and inline spinners (e.g. Roostertails) for winter action.

Leapfrogging is a great way for two people to work a canal. The first person is dropped off and the second person drives the vehicle up a ways and starts fishing. When the first angler gets to the vehicle, he or she leapfrogs ahead, and the process continues. Winter anglers score big on catfish utilizing this technique.

Please note that the irrigation district has trespassing regulations and many canals are posted. But enforcement is minimal—maybe because fishing is a big draw and helps the local economy. The small towns in the valley offer food, lodging, bait and tackle, etc. The El Centro Chamber of Commerce, (760) 352-3681, offers a county map showing the main canals, as well as information on county and private campgrounds and BLM camping in the vicinity of the canals. The Imperial Irrigation District, (760) 339-9416, sells a detailed canal map.

Eastern Sierra Freshwater

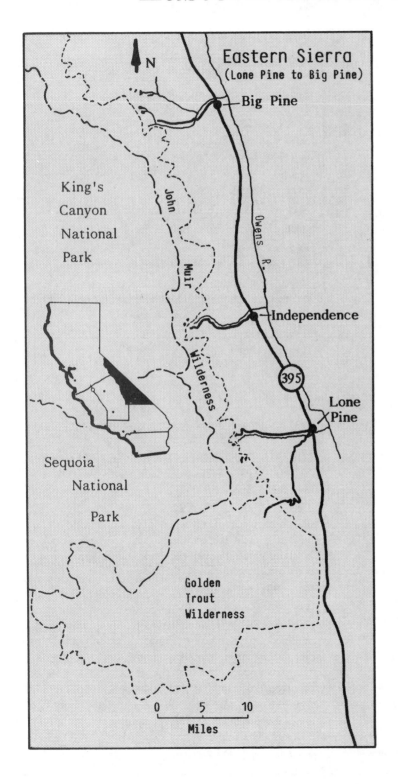

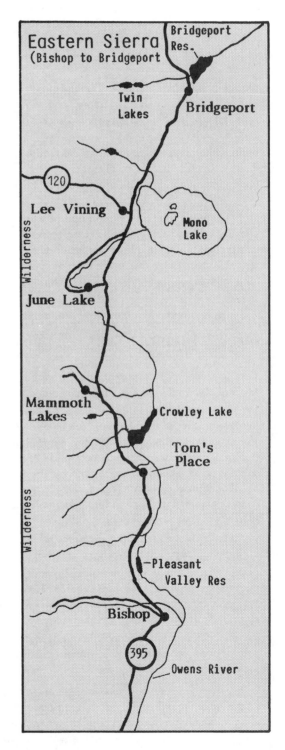

Eastern Sierra Freshwater Fishing

Freshwater fishing in the Eastern Sierra (the stretch of California that parallels Hwy. 395) means almost exclusively "trout fishing." And we're not just talking run-of-the-mill trout fishing. That's because the Eastern Sierra region is the premier trout territory in California—both in terms of size of fish and numbers of fish. And because of this special stature, the Eastern Sierra are covered in great detail in a sister publication, *Trout Fishing in California*, Marketscope Books. A somewhat condensed version of this coverage, with special emphasis on several of the Eastern Sierra major lakes, is presented below.

Trout fishing takes the angler to some of the most beautiful spots in this most beautiful state. Nowhere is this more true than in the Eastern Sierra. The point was eloquently made back in 1894 when David Starr Jordan, at the conclusion of a State Fish Commission report, said, "In writing on the trout of California, one does not willingly lay down the pen at the end. The most beautiful of fishes, the most charming of lands, where the two are connected, one wishes to say something better of them than has been said. It is with regret that he lets fall the pen in confession of inability to say it." Much has changed in California in the last 90 or so years. But the beauty of many of our Eastern Sierra mountain lakes and streams and our trout has not.

The success of a stream fishing experience depends on many factors including the amount of snowfall, the runoff, timing of insect hatches, weather patterns, etc. Generally, trout fishing is better in the spring and fall than it is in the summer. But summer fishing is often productive. When summer comes on, veteran stream anglers follow 60-65° water temperature up to higher elevations as back roads become passable. In July and August, a good spot is the cool tailwaters below dams.

One approach that always seems to produce more and larger trout is to contradict human nature. Most anglers park at a stream access point, walk to the water and begin to fish. So the pros have found that it's always better to hike for about 15 minutes along a stream before fishing. This will get you beyond the overworked and underpopulated spots and into some really good fishing action. Once fishing in a stream, the most productive anglers aren't afraid to get into the water. Don't just wade around the edges and fish from convenient spots. Get in the water with chest waders, if necessary, and move to the spots that provide access to the most likely holes.

In this chapter, Eastern Sierra waters are organized from south to north. By the way, the Southern California Automobile Association (AAA) publishes "A Guide to the Eastern Sierra" You'll find it quite useful and informative. With some variation, the trout season in the Eastern Sierra runs from the last Saturday in April through October 31st.

Inyo Early Trout Opener

Many stream trout anglers have trouble waiting for the general trout opener that comes each year on the last Saturday in April. They want to get going and catch some fish. Fortunately, there are some lower elevation trout streams and lakes, adjusted regulations, and willing host communities that are ready to accommodate trout-anxious anglers. Here are the specifics.

Southern Inyo County's trout season begins on the first Saturday in March. In the area which is bordered by Independence Creek (at Independence) to the north, Hwy. 395 to the east, and the Inyo County lines to the west and south, there are dozens of trout streams and several lakes that are primed for trout anglers. In many years the Department of Fish and Game even enhances these fisheries by planting big brood stock trout. And the local communities and merchants sponsor several fishing derbies. One is at Diaz Lake. The other is at Pleasant Valley Reservoir and the Lower Owens River below the dam (these two waters, by the way, are open to fishing all year long). There is more on Pleasant Valley and the Lower Owens River later in this chapter.

Usually, some of the best stream bets include Independence, Symmes, Piñon, Shepards, North and South Bair, Georges, Lone Pine and Cottonwood (open from Little Cottonwood on down). Most streams have roads or jeep trails along them, but some just have trails. Anglers move upstream, hitting good spots. Access isn't a problem since most of the streams are on U.S. Forest Service or BLM lands. Most anglers use bait (e.g. Power Bait, salmon eggs) or tiny spinners like Roostertails. Information: Bishop Chamber of Commerce, (760) 873-8405; Lone Pine Chamber of Commerce, (760) 876-4444.

Pack-in Fishing (map - p. 145)

As you can see on the full-size map that leads off this chapter, wilderness areas and national parks line the entire western side of the Eastern Sierra. This geographical proximity and multiple access point along Hwy. 395 make the region the focus for many backpack and horsepack anglers.

The Eastern High Sierra Packers Association publishes a wonderful little brochure each year that describes each member's services and the high country lakes and streams they access. See the illustration on the opposite page. The accompanying "Type of Pack Trips" information presents other highlights from this publication.

Types of Pack Trips

Spot Trips. You are taken by horseback, your gear and provisions by pack animal, to a desirable campsite on a lake or stream. The stock and pack return for you on a predetermined date. This type of trip has the desirable features of moderate riding, camp comfort, hiking to nearby areas and economical charges for the pack services. Your length of stay does not affect the charges. The party is expected to furnish its own camp gear and food. Variations in rates occur because of the distance, number in the party and the amount of your gear.

All Expense Trips. The stock, packer, food, cook and camping gear are provided by the pack outfit for the duration of the trip. This type of trip has many advantages, including the planning, preparation and cooking, all of which are done by the pack outfit.

Continuous Hire of Stock and Packer. The packer and stock remain with your party throughout the duration of the trip. Camp gear and provisions are normally provided by the party. The amount of moving and excursions may be determined by the individual party during the trip, or itineraries my be planned in advance. This type of trip features mobility and flexibility. The amount of horseback riding varies with the interest and desires of the party.

Dunnage Packs. The pack outfit packs the gear for a hiking party. The charges are based on the number of pack animals and packers required. This my be either a traveling trip or a pack to a predetermined area.

Day Rides. Available with or without guides. Guided open-group trips are available.

How to Arrange Your Pack Trip. You are encouraged to write the packer for information and assistance in planning your trip. The packer will be happy to provide suggestions and recommendations to make your trip enjoyable.

In your correspondence with the packer of your choice you should indicate:

1. The approximate dates of your trip
2. The type of trip you desire
3. The number of people you expect in your party
4. If known, the area or lakes you desire

Bishop Area Trout (map - p. 146)

The town of Bishop is one of the centers for eastern Sierra trouting. Elevation varies in the Bishop area from 7,000 ft. to 9,000 ft. Lower elevation fishing is usually more popular in cooler months. Streams and lakes at higher elevations are more popular in the warmer months since air and water temperatures are cooler and most of the higher elevation waters are closed to fishing early in the season. The main streams and lakes in the Bishop area are shown on the map accompanying this section.

Four streams in the area (South Fork of Bishop Creek, North Fork of Bishop Creek, Upper Rock Creek and Big Pine Creek) have much in common. They are all stocked nearly weekly with catchable-sized rainbows. Typical fish are 8 to 12 inches, but a special program has seen the stocking of trophy fish in recent years. This maintains a high catch-per-angler ratio throughout the summer months. Also these streams are all about the same size—about 10 to 12 feet wide. Average water depth is several feet but there are holes five to six feet deep.

Lower Rock Creek, which runs from Tom's Place parallel to Rte. 395 to Pleasant Valley Reservoir is a very special trout stream. This stream holds both wild and planted fish including some very large browns and rainbows. The upper reaches of the stream, accessible by a good trail, is a small clear water area that harbors many wild brown trout.

The last mile of Lower Rock Creek, before it empties into Pleasant Valley Reservoir, has an entirely different character. At the Los Angeles DWP power plant, Lower Rock Creek is joined by waters from Pine Creek and the Owens River Aqueduct system to produce a large river. Here trophy-sized

Eastern High Sierra Packers Association

Agnew Meadows Pack Train
Bob Tanner
P.O. Box 395, Mammoth Lakes, CA
   93546
(760) 934-2345
(800) 292-7758

Bishop Pack Outfitters
Mike Morgan
247 Cataract, Bishop, CA 93514
(760) 873-4785

Cascade Stables
H.R. Ebright
P.O. Box 7034, So. Lake Tahoe, CA 96158
(530) 541-2055

Cottonwood Pack Station
Dennis Winchester
Star Rt. 1, Box 81-A, Independence, CA
   93526
(760) 878-2015

Frontier Pack Train
Dave Dohnel
Star Rt. 3, Box 18, June Lake, CA 93529
Summer: (760) 648-7701;
Winter: (760) 873-7971

Glacier Pack Train
M. Stewart
P.O. Box 321, Big Pine, CA 93513
(760) 938-2538

Kennedy Meadows Resort and Pack Station
Matt Bloom
P.O. Box 4010, Sonora, CA 95370
Summer: (209) 965-3900;
Winter: (209) 928-1239

Mammoth Lakes Pack Outfit
John and Loree Summers
P.O. Box 61, Mammoth Lakes, CA 93546
(888) 475-8747

McGee Creek Pack Station
Lee and Jennifer Roeser
Rt. 1, Box 162, Mammoth Lakes, CA
   93546
Summer: (760) 935-4324;
Winter: (760) 878-2207

Mt. Whitney Pack Trains
Bob Tanner
P.O. Box 248, Bishop, CA 93515 or
P.O. Box 395, Mammoth Lakes, CA
93546
(760) 872-8331

Pine Creek Pack Trains
Brian and Danica Berner
P.O. Box 968, Bishop, CA 93515
(760) 387-2797
(800) 962-0775

Rainbow Pack Outfit
Bill Draves
P.O. Box 1791, Bishop, CA 93515
(760) 873-8877
(800) 443-2848

Red's Meadow Pack Train
Bob Tanner
P.O. Box 395, Mammoth Lakes, CA
   93546
(760) 934-2345
(800) 292-7758

Rock Creek Pack Station
Herbert and Craig London
P.O. Box 248, Bishop, CA 93515
Summer: (760) 935-4493
Winter: (760) 872-8331

Sequoia Kings Pack Trains
Brian and Danica Berner
P.O. Box 209, Independence, CA 93526
(760) 387-2797
(800) 962-0775

Troy Meadows Outfitters
Stanley Carver
P.O. Box 1402, Lake Isabella, CA 93240
(760) 379-3148

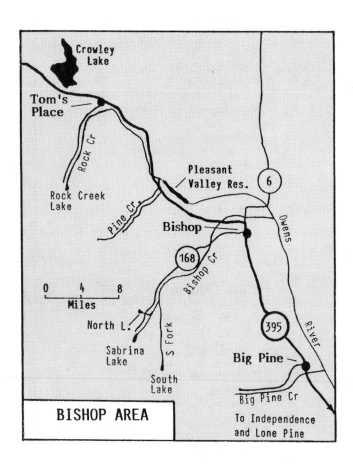

BISHOP AREA

Pleasant Valley Reservoir and the Lower Owens River

Most anglers wait for the last weekend in April to fish the Eastern Sierra, but Pleasant Valley and the Lower Owens River offer super trout action year-round, especially in late winter and early spring.

At Pleasant Valley, anglers frequently take limits of rainbows in the 12-15 inch class, and browns weighing 10 pounds are hauled in. Rainbows are easiest to catch, but if you want to go after the big browns, take along some Rapala and Rebel plugs that resemble small rainbows. The browns eat small rainbows for lunch. But you can't troll at Pleasant Valley because boats aren't allowed; therefore, you must use longer rods and heavier line to increase casting distance. Work the deeper holes at dawn or dusk, or even better, at night. Night fishing is legal in Inyo County—many big browns are taken then. The best brown angling is at the power plant end of the lake.

Both bait and lures produce stringers of mid-size rainbows. Lures are best when used early in the morning. Small (1/4 to 1/2 ounce) Kastmasters, Z-Rays, Roostertails and Phoebes, or anything shiny on 4-6 pound line is the way to go. Baits that float off the bottom (Zeke's, marshmallows, inflated nightcrawlers) are all good. After a rain, work the inlet area with nightcrawlers.

Pleasant Valley Lake Facts
Location: Pleasant Valley Road, the access to the dam end (southern end) is 7 miles north of Bishop via Hwy. 395. Six miles farther north on Hwy. 395 is another access via Gorge Road to the power plant end/inlet of the lake.
Species: Planted and brood stock rainbow and brown trout
Boating: No boats are permitted.
Access: There is a service road (no vehicles allowed) along the east shore. The west shore is steep and rocky.
Facilities: There are parking lots at both ends of the lake. Camping is provided along the Owens River, south of the lake.
Information: Bishop Chamber of Commerce, (760) 873-8405

Anglers attacking the Lower Owens (the river below Pleasant Valley) should watch reports of stream flow and be aware of special regulations. Whenever releases are made from Pleasant Valley Dam, the river can be high and challenging. There is a wild trout section on the river that goes

browns and rainbows are caught. Nightcrawlers, Rapalas, Rebels, as well as Mepps and Roostertail spinners are the top producers.

And don't overlook the fine little lakes in the Bishop area. There is South, Sabrina and North Lake off Bishop Creek Road, all accessible by car. Boats can be rented at South and Sabrina Lakes. And at the head of Rock Creek is Rock Creek Lake which also has boat rentals.

Maps of the region are available by writing Inyo National Forest, 798 Main St., Bishop, CA 93514. Their phone number is (760) 873-4207. The John Muir Wilderness Map is available, and it has topographical information. The Bishop Chamber of Commerce can be reached at (760) 873-8405. Fishing information is available at Culver's Sporting Goods, (760) 872-8361 and Brock's Sporting Goods, (760) 872-3581.

from the Dam down about seven miles to Five Bridges. The best time on this wild trout stretch is just after the river drops. Oxygen levels decrease with the water level so the caddis larvae move into the current where wild browns gobble them up. When the water is high, fly anglers use a dropper and fish tight in along the banks, no more than two feet out. Be aware of regulations along this portion of the Lower Owens. Below Five Bridges there are no special regulations. The river's serpentine and brush-lined course easily accommodates moderate fishing pressure. Dirt access roads run along much of the river for miles and miles south of Bishop. Get to the river by taking side roads (like East Line, Warm Springs, Collins, Rte. 182, Stewart Lane) of Hwy. 395. Most anglers pursue the rainbows that are planted at these access crossings, but there are also large browns. Earthen banks provide abundant worms, larvae, crickets and hellgrammites. One way to get browns is to use a natural presentation of these common foods. Fly anglers score by taking advantage of spring, summer, and early fall hatches of mosquitoes, gnats and other insects.

Crowley Lake (map - p. 148)

Crowley Lake is probably the most popular mountain trout lake for Southern Californians. Crowley is planted each summer with hundreds of thousands of small rainbow. By the next trout season opener in late April, these plantings average almost a pound each. And in the early 1970's, Crowley held the state record for brown trout at 25 lbs. 11 oz.

The fishing season kicks off at Crowley on the last Saturday in April. Every year over 5,000 people fish the lake on opening day! It's a gala weekend and a sight to behold. Crowley is open to fishing up until October 31st. But gear and limit regulations change for the trophy trout season. Be sure to check a copy of the regulations for current rules. Also, usually in June and lasting into the fall, the Sacramento perch bite comes on. So there is a lot of variety and a lot of action at Crowley.

Crowley Lake is about four miles long, and there are complete boating facilities. It is located about 300 miles from Los Angeles, via Rte. 395.

Crowley Fishing Seasons													Good: ▨ Fair: ▧
	J	F	M	A	M	J	J	A	S	O	N	D
Trout				▨	▨	▨	▨	▨	▨	▨		
Sacramento Perch				▧	▧	▨	▨	▨	▨	▧		

Crowley Fishing Tips

Historically, Crowley Lake has yielded many trout in the opening weeks of the season. But the larger trout are caught later in the season. This is also the time when Sacramento perch fishing is coming alive. Here's a look at the best techniques to use at Crowley as the season progresses.

Bait anglers do really well at Crowley in the early season. A sliding sinker rig with bait that floats up off the bottom is the way to go. Use a 2-4 pound leader about two feet long and a size 16 or 18 treble hook. Casters score with Mepps, Kastmasters, Rapalas and similar offerings. Early season bait anglers and lure casters are advised to concentrate around the many tributaries that enter the lake. Spring rainbows move to these areas as they attempt to spawn.

Trollers also do well in the spring. Two good areas are McGee Bay and the Old Owens River channel along the east shore. In shallow McGee Bay, troll a flasher in front of a nightcrawler or Needlefish. In the deeper river channel, leadcore is needed. Let out only 3 to 6 colors early in the season. By mid-summer, you may need to let out 7 to 10 colors.

In early summer, bait becomes less effective as the smaller stocked rainbows are caught or move away from shore. But bait anglers continue to catch fish by anchoring out in the McGee Bay near the river channel. Usually in June fly fishing (either with fly equipment or with a Cast-a-Bubble on spinning equipment) gets hot. Anglers score by casting Elk Hair Caddis, smaller emerger patterns and Olive Matukas in front of crossing fish.

When the trophy season starts, anglers are restricted to artificial lures with barbless hooks. The daily limit is two fish with an 18-inch minimum. Most fish caught during the trophy season are 14-17 inch rainbows that are holdovers from the previous year's plant. But there are also second year, 18-23 inch rainbows that were up in Crowley's tributaries during the spring spawn. These can weigh up to 3-4 pounds. Finally, there are also browns that reach up to 8 pounds.

By August, Crowley is usually lined with weed beds. Trout cruise through the channels in the weeds chasing perch minnows. Casting from shore can be a difficult task due to the weeds. Float tubes are the way to go. Quietly kick out into the channels where trout are feeding. Cast ahead of cruising fish or swim your offering deeper along the weed lines. Fly rodders throw Olive Matukas. Spin anglers toss small Rebel or Rapala plugs (rigged with barbless hooks) or a fly and casting bubble combination.

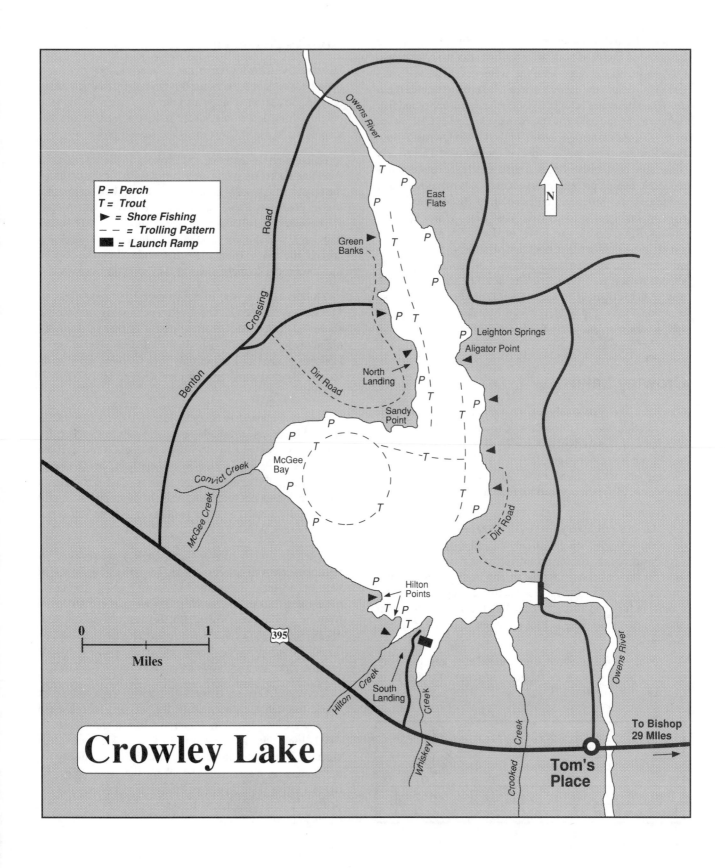

Crowley Lake

Jim Matthews, an outdoor writer and veteran of Crowley's trophy trout, says that most fly rodders carry both a 10-foot sink-tip line and a full-sink or sinking head so they can fish deeper by degrees until they find fish. Lure anglers use crankbaits with large tips that take plugs down, or they use "countdown" lures. Matthews recommends 12-15 pound line. During the "weed" season, the bite is either in the early morning or evening. Good spots include the west flats of the Owens River arm, Hilton Bay, Whiskey Bay, Crooked Creek Bay, Leighton Springs Bay and Christmas Bay.

In October, if the weed beds are dying off, the trout relocate along old stream channels and drop-offs; therefore, they are more difficult to find. But brown trout are now into spawning, so anglers concentrate around the mouth of the Owens River or any of the small creeks that enter the lake along the western shore. Tackle and lure selection stay the same. Try to draw instinctive strikes.

Finally, some tips on the Sacramento perch. Historically, late May through mid-July have been the top producing months. Like crappie, these perch school up and move into the shallows to spawn. Finding a school means frantic action. They run from 1/2 to almost 4 pounds and are very good eating. Drifting has proven to be the best method of finding fish. Mini-jigs or white Marabou jigs tipped with a bit of worm is the technique of choice. One good place to try is the open areas that form in the weed beds. Shallower water, 4 to 8 feet deep in McGee Bay, Hilton Bay, Leighton Springs Bay, and the east shore from Alligator Point to the mouth of the Owens River, are good bets. Use light or ultralight spinning tackle.

Crowley Lake Facts

Location: Crowley Lake is located about 29 miles north of Bishop via Hwy. 395.

Species: Rainbow trout, brown trout, Sacramento perch

Facilities: Camping at the North Landing and South Landing, full-service marina, launch ramp and boat rental. The City of Los Angeles manages the facilities.

Information: Mammoth Sporting Goods, (760) 934-8474; Culver Sporting Goods, (760) 872-8361; Brock's Sporting Goods, (760) 872-3581; Bishop Chamber of Commerce, (760) 873-8405; Crowley Lake Fish Camp, (760) 935-4301

Convict Lake, Hot Creek and Upper Owens

Convict Lake is just up Rte. 395 a short ways past Crowley lake. Many consider it one of the most beautiful spots in the Eastern Sierra, with rigged peaks surrounding clear, cold waters. Launch ramp, cabins, boat rental, grocery, restaurant, etc. support anglers in pursuit of rainbow and brown trout. Fishing is best in late spring and early fall, but also holds up well in the summer months. From this base camp, it's possible to hike to about six small mountain lakes and numerous streams to enjoy fine fishing and spectacular scenery. Convict Lake itself is about one mile long and one-half mile wide. It is at an elevation of 7,600 feet, so summer daytime temperatures are in the mid 70's.

Hot Creek gets its name from the hot springs naturally heated waters. Although the upper part of this stream is private, there is a wild trout fishery in the one-mile long Hot Creek gorge stretch. The hot springs are also located in the gorge. Fishing here is catch-and-release, barbless, and artificial flies, and the quarry is wild brown trout and rainbows. A well-maintained gravel road leads to Hot Creek. It's about 30 miles north of Bishop. Turn right near the northwest end of Long Valley Airport. Hot Creek is considered one of the best fly fishing streams in the West.

The Upper Owens River feeds Crowley Lake. It is a meadow stream with open banks. It's a good fly fishing stream. Concentrate on the undercut banks in late evening. Several-pound browns hold in these areas. Access to the Upper Owens River is at Benton Crossing. Go north from Rte. 395 at Witmore Hot Springs for about six miles. You can fish upstream or downstream from Benton Crossing. Going downstream early in the season might catch you some rainbows that come up from Crowley Lake to spawn. Locals use streamers and nymphs, and check your regulations booklet for gear and limit restrictions.

Mammoth Lakes Area Trout

The Mammoth Lakes Area is only a short way (about 12 miles) up Rte. 395 from Crowley Lake. The town of Mammoth Lakes serves as a launching point for a wide variety of trout fishing experiences, including lake fishing, stream fishing, day-hike fishing and pack-in fishing. There is an immense assortment of twisting creeks and secluded mountain lakes. Lodging, camping facilities and other amenities are plentiful in the Mammoth Lakes area.

One of the most popular destinations here is Twin Lakes. They are just out of town on Highway 230. They offer complete facilities and good fishing. Twin Lakes is actually three lakes joined by a small stream. They are weedy and range in depth to about 40 or 50 feet. Brook trout, browns and rainbow are all available. Most trout are pan-sized, but some range up to 5-6 pounds.

Also accessible by car are four more lakes located right near Twin Lakes. Lake Mary, Lake Mamie, Horseshoe Lake and Lake George all offer housekeeping cottages and/or camping facilities and good trouting. Lake Mary is the largest of the four, with depths of up to 60 feet, and is a favorite for trolling. The other three are productive, using a variety of techniques. After the ice clears, they are planted regularly during the summer.

Some of the favorite day-hike fishing lakes in the Mammoth Lakes area are Arrowhead, Skelton, Wood and Barney Lakes. These lakes are generally not reachable early in the trout season because of snow on the trails. But they are all along the same trail. It begins near the Lake Mary campground.

If you're interested in other day-hike and pack-in fishing excursions in the Mammoth Lakes area, the Mammoth Ranger District of the Inyo National Forest offers a Mammoth Trails Booklet. It provides complete information on about 15 different hikes of varying length and degree of difficulty. The Mammoth Ranger Station is at Box 148, Mammoth Lakes, CA 93546.

Fly anglers new to the area should check with Mammoth tackle outlets to determine which offering works best in these waters. A good source is Mammoth Sporting Goods, (760) 934-8474. Mammoth Visitors' Center can be reached at (800) 367-6572, and the Mammoth Lakes Chamber of Commerce is at (760) 934-3068.

June Lake Loop Trout

The next fine fishing spot, known as June Lake Loop, is about 18 miles north of Mammoth lakes up Rte. 395. It consists of four lakes off of Rte. 395. They are all reached by taking Hwy. 158 out of June Lake Junction. The first lake you'll hit, just about two miles out of town, is June Lake (160 acres). Next, comes Gull Lake (64 acres), Silver Lake (80 acres) and finally Grant Lake (1,100 acres). These lakes are at an elevation of about 7,000 feet and offer spectacular Eastern Sierra mountain scenery. All these lakes have developed facilities including campgrounds, boat rentals, etc. Lodging is available at some lakes as well as in the town of June Lake.

In June Lake itself, trolling and casting are probably the most popular and productive approaches. Good offerings include Roostertails, Mepps, Super Dupers, Rapalas and Rebels. Spinners are best in yellow or black while Rapalas and Rebels are good in silvers and golds.

Gull Lake, the littlest, is regarded as a good baitfishing opportunity. There are both rainbow and brook trout in Gull Lake that go for nightcrawlers, cheese, salmon eggs and worms. The bottom of Gull Lake is a little marshy, so it's best to try and float your offering up off the bottom. Use a worm inflator, floating bait or marshmallow combination to accomplish this.

In Silver Lake and the inlet area of Rush Creek, both bait and lures are productive. In Rush Creek proper, above Silver Lake, worms and salmon eggs take both stocked fish and wild trout.

Grant Lake is another spot for the trollers. They use flasher/nightcrawler combinations, Rapalas and Phoebes. Bright colors, like gold, work well in this lake. Grant Lake also offers good shore fishing opportunities. Toss spinners or bait like cheese, eggs or worms.

Information on the June Lake Loop area is readily available. For general and accommodation information, call the Chamber of Commerce at (760) 648-7584. Camping information is available from the United States Forest Service in the town of Lee Vining at (760) 647-6525. A good source of fishing info is Ernie's Tackle at June Lake (760) 648-7756.

Bridgeport Reservoir (map - p. 152)

Bridgeport Reservoir is the northern anchor of the "trout alley" that runs along Hwy. 395 for almost 150 miles from Lone Pine on up to the town of Bridgeport. And this lake is a fitting landmark because it has put out big numbers of trout in both quantity and size.

Planted fish grow fast here because of the abundance of food. The reservoir is about 5 1/2 miles long and covers almost 4,500 acres. But Bridgeport is not deep, so the water warms up in the summer months. This contributes to moss and algae growth, and affects fishing techniques and hot spots. There are complete boating facilities at the lake. And the town of Bridgeport and surrounding area provide a full range of resort and camping facilities. The Sacramento perch bite provides a change of pace as well as some good eating.

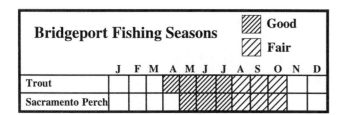

Bridgeport Fishing Seasons		J	F	M	A	M	J	J	A	S	O	N	D
Trout					▨	▨	▨	▨	▨	▨	▨		
Sacramento Perch						▨	▨	▨	▨	▨	▨		

Good / Fair

Bridgeport Fishing Tips

In the springtime, trolling worms behind flashers is the most popular and productive technique. Shore fishing, especially with nightcrawlers, is also productive at this time since the trout are still in shallow water near shore. Concentrate on stream inlets and near the dam. Casting gold Phoebes and Kastmasters (about 1/4 ounce size) and Rapala-style lures can be good. These can also be trolled. Fly anglers can also do well at stream inlets in the cooler months.

In the warmer months, most trout are taken by boat in the deepest part of the lake by stillfishermen. They use inflated nightcrawlers and other baits that float up off the bottom. Most summer fish are carryovers that were planted the previous fall. They exceed the one-pound level and are pink-meated and deep-bodied. Use a sliding sinker above a swivel and tie on a 2-3 pound test leader before the hook. Some of the best stillfishing sites are off Falling Rock Marina, Rainbow Point and Sandy Point. A consistently good spot for bank angling is along both shores near the dam.

Angling for brown trout in the 5-8 pound range can be very good in the summertime, especially when there is little or no moonlight. That's when browns are taken near the dam during the last hour of daylight. Bank anglers toss Rapala-type lures (rainbow patterns or silver and black) and use a quick return. Local experts speculate that the browns are in a Sacramento perch feeding frenzy. Trollers pulling Rapalas (size No. 7) are also taking browns in the narrow north end of the lake.

Summertime is also prime Sacramento perch fishing season. The good-eaters were illegally introduced into the lake in the early 1980s and have expanded to become a popular fishery. At times, anglers toss yellow-white mini-jigs or red worms to pull in 60 to 80 perch per hour. They range from hand-sized to 1 1/2 pounds.

Bridgeport Reservoir Facts

Location: Just north of the town of Bridgeport; take Hwy. 182 north off Hwy. 395 to reach most facilities.

Size: Bridgeport is 5 1/2 miles long, 1 1/2 miles wide, and covers 4,400 acres

Species: Rainbow trout, brown trout, Sacramento perch

Facilities: There are several full-service marinas, campgrounds and launch ramps on Bridgeport Reservoir. All are located off Hwy. 182 along the east shore of the lake. There are also U.S. Forest Service campgrounds in the area.

Information: Falling Rock Marina, (760) 932-7001, Ken's Sporting Goods, Bridgeport, (760) 932-7707; Toiyabe National Forest, (760) 932-7070.

Bridgeport Area Waters (map - p. 153)

Our next locale up Rte. 395 in the Eastern Sierra is Bridgeport. It offers an excellent and widely diverse trouting experience. Here in a beautiful setting are lakes, rivers and streams that provide may trout, some very large. All these waters are located within 20 miles of Bridgeport, a full facility resort town.

Flowing out of Bridgeport Reservoir toward Nevada is the East Walker River. This is a trophy brown trout fishery. Browns average 3/4 to 2 pounds here, but range up to 9 pounds. Minimum size in the East Walker is 14 inches with a two-fish limit. Only barbless hooks on artificial lures may be used. Anglers wade this river in chest waders. Submerged roots and overhanging branches add to the character of the East Walker. Anglers use spinning gear or fly casting equipment. Fly anglers use a 4-pound test tippet for dry flies and an 8-pound for streamers. Good fly patterns include Mayflies, Caddis, Grasshoppers, Yellow Stoneflies and Woolly Worms. Best streamers are No. 2 black-white and No. 2 black-yellow Marabous. Dawn and dusk are the best times to fish the undercut banks of this sizeable stream.

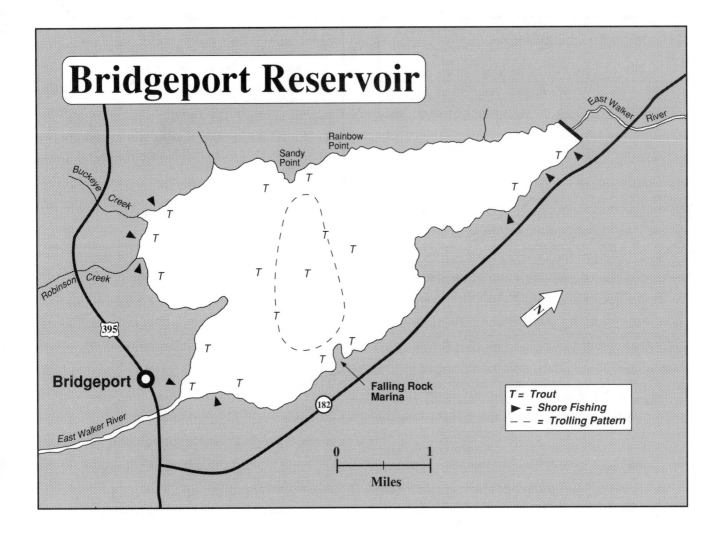

Another gem (or should we say gems) is Twin Lakes. Big browns are also the order of the day here. Fish in the ten-pound range are not uncommon. And Lower Twin currently holds the California brown trout record at 26 lbs. 8 oz. set in May 1987. Fishing techniques are similar to those in the Bridgeport Reservoir, but weed growth is not a problem in the Twins. These big browns feast on planted rainbows, small kokanee salmon as well as crawdads. Troll Rapalas and Rebels that imitate these. Best fishing for very large brown trout in the Twin Lakes is late April to early May, and then again near the end of the season in late October. Twin Lakes are located about 12 miles southwest of Bridgeport at an elevation of about 7,000 feet. There is camping and a full-service marina at the lake.

By the way, planted brood stock rainbow, pan-sized planted rainbow and small kokanee are abundant in Twin Lakes.

Trolling works well on all these fish throughout the summer months. Go deeper as the water warms up.

Upper Robinson Creek, which flows into the Twin lakes, is a good rainbow fishery. Spinning anglers use spoons such as Hot Shots and Phoebes. Fly anglers score with floating line and Zug Bug Nymphs.

In addition to Robinson Creek, there are literally scores of other small, productive trout streams. Some of the best known are Buckeye, Eagle, Swauger, Leavitt, Sardine, Wolf, Silver, West Walker and Molydenite. Many smaller streams are lightly fished. But it's important to remember to fish these waters slowly and carefully. Walk quietly. Crawl up to pools in meadows. Keep your shadow off the water. Move upstream so you stay behind the fish. Trout fishing in small streams is akin to stalking in a hunt.

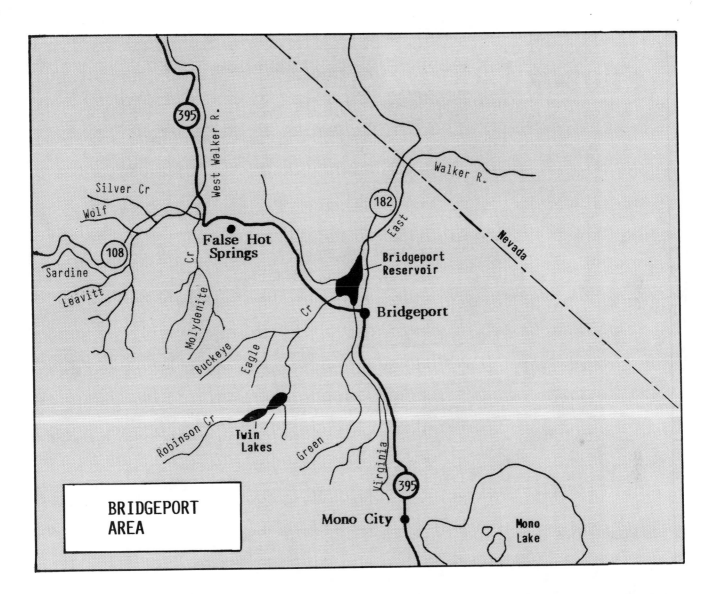

BRIDGEPORT
AREA

Trail and camping information in the Bridgeport area is available from the United States Forest Service, Bridgeport Ranger District, Box 595, Bridgeport, CA 93517, (760) 932-7070. Fishing information is available at Ken's Alpine Shop and Sporting Goods in Bridgeport at (760) 932-7707.

Topaz Lake (map - p. 154)

We started out this chapter with the early trout opener in Southern Inyo County, so it only seems fitting that we close it out with another early season trout opener. But Topaz is more than an early season possibility—it's a trophy trout factory. Most Southern Californians never go farther north than Bridgeport to find trout. But knowing winter and spring anglers stay on Hwy. 395 a little longer and find a gem called Topaz Lake. Another plus is that Topaz gets light fishing pressure—partly because the best angling is from February to May, and also because it's pretty much in the middle of nowhere. Topaz straddles the Nevada-California border so local casinos may be enough to entice some anglers to make the drive. Only a California or Nevada fishing license is required to fish the entire lake.

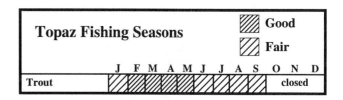

Topaz Fishing Seasons													▨ Good ▨ Fair
	J	F	M	A	M	J	J	A	S	O	N	D	
Trout												closed	

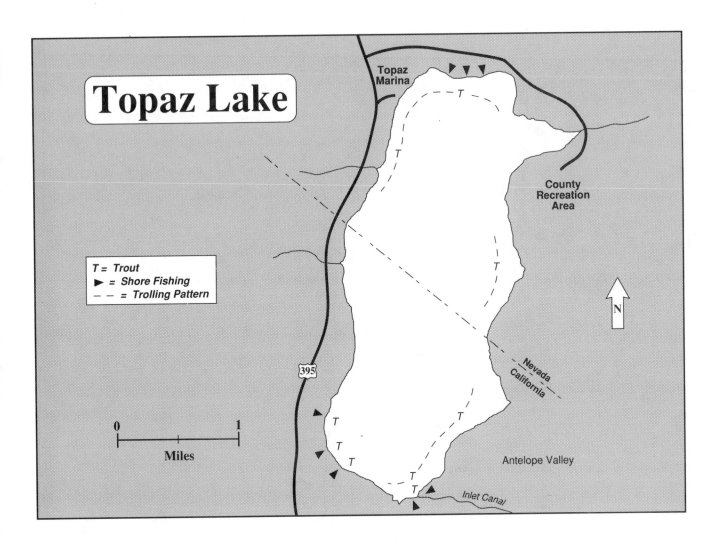

Topaz Fishing Tips

Topaz is heavily planted by both California and Nevada agencies. During the closed season (October-December) these planted rainbows grow to 12-16 inches. There are also holdovers and wild browns. Browns weigh up to 8 pounds! Rainbow action starts in February. Big browns become active around the middle of March and keep biting until early June. Local experts agree that trolling is the way to go early in the season, but stillfishing gets the nod in May and June when temperatures rise.

Trollers find success pulling nightcrawlers behind flashers or Floating J7 or J9 Rapalas of various colors. Early in the season most of the bigger fish are caught in water from 5 to 15 feet deep and near the shoreline. Shore anglers who concentrate their efforts at the southern end of the lake where the Walker River canal enters the lake find good fishing in March and early April as the rainbows gather in this area for their spawning run. The same holds true in September for

fall-spawning browns. Inflated nightcrawlers and floating baits are the best trout getters.

Topaz Lake Facts
Location: Topaz is located where Hwy. 395 crosses the California-Nevada border. It's 135 miles north of Bishop.
Size: The reservoir covers 1,800 acres and has 25 miles of shoreline.
Species: Rainbow and brown trout
Facilities: There are three campgrounds on Topaz: Douglas County Recreation Area Campground, (775) 266-3343, Topaz Marina, (775) 266-3550, Topaz R.V. Park, (530) 495-2357. Launching is at the marina. Other services are available in the town of Topaz, south of the lake.

Special: Walker Lake

Eastern Sierra anglers who are looking for a change of pace need only take a short trip into Nevada. At Walker Lake they will find trophy Lahontan cutthroat trout, fishing derbies, casinos, western hospitality and all the creative comforts of home. Walker cutts flourish in this alkaline water, with catches ranging from 2 to 15 pounds! Often the average catch measures 16 to 19 inches and weighs in at 2 to 3 pounds.

Walker Lake is the terminus of the Walker River drainage system that originates in the Sierra east and south of Bridgeport, CA. It has much in common with its cousin to the north, Pyramid Lake (covered in detail in *Fishing in Northern California*). Both are high elevation natural desert lakes with lots of big cutts. At one time, a giant inland sea, known as Lake Lahontan, included both Pyramid and Walker Lakes. Nevada cutthroat trout are closely related to the coastal cutthroat that migrate into the Pacific Ocean.

The Nevada Department of Wildlife plants hundreds of thousands of cutts into Walker Lake each year. They thrive on a diet of tui chub, an abundant baitfish. Walker is a big lake, measuring 16 miles from north to south and six miles in width, so wind is always a concern. Large whitecaps can come up quite quickly. Fortunately, many of the most productive fishing waters are within a comfortable distance of protected waters and launch ramps. Wind is only one element of the weather picture at Walker. Cool to downright cold temperatures are another during most of the good fishing months. So dress appropriately, preferably in layers.

There are two major fishing derbies at Walker Lake offering a wide range of cash and merchandise prizes. The Mineral County Chamber of Commerce along with Hawthorne merchants sponsor an annual Thanksgiving weekend fishing derby. Top prize is $10,000 for taking the properly tagged cutthroat trout. Usually there are about 60-70 other cash prizes, mostly of about $50 each. A final enticement is a boat and trailer raffle prize.

The other derby is a season-long affair sponsored by the El Capitan Lodge and Casino, kicking off in November and running through the end of April. In the past the grand prize has been a fully outfitted boat package. Weekly cash prizes are also awarded. A ten-pound trophy has a good chance of winning this derby.

Historically, the Walker Lake fishery gets serious attention around the first of November with the bite usually peaking in early spring. Trollers have the advantage early in the season when most hits are down 40 to 80 feet. Productive trolling lures include Kwik-Fish, Tor-P-Dos, Mepps Cyclops and Flatfish. Lures in the 2 1/2- to 3-inch size range are best with green frog or red and black coloration. Most trollers round out their equipment list with fishfinders and downriggers.

Fishing is consistently best in the months of March, April and on into May when the trout move into the shallows to spawn. It's during this time period when shore anglers do very well. One technique is to cast spoons such as Daredevils, Krocadiles, Little Cleos or Mepps Cyclops. A local color favorite is chartreuse with red or black dots. Bait fishing is also an excellent shore-fishing technique. Most anglers use strips of tui chub, nightcrawler or floating baits such as Zekes or Power Bait.

Boat anglers troll tight to shore in five to ten feet of water during the spring spawn. Apex and Flatfish lures are good, as are gold minnow imitation lures. Following the spawn the fish scatter, so trollers dominate the action from May to the next February.

Most of the best fishing areas at Walker are along the western shoreline, for both boat and shore anglers. At the north end of the west shore the Walker River inlet, when flowing, brings in food-rich, cool, oxygenated water. It's a good choice, especially in the summer months.

On down the western shore, the next hot spot is Sportsman's Beach. Trollers and bank anglers do well here. Onshore facilities include improved campsites with covered tables, fire pits and a launch ramp. Just south of Sportsman's is an area known as the cliffs, possibly the most popular trolling area on the lake. Its rocky bottom area draws baitfish followed by hungry cutts. Water depths vary from 30 to 90 feet. The steep shoreline limits bank access. Next on down the western shoreline comes the State Park area. Shore anglers and trollers both do well here. Finally, on the eastern shore, the Sand Point area can be good for trollers.

There are three free launch ramps at Walker. During low water periods, the ramp at State Park Beach is limited to small craft. The ramp at Sportsman's Beach and Cliff House can handle a larger variety of watercraft. There are no boat rentals at Walker, but fishing guides are available.

Walker Lake is located north of Bishop via Highway 6 to Highway 95 north. Travel time is about the same from Bishop to Walker Lake as it is from Bishop to Bridgeport. Complete services are available in the town of Hawthorne, south of the lake. A Nevada three-day fishing license and trout stamp is less than $25. Season permits are also available. The cutthroat limit at Walker is five fish per day, with no minimum size. For more information, contact the Nevada Department of Wildlife, (775) 688-1500, and the Mineral County Chamber of Commerce at (775) 945-5896.

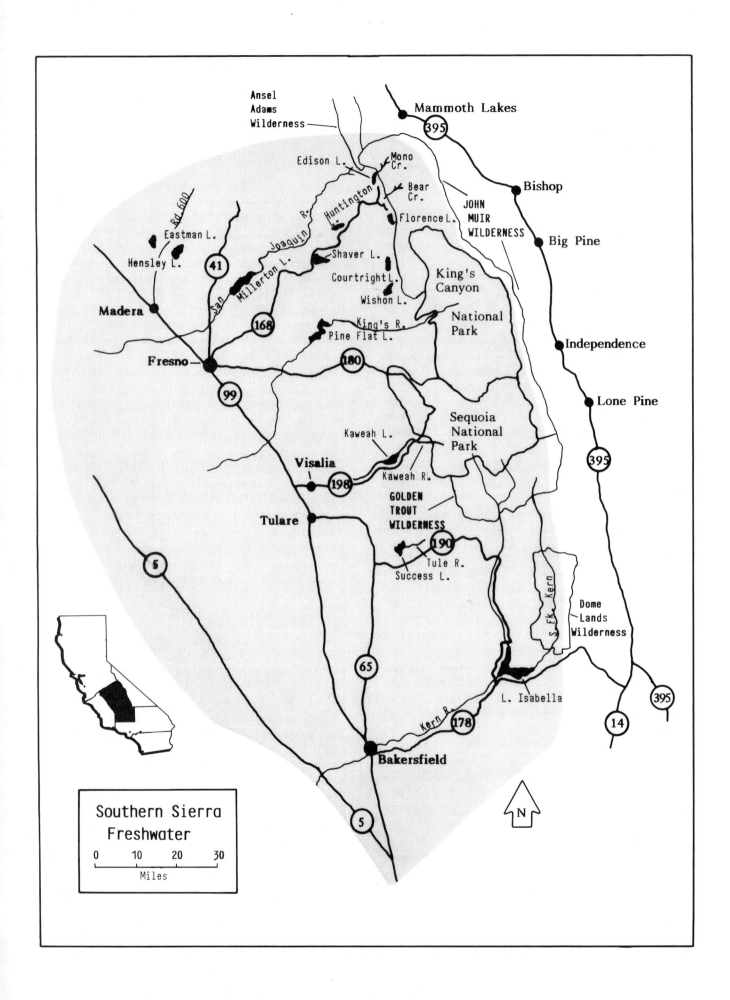

Southern Sierra
Freshwater

0   10   20   30

Miles

Southern Sierra Freshwater Fishing

The Southern Sierra Mountains shelter a marvelous collection of freshwater fishing possibilities. Let's start in the foothills and work our way up the slopes, as if breezing along in a low-flying balloon and looking down at the wonders.

First comes the foothill reservoirs: places like Eastman, Hensley, Millerton, Pine Flat and Success. These are large bodies of water which primary focus are warm-water species like largemouth bass, catfish and striped bass. But most are also fully developed recreational destinations for boaters, campers, picnickers, and entire families as well as anglers. These conveniently located spots also provide planted trout fishing in the late winter and spring months. Lake Isabella, although it is at about 2,500 feet in elevation, has much in common with the foothill reservoirs.

Flowing into and out of the foothill reservoirs are the rivers that bring water down from the snow-packed summits. There are miles and miles of planted and native trout waters in the San Joaquin, Kings, Kaweah, Tule and Kern drainages. Look down and pick out the holes and riffles where you'd like to wet a line. Happily, you can probably really work these spots because highway access along most rivers is excellent.

Next up the western slopes come the good-sized, higher elevation, cold-water trout lakes. Anglers here pursue large rainbows and browns from trailer boats, rental boats and from shore. As you can see, there are also established resorts and campgrounds at Edison, Florence, Huntington, Wishon and Shaver Lakes.

As our mystical balloon nears the summit of the Southern Sierras, at 8,000, 10,000 or even 12,000 feet above sea level, we're cruising over gorgeous, pristine, rugged high country. See the hundreds of tiny lakes and narrow, tumbling streams. This is golden, brown and brook trout territory at its most magnificent best. Read up on the Golden Trout Wilderness, John Muir Wilderness, Ansel Adams Wilderness, Dome Lands Wilderness and the Sequoia National Park, and then set your arm chair balloon down and go fishing.

Dinkey Creek, Courtright and Wishon Reservoirs

The first stop on our word tour is Dinkey Creek, a tributary of the King's River. When it comes to trout, Dinkey Creek is "dinkey" in name only. Dinkey Creek can be reached by taking Dinkey Creek Road east from Hwy. 168. The junction is just south of Shaver Lake Highlands near Shaver Lake. It's about a 10-mile drive. There are miles of stream here with sparkling clear water and beautiful holes. However, many of the best spots are accessible only after a long climb down. And often a climb back up and down again is required to reach the next good spot. But the trout population is very high in much of Dinkey Creek exactly because of this remoteness and inaccessibility. Some local experts say that at times you can catch and release beautiful trout until you get too weary to continue. There are several public campgrounds in the vicinity of the town of Dinkey Creek. Ambitious Shaver Lake anglers often head to Dinkey Creek for a pleasant change of pace.

Proceeding east of Dinkey Creek on McKinley Grove Road takes anglers to two fine trout lakes—Wishon and Courtright. Wishon Village, (559) 865-5361, offers campgrounds, boat rentals, etc. at Wishon Lake. There are also U.S. Forest Service campgrounds in the vicinity of both lakes.

Eastman & Hensley Lakes (map - p. 158)

Here are two lakes that are as close to being twins as just about any two lakes in California. Each is in the 1,700 surface acre range, each is administered by the Corp of Engineers, and they are less than 15 miles apart as the crow flies. Best of all, they both offer good warm-water fishing (largemouth bass, catfish, crappie, bluegill) and planted rainbow trout fishing in the winter and spring.

Both of these reservoirs are north and somewhat west of Madera in the Sierra foothills. Specifically, they're about 20

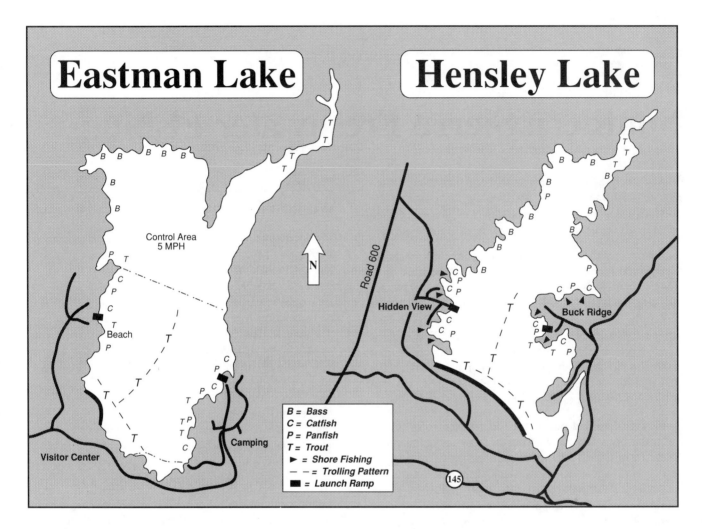

miles from Madera, and about 25 miles east of Chowchilla. Both lakes have two paved launch ramps and several campgrounds and swimming beaches. Waterskiing and other summer recreation activities are popular at these lakes, but angling at this time is still productive, especially in the northern reaches.

Eastman & Hensley Fishing Seasons													
	J	F	M	A	M	J	J	A	S	O	N	D
Bass													
Catfish													
Panfish													
Trout													

Good / Fair

Eastman & Hensley Fishing Tips

Bass fishing is usually hottest in April. Those with boats head up to the northern end of the lakes. That's where trees and cover are best. Work each cove thoroughly. A local favorite is a 1/2 to 3/8 ounce, double-bladed spinnerbait. Try chartreuse or chartreuse and blue skirts. Another good bait is a split-shot worm. They produce near the dams. Most largemouths are in the 2-3 pound range, but they go up to 6-8 pounds.

Channel catfishing is at its best in the summer and early fall. It's not unusual to catch six-pounders, and fish up to 20 pounds are taken. Nightcrawlers, stinkbaits, chicken livers and anchovies all produce at times. Try some summertime night fishing.

Winter and spring trout anglers do very well from shore in the areas around the launch ramps. Shore fishing access is also good in these areas for catfish and bluegill. Shallow trolling for rainbows is another good option. Crappie fishing is best in the coves of the upper parts of the lakes.

Eastman and Hensley Lake Facts

Location: Both lakes are 20 to 25 miles north and west of Madera and Chowchilla.

Size: Eastman—1,780 acre feet; Hensley—1,570 acre feet

Species: Largemouth bass, catfish, crappie, bluegill and rainbow trout

Facilities: Both lakes have launch ramps, camping, hiking, swim beaches and picnic areas.

Information: Eastman—(559) 689-3255; Hensley—(559) 673-5151

Edison & Florence Lakes

Edison and Florence Lakes are situated at 7,500 feet in a beautiful Sierra basin. These excellent trout lakes are located at the very end of Hwy. 168. Before getting here, the two-lane road turns into one lane, as it twists and winds through pine forests and giant boulders. Motor homes and vehicles pulling trailers need to take extreme care, or if too large, they must stop at Shaver Lake or Huntington Lake, farther back toward Fresno. Edison and Florence Lakes are only about 20 miles above Huntington, but the drive can take quite some time.

There are a number of people who make the trip up here to visit Mono Hot Springs. This resort, located just before the junction to Florence and Edison Lakes, has a store, cabins, a restaurant, and hot mineral baths. But for most, the main attraction here is the fishing in the lakes. Plus there is a ferry shuttle service at each lake that takes hikers and backpackers into the John Muir and Ansel Adams Wilderness, just above the lakes. There is much more on these areas in that specific section of this chapter.

Trouting is good in both lakes, in smallish Ward Lake (off the road to Florence), and in the surrounding streams in the area. Both Edison and Florence receive stocks of rainbow trout in addition to the German browns and brookies that call these waters home. There are some browns of monster proportions. Ward has wild browns only. One consistently good approach is to troll a Rapala, or other minnow-type plug, along the shoreline. Many hookups are in the 15-18 inch range, and six pounders-plus are not infrequent. Bait anglers do well with nightcrawlers/marshmallow combinations. Fishing boats and canoes are available to rent. There

are U.S. Forest Service campgrounds in the area, and Vermillion Valley Resort at Edison offers cabins, a restaurant and a store.

These lakes are in the high Sierra. Roads may not be open until sometime in early summer. For information contact the U.S. Forest Service, P.O. Box 300, Shaver Lake, CA 93664, (559) 855-5355.

Golden Trout and Domeland Wilderness Areas (map - p. 160)

In the How to Catch . . . Golden Trout section of this book, it was noted that golden trout were first discovered in the Kern River System around the turn of the century. As can be seen on the accompanying map, goldens inhabited much of the Little Kern River and the South Fork. Today much of this territory is in the Domeland Wilderness and the Golden Trout Wilderness.

First let's look at the Domeland Wilderness. This is where the South Fork of the Kern flows for miles through a deep rock-strewn gorge located between the majestic spires and great white domes of the wilderness to the west and the massive cliffs of the Kern Plateau to the east. Access is from the BLM Long Valley Campground. To get there, take Hwy. 178 out of Bakersfield past Lake Isabella and onto the Chimney Recreation Area turnoff (Cranebrake Road). Go eight miles north, turn west, and follow the signs. An alternate route is to take Nine-Mile Canyon Road west from Rte. 395. Go one-quarter mile past the BLM fire station, turn south, and follow the signs.

The trail leading from Long Valley Campground is rocky and steep, and rattlesnakes inhabit the area. But the adventurous angler, willing to travel through heavy undergrowth, over slick rocks, and between boulders to the bottom of the South Fork trail, will be rewarded with big native rainbows at the end of almost every cast. Also expect some healthy-sized browns. Much of the fishing here is dropping bait or small spinning lures into pockets, through riffles and under overhanging brush. No. 0 Mepps and Roostertails are recommended by one expert. The terrain makes fly casting iffy. Light spinning equipment is a better bet.

This area is seldom fished and is not for tenderfoots. The northern portions of the South Fork in the Domeland is paralleled by the Pacific Crest Trail. Access is via Nine-Mile Canyon Road (off Hwy. 395) to Kennedy Meadow Road (J-

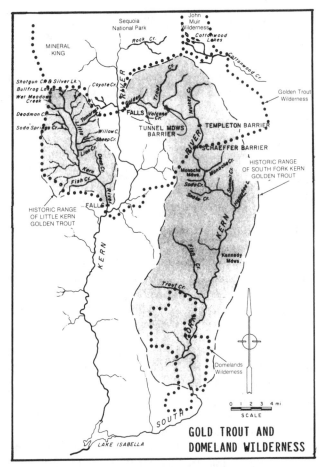

GOLD TROUT AND DOMELAND WILDERNESS

41). For information contact the U.S. Forest Service at Kernville, CA, (760) 376-3781, and the Bureau of Land Management (BLM) in Bakersfield, CA, (805) 391-6000 (ask for the "Chimney Peak Recreation Areas" brochure).

Anglers horsepacking or backpacking into the Golden Trout Wilderness have a chance at four trout species in vast, unspoiled country. In fact, there are four million acres of rugged mountain wilderness. The fishing season runs from June to about October. Be prepared for 90-degree heat, below freezing nights, rain and maybe snow. Many first-time visitors choose the horsepacking option and also hire a professional guide. A typical pack mule can carry 150 pounds of gear more than 20 miles a day. This method allows you to bring along a variety of fishing gear, tents, good food, frying pans, etc. It also reserves your energy for fishing rather than packing with 40 pounds on your back. There are good waters and not so good waters in the Golden Trout Wilderness. Experienced guides can take guests to they types of waters they want and provide insights that produce hookups. Adaptability is the key, for both tackle and tactics. Bring along both fly and spinning equipment. Both standard length and shorter six-foot fly rods with four or five weight lines are useful. Fly selection isn't critical. Bring standard nymphs and dry flies. A five-foot spinning rod teamed with spinners like Roostertails is a solid bet. And don't expect to just hook into some smallish goldens. For example, the Kern, between Little Lake and Mt. Whitney, holds some trophy-sized fish. Creeks and the river have produced browns of 15 to 18 inches, rainbows 8 to 16 inches, and goldens up to 15 inches.

There are several trail heads and pack stations out of Porterville via Hwy. 190. However, the most popular access is probably out of Lone Pine along Hwy. 395 in the Eastern Sierra.

Huntington Lake (map - p. 161)

Huntington lake, located above Fresno via Hwy. 168, combines fine trout and kokanee angling, excellent facilities and a picturesque mountain setting. The lake itself is filled with mountain runoff, so it's cold year-round. This causes some problems for swimmers and waterskiiers, but the fish flourish and grow. They range in size from pan-sized on up to those that exceed 20 inches. Rainbows average 12 to 16 inches. There are also some big German browns. Huntington has about a half a dozen resorts, as well as a number of Forest Service campgrounds. Another nice aspect of Huntington Lake is that shore anglers have just as good a chance of catching a limit as do boat anglers. That's because there are stream inflows, mostly on the north shore, that attract trout to this mostly manageable terrain. Stream angling is also quite productive. The Kaiser Wilderness, just north of the lake, provides a great hike-in and pack-in option to more adventurous visitors.

A note about winds: They come up consistently at about 10:30 in the morning, and then die down about 5:30 in the afternoon. This means anglers do best from sun up to about 9:30 a.m. and again in the evening. Sail boating is quite popular at midday.

Huntington Fishing Seasons													
	J	F	M	A	M	J	J	A	S	O	N	D
Trout					░	░	░	░	░	░		
Kokanee							░	░	░	░		

Good ░ / Fair ░

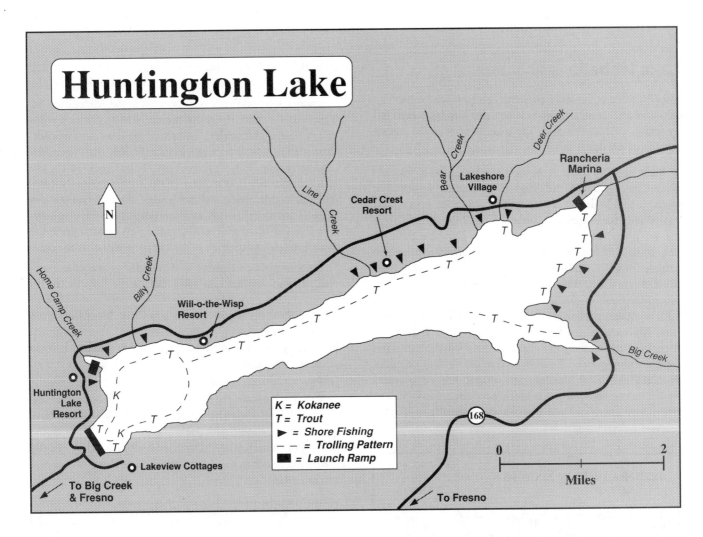

Huntington Fishing Tips

Fishing is good throughout the late spring, summer and early fall. May, June and September are especially good, with the best brown trout action coming in early fall. Kokanee usually turn on in July. Nightcrawlers are king at Huntington. That's because all of the major streams wash nightcrawlers into Huntington, so the native and planted trout both get used to munching on them. Two other good baits are salmon eggs and red worms. When the trout are near shore or near the surface, many Huntington regulars fish crawlers with only a small split shot up the line. Drifting from a boat or hanging them below a bobber also works. As trout move to the bottom (either later in the day or later in the season) use a sliding sinker rig and float them up with an inflator or with a marshmallow. Shore angling is good along much of the north side of the lake, especially at stream inlets. The east shore is also good.

Trollers score by pulling nightcrawlers. Top hardware, for casting or trolling, includes Kastmasters and Phoebes in gold. Big Rapalas are tops for browns over by the dam. Stream anglers hit with crickets, grubs and salmon eggs.

Home Creek, Rancheria Creek and Line Creek are most popular with fly anglers. Use California Mosquitoes, Black Gnats, Woolly Worms and Woolly Buggers.

Near the dam is the hot spot for kokanee. Use a full kokanee rig and troll deep. Leadcore line is one way to get down deep enough.

Huntington Lake Facts

Location: On the western slope of the Sierras at 7,000 feet, about 80 miles northeast of Fresno via Hwy. 168.

Size: Huntington is about 6 miles long and roughly 1/2 mile wide.

Species: Rainbow trout, brown trout, kokanee salmon

Facilities: There are a number of resorts with a range of facilities. These include Huntington Lake Resort, (559) 893-3226 and Cedar Crest Resort, (559) 893-3233. The U.S. Forest Service maintains several campgrounds. Rancheria and Deer Creek, located right on the lake, are considered the most desirable.

Information: U.S. Forest Service, Pineridge District, Shaver Lake, (559) 855-5355. Also see the phone numbers above.

Lake Isabella (map - p. 163)

Isabella is one of several fine Sierra fishing lakes available to Southern and Central California anglers. This big lake is fed by snows of Mt. Whitney, the highest peak in the nation outside of Alaska.

Most noteworthy at Isabella is the largemouth bass angling. Twenty-seven thousand Florida-strain largemouth were planted in the early 1970's. Since then the lake record has steadily moved up to a current 18 lbs. 14 oz.! And fish in the 4-5 pound class are not uncommon. Rainbow trout hit year-round, but tend to go much deeper in the late spring and summer months. Catfish anglers do best from shore, catching 1-3 pounders, with an occasional lunker. Crappie and bluegill abound in the lake. Isabella has complete facilities with eight campgrounds around the lake. One note of caution: High winds can be a problem to boaters at Isabella, especially in the spring months. Find out about the high wind light warning system. Boaters need to get a safety permit at French Gulch Park Headquarters, during regular business hours, before launching. Complete services are available in the nearby towns of Lake Isabella and Kernville.

Isabella Fishing Seasons	J	F	M	A	M	J	J	A	S	O	N	D
Bass		Good	Good	Good	Good	Good	Good	Good	Good	Good	Good	
Catfish				Fair	Good	Good	Good	Good	Good			
Panfish		Fair	Good	Good	Good	Good	Good	Good	Good	Fair		
Trout	Good	Good	Good	Good	Good	Good	Good	Good	Good	Good	Good	Good

Legend: Good (cross-hatch), Fair (single hatch)

Isabella Fishing Tips

Bass is king at Lake Isabella. Good spots include the upper reaches of the north fork, where the old river channel is lined with dead trees. Another bass hot spot is the submerged Edison Canal. It is about 25 feet high and wide and runs from up on the north fork to Engineers Point at the dam. This is a huge reef-like structure that provides an excellent habitat for crawdads and big bass. A depth finder will help you trail it. Locals also watch the way gulls feed on the water. On an east wind, anglers work the north end of the canal. On southwest winds, they fish the northwest part of this structure. Live crawdads, plastic worms, Pig 'n Jigs and deep-diving plugs are all good. Other good bass spots include the Rocky Point

area, Boulder Gulch, the trees along the north fork, Stine Point, Piney Point, and from French Gulch to the dam.

Shore anglers do very well on trout in the colder months. This action usually holds up into early May. Salmon eggs, Power Bait, nightcrawlers, and marshmallows are favorites. Consistently good spots are French Gulch, the north fork sand bar, Ramp 16 in the South Fork, Tillie Creek Gulch, and near the dam. Shallow trolling works with Rapalas, Needlefish and nightcrawlers behind blades. Favorite spinners at Isabella are nickel or copper Blue Foxes and black-yellow-spot Panther Martins. Trolling is the only way to go in the summertime. Concentrate in the deeper water near the dam.

Catfishing is productive and popular at Isabella, especially in the summer and early fall. Some famous catfish haunts are at the north Fork around the airport, around Rocky Point to Stine Point and at Robinson Cove. Most catfish are caught from shore on nightcrawlers and other traditional baits. Lanterns and lawn chairs are used to fish late into the evening. Blue channel, white catfish and bullheads are all taken.

Isabella is known for its crappie, some up to two pounds. A local club planted fish and improved habit so the long-term prospects are good. Look for them around trees in both the north and south forks. Bluegill are abundant. They usually start coming out in good numbers in June. Meal worms are the main bait.

Isabella Lake Facts

Location: In the Sierras, about 45 miles out of Bakersfield via Hwy. 178

Size: Isabella is large, covering 11,400 acres. It's 9 miles in its longest direction and has 38 miles of shoreline.

Species: Largemouth bass, rainbow trout, channel, blue and white catfish, bullheads, crappie, bluegill

Boating: High winds are common at Isabella. Be aware of the wind warning light system. Boaters need to get a safety permit at the French Gulch Point Headquarters, during regular business hours, before launching.

Facilities: The U.S. Forest Service operates a number of campsites around the lake. There are over 600 developed sites and over 1,200 underdeveloped sites. There are several launch ramps around the lake plus a full-service marina at French Gulch. The nearby towns of Kernville and Isabella have motels, restaurants, stores, etc.

Information: U.S. Forest Service, (760) 379-5646; Kern River Valley Chamber of Commerce, (760) 379-5236; Kernville Chamber of Commerce, (760) 376-2629; French Gulch Marina, (760) 379-8774

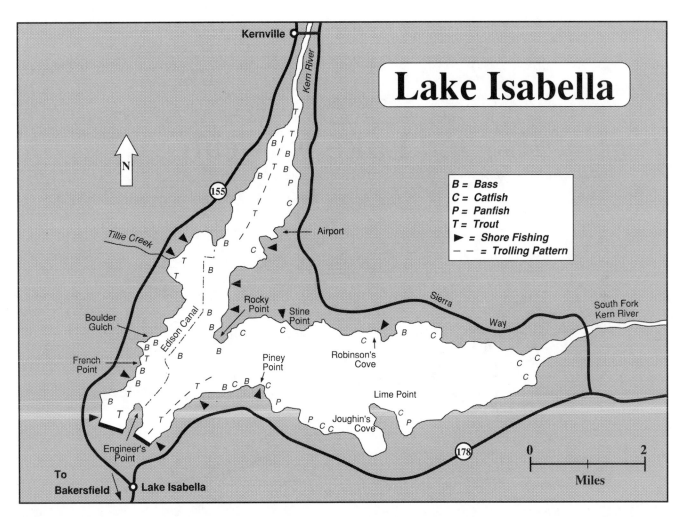

Map showing Lake Isabella with legend: B = Bass, C = Catfish, P = Panfish, T = Trout, ► = Shore Fishing, – – = Trolling Pattern. Locations include Kernville, Kern River, Tillie Creek, Boulder Gulch, French Point, Engineer's Point, Rocky Point, Stine Point, Piney Point, Robinson's Cove, Lime Point, Joughin's Cove, Sierra Way, South Fork Kern River, Airport, Edison Canal, To Bakersfield, Lake Isabella. Highways 155 and 178.

Lake Kaweah (map - p. 164)

Lake Kaweah has rebounded from a problem it had in the late 1980's and is now a good trout and warm-water fishing spot. In the fall of 1987 all fish were eliminated from this lake to prevent Kaweah's white bass from possible migration to the California Delta. The Department of Fish and Game is following a program to rebuild the trout, black bass, catfish and panfish populations. It's now the home of burgeoning bass, panfish and catfish population. It also receives a heavy winter-spring planting of rainbow trout.

Kaweah is a good-sized lake (almost 2,000 surface acres) with 22 miles of fairly steep shoreline. It is located about 17 miles from Visalia and a similar distance from the entrance to Sequoia National Park. Kaweah is maintained and operated by the U.S. Corp. of Engineers. A full-service marina offers complete facilities, including houseboat rentals. This is a good shore-fishing lake. Bank anglers work the entire southern shore, from the launch ramp area all the way to Horse Creek. Shore angling in the Kaweah River, above the reservoir, is also quite good.

Kaweah Fishing Seasons		J	F	M	A	M	J	J	A	S	O	N	D
Bass			▨	▨	▨	▨	▨	▨	▨	▨			
Catfish				▨	▨	▨	▨	▨	▨	▨			
Panfish					▨	▨	▨	▨	▨	▨			
Trout		▨	▨	▨	▨	▨	▨						▨

Legend: ▨ Good, ▨ Fair

Kaweah Fishing Tips

Trout fishing is good all winter and spring. Both pan-sized planters and brook stock are transferred to Kaweah, so anglers have a chance to hook into some really large rainbows. Trollers take trout with Kastmasters, Needlefish, or a yellow Roostertail. The best routes in an elongated circle around the

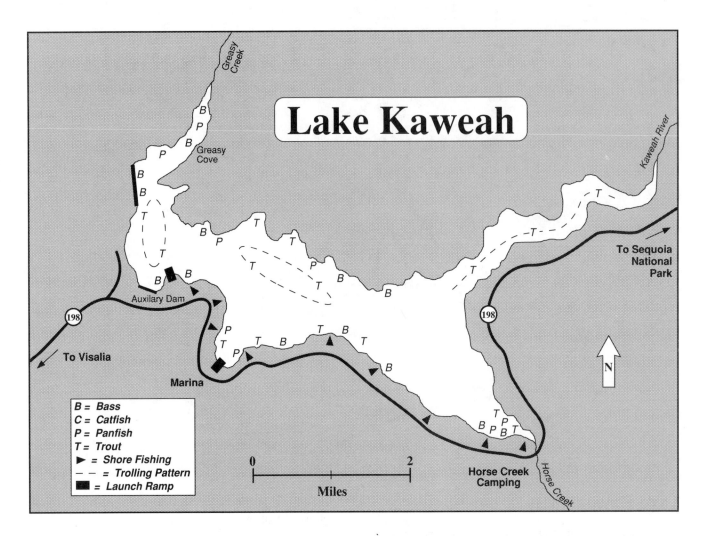

middle of the lake, out in front of the north shore, or in front of the dam. Best bait angling is from the south shore or from a boat along the north shore. Power Bait, nightcrawlers and salmon eggs are some of the top baits. When the lake starts filling (usually around April 1) the best trout angling often takes place near the Kaweah River end of the reservoir.

Kaweah has both northern largemouths and Florida large-mouths. Look for them up in the shallows both in April, and early and late in the day, later in the season. They suspend or hold near the shoreline in deeper water in warmer months. Top baits are plastics in motor oil, clear pepper and sparkle, smoke sparkle, green weenie, and electric blue. A chartreuse or pink fintail is good on worms. Crawdads and shad-colored crank-baits are also producers, as are spinnerbaits with light-colored skirts and nickel blades.

Crappie fishing also heats up in April as the lake fills. Horse Creek and the marina area are two traditional hot spots. But it pays to hunt around for good concentrations. Most are hand-sized, but some range up to one or two pounds. Crappie like to crunch small minnows, either free-lined or below a bobber. The best mini-jig color at Kaweah is white tail and red bodies.

Another option for trout is the Kaweah River which paral-lels Hwy. 198 from the lake into Sequoia National Park. Many anglers concentrate on the section just above the reservoir. There is good bank access from the highway. If you want to get away from fellow anglers, move further on up stream. For one thing, fly fishing is better up there. But stealth is called for. The water is usually very clear and shallow. All but the north fork is fishable the entire summer.

```
┌─────────────────────────────────────────────┐
│              Kaweah Lake Facts               │
├─────────────────────────────────────────────┤
│ Location: Kaweah is in the rolling foothills │
│ of the Sierras below Sequoia National Park   │
│ about 20 miles east of Visalia via Hwy. 198. │
│                                              │
│ Size: Kaweah covers 2,000 acres at full      │
│ pool, is about six miles long, and has 22    │
│ miles of shoreline.                          │
│                                              │
│ Species: Rainbow trout, largemouth bass,     │
│ catfish, crappie and bluegill                │
│                                              │
│ Facilities: There are two launch ramps, a    │
│ marina, camping (78 sites at Horse Creek),   │
│ fishing boat rentals, and houseboat rentals. │
│                                              │
│ Information: Corp. of Engineers, Lemon Cove, │
│ CA 93244, (559) 597-2301; Kaweah Marina,     │
│ (559) 597-2526.                              │
└─────────────────────────────────────────────┘
```

Kern River

Many associate the Kern River with golden trout and back country wilderness fishing, and rightly so. But there is another Kern River when it comes to fishing. It's the portion of the Kern immediately above and below Lake Isabella. In fact, when trout angling slows in the heat of summer at Isabella, in contrast, it just keeps humming along in the Kern River. And we're not just talking pan-sized planters. Rainbows move out of Isabella in the summertime in pursuit of colder water. Some run up to 2 to 4 pounds.

The Kern River above Isabella is parallel for 25 miles or more along Hwy. 155 from Kernville all the way to the Johnsondale Bridge east of Johnsondale. Access is excellent here and there are a number of U.S. Forest Service campgrounds for overnighting. Besides holdover trout from Isabella, the Kern above Isabella is planted year-round, in some sections, weekly, and in others, every other week. Locals in the know recommend these hot spots (moving up river from Kernville): the Kernville Park, the hole above the bridge in Kernville, at the KR3 power plant, at the Hospital Flat Campground, Gold Ledge Campground, Corral Creek Campground, above and below the Fairview Dam, Limestone Campgrounds and the Johnsondale Bridge. Above the Johnsondale Bridge note the special lure and take restrictions.

Anglers working below the Lake Isabella dam find fish all the way from the dam outflows to the mouth of the Kern River Canyon. Planting is done from Isabella Dam to Democrat Hot Springs. Hot spots are the campgrounds at Democrat, Sandy Flats and Hobo. All are accessible from Hwy. 178 and have good bank fishing. Further upstream, trout are taken below the main dam and the auxiliary dam, depending on water flow. For information contact the Department of Fish and Game, Kernville, (760) 376-2846.

Kings River

The Kings River, which runs from Kings Canyon National Park down into Pine Flat Reservoir and then down into the San Joaquin Valley offers some good spring and early summer trout prospects. To reach the Kings, take Hwy. 180 east out of Fresno and then follow Trimmer Springs Road toward Pine Flat. In the lower river, below the dam at Pine Flat, there are three popular and productive spots to pursue stocked rainbow: 1) in Winton Park below the town of Piedra, 2) at Chonumni Park in the bend of the river above Piedra, 3) around the bridge at the dam. Cold outflows from the base of the dam make for good trouting. Bait anglers do best in these waters.

Fly anglers and those looking for a change of pace should head upriver to the Kirch Flats Campground above the lake. Good fly waters run from there on up the main river all the way to Garlic Falls—about a 10-mile stretch. There is good access via the road that runs to Garnet Dike, about three miles above Kirch Flats, and then from a trail that leads to the falls. Local experts recommend working tailouts and riffles. Catch rates are not high, but there are some good-sized rainbows along here. Check for catch restrictions in these waters. Best time in the upper river is usually in June. Try the Elk Hair Caddis.

The north fork of the Kings River is another choice. It breaks off the main river just above Kirch Flats campgrounds. Anglers work all along the 20-mile stream until it reaches Blackrock Reservoir. Black Rock Road provides access. Black Rock Reservoir, which has a Forest Service campground, is good bait and lure water. For information contact the Department of Fish and Game, Fresno, (559) 222-3761 or use a Sierra National Forest map.

Millerton Lake (map - p. 167)

Millerton Lake offers a broader selection of fishing opportunities than most other lakes in California. This large, 5,000 surface acre impoundment features spotted bass, striped bass, smallmouth bass, largemouth bass and American shad fishing, as well as catfish and panfish. For the angler who is looking for a change-of-pace this is just the lake to try next.

Most spotted bass are small, so anglers catch many below the legal size. Many sub-legal smallmouths are also hooked, but bronzebacks run to up four pounds. It's not unusual to take striped bass in the 4-8 pound range. Shad are caught when they make a spawning run up in the headwaters and rivers. Millerton is a fully developed lake recreation facility. There are campgrounds, hiking, all types of boating, a swimming beach and full-service marina. Millerton Lake is located about 20 miles from both Fresno and Madera in the Millerton Lake State Recreation Area.

Millerton Fishing Seasons	J	F	M	A	M	J	J	A	S	O	N	D
Bass, Smallmouth			Fair	Good	Good	Good	Good	Good	Good	Good	Fair	
Bass, Spotted			Fair	Good	Good	Good	Good	Good	Good	Good	Fair	
Catfish				Fair	Good	Good	Good	Good	Good	Fair		
Panfish			Fair	Good	Good	Good	Good	Good	Good	Fair		
Striper		Fair	Good	Good	Good	Good	Good	Good	Good	Good	Fair	

Legend: Good, Fair

Millerton Fishing Tips

Millerton has 43 miles of shoreline, is three miles at its widest point, and it stretches more than 16 miles. So there is lots of territory to cover. The premier attraction at Millerton, for anglers in the know, are smallmouths. Some say it's the best bronzeback lake in the area. Here are the areas to concentrate on. The rocky points and coves on the north side of the dam are good. Across the lake, don't overlook Winchell Bay. The big rocks, rocky points and walls are all good. Moving uplake again, the Finegold arm area is excellent smallmouth territory—a split shot works well here. Use grubs or four-inch plastic worms in brown with orange or chartreuse tails. Above Finegold in the narrows concentrate your effort on the south shore. You may even hook up with some largemouths here.

All the way up at Temperance Flat, variety is the name of the game. Here anglers hook into smallmouths, largemouths, spots, maybe even a stray trout from upriver, and of course, stripers. Millerton has lots of striped bass which can weigh up to 25 pounds or more. Most linesides are taken by drifting jumbo-sized minnows or by trolling large plugs like Rebels, Cordell Spots or Rapala Fat Raps. Early and late the fish are in shallow water, but during the day they're down 20-40 feet. Good spots include the face of the dam in the main lake and up the San Joaquin arm.

There are some classic brushy largemouth flats in the main body of the lake. The most popular offerings for spotted bass are small plastic worms and plastic grubs. Top-water bass lures sometimes work early in the morning. One of the most consistently productive areas for spots is the Finegold arm. Anglers hunting for large spots (up to five pounds) should try live crawdads. The most popular shad lure is probably the small, white jig. For more information on shad fishing, see Marketscope's *Fishing in Northern California* book.

Millerton Lake Facts
Location: Millerton lake is located about 20 miles from both Fresno and Madera, in the Millerton Lake State Recreation Area.
Size: Millerton covers 5,000 acres and has 43 miles of shoreline.
Species: Smallmouth bass, largemouth bass, spotted bass, striped bass, catfish and panfish.
Facilities: There are almost 200 campsites (including some boat-in and boat access sites), small launch ramps, a full-service marina, boat rental, picnic areas, and swim beaches.
Information: Millerton Lake State Recreation Area, (559) 822-2225; Department of Fish and Game, Fresno, (559) 222-3761

John Muir and Ansel Adams Wilderness

As noted earlier in this chapter, Edison Lake and Florence Lake are jumping off points for backpackers and anglers looking forward to experience some spectacular wilderness fishing. Both lakes operate ferries which carry backpackers, hikers, and people and horses from nearby park stations to the lakes' far ends. Once dropped off, the trails lead to some fine golden, brook, and brown trout waters. The Edison Lake ferry departs at 9 a.m. and 4 p.m., while the Florence Lake ferry operates every two hours beginning at 8:30 a.m.

The Edison ferry leads to the Mono Creek drainage. This area, above Edison lake, has 31 lakes ranging in size from

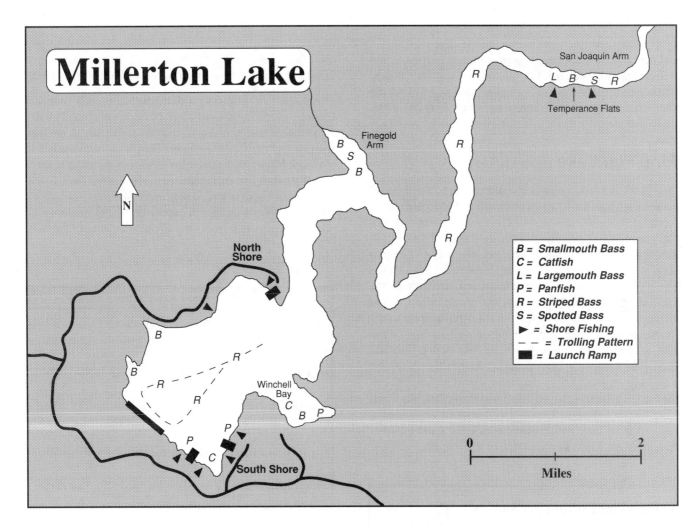

Millerton Lake

San Joaquin Arm

R

L B S R

Temperance Flats

Finegold Arm

B
S
B

R

R

North Shore

R

B

R

B

R

R

Winchell Bay

C

B P

P

P

C

South Shore

N

B = Smallmouth Bass
C = Catfish
L = Largemouth Bass
P = Panfish
R = Striped Bass
S = Spotted Bass
► = Shore Fishing
– – = Trolling Pattern
■ = Launch Ramp

0   2

Miles

acre to over 70 acres. These and the connecting streams provide some fine trouting, especially for golden trout. The Pacific Creek Trail also passes by the upper end of Edison. It provides access, both in the north and south directions, to other trout opportunities.

Florence Lake is on the south fork of the San Joaquin. Its ferry provides access to trails that lead to the Upper San Joaquin, Piute Canyon, French Canyon and Humphrey's Basin. These are all premier golden trout haunts. Many anglers access these spots from trail heads along Rte. 395 in the Eastern Sierra (see that chapter for more specifics).

There is one more option above Florence Lake along the San Joaquin. It's the Muir Trail Ranch. At the ferry drop-off, ranch hands will meet you for a five-mile horseback ride (about two hours) that passes through spectacular scenery and leads to the ranch. It offers on-ranch, fly-only golden trout fishing, accommodations, wonderful food, horses and odor-free hot springs. For information write Muir Trail Ranch, P.O.

Box 3005, Ahwahnee, CA 93601 (November to May), or P.O. Box 176, Lakeshore, CA 93634 (June to October).

Another great place is the Bear Creek drainage. Here there are over 50 lakes, miles and miles of streams, and you can catch all four trout species (golden, brown, brookies, rainbow) in the same day. Actually, you can catch all four in Bear Creek. Bear Creek joins the San Joaquin River near Mono Hot Springs. Access is either from the trail head at Bear Creek Diversion Dam out on Mono Hot Springs or via the Edison ferry from the top of the lake.

Bear Creek has everything: deep pools, sustained runs, riffles and a rocky bottom. Look for goldens in the upper reaches of Bear Creek, its east, west and south forks, and along the Hilgard and Orchard Creek tributaries. Good golden lakes include Seven Gables, Beverly, Sandpiper, Three Islands, Rose, Apollo, Orchard and Vee. One pleasant aspect of the Bear Creek drainage is that its golden trout waters are not above the timber line. Streams are lined with quaking aspen and cottonwood trees amid a predominantly lodgepole and Jeffrey pine forest cover. For information contact the U.S. Forest Service at Mono Hot Springs at (559) 877-3138 or the main office of the Sierra National Forest at (559) 297-0706.

Pine Flat Lake (map - p. 169)

Pine Flat Lake is a fine fishing resource. This 21-mile long, meandering lake has 67 miles of shoreline. It is located in the foothills about 30 miles east of Fresno, in the King's River Canyon. Fishing opportunities include spotted and small-mouth bass averaging about three pounds, with a few up to six pounds. Trout, both rainbow and browns, are large at Pine Flat. Five pounders are not that unusual. Catfish are on the small side (averaging 1 1/2 pounds) but are plentiful. Crappie fishing heats up in late February and they can average three-quarter pounds. There are three full-service marinas on the lake, all with launch ramps, boat rental, etc. Both private and U.S. Forest Service campgrounds are nearby. Also, the King's River itself offers outstanding trout angling. Below the Pine Flat Dam is planted water, and above Pine Flat Lake, from Garnet Dike upstream, is a wild trout fishery allowing only artificial lures with barbless hooks. For more information, read the Kings River section of the chapter.

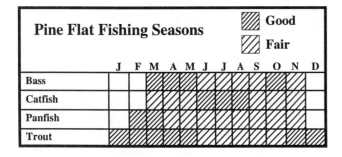

Pine Flat Fishing Seasons													Good Fair
	J	F	M	A	M	J	J	A	S	O	N	D	
Bass													
Catfish													
Panfish													
Trout													

Pine Flat Fishing Tips

As is true at many Sierra lakes, spring is the best time at Pine Flat Lake for trout, bass and crappie. And since this lake is farther south than many others, spring comes earlier. If the water is murky from runoff, bright offerings or bait work best. Bass go for crawdads and minnows. White spinnerbaits are also good, and plastic worms (purple and black) produce. Crickets are good for smallmouths. Use just enough split shot to reach the target area. Crappies go for red and white mini-jigs and live minnows. Needlefish in nickel, frog or red-dotted are productive for trout trolling. Big Creek Cove is one good

shore fishing area for trout in the spring. Lake elevation is only 1,000 feet, so wintertime anglers usually have decent weather.

At times there is also a good crappie bite in early summer. Crappie, averaging about 12 inches, are taken around all the docks on mini-jigs or small minnows. Catfish is another summer and early fall highlight. They're mostly small, but plentiful. Minnows, chicken livers, anchovies and mackerel are all good. A hot area is the north shore from Deer Creek to Trimmer. Night fishing is permitted. Summertime bass go for Green Weenies, salt-and-pepper grubs and minnows. A good place to work is from Deer Creek to the head of the lake.

Pine Flat Lake Facts

Location: Take Hwy. 180 east out of Fresno. In Sanger, head towards Piedra via Rainbow Ave. and then Trimmer Springs Rd.

Size: Pine Flat is narrow and 21 miles long. There are 67 miles of shoreline.

Species: Rainbow trout, smallmouth bass, spotted bass, largemouth bass, catfish, crappie and bluegill

Facilities: There are three full-service marinas, boat rental, and several private campgrounds and resorts as well as public campgrounds.

Information: Pine Flat Lake, Piedra, (559) 787-2589; Doyle's, (559) 787-2387

Sequoia National Park

Highway 198 out of Visalia leads to Sequoia National Park. For some fine high-country trouting take the Mineral King Road entrance into the park. It cuts off Hwy. 198 four miles beyond Three Rivers. At the end of the road you'll be in the Mineral King Basin. Within a 4-5 mile radius there are 16 fishable lakes. Most hold eastern brook trout. Fishing is best early in the season and from late August through October. Anglers also fish the east fork of the Kaweah River, both above and below the Mineral King's store.

Mineral King is also a convenient launching point for a back-country trip to the Little Kern River drainage in the Golden Trout Wilderness five miles south of Mineral King. The head waters of the main Kern River drainage are also in the Sequoia National Park, about 12 miles to the east. Pack-in anglers work the Kern itself as well as some fine inflows such as Golden Trout Creek which is just inside the Golden

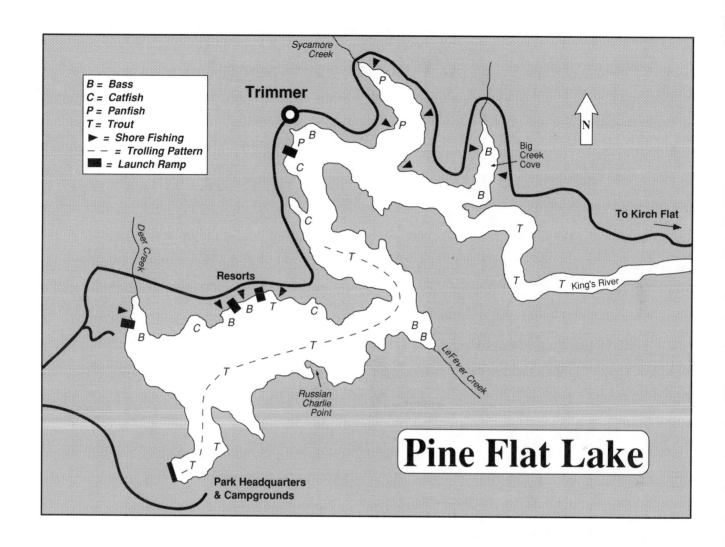

Shaver Lake (map - p. 170)

Shaver Lake is a premier trout and kokanee salmon lake in central California. At 5,500 feet and surrounded by forest, it's a high mountain delight. As part of the Southern California Edison hydroelectric system, there are fine camping facilities provided by Edison and the U.S. Forest Service. Shaver Lake is about 45 miles up the Sierras from Fresno and is accessible and fished all year long.

Shore fishing for trout at many spots along the west shore is best from December to the end of April. This is also the time for shallow trolling. Brown trout in Shaver are large (many over four pounds), and taken mostly in the spring. Rainbow are both pan-sized planters and 2-7 pound planted brood stock. Shaver also offers bass (mostly smallmouth), catfish and panfish. The crappie season peaks in April and May, but there are both good and spotty years for these slabslides.

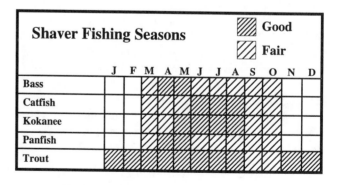

Shaver Fishing Seasons												▨ Good ▨ Fair
	J	F	M	A	M	J	J	A	S	O	N	D
Bass			▨	▨	▨	▨	▨	▨	▨	▨		
Catfish			▨	▨	▨	▨	▨	▨	▨	▨		
Kokanee			▨	▨	▨	▨	▨	▨	▨	▨		
Panfish			▨	▨	▨	▨	▨	▨	▨	▨		
Trout	▨	▨	▨	▨	▨	▨	▨	▨	▨	▨	▨	▨

Shaver Fishing Tips

Shore trout anglers score with nightcrawlers, crickets and salmon eggs. Try inflating your nightcrawlers with a worm blower to keep them off the bottom. Another local trick is to use vacuum-packed salmon roe. It "milks" in the water,

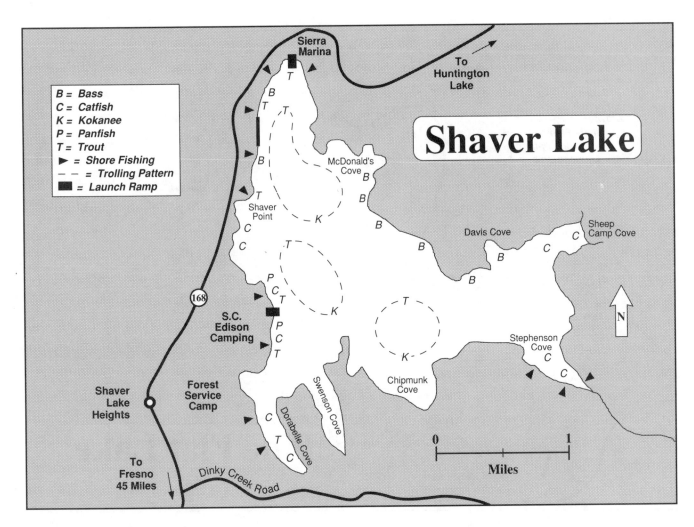

attracting the trout. Casting spoons and spinners also work early and late in the day. Trolling is the big on-the-water technique at Shaver. In cooler months use mono line, Cowbells or Half-Fast flashers and a three-foot leader tied to a hooked nightcrawler, a Triple Teaser or a Needlefish. The following are some local tricks. If #1 Needlefish are bringing in 12-inch rainbows, switch to #3 in the same pattern to score bigger fish. Also try Rebels and Rapalas up to six inches in a trout finish. The big browns and rainbows eat the little guys. Finally, try fishing at night. This is when nightcrawlers on the bottom score big browns.

Kokanee are caught by trout trollers. Summertime trollers need to go deeper with leadcore line or downriggers. Four or five colors of leadcore may be just about right. The slowest trout months are September and October, but fish are taken even then. Brown trout fishing seems best in late fall and early spring. This is also true of Shaver's brook trout. Rainbows are consistent all year, but the size of the catch varies.

Smallmouth bass are most commonly found near the dam and along the rocks from McDonald Cove all the way east past Doris Cove. Gitzits are a top producer.

<table>
<tr><td colspan="1">Shaver Lake Facts</td></tr>
</table>

Location: Shaver Lake is about four and a half or five hours away from metropolitan Los Angeles via I-5, Hwy. 99 and Hwy. 168. Fresno is 45 miles away.

Size: Shaver covers 2,000 acres with 13 miles of shoreline.

Species: Trout (browns, rainbow, brook), kokanee, bass (largemouth and smallmouth), crappie, bluegill

Camping: The U.S. Forest Service has 67 developed sites at Dorabelle Cove, (559) 855-5355. Camp Edison has 150 developed sites plus a small boat launch ramp, (559) 841-3134.

Other Facilities: There are full marina services at Sierra Marina, (559) 841-3324. Shaver Lake Heights has restaurants, tackle stores, etc.

Information: See the telephone numbers listed above.

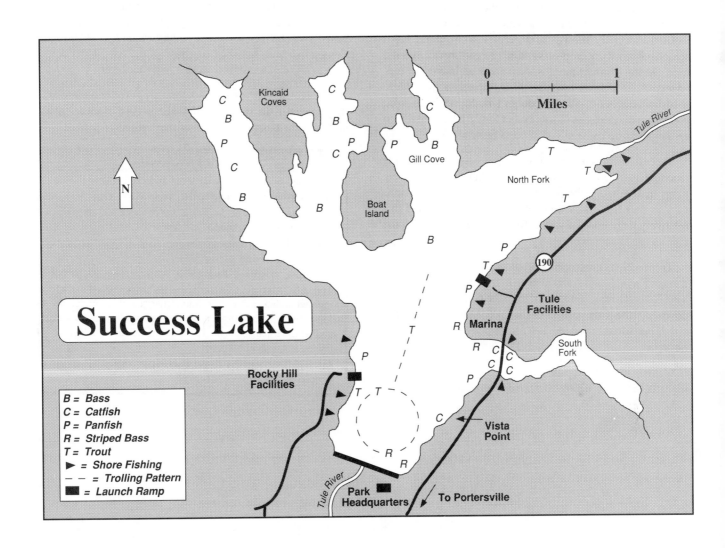

Success Lake (map - p. 171)

Success Lake is a popular fishery outside of Porterville at an elevation of 640 feet in the Southern Sierra foothills. This reservoir, which is under the jurisdiction of the U.S. Army Corp. of Engineers, features trout, largemouth bass (northern strain), catfish, crappie, redear sunfish, bluegill, as well as good striped bass action. This combination provides year-round activity for Success anglers.

There are complete facilities, and all types of water sports are permitted including waterskiing and swimming. A wildlife management area, which surrounds the Kincade Coves, permits in-season, shotgun-only hunting.

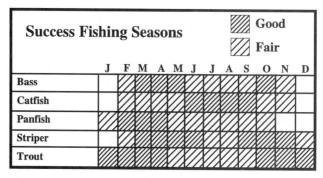

Success Fishing Seasons		Good												
				Fair										
	J	F	M	A	M	J	J	A	S	O	N	D		
Bass														
Catfish														
Panfish														
Striper														
Trout														

Success Fishing Tips

Largemouth bass anglers concentrate on the coves at the north end of the lake when the fish move into shallow water to spawn. Live baits, including shad from the lake and waterdogs, are productive this time of year. Another good bet is plastic worms, especially browns and purples with glitter. Later season bassers work drop-offs and other structures all over the lake. During summer months, bass show an interest in top-waters. A local favorite is the 11-S Rapala—a long, slim, shad-imitating lure. Success doesn't boast the large-sized black bass that are seen in some other SoCal lakes, but five to six pounders do come out of Success quite often.

Success stripers average four to five pounds, with some reaching up to 15 pounds. Most are caught by trollers pulling plugs that imitate either trout or large shad. Best locations vary as bait fish and schools of stripers move around this relatively large body of water. But near the dam and off the marina are always worth a try.

Trout seekers most often find success by working near the dam and launch ramp, and also up in the northern fork of the Tule River. Often planted trout from the river work their way down into the Tule portion of the lake. Most trout are pan-sized, but some brood-stock-sized rainbows are planted in Success.

Catfish in Success run from 3-15 pounds, with a few monsters running up to 30 pounds. In summertime, early mornings and late evenings are the best fishing times. Some good spots are by the dam, along Vista Point, in the original Tule River channel, and at the south fork, Hwy. 190 bridge. Top catfish baits are shad (because of the cats' local diet), anchovies, nightcrawlers, worms and mackerel.

The Kincaid Coves are also great areas for crappie when they spawn in the spring. And the upper end of these coves are good for bluegill throughout the summer.

Success Lake Facts

Location: Success is located about midway between Fresno and Bakersfield, near Porterville, off of Hwy. 190.

Size: This reservoir on the Tule River covers 2,400 acres and has 30 miles of shoreline.

Species: Rainbow trout, largemouth bass, striped bass, catfish, crappie, redear sunfish, bluegill

Facilities: There are about 100 developed campsites at the Tule area. All types of water activities are permitted including swimming and waterskiing. Other facilities include a full-service marina, three launch ramps, store, hot showers and wildlife management area. Boat rental services include fishing boats and houseboats.

Information: Success Lake, Porterville, (559) 784-0215; Success Marina, (559) 781-2078.

Special: Float Tubing

There was a time not too many years ago when float tubes were not allowed on many SoCal waters. But things have changed. Float tubes, which fill the void between shore fishing and boat fishing, have arrived. The logic of float tubes cannot be denied. Shore fishing is inexpensive and convenient. But access is restricted. Boat fishing provides access to most good spots, but it expensive and cumbersome, at times. Float tubes allow shore anglers to move out onto the water like boaters, but with equipment that fits in the trunk of a car and costs only $100-$200.

Float tubes have come a long way. Originally, they weren't much more than a device that converted a 16-inch auto tire inner tube into a floating seat. Now they're made of high-quality nylon and feature shoulder straps, numerous storage pockets, back rests, quick-release buckles, D-rings, handles, etc.

Float tubes are extremely stable and maneuverable vessels. Their seat is located to provide a low center of gravity so capsizing is difficult. Swim fins provide steering and propulsion. Some say sitting in a float tube is not unlike lounging in an easy chair. If you have concerns or trepidations, borrow one from a friend and try it out in a small pond or swimming pool. Standard size 20-inch tubes are sufficient for most individuals. Several manufacturers also offer a 22-inch model. A Coast Guard approved flotation vest is strongly recommended.

Float tube swim fins come in the traditional front flipper version and in a heel flipper version. Front flippers provide the most propulsion but, of course, they move the tuber backwards. They are also difficult to walk in. Heel flippers offer less propulsion, but if you're angling where you're in and out of the water a lot, they may be best. Where large distances need to be covered on the water, front flippers provide the needed range. Some float tube anglers take advantage of the front flipper locomotion to "troll" bait or plastics along the bottom.

Except in the warmest of water, chest-high waders are essential. Most anglers use latex or neoprene. Waderless tubers wear long pants to protect legs from brush, tules, sunken debris (like old car bodies), etc. An old pair of soft shoes rounds out the basic equipment.

Actually, float tubers have a stealth advantage over boaters. Tubers make no sound and have a very low-to-the-water profile. Most new tubers report with surprise on how well they blend in with nature. Fish just don't seem to consider a float tuber as an intruder. And the small size of a float tube allows anglers to fish spots that not even a small boat could reach. One hint: make sure all your underwater attire is dark so you don't spook the fish.

Float tubers can use just about any fishing techniques that boat anglers use. We've already mentioned trolling. Flipping is also as natural, as is live bait and dry flies. Long casts are typically not necessary with lures, bait or flies. Tubers just move in closer than boat anglers and then just flip or pitch out their offering. Fly casters need to adjust the back cast to avoid skimming the water behind them. Fly rod float tubing on still water has many of the same appeals as stream wading.

Space to "put things" and to "put down" things is limited on float tubes. Some type of rod holder is essential. If your tube doesn't have one, purchase a strap-on model. All float tubes have built-in storage space for small tackle items, lures, first aid items, insect repellent, tools, a puncture repair kit, air pump, clothing item, etc. If you need more storage, strap-on accessories are available. Don't forget a landing net and stringer. They attach conveniently to the tubes D-rings.

Float tubing opportunities are mushrooming in Southern California. For example, in 1991 the lakes along the State Water Project were opened up to float tube anglers. So now some of the best fishing in the state for spotted bass, large-mouth bass, trout, panfish and even striped bass is there for the picking at Pyramid, Perris and Silverwood Reservoirs. When you travel north, don't forget your tube since this agreement also opens up San Luis, Del Valle and Oroville Reservoirs. Regulations require float tube anglers on these waters to remain within 150 feet of the shoreline, wear a Coast Guard approved floatation device, carry a whistle or horn, wear waders and shoes and show at least 12 square inches of orange material a foot above the water line (a hunting cap is the ticket).

Another great set of SoCal lakes that permit float tube angling are the City of San Diego lakes: Otay, Hodges, El Capitan, Sutherland, San Vicente and Miramar. These lakes, of course, are famous for their monster Florida-strain large-mouth bass. Trout fishing in the winter months can also be excellent. There are two other San Diego lakes not in the city chain that also permit float tubing—Lake Morena and Lake Cuyamaca. By the way, the safety regulations described above for the State Water Project reservoirs apply to almost all lakes that permit float tube angling.

In the San Bernardino mountains, there are two good opportunities—Lake Gregory, near Crestline, and the famous Big Bear Lake. Both require purchase of a launch ticket so check on local requirements.

Oso Lake, a privately operated catch-and-release basswater located in Orange County, is now also open to float tubes.

Of course, many lakes in the Southern and Eastern Sierra are perfect float tube hangouts, with the fall season at Crowley Lake being the most famous.

Finally, don't overlook the miles and miles of great float tubing waters in the Colorado River system. The tule and brush-filled, slow-moving backwaters are great for bass and panfish. Some of the best are the Topock Marsh area north of Lake Havasu, Palo Verde south of Blythe and the whole section of backwaters stretching from the Imperial Dam and Martinez Lake just above Yuma all the way to Cibola Wildlife Reservation.

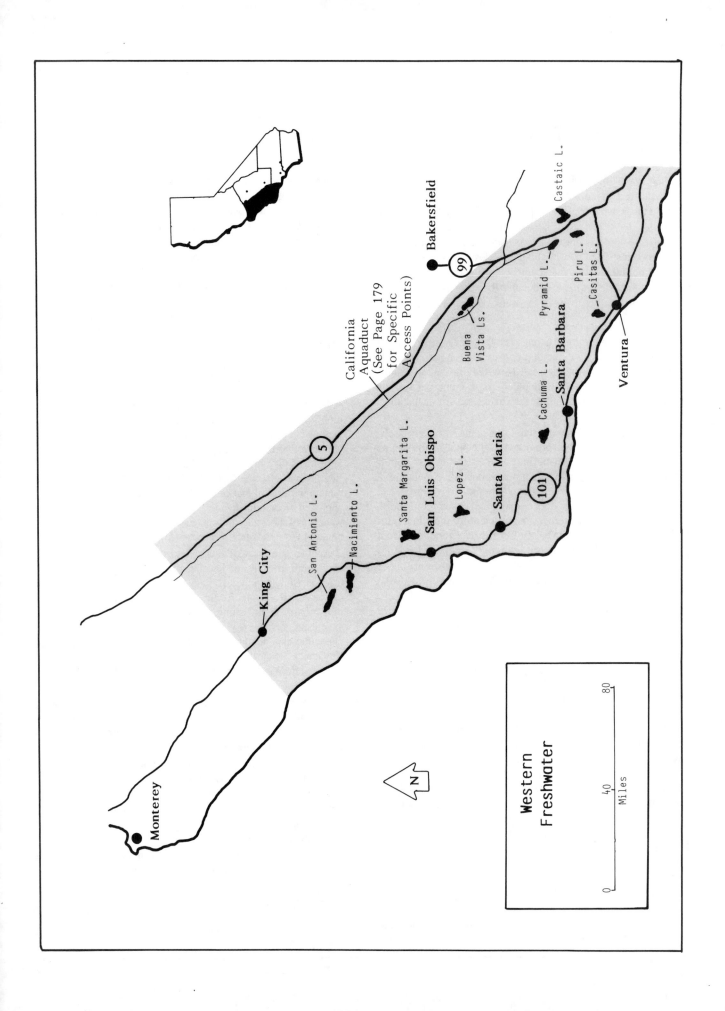

Western
Freshwater

Miles

California
Aquaduct
(See Page 179
for Specific
Access Points)

Bakersfield

Castaic L.

Piru L.

Pyramid L.

Casitas L.

Buena
Vista Ls.

Ventura

Cachuma L.

Santa Barbara

Lopez L.

Santa Maria

San Luis Obispo

Santa Margarita L.

Nacimiento L.

San Antonio L.

King City

Monterey

Western Freshwater Fishing

Generally speaking, the lakes in Southern California are on the smaller side. Of course there are exceptions throughout the Southland, and in the Western Freshwater Fishing region, the exceptions dominate. The primary fishing lakes, all of which are featured in this section, are almost all quite large—some are miles and miles long. So at most locales there is lots of room for waterskiing, camping and hiking, as well as for fishing.

Two other distinct characteristics of the lakes in this area are the variety and size of the fish available. Four waters (Buena Vista, Pyramid, San Antonio, and the California Aqueduct) produce many striped bass in the 5 to 10 pound range, and some up to 30 pounds plus. Both Casitas and Castaic are known for the size of their largemouth bass—some weighing up to 20 pounds. And then there is the excellent white bass fishing at Lake Nacimiento. This is all topped off by the California Aqueduct—the longest fishing hole east of the Pacific Ocean.

All of the waters described in this chapter are shown on the map on the opposite page. Read up on them and then hit the water—you won't be disappointed!

Buena Vista Lakes (map - p. 176)

Buena Vista Lake combines fine year-round fishing with a modern, complete, 1600 acre recreational facility. Lake Evans, the smaller (86 acres) of the two Buena Vista Lakes, is dedicated to angling. A main attraction is the trout planting program (nothing less than 3/4 pounds) that runs from November to early April. Lake Webb is much larger (873 acres) and provides excellent bass fishing (both largemouth and striped) as well as sailing and waterskiing. Webb Lake is one of several lakes along the California Aqueduct that is known for its fine striped bass fishing. Facilities at Buena Vista include over 100 developed campsites, bait and tackle shops, picnic areas, snack bar, grocery store, and laundromat. Each lake has paved launch ramps. Buena Vista Lakes (formally called the Buena Vista Aquatic Recreation Area) is 23 miles southwest of Bakersfield and about 115 miles north of Los Angeles.

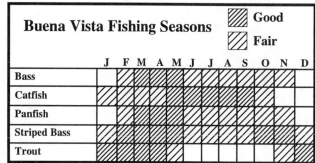

Buena Vista Fishing Seasons													Good
													Fair
	J	F	M	A	M	J	J	A	S	O	N	D	
Bass		▨	▨	▨	▨	▨	▨	▨	▨	▨	▨		
Catfish	▨	▨	▨	▨	▨	▨	▨	▨	▨	▨	▨	▨	
Panfish			▨	▨	▨	▨	▨	▨	▨	▨	▨		
Striped Bass	▨	▨	▨	▨	▨	▨	▨	▨	▨	▨	▨	▨	
Trout	▨	▨	▨	▨							▨	▨	

Buena Vista Fishing Tips

Both Evans and Webb lakes are home to a variety of warm-water species: stripers, largemouth bass, catfish, crappie and bluegill. But the smaller lake, Evans, is really the fishing lake—in winter because it is stocked with 10-12 inch trout plus some trophies up to 9 pounds, and in summer because there is a 5 m.p.h. boat speed limit. Lake Webb is very popular for waterskiing, etc., but off-season anglers and early and late anglers do just fine there.

During stocking months trout are taken all day at Evans, but morning and late afternoons are consistent winners. Both lakes are primarily irrigation ponds, and when water is pumped in or out, fishing usually improves for all species. During pumping the top fishing areas at Evans are at the inlet where the water flows into Lake Evans from the California Aqueduct, and at the outlet area where the water is pumped between Lake Evans and Lake Webb. When the water isn't circulating, shore anglers do well all around Evans. Boat anglers find good action around the islands. Evans is shallow, averaging about 11 feet, so trollers pull small spinners and spoons with no weight.

Stripers up to 30 pounds have been taken from both lakes—average stripers are in the 7 to 10 pound range. Best baits are blood worms, shad or anchovies. Trollers pull Rattlin' Spots

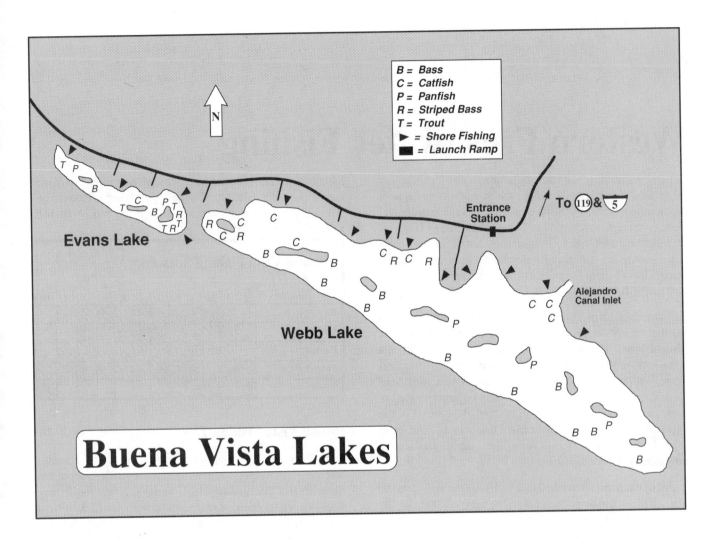

B = Bass
C = Catfish
P = Panfish
R = Striped Bass
T = Trout
► = Shore Fishing
■ = Launch Ramp

Evans Lake

Webb Lake

Entrance Station

To 119 & 5

Alejandro Canal Inlet

Buena Vista Lakes

or broken-back Rebels. At Evans, fish the inlet and outlet areas and around the islands. At Webb, concentrate on the west end of the lake where the water is pumped into Lake Evans and at the gas dock. A local secret is to fish both lakes with live shad. Hook them just under the backbone or through the tip and free-spool them. When you find the shad schools in the lakes, you'll find the striper.

Most largemouths are in the 1 1/2 to 4 pound range. At Evans, fish the tules, around the islands, off the rocky points and any drop-offs. Plastic worms, nightcrawlers and spinnerbaits are tops at both lakes. In Webb, the best bucketmouthing is off the rocky points on the south side of the lake. Also work the weedy areas around many of the islands.

Evans has yielded catfish up to 30 pounds. Cut mackerel, anchovies, liver or prepared baits are effective enticements. Evans catfish are all over, but the inlet and outlet areas are tops when water is circulating. At Webb, cats can be had in the outlet area or in the deeper holes.

At Evans, crappies in the 1-2 pound range are common. Mini-jigs and meal worms are fish-getters. Work offerings off docks and in the short brush areas around the islands.

Buena Vista Lake Facts
Location: 115 miles north of Los Angeles and 23 miles southwest of Bakersfield. The lake is 6 miles west of I-5. Use the Hwy. 119 exit.
Size: Lake Evans covers 86 acres and is a fishing-only lake. Lake Webb covers 873 acres and provides water recreation and fishing.
Species: Striped and largemouth bass, trout (in Evans), catfish, crappie, bluegill
Facilities: Campgrounds, store, snack bar, laundromat, picnic area, swimming beaches, launch ramps, and boat rental
Information: Kern County Parks (661) 868-7000; Buena Vista (661) 861-2063

Cachuma Lake (map - p. 178)

Lake Cachuma is an excellent fishing lake in a beautiful setting in the Los Padres National Forest where oak trees and chaparral rise up on the slopes surrounding the lake. The lake itself is about 7 miles long, one mile wide, and covers just about 3,200 surface acres. Rainbow trout are planted from October to March, and catches are typically in the one- to two-pound range. But six-pound trout are caught at times. This is also an outstanding bass lake because of its rocky drop-offs, shallow areas and weed beds. Cachuma offers both bragging-size largemouths and smallmouths. Catfishing, peaking in August and September, is also excellent, as is the panfishing (redear sunfish, crappies and bluegill). The lake record largemouth was 14 3/4 pounds, the largest catfish taken weighed in at 32 3/4 pounds, and the rainbow record exceeds 9 pounds.

There is no swimming or waterskiing at Cachuma, so life is a little more pleasant for the summertime angler. Adding to this tranquil, oak-covered hills setting is the abundance of wildlife, including deer, bobcat and quail. Lake Cachuma is located 25 miles north of Santa Barbara, and has more than 400 campsites which are close to the lake and some have hookups.

The largest bucketmouths at Cachuma are caught in the winter months (January through March). But greater numbers are caught in the summer. Successful winter anglers fish on the bottom and move their lines slowly. The Pig 'n Jig (lead-head jig with a plastic skirt and pork rind trailer) is the most consistent winter producer. During the rest of the year, plastic worms and nightcrawlers are the big winners. Worm color doesn't seem to be too important, but using a split-shot rig (see the Lake Castaic Fishing Tips section) is definitely the way to go. The most productive areas for bass at Cachuma are in canyons, along walls, and at shelves in water that range from 15 to 30 feet deep. Electronic fish finders are extremely helpful. Surface lures are a good choice in the early morning hours over weed cover.

August, September and October are the best months for channel catfish at Cachuma, although they are taken in all months of the year. Most cats are taken in 5 to 25 feet of water. Shrimp, mackerel and nightcrawlers are best for catfish when using a sliding sinker rig at dawn or dusk. Crappies fall to 1/16 and 1/32 ounce mini-jigs in white or yellow. Anchor near submerged trees and fish from 10 to 25 feet down. Bluegills go for meal worms and red worms on No. 6 or No. 8 hooks. When you find a school, stay put.

Cachuma Fishing Seasons — Legend: Good, Fair

	J	F	M	A	M	J	J	A	S	O	N	D
Bass	Fair	Good	Good	Good	Good	Good	Good	Good	Good	Good	Fair	
Catfish			Fair	Fair	Fair	Good	Good	Good	Good	Fair		
Panfish			Fair	Fair	Good	Good	Good	Good	Fair	Fair		
Trout	Fair	Good	Good	Good	Good	Good	Good	Good	Good	Good	Good	Fair

Cachuma Fishing Tips

Trout can be caught near the surface (from shore or boat) in the cooler months. But deep trolling out in the lake (from the mouth of Cachuma Bay to the dam, east side of Chalk Bluffs to Santa Cruz Point, and from the Cistern to the barrel line at the dam) is necessary in summer. Leadcore line trollers go out as many as nine colors in August. No. 2 Needlefish, Kastmasters and Phoebes are most popular. Summer trout bait anglers fish as deep as 60 feet off the Cistern, at the entrance to Cachuma Bay, Santa Cruz Bay and their inflows.

Lake Cachuma Facts

Location: Cachuma is located on Hwy. 154, about a 40-minute drive north of Santa Barbara. The old world Danish village of Solvang is about another 20 minutes northwest of Lake Cachuma via the San Marcos pass.

Size: Cachuma is one of the larger reservoirs in Southern California. It's about 7 miles long and one mile wide at its widest.

Species: Large and smallmouth bass, rainbow trout, catfish, redear sunfish, crappie and bluegill

Water Use: No swimming or waterskiing

Facilities: Cachuma has extensive developed camping facilities, a full-service marina, multi-lane launch ramp, a general store, boat and bicycle rental and a laundromat.

Information: General and camping reservations, (805) 688-4658; boat rental (805) 688-4040

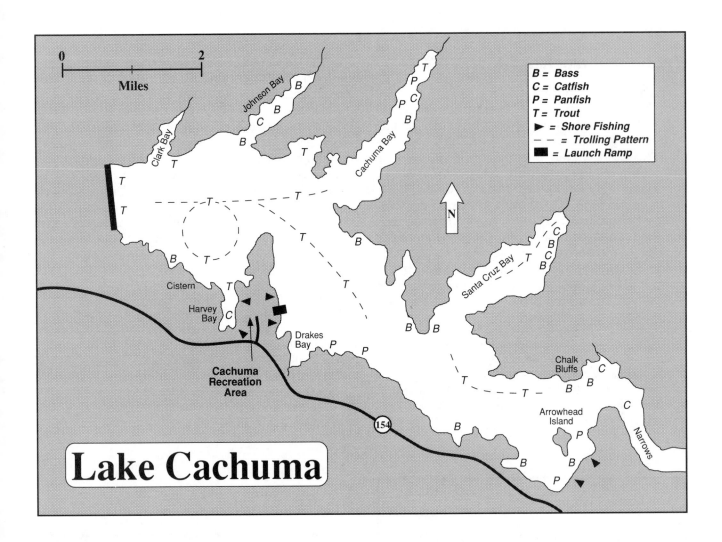

B = Bass
C = Catfish
P = Panfish
T = Trout
► = Shore Fishing
– – – = Trolling Pattern
■ = Launch Ramp

Lake Cachuma

The California Aqueduct (map - p. 179)

The California Aqueduct has to be one of the most unique fishing locales in the entire world. It extends 444 miles from the Sacramento Delta, where water is pumped in at Bethany Reservoir in Alameda County, south through the San Joaquin Valley and over the Tehachapi Mountains, to its termination point at Perris Lake in Riverside County. On its way, it provides over four million acre-feet of water annually, mostly for agriculture, but also for cities, industry, recreation and even some fish and wildlife enhancement. South of the Tehachapis, the west branch of the aqueduct supplies water to Los Angeles and Ventura counties. The east branch serves San Bernardino, Riverside, Orange and San Diego counties. Flood control, water quality improvement, and hydroelectric power production are also functions of the California Aqueduct System, a major part of the California State Water Project developed in the mid-1950s.

The aqueduct provides 343 miles of open canals for public fishing, including 18 specially designed access sites. Striped bass, largemouth bass, catfish, crappie, green sunfish and bluegill have traveled the aqueduct's pumps and penstocks and are now spread throughout the system. The entire California Aqueduct System is open to anglers, with the exception of a few locations around pumping plants and two stretches that are below ground. Open areas of the aqueduct are fenced on both sides of the channel, with approximately 100 yards of open space on each side. The aqueduct is accessible at each public road crossing unless posted. Fishing from bridges is not permitted.

The California Department of Water Resources offers some cautions on use of the aqueduct. The concrete sides of the aqueduct are steep and made slippery by algae. If you happen to fall into the aqueduct, try to reach one of the safety ladders spaced every 500 feet on alternate sides of the chan-

CALIFORNIA AQUADUCT

- - - - - - - Underground sections
─────── Aqueduct

nel. Do not deliberately go into the water for any reason. The canal water can be almost static one minute, and moving rapidly the next. Suction can occur and, without help, it is impossible to get out. If you drop fishing gear or anything else into the water, let it go. The risk is not worth the salvage effort. Boats are not permitted in the canal system.

The San Joaquin Valley section of the aqueduct runs somewhat parallel to I-5 from Los Banos to the Tehachapis Mountains. Here are the developed access sites:

- At the Canyon Road crossing, eight miles south of Los Banos
- Where Marvel Road crosses the canal, 11 miles southwest of Los Banos
- At Fairfax, just west of Mendota
- At Three Rocks, just east of Hwy. 33
- Near Huron at the Hwy. 198 crossing
- At the Avenal Cut-off, crossing the canal
- At the Hwy. 41 crossing at Kettlemen City
- At Lost Hills at the Hwy. 46 crossing
- At Buttonwood where Hwy. 58 crosses the canal
- At the Cadet Road crossing near Toft

The southern portion of the California Aqueduct extends for 105 miles from Quail Lake and runs westerly to just north of Silverwood Lake in San Bernardino County. There is a developed bikeway that makes it possible for anglers to quickly move along the canal to reach more remote fishing spots.

Developed access sites along the southern channel are listed below:

- At the Munz Road crossing near Fairmont in the Antelope Valley
- At the end of 70th Street in Quartz Hill
- At Avenue S. near Palmdale
- At 77th Street East in Littlerock
- At the Longview Road crossing near Pearlblossom

California Aqueduct Facts	
Location:	See the accompanying map
Size:	343 miles of open canal for public fishing
Species:	Striped bass, largemouth bass, catfish, crappie, green sunfish, bluegill
Facilities:	There are 18 developed access sites. Access is also permitted at most road crossings.
Information:	Your local Department of Fish & Game Office

Casitas Lake (map - p. 180)

Lake Casitas is a famous Southern California fishing lake, not only because it provides excellent fishing, but because three state record fish were caught here in recent years: a 21 lb. 3 1/2 oz. largemouth bass in March 1980, a 41 pound channel catfish in August 1982, and a 3 lb. 7 oz. redear sunfish in August 1976. Casitas has both largemouth bass and Florida-strain largemouth that grow big and fast. Rainbow trout are stocked in Casitas from October to May. Catfishing is good in the heat of the summer, or whenever it rains. Casitas has 32 miles of shoreline around its 2,700 surface acres of water. Facilities at Casitas are complete. There are 480 developed campsites. No bodily contact with the water is allowed. Lake Casitas is located 78 miles from Los Angeles (12 miles north of Ventura) in the oak-studded hills west of Ojai.

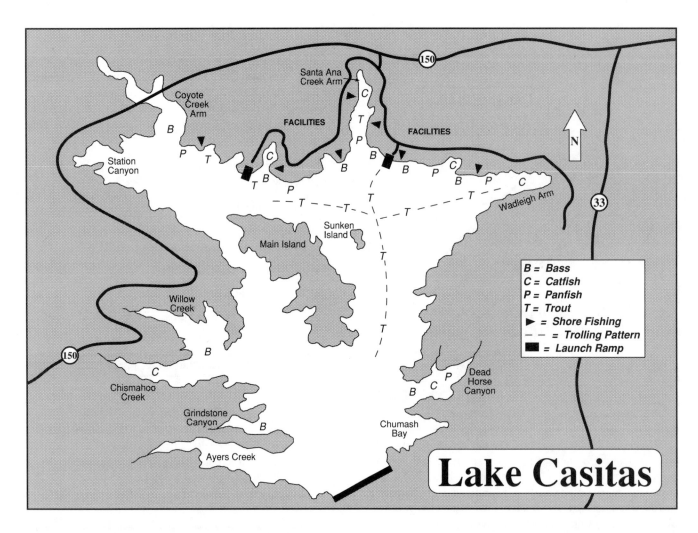

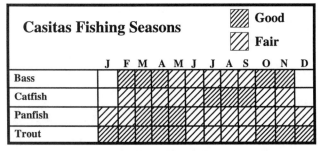

Casitas Fishing Seasons												
	J	F	M	A	M	J	J	A	S	O	N	D
Bass												
Catfish												
Panfish												
Trout												

Good — Fair

Casitas Fishing Tips

Large bass can be caught anywhere in the lake. The entire shore is lined with small coves. One favorite spot is just outside the marina in the Santa Ana Creek channel. This area known as the Rockpile is about 20 yards east of the main ramp buoy line and within easy casting range from shore. Live crawdads are the most popular bait for super-big bass. And surprisingly, bass in the 10-15 pound range are not unusual at Casitas. Here's the basics of early spring big bass fishing at Casitas. Casitas waters are unusually clear, so monofilament in the 6-10 pound range is appropriate. Use a 6, 8 or 10 sized bait hook, depending on the size of the crawdads. Some anglers put a little split shot up the line to help keep the crawdad near the bottom. Crawdads are worked along the bottom just like you would fish a plastic worm. Crawl them slowly along the bottom. When you see a twitch, that is the bass picking up your offering. As he moves off with the bait, the belly will come out of your line. Let the bass run a few feet and then set the hook hard. Don't allow any slack in your line when playing the fish. Fish the rocky points, drop-offs and ledges. Bassing starts in the north end of the lake in early spring and then opens up all over the lake as the water warms. Some anglers will work a good spot from an anchored boat for hours. Lead-head jigs and plastic worms are also productive at Casitas, as are popular lures like Rapalas, Rebels, Lucky 13's, Jitterbugs and Devil's Horses. In lower water years some of the biggest bass are taken in the Deep Cat area west of the auxiliary ramp, in Deadhorse Canyon, in Chismahoo Creek, and in the numerous points and coves on the west side of Main Island.

Trout fishing is consistently good throughout the stocking months. Shore angling can be quite productive. But often the biggest trout of the year at Casitas are caught during the summer. That's when anglers score on holdover rainbow in the 2 to 5 pound range. Work the buoy line near the dam in water from 50 to 80 feet deep. Trolling with leadcore line or downriggers is a good approach. Pull spoons or minnow imitation plugs. Another way is to bait fish from an anchored boat using a sliding sinker rig. Bait that work include salmon eggs, Zeke's garlic-flavored bait, Berkley Power Bait, and the salmon egg-marshmallow combination. The top trolling area in the winter is from the marina to the northeast side of Main Island. Winter trout bank anglers move to the north end of the lake. The Wadliegh and Santa Ana Creek arms are the two top areas, but the waters along the Coyote Creek boat ramp can also produce. Winter boat anglers find trout in the Santa Ana and Coyote Creek arms as well as near Grindstone, Station and Deadhorse canyons.

Most winter anglers pursue trout, but surprisingly some of the best catfishing at Casitas is also in the winter—after a good rain. That's when these prowlers leave their 80-90 feet deep haunts and move right up into the shallows to feed on whatever is flowing in on swollen streams. Best areas include the Santa Ana arm (around the boat dock and off the points) and in the Coyote and Chismahoo creek inflows. Summertime baits like cut mackerel, anchovies, nightcrawlers and commercial products all work. Expect to catch big catfish at Casitas during both winter and summer. Ten pounders are not unusual and many are taken in the 5-6 pound range.

Crappie run up to 3 pounds, while redear sunfish are typically in the 1/2 to 3/4 pound range. Crappie go for 1/64 to 1/32 ounce crappie jigs. Red and white, all white, red and yellow, all yellow, smoke flake, and silver flake are the better colors. Top crappie areas are the Santa Ana Creek and Wadliegh arms. Redear are taken all along the north shore. In winter, crappie can be taken over some old submerged oak trees just off the main boat ramp. Use your electronics to find them from November through February.

Casitas Lake Facts

Location: Casitas is located northwest of Ventura just off Highway 150.

Size: This reservoir has 2,700 surface acres of water and a shoreline of 32 miles when filled to capacity.

Species: Largemouth bass, rainbow trout, channel catfish, crappie and redear sunfish

Water Use: No bodily contact with water

Facilities: Complete boating and camping facilities, including marina, two multi-lane launch ramps, general store, boat rental and over 450 developed camp sites. Total recreation area is 6,200 acres.

Information: Lake Casitas Recreation Area, (805) 649-2233. Casitas Boat Rental, (805) 649-2043.

Castaic Lake (map - p. 182)

Castaic, from an angler's point of view, has a lot going for it. Recently its been consistently booting out some monster largemouths in the 20-pound class. It holds scads of catfish in the one to three pound range and ten-pounders are taken frequently. Trout are planted by the Department of Fish and Game for nearly nine months each year. Add to all this the fact that Castaic is very conveniently located right off I-5 and only 45 miles north of Los Angeles. Plus waterskiing is prohibited in the fish-rich east arm of the lake. But there is one minor drawback: Castaic, part of the California State Water Project and operated by Los Angeles County, has no on-site camping. Fortunately, there is a nearby campground and R.V. park, and a good selection of motels in the vicinity.

Castaic is actually two separate waters. The main 2,500 surface acre lake provides the bass and trout action. It has the boating restrictions noted on the accompanying map and can be fished only in daylight. The 180-acre afterbay permits only non-power boats, but anglers can work these waters 24 hours a day. Catfish are king here, although bass, trout and panfish are also taken.

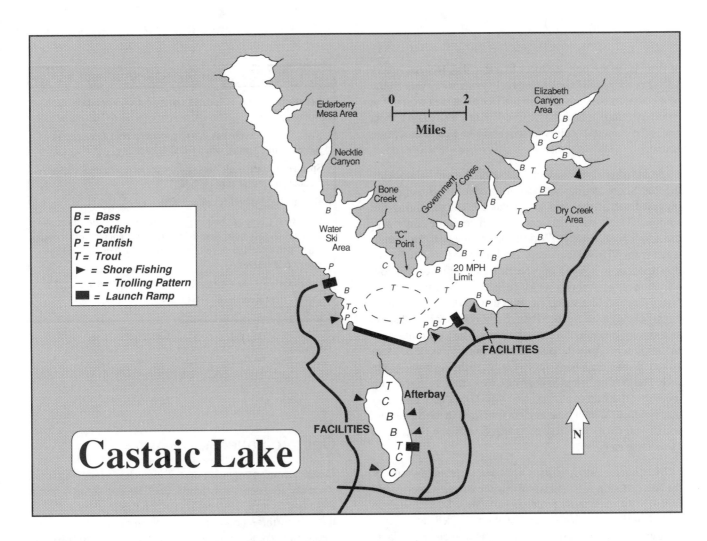

Castaic Lake

Castaic Fishing Seasons														Good
														Fair
	J	F	M	A	M	J	J	A	S	O	N	D		
Bass														
Catfish														
Panfish														
Trout														

Castaic Fishing Tips

In the 1987-1988 period, two Florida-strain largemouth were taken from Castaic that exceeded 18 pounds. This action was followed by a 19.04-pound giant in the spring of 1989, and a 22.01 monster in March 1990. The 22.01 pounder, taken by Los Angeles policeman, Bob Crupi, measured 29 1/4 inches long and had a girth of 28 inches. It was only 4 ounces off the world record! He caught it by slowly working a live crawdad along the bottom in 36 feet of water after graphing the huge bass on his fish finder.

There is a good deal of bass fishing pressure at Castaic because of its reputation for big bass and because of its accessible location. Shoreline structure fishing early and late in the day and during the spawn produces bass, but many Castaic bass have become "educated" to avoid these high-risk zones. Therefore, successful largemouth angling at Castaic (and other popular SoCal bass lakes) often means probing areas beyond and away from the shoreline.

One approach is to vertically work specific deep-water targets from a boat with plastic worms; this technique is called "doodling" or "shaking." Use green weenies, or browns, purple and blue mix worms. A second method, maybe the most popular, is called "split shotting." A No. 2 or larger split shot is placed from six inches to three feet above tiny 3-4 inch plastic worms or leach-like reapers in colors like pale cinnamon, smoke or salt and pepper. Using six-pound or less line, these offerings are drifted or dragged over reefs, flots and bars. "Doodling," "shaking" and "split shotting" are described in detail in *Bass Fishing in California* (Marketscope Books). Primary bass areas at Castaic are all the coves and points of the east arm.

Rainbow trout are most easily taken by trollers. Popular lures are the No. 2 Needlefish and Kastmasters. Shore fishing is also good when the surface water temperature is low. Baits like salmon egg/marshmallow combinations and inflated nightcrawlers score. Average trout are in the 1/2 to 2-pound range.

Some good catfishing haunts are off "C" Point, near the boat ramps on either side of the dam and up in Elizabeth Canyon near the sand bars. Many of the coves in the main lake hold catfish. And don't overlook the afterbay, especially after dark. Cats like mackerel, sardines, anchovies and prepared baits.

Bluegill angling is good in many of the coves. They take grubs and flies. One of the best crappie areas is the brush-filled Hawk's Nest Cove.

Castaic Lake Facts

Location: 45 miles north of Los Angeles vis I-5; take the Hughes exit.

Size: The main lake has 2,500 surface acres of water and 3.5 miles of shoreline.

Species: Florida-strain largemouth bass, rainbow trout, catfish, crappie, bluegill

Facilities: Picnic areas, 2 multi-lane launch ramps, docks, snack bar, boat rental, marina, bait and tackle. Swimming permitted in the afterbay. Camping and motels nearby.

Information: Castaic Lake Recreation Area, (661) 257-4050, Castaic Boat Rental (661) 775-6232

Lopez Lake (map - p. 184)

Lopez Lake, located between San Luis Obispo and Santa Maria off Hwy. 101, provides excellent angling for trout, bass, catfish and panfish. Known by some as an outstanding sailboarding spot, it's also a fine boating, camping and fishing locale. Its 22 miles of drop-offs, rocky points and coves encompass 950 surface acres of water. The lake is in a beautiful, hilly setting, surrounded by oak trees. Almost

100,000 trout are planted by a combined effort of the Department of Fish and Game and San Luis Obispo County. Lopez is open all year and has campsites, bait and tackle, grocery store, picnic areas and hiking trails.

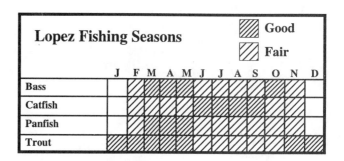

Lopez Fishing Seasons	J	F	M	A	M	J	J	A	S	O	N	D
Bass			Good									
Catfish												
Panfish												
Trout												

Good / Fair

Lopez Fishing Tips

Trout fishing is at its prime in the winter and spring months, but dress warmly because the breeze off the Pacific can be chilling this time of year. Rainbows range from pan-sized to about 3 pounds. But Lopez is a steep, deep canyon reservoir so holdover trout flourish. Some are taken up to 8 pounds. Trolling, near the surface in cool months and as deep as 40-60 feet in the summer, is the most productive approach. Lures like Super Dupers, Kastmasters and nightcrawlers are all good. Some of the best trolling is near the dam. If it gets too windy there, head up into the Lopez arm. There are lots of trout in these areas in the cooler months, and it's quiet and peaceful. You can troll, stillfish or drift. Shore trout angling is most productive in Cottonwood Cove in the cooler months. Nightcrawlers are the number one trout taker, followed by Power Bait. Casting and counting down Kastmasters, Super Dupers or other spoons produces early and late in the day.

Lopez has populations of both smallmouth and largemouth bass. But the structure, rocky old creek beds, outcroppings, etc. favor smallmouths. There is no wood structure or ledges to speak of. Bass are found primarily at points and then in coves, but there are no particular hot spots. The single-most popular bass bait is the single blade spinnerbait with a white-green skirt. The lake record largemouth is 10 lbs., 1 oz. while the record smallmouth is 4 lbs., 10 oz. But the average catch for either species is around two pounds.

Catfish for all three species (channel, blue, bullhead) is probably best right off the marina. Sardines, mackerel and chicken livers are top baits. Average blues and channels run from three to five pounds. Bullheads come in at around a pound.

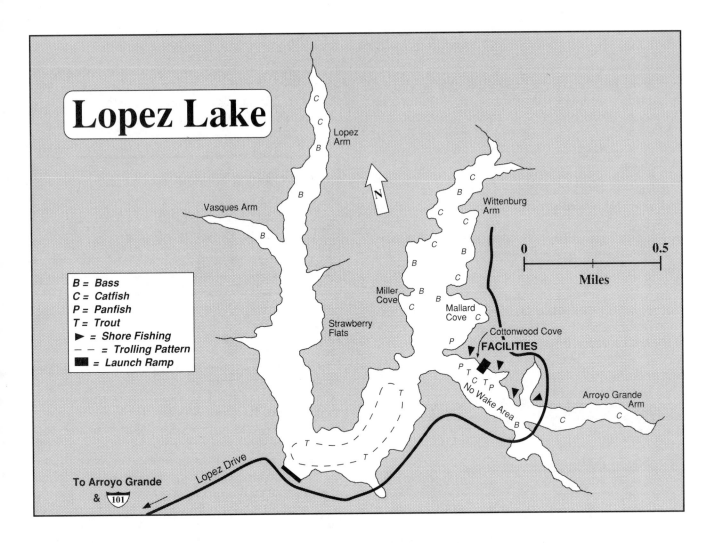

Bluegill are taken all over the lake in coves on worms and flies. Crappie go for red-white, red-yellow and green-white jigs. Look for them off sharp cliffs.

Lopez Lake Facts
Location: About halfway between San Luis Obispo and Santa Maria, at Arroyo Grande, about 8 miles off Hwy. 101.
Size: 950 surface acres of deep water in a canyon-type reservoir
Species: Smallmouth and largemouth bass, rainbow trout (both planters and carry-over fish), catfish, crappie and redear sunfish
Facilities: There are 365 campsites ranging from walk-in to full hookup. Boat rental, marina, multi-lane launch ramp, snack bar, tackle shop, laundromat and water slide.
Information: Lopez Lake, (805) 489-2095. Lopez Marina, (805) 489-1006

Lake Nacimiento (map - p. 185)

Lake Nacimiento, which is just south of San Antonio Lake, provides one of the few white bass fisheries in California. White bass are prolific and can damage trout and striped bass fisheries. Therefore, the limit at Nacimiento for white bass has been removed, but no **live** white bass may be in possession. No one wants white bass to take over other lakes. In addition to the excellent white bass fishing, there is also black bass, crappie, catfish and carp in Lake Nacimiento.

This is a beautiful, big lake (18 miles long) that has an unusually large number of long narrow fingers and coves. Facilities at Nacimiento include a store, campground and launch ramp. The lake has 165 miles of shoreline, surrounding 5,400 acres of water. It is located 17 miles northwest of the town of Paso Robles, and 241 miles from Los Angeles via Hwy. 101 to Paso Robles.

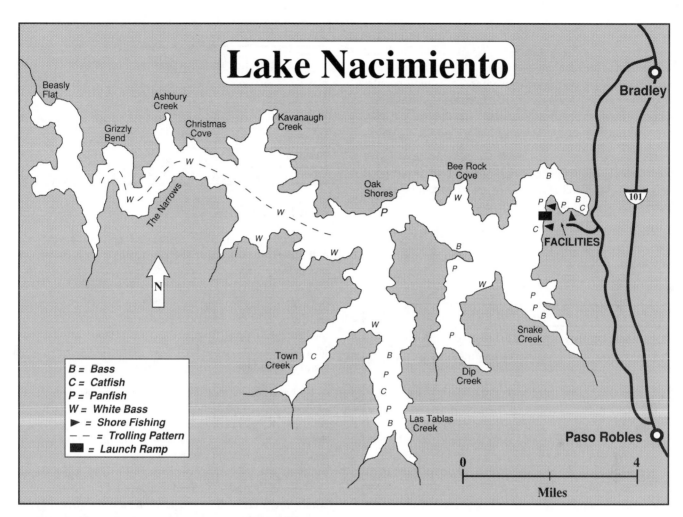

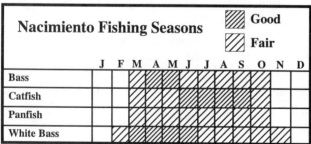

Nacimiento Fishing Seasons												
	J	F	M	A	M	J	J	A	S	O	N	D
Bass			▨	▨	▨	▨	▨	▨	▨	▨		
Catfish			▨	▨	▨	▨	▨	▨	▨	▨		
Panfish			▨	▨	▨	▨	▨	▨	▨	▨		
White Bass		▨	▨	▨	▨	▨	▨	▨	▨	▨	▨	

Legend: ▨ = Good, ▨ = Fair

Nacimiento Fishing Tips

White bass at Nacimiento spawn in the spring in the river that feeds the lake. This usually occurs in mid-April, when fishing is tremendous. Anglers boat up and then wade the river. Good lures are small feathered crappie jigs (white or yellow) or spinners. The key is to be careful not to spook the fish. Cast the lure in front of them and let it sink to the bottom. Retrieve in little jumps, and you'll catch all the white bass you want. By sometime in May, all the white bass have moved out into the main lake. Anglers cast into feeding schools, at varying depths. Minnow-mimicking plugs like Rebels, Rapalas and Thin Fins with blue, black or gray backs and light-colored bellies are popular. Good spinners include yellow and white Panther Martins and Roostertails. White bass average 2-3 pounds. Bait anglers take them on live minnows.

For a change of pace, try largemouth and smallmouth bass. Since smallmouth predominate, most anglers stick with tackle and techniques best suited to bronzebacks. Look for action along break lines, abrupt ledges and rocky points. Salt-and-pepper grubs and Pig 'n Jig combinations in brown and black take a lot of fish. Small silver Kastmasters also take fish. Two top areas are Los Tablas Creek and the cliffs across from the dam. Expect to hook many fish below legal size and a few up to 3 pounds.

Nacimiento can be a fantastic crappie lake at times. A family of anglers has been known to take five or six dozen. They average 3/4 of a pound. Submerged brush and other cover around Dip Creek, Las Tablas Creek, Snake Creek and in the marina area are all good spots. Tiny jigs in red-white and yellow-white are the local favorites. The crappie population is diminished in some years, but even then good numbers can be taken. Bluegill are available throughout the lake, especially at drop-offs and coves. Meal worms are suggested.

Catfishing is one of the most popular attractions in the summertime. Night fishing, from shore or boat, is one good way to go. Mackerel is the most popular bait, followed by anchovies, nightcrawlers and crawdads.

There are lots of carp in Nacimiento. Anglers pursue the big guys with dough bait, etc. Spring is a good time for bowfishing for carp.

Lake Nacimiento Facts

Location: Off Hwy. 101, 17 miles north of Paso Robles.

Size: 5,370 surface acres of water with 165 miles of wooded, rolling shoreline

Species: White bass, largemouth and smallmouth bass, catfish and panfish

Facilities: Almost 400 campsites, some with full hookups. There is also a store, marina, laundry, restaurant, rental boats and multi-lane launch ramp.

Information: Lake Nacimiento Resort, (805) 238-3256, Nacimiento Marina, (805) 238-1056

Piru Lake (map - p. 187)

Lake Piru is a fine all-around, outdoor recreation facility that is about 50 miles north of Los Angeles. The fishing is good throughout the year, camping and other facilities are very nice, and all water sports (including waterskiing and swimming) are permitted.

At capacity, Piru covers 1,200 surface acres. There are about 250 campsites, a five-lane concrete launch ramp, a tackle shop, snack bar and boat rental. Rainbow trout are planted in the winter months, and this is the best angling time, especially for shore anglers along the west shore. But trollers who can get down will catch fish in the summer. Bass at Piru are the northern largemouth. These do not get as big as the Florida-strain, but most agree, they are easier to catch. Catfish, crappie and bluegill are also plentiful.

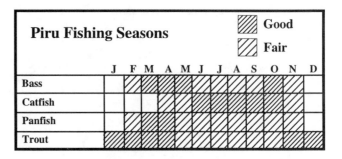

Piru Fishing Seasons	J	F	M	A	M	J	J	A	S	O	N	D
Bass		Fair	Good	Good	Good	Good	Good	Good	Good	Good	Fair	
Catfish				Fair	Good	Good	Good	Good	Good	Good	Fair	
Panfish			Fair	Good	Good	Good	Good	Good	Good	Good		
Trout	Fair	Good	Good	Good	Good	Good	Good	Good	Good	Good	Good	Fair

Legend: ▨ Good ▨ Fair

Piru Fishing Tips

In the winter months, shore trout anglers work the west side of the lake. Floating baits like Zeke's and Velveeta cheese are productive. Casters also score with Kastmasters, Rooster Tails and Needlefish. Winter trolling is up near the surface, but summertime trolling means getting down 20 to 60 feet, usually with Needlefish, near the dam, or down the center of the lake. Stillfishing from a boat is also a good bet, particularly near the dam. Berkeley Power Bait and Zeke's Floating Bait both produce.

Early season largemouth bass anglers also work deep off the bottom in 15-60 feet of water. Plastic worms, live crawdads, Pig 'n Jigs and even inflated nightcrawlers score. When the bass come to shallow water to spawn (April), shore anglers toss plastic worms into Bobcat Cove and along east shore locations between Cow Cove and Santa Felicia Cove. Crappie season usually peaks in March and April. Fish brushy areas with white, green/yellow and pearl crappie jigs. Bluegill take over the panfishing action in the summer months. Use meal worms back in the coves.

Catfishing is popular, with the best angling starting around Memorial Day to the end of October. Best spots include the north end of the lake, Cow Cove and Felicia Cove. Catfish average about 2-4 pounds and favor cat mackerel.

Piru Lake Facts

Location: Lake Piru is located five miles north of the town of Piru and 50 miles north of Los Angeles.

Size: When full, Piru has 1,200 surface acres of water.

Species: Rainbow trout, largemouth bass, catfish, crappie and bluegill

Facilities: There are over 200 campsites for both tents (187) and R.V. with electric hookup (62). Facilities also include a multi-lane launch ramp, picnic area, marina and store.

Information: Piru Lake, (805) 521-1500. Piru Marina (805) 521-1231

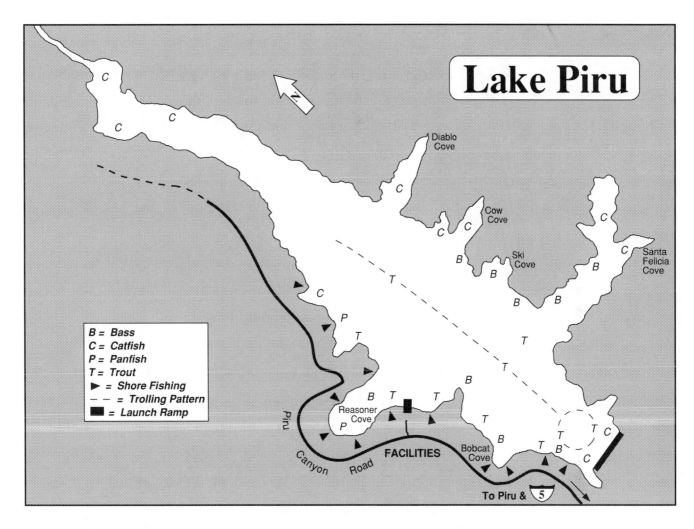

Lake Piru

B = Bass
C = Catfish
P = Panfish
T = Trout
► = Shore Fishing
– – = Trolling Pattern
■ = Launch Ramp

Diablo Cove
Cow Cove
Ski Cove
Santa Felicia Cove
Reasoner Cove
Bobcat Cove
Piru Canyon Road
FACILITIES
To Piru & 5

Pyramid Lake (map - p. 188)

There are three major reservoirs in the high country along I-5 and north of Los Angeles. Castaic is known for its outstanding Florida-strain largemouth fishing. Piru is an all-around fishing and water sports haven. And then there is Pyramid. It too is popular with water sports enthusiastics, especially in the summertime, but to the angler, Pyramid provides anglers a chance at some fine striped bass fishing. Some say that Pyramid produces more stripers per angler than any other lake in California. In addition, Pyramid Lake has large and smallmouth bass, catfish and panfish. Trout were planted in the lake on a regular basis throughout most of the year, but the Department of Fish and Game stopped the program. It could resume in the future.

The terrain surrounding Pyramid Lake is rugged, so most of its shoreline is accessible by boat only. But there is plenty of area for bank anglers. Most is near the facilities at the north end of the lake.

Facilities include a picnic area, marina, campgrounds, boat launching, hiking trails and store. Both swimming and water skiing are permitted. This is a very popular summer facility. It's so popular, in fact, that many anglers prefer to come to the lake in the off season, when the fishing is at its peak and most of the people are somewhere else.

Pyramid Fishing Seasons	J	F	M	A	M	J	J	A	S	O	N	D				Good / Fair
Bass		▨	▨	▨	▨	▨	▨	▨	▨	▨	▨					
Catfish			▨	▨	▨	▨	▨	▨	▨	▨						
Panfish			▨	▨	▨	▨	▨	▨	▨	▨						
Striped Bass	▨	▨	▨	▨	▨	▨	▨	▨	▨	▨	▨	▨				
Trout		▨	▨	▨	▨	▨	▨	▨	▨	▨	▨					

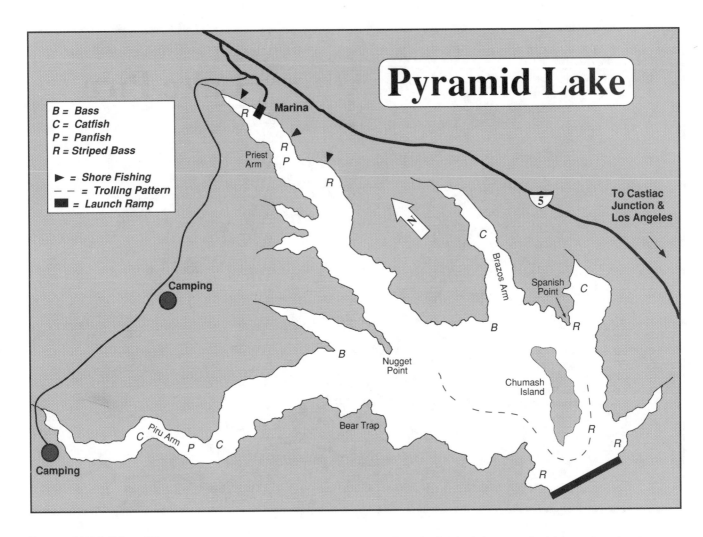

Pyramid Fishing Tips

Stripers taken at Pyramid generally average 3 to 5 pounds, with an occasional lunker in the 10-pound class. Striped bass are nocturnal feeders, so many striper anglers concentrate their efforts at Lake Pyramid in the hours following dawn and before dusk. In fact, the avid striper hunters will get to the lake while it's still dark and wait for sunrise. The two most popular areas to fish for striped bass are near the park entrance and at the extreme other end of the lake near the dam. Binoculars are useful to scan the water for striper feeding activity. Frequently stripers will surface near the dam. Casting surface plugs and spoons hooks these fish. LCD recorders are also useful in finding striped bass. Jigging a spoon or lead-head jig is the best for stripers located down deep. Fishing for stripers soon after a trout plant, in the area of the plant, works well. Trolling is also productive near the dam and along the rock wall just below I-5.

Since shad and rainbows are both big on the striper's menu, plugs that resemble them are always a good bet. Redfin, Pencil Poppers, Rattletraps and Shad Raps in rainbow patterns are all good, at times. A good way to make sure you're heading out onto the water with the best offerings is to check at the lake store. They keep close tabs on what's working and where the current lake hot spots are, and they're happy to share this information.

The ability to make long casts is often critical from shore or boat. So many anglers use surf equipment with 10-20 pound line. Some anglers also find stripers by trolling or drifting. Try slow trolling a big white jig like a Striper Slayer. Anchovies or blood worms trailing behind a drifting boat takes many striped bass. Electronic fish finders are a great asset to both trollers and drifters since Pyramid is a good-sized, deep lake.

The official Pyramid largemouth bass record is 9 3/4 pounds. Two top bass takers are rootbeer-colored plastic worms and salt-and-pepper green weenies. Recently, small-mouths were introduced at Pyramid. They should flourish in this rocky, deep environment—so expect some battlers.

Catfishing is best in the warmer months. They are taken all over the lake, but two consistent producers are Brazos and Posy Coves.

Pyramid Lake Facts

Location: Pyramid Lake is located about 60 miles northwest of Los Angeles on the west side of I-5. Drive past the Castaic Junction to the Hungry Valley Road exit, cross under the freeway and follow the signs.

Size: Pyramid covers 1,297 acres, with 22 miles of rugged shoreline. It is over 750 feet deep in places.

Species: Small stripers enter Pyramid via the California Aqueduct from the Delta. Other species include largemouth and smallmouth bass, catfish, crappie and bluegill.

Facilities: There is a marina, store, multi-lane launch ramp and boat rental at the north end of the lake. There are about 125 U.S. Forest Service sites (some developed) within several miles of the marina.

Information: Pyramid Lake, (661) 295-1245; Marina, (661) 257-2892

San Antonio Lake (map - p. 190)

San Antonio Lake is located in the extreme southern end of Monterey County. Although this may not seem like a convenient Southern California fishing locale, it is actually closer (250 miles) to Los Angeles than Crowley Lake (300 miles), for example, is to Los Angeles. San Antonio provides very good fishing for the usual species (black bass, catfish and panfish), but in addition, it offers excellent striped bass fishing. The average striper caught is in the 15-pound range. Like Nacimiento, its sister reservoir, San Antonio is large (16 miles long, 5,000 surface acres). Its facilities are operated by the Monterey County Parks and Recreation Department. There are camping and launch ramps at three locations on the lake, as well as a restaurant, store and swimming.

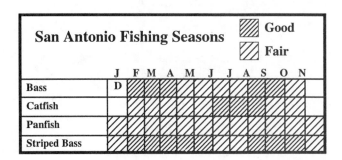

San Antonio Fishing Seasons												Good / Fair
	J	F	M	A	M	J	J	A	S	O	N	
Bass	D											
Catfish												
Panfish												
Striped Bass												

San Antonio Fishing Tips

One rule that seems to apply to all the fisheries in San Antonio is that the bite is best near shore early in the day and then moves into deeper water later in the day. So, if the action slows, move into deeper water rather than quit. Stripers are big at San Antonio. The lake average is in the 15-pound range and the lake record is 36 lbs. 2 oz. Another wonder is that they bite year-round although there are 2-3 week lulls, at times. Shallow trolling, deep trolling (with downriggers), bait fishing, and casting to surface feeders all produce fish, depending on the season and feeding pattern. Casting to the shoreline in the early morning and late evening with surface and shallow offerings is always a fun way to go, as is casting to boils of surface feeders. Top striper artificials are Hopkins Spoons, 1/2-ounce Kastmasters, Hair Raisers, Twin Spins, and Big Macs. Shad minnows are great for bait dunkers. Three of the top striper hangouts are the Dam, White Chalk Cliffs and Three Fingers.

Lee Cisneros, a San Antonio Park Ranger, is an avid angler. Here's his rundown on the other San Antonio attractions:

For largemouth bass averaging two pounds, the best months are September through November, and January through June. Top lures are red, black or blue plastic worms, and shad, bass or crawdad-finished crankbaits. A great winter bait is lead-headed jigs, and they should be retrieved slowly.

Hot spots are Bee Rock Cove, Harris Creek, the White Chalk Cliffs, Cemetery Cove, Twin Coves and the Shallows. The lake record is 9 lbs., 1 oz.

March through May are the months for the smallmouth bass that average 1 1/2 pounds, with a 4 lbs., 11 oz. lake record. The Pleyto Points (North Shore), Harris Creek and the White Chalk Cliffs are the spots. Shad-finished crankbait and Mepps lures are the fish getters.

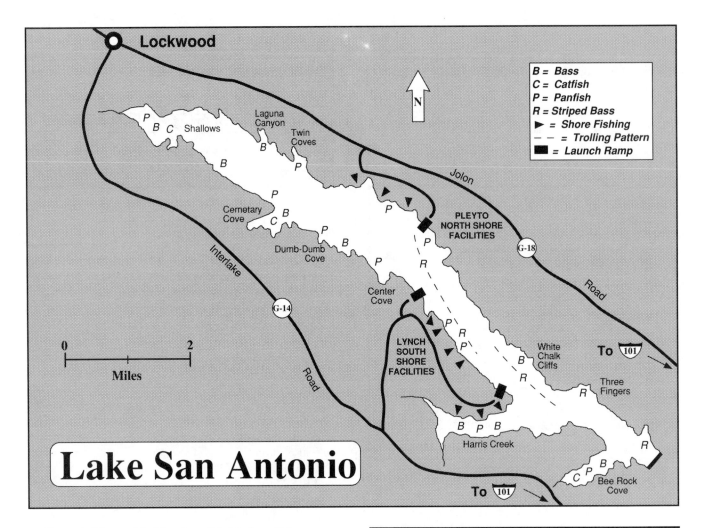

Lake San Antonio

Channel, blue and bullhead catfish hit from February to November on anchovies, crawdads, sardines, chicken livers, nightcrawlers, waterdogs and dead shad. When I'm going for the "cats," I hit the Dam, Bee Rock, the Shallows and the rocky points around the lake. Channels and blues average a huge 12 pounds with the bullheads coming around one pound. The lake record is a 25-pound channel cat.

Crappier averaging a monstrous 1 1/2 pounds strike from October through May on red/white mini-jigs, chartreuse Puddle Jumpers and hard-to-get minnows. Harris Creek, the Marinas, Dumb Cove and all of the brushy coves really produce. The lake record is 3 lbs. 8 oz.

Redear perch and bluegill are on the bite all year at the Lynch Area, Bee Rock Cove, Three Fingers, the Pleyto Points, and the Shallows. The Shallows features a lot of brush and stickups on the north end. Night fishing is allowed for all species, and can be quite good for bass, crappie and catfish.

San Antonio Lake Facts

Location: San Antonio Lake is located west of Hwy. 101 between Paso Robles and King City. Take the Jolon Rd. exit and then follow G-18 for the north shore and G-19 to G-14 for the south shore.

Size: San Antonio is large. It has 60 miles of shoreline, is 16 miles long and has 5,500 surface acres of water.

Species: Striped bass, largemouth and smallmouth bass, crappie, redear sunfish, bluegill, catfish

Facilities: San Antonio has extensive facilities. Campsites at Pleyto, Lynch and Harris Creek total 650. There are three multi-lane launch ramps, two marinas, stores, a restaurant, boat rentals (including houseboats), picnic areas, hiking trails, swimming beaches, etc.

Information: Monterey County Parks Department, (805) 472-2311; San Antonio Marina, (805) 472-2818

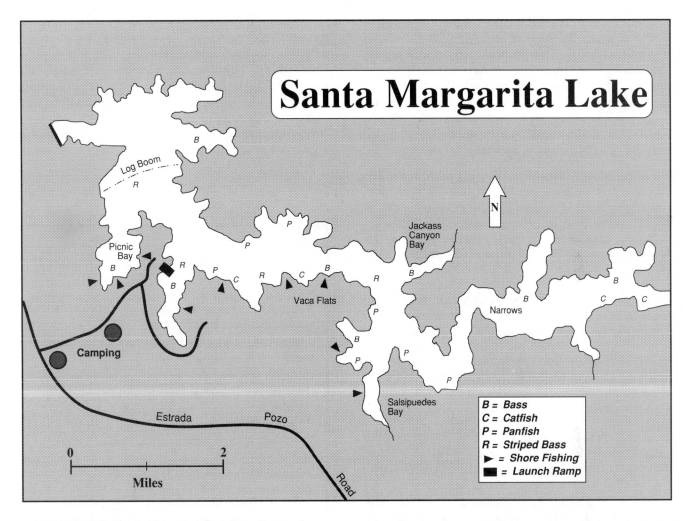

Santa Margarita Lake (map - p. 191)

Santa Margarita is an outstanding anglers' lake. It is open throughout the year, has abundant supplies of striped bass, largemouth bass (northern strain), catfish (white, yellow and channel), crappie and bluegill. Trout are also planted in the winter months. And summertime anglers will be happy to know that no waterskiing is permitted. In fact, swimming and wading are not allowed either (but there is an olympic-sized swimming pool for visitors). Other facilities include a picnic area, full-service marina and store. There is no camping in the park itself, which is operated by San Luis Obispo County, but there are two private campgrounds just outside the gate (within several hundred yards of the lake). Santa Margarita Lake is a long (7 miles), narrow lake that covers 1,100 surface acres. There are 22 miles of shoreline, surrounded by tree-studded foothills.

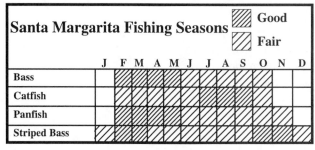

Santa Margarita Fishing Seasons												Good Fair
	J	F	M	A	M	J	J	A	S	O	N	D
Bass		▨	▨	▨	▨	▨	▨	▨	▨	▨		
Catfish		▨	▨	▨	▨	▨	▨	▨	▨	▨	▨	
Panfish		▨	▨	▨	▨	▨	▨	▨	▨	▨	▨	
Striped Bass	▨	▨	▨	▨	▨	▨	▨	▨	▨	▨	▨	▨

Santa Margarita Fishing Tips

Striped bass can be taken year-round. In springtime, anglers troll. The fish are suspended so it helps to have an electronic fish finder. Trollers score right on through the summer. Best lures include Li'l Macs, Redfin, Hair Raiser jigs (one ounce in white or red-white) of Rebels and Rapalas (five inch in silver and black). Spinning tackle is okay, but a levelwind conventional reel with ten-pound monofilament is another good choice. Summer also sees stripers very active on the surface, as they chase threadfin shad. Cruising anglers, spotting surface activity, cast lures to boils. Use Zara Spooks, Pencil Poppers and one-ounce Kastmasters with bucktails. Hair Raisers are also good. When stripers are down deep, the vertical jigging technique is a winner.

Largemouths at Santa Margarita are northern-strain. The lake record is 10 lbs. 2 oz. Biggest bass are taken from February through March. April can also produce some six to eight pounders. In summer, work surface plugs in the shallows early and late in the day. Slowly working worms and jigs in deeper water off the rocky points will produce in the daylight hours.

Trout are best from November through April, with the most action at the narrows and the dam. Trollers score best with Needlefish, while bait fishermen usually rely on Power Bait.

Peak catfishing is from July through September. Sloping, muddy banks are the best choices. The lake record channel cat is 22 lbs. 12 oz. Frozen anchovies, frozen shad and cut mackerel are the top baits.

Bluegill are prolific at Santa Margarita. They can be taken anywhere there is a tule patch. Crappie start biting just before the bass do in spring, but hang out in deeper water. Miniature jigs in yellow, white, red-yellow and red-white are best. As the weather warms, crappie should be hunted in brush piles in 10 to 20 feet of water. An average crappie goes one to two pounds.

The southern shore of Santa Margarita Lake, from Picnic Bay east to Salsipuedes Bay, provides a very long (7 miles) access area for shore anglers. However, there are numerous weed beds that limit shore angling in many portions of this stretch. But persistent anglers are successful in locating fishable spots by exploring the shoreline. Summertime bass anglers take advantage of these weedbeds and rocky areas by working surface plugs near them in the early morning and late evening hours. Catfish chasers also do well.

Santa Margarita Lake Facts

Location: Santa Margarita Lake is located about 220 miles north of Los Angeles, 8 miles off Hwy. 101, north of San Luis Obispo.

Size: The lake is about seven miles long and covers 1,100 surface acres. There are 22 miles of shoreline.

Species: Striped bass, largemouth bass, catfish, crappie, bluegill

Facilities: At the lake there is a multi-lane launch ramp, full-service marina, docks, boat rental, store and picnic area. Two campgrounds are located along the entrance road, right near the lake facilities.

Water Use: No waterskiing or body contact, but there is a large swimming pool.

Information: Santa Margarita Marina, (805) 438-4682; Santa Margarita Campground, (805) 438-5485, Rinconado Camp, (805) 438-5479, KOA Santa Margarita, (805) 438-5618

Salton Sea Fishing

The Salton Sea, to say the least, is a unique place to fish. This is a very large (45 miles by 17 miles) inland saltwater sea. Its water level is about 230 feet below sea level, and it is a little more salty than the Pacific Ocean. Four species of saltwater fish provide great fishing action in this shallow (average depth is less than 20 feet) oval. Species include the orangemouth corvina that average 5-15 pounds, as well as several smaller fish that make the Salton Sea a great place for kids to experience the joy of catching lots of fish. As a matter of fact, the catch rate per angler here is greater than at any other inland fishing locale in California. This is the result of diligent Department Fish and Game efforts that began in the 1950s.

The Salton Sea is located about 140 miles southeast of Los Angeles and is surrounded by desert. The climate is very enjoyable in the cooler months. Summer temperatures often rise over 100°, moving anglers to fish early and late in the day. Surface water temperatures reach over 90° in the summer and fall to as low as 55° in the winter.

There are good facilities here, including the Salton Sea Recreation Area. Marinas, launch ramps, boat rentals, motels and campgrounds are mostly near the Salton Sea State Park or near Salton City. There is also a marina at Red Hill. All together there are about 10 launching facilities.

The fishing is good almost all year at the Salton Sea. But the bite of the various species varies a great deal, depending on the season.

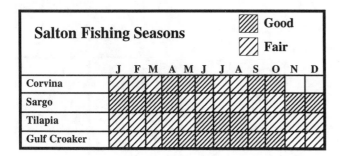

Salton Fishing Seasons	J	F	M	A	M	J	J	A	S	O	N	D
Corvina		Fair	Fair	Fair	Good	Good	Good	Good	Good	Fair		
Sargo		Good	Good	Good	Good	Good	Good	Good	Good	Good	Good	
Tilapia		Good	Good	Good	Good	Good	Good	Good	Good	Good	Good	
Gulf Croaker		Good	Good	Good	Good	Good	Good	Good	Good	Good	Good	

Good — crosshatch / Fair — crosshatch

Catching Corvina

Orangemouth corvina is by far the largest and most sought after fish in the Salton Sea. The lake record fish (and world record) is 36 lbs. 8 oz.! Many are caught in the 5-15 pound range. And this long, sleek fish is fantastic eating. Many compare it favorably with such great ocean-caught eating fish as halibut and rockfish.

There are several ways to take these fish, depending on the season. Corvina seek water temperatures in the 70-85° range. This means they are in shallower water in the late spring and early summer, then retreat to deeper water in the heat of late summer. In winter, when climatic conditions are right to produce warmer shallow water in the Red Hill area, they move to feed in water as shallow as 4 feet. Their other winter hangout is down deep.

Trolling, casting and live bait fishing are all productive at the Salton Sea, depending on the season and on what seems to be working. Among the trolling lures that produce, the most popular is the Thin Fin Shad (about 3 1/2"). Use the sinking type in red, green or yellow. The locally produced Lunker Shad is also popular, as are Hopkins Spoons, Kastmaster and Krocodile Spoons (all in 1/2-3/4 ounce). Minnow-shaped plugs like Rebels also produce. Troll slowly, and make sure the lure taps the bottom once-in-a-while.

When the corvina are in deeper parts of the lake, vertical jigging with a wobbly spoon (like a Hopkins) is productive. Jig up and down from the bottom to 2 feet above the bottom. Some anglers leave their motor running and chum with canned corn. The noise and the corn seem to stimulate a bite.

Live bait fishing is a tried-and-true method of taking corvina, especially from late spring to mid-July. The most popular bait is mudsuckers. Tilapia, sargo and croaker are also used. From shore, live bait fishing is done on the bottom using a slider sinking rig. Match hook size to bait size.

Bait is either nose hooked or the hook is put through the back at the dorsal fin. From a boat, most anglers use a rubber core sinker, about 3 feet up from the hook.

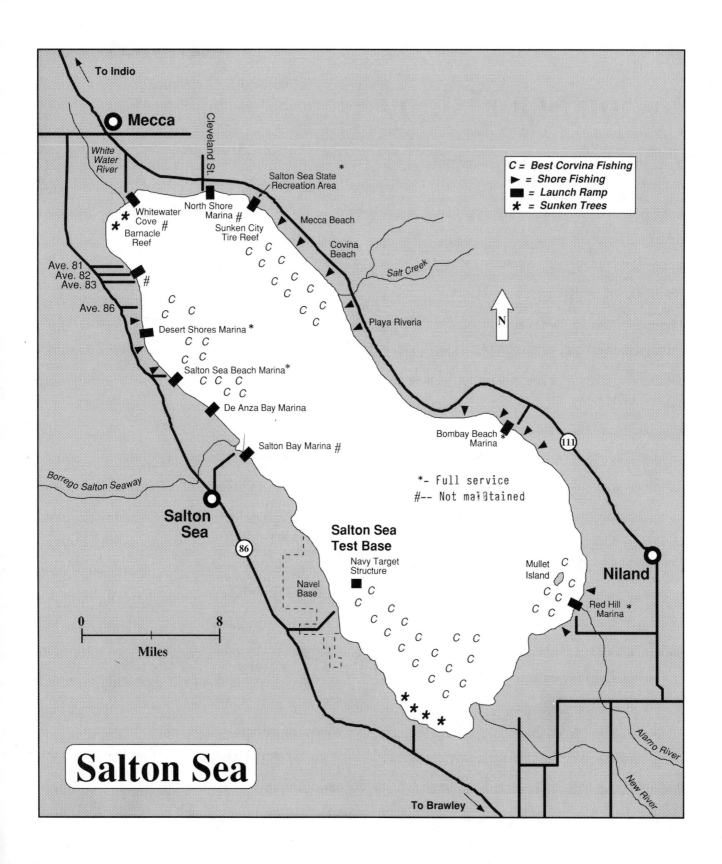

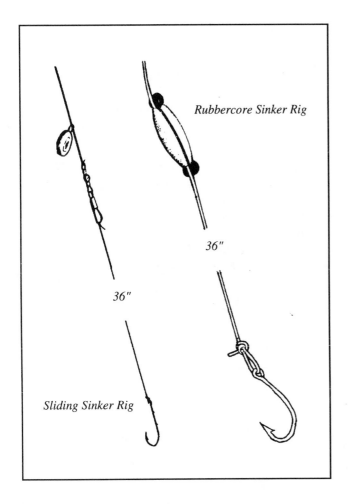

Rubbercore Sinker Rig

36"

36"

Sliding Sinker Rig

In the winter, the corvina are sometimes found in a feeding boil in shallow water in the Red Hill area. A most productive approach is casting a Thin Fin type lure, and retrieving it medium to slow, yet with an erratic action.

Many a corvina are caught by shore anglers at the sea. One technique (called "arm pit fishing") is popular. After wading out from a beach, anglers either cast out live bait or cast and retrieve lures (the same as used in trolling). Several jetties around the lake also produce corvina for shore anglers.

A tip on water color: don't fish in green water. Most local experts agree that "chocolate" or "chocolate-pink" water is the right color for corvina action. Depending on the season, some of the most consistent producers of large corvina are the north shore, Salt Creek, Bombay Beach, Red Hill, Black Rock, Basketball Court, New River, Alamo River, Mullet Island, Navy Target, DeAnza Bay, Salton Beach and Desert Shores.

Catching Tilapia

Tilapia, originally a native of the Middle East and Africa, are prolific breeders and there are literally millions in the Salton Sea. These good eating fish are generally caught in the 1/2-3 pound range.

The most popular method for catching tilapia, especially from shore, is to use bait on what is basically a surf fishing rig or crappie rig, as shown on the next page.

Popular baits include a piece of nightcrawler or a whole red worm. It sometimes helps to keep bait moving, and at times, anglers put a kernel of corn on the hook before the worm. This rig can be fished under a bobber or from a boat.

Jigging Kastmasters and Hopkins Spoons (about 1/2 ounce) up and down right off the bottom in 10-20 feet of water is often a good way to take larger tilapia. This is done from a drifting boat. A good spot is from Avenue 81 south to Desert Shores.

Catching Sargo

Sargo are native to Southern California ocean waters where they are called China croaker. These 1/2-2 pound fish like to hang out around old submerged buildings, trees or rock jetties. Boat anglers like to fish the sunken buildings just south of the town of North Shore. The Salton Sea State Recreation Area has a good jetty for sargo fishing.

Sargo should be fished right on the bottom. Popular baits are nightcrawlers, shrimp or canned whole-kernel corn. Corn is the most productive. Anglers put 3 or 4 kernels on one hook. Chumming, or throwing corn into the water, is often done to stimulate a bite. This is legal in the sea.

The same rig as used for tilapia can be used for sargo. Or a one hook or two hook sliding sinker rig can be used, as shown below.

Catching Gulf Croaker

Gulf Croaker, averaging in the 8-12 inch range, are easier to catch in the warmer months. They travel in large schools, and are not fussy eaters. Popular offerings include minnows, nightcrawlers, red worms and pieces of anchovy. They can be caught all over the lake in summertime using a tilapia rig. Casting small trout spoons and spinners also works. Whole croaker are popular bait for corvina fishing.

Tackle, Cleaning and Cooking

One of the beauties of Salton Sea fishing is that only one rod and reel combination is needed to participate in all the fishing fun. The most popular rig is the following:

- Spinning reel
- 6 1/2 - 7 1/2 foot medium action spinning rod
- 10-15 pound monofilament line

Bait casting equipment is also popular, as is spin surf casting equipment for long-cast shore fishing. Boat anglers need a landing net.

Corvina are most often filleted. The white, sweet meat is delicious prepared almost any way. Tilapia are also filleted. Try to avoid cutting into the stomach cavity. It has an unpleasant odor. Skinless fillets can be baked, broiled, fried, poached or smoked. Sargo are also filleted. Remember to remove the dark meat along the lateral line. Sargo are excellent smoked, or fillets are excellent when breaded and deep fried. Gulf croaker are filleted, but even with the skin on they have a mild flavor. Deep frying is a popular preparation method.

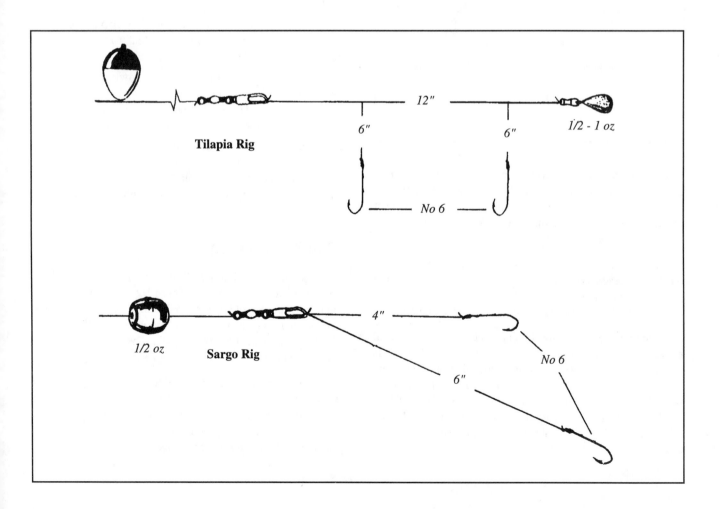

Tilapia Rig

12"

6"   6"   1/2 - 1 oz

No 6

1/2 oz   Sargo Rig

4"

No 6

6"

Colorado River and Lakes Fishing

The Colorado River is an amazing fishing resource for Californians. Striped bass and largemouth bass angling is excellent. There is some of the best catfishing to be found anywhere. And there is even good rainbow trout and panfish action.

In 1935, Hoover Dam was completed to form Lake Mead. Three years later, Lake Havasu was formed by the completion of Parker Dam. And then in 1953, Davis Dam was completed to form Lake Mohave. Besides satisfying hydroelectric, water storage and flood control needs, these dams have created three marvelous, huge, year-round fishing and recreation lakes. As an added bonus there are another 140 miles of the Colorado River south of Lake Havasu where the angling pressure is lighter and the fish just as big or bigger.

There are excellent facilities on each of the lakes and along the river sections of the Colorado. These include recreation-oriented communities, resorts, marinas, golf courses, boat rentals, house boating, boat-in campgrounds, R.V. parks, and traditional campgrounds. Of course, water skiing, jet skiing, swimming and sunbathing are also part of the Colorado water sports scene. Finally, add in the night life and gambling possibilities for those who are so inclined—Las Vegas is just 20 miles east of Lake Mead, and booming Laughlin, Nevada, on the western shore of upper Lake Havasu, is just south of Davis Dam.

A note in fishing regulations: remember that Lake Mead and Lake Mohave are in Arizona and Nevada. And the remainder of the Colorado River is on the border of California and Arizona. Different licensing and other fishing regulations are in effect than in California proper. Check into the local requirements and purchase the proper licenses.

The Automobile Club of Southern California publishes the *Guide to the Colorado River*. It maps and describes in detail all the dams, place names, highways, road accesses, resorts and campgrounds from Lake Mead down to the Mexican border. This invaluable guide is in a convenient map-type format and is available to AAA members (and their friends).

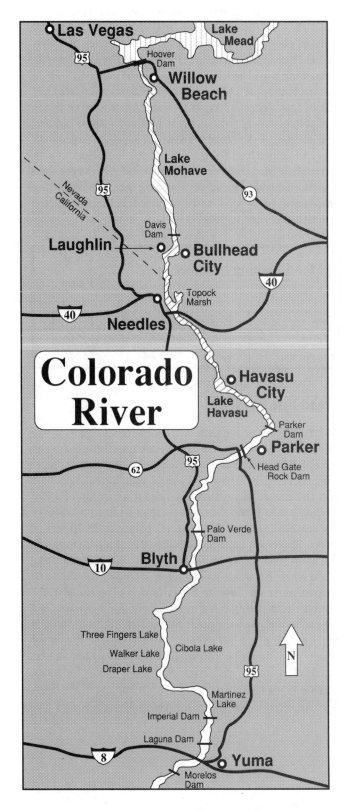

Lake Mead (map - p. 199)

Lake Mead is an immense reservoir that was formed in the mid 1930's by the completion of Hoover Dam. It has 550 miles of shoreline surrounding 225 square miles of water. This ever-changing shoreline is highlighted by steep canyon walls, wide gravel beaches and hundreds of little coves. From one end to the other, Mead measures 115 miles. Located just east of Las Vegas, all types of water-related activities are available including fishing, house boating, water skiing and boat camping. Lake Mead is known for excellent largemouth bass and striped bass fishing. Other fisheries include catfish and panfish. Mead has been the sight of countless largemouth bass tournaments. But surveys indicate that 60% of angling time, on a year-round basis, is aimed at stripers. In the summer, this rises to 90%!

Mead Fishing Seasons (Good / Fair)

	J	F	M	A	M	J	J	A	S	O	N	D
Bass		Fair	Good	Good	Good	Fair	Fair	Fair	Fair	Good	Fair	
Catfish		Fair	Fair	Fair	Fair	Good	Good	Good	Good	Fair	Fair	
Striped Bass		Fair	Good	Good	Good	Good	Fair	Fair	Fair	Good	Good	Fair

Mead Fishing Tips

Since this is such a big lake, and since striper move from day to day and by season, the key to catching them is finding them. Some anglers first make telephone calls to bait shops, marinas, etc. to help narrow down the search area. Electronic fish finders are also extremely helpful as are tip-offs like feeding birds. When the stripers aren't in shallow water or surface feeding, look for them off points in 20-70 feet of water. Stripers at Lake Mead follow their favorite food, the threadfin shad. In winter the stripers are down deep, eating those shad. As water temperatures increase, the shad and stripers move up closer to the surface. By late summer, the shad are often being eaten by stripers in shallow water. But no matter the season, stripers are feeding nearer to shore in early morning and late evening. At midday, the sun on the water drives the stripers down. A favorite among bait anglers at Mead is frozen anchovies. A popular spoon for spoon jigging is the Hopkin's Shorty 45. Trollers use Sassy Shad, Cordell Redfin, large Rebels, Rapalas, etc.

Downrigger trolling is becoming more and more popular for striper hunters at Mead, especially in the cooler months. Top-water action for stripers is fantastic from July to November, but as the water cools below 70°, shad and stripers head down. November and December finds them suspended from 75 to 135 feet deep—perfect for downriggers. But Mead waters can be very clear from November through early March. Stripers spook easily, so local experts troll very slowly (using an electric trolling motor), use lighter line (6-10 pounds), smaller offerings (i.e. 1/4 ounce white bucktail jig with a twist tail), and set the lure as much as 150 feet behind the boat.

Spring and early summer striper anglers take striper (average Mead stripers are in the three to four pound range) by spoon jigging, drifting or bottom fishing frozen anchovies, or by trolling. Many Mead bait anglers cut off the head and tail of anchovies and hook them through the backbone on about a 1/0 hook.

Plugs are a favorite when the striper bite moves up to the

Lake Mead Facts

Location: About 20 miles east of Las Vegas

Size: Lake Mead covers 225 square miles and has 550 miles of shoreline. From one end to the other, it measures 115 miles!

Species: Striped bass, largemouth bass, catfish, crappie and carp

Facilities: There are 10 major launching areas on Lake Mead. These are listed below and keyed on the accompanying map. Those with an asterisk have full marina facilities.

1 Overton Beach Resort*—(702) 394-4040

2 Stewarts Bay*

3 Echo Bay Resort*—(702) 394-4000

4 Callville Bay Resort*—(702) 565-8958

5 Las Vegas Bay Marina*—(702) 565-9111

6 Lake Mead Marina , Resort*—(702) 293-3484

7 Hemenway Harbor*

8 Temple Bar Resort*—(520) 767-3211

9 South Cove

10 Pierce Ferry

Information: Lake Mead National Recreation Area, 601 Nevada Highway, Boulder City, Nevada 89005, (702) 293-8990

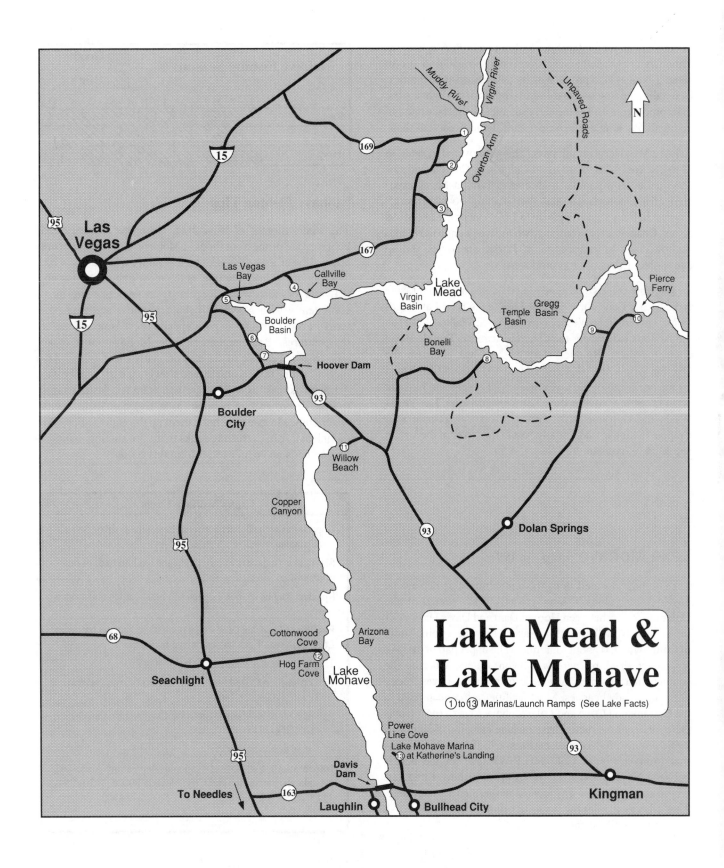

Lake Mead & Lake Mohave

① to ⑬ Marinas/Launch Ramps (See Lake Facts)

surface. Locals prefer Zara Spooks, Bomber Long A's, Jumpin' Minnows and Cordell Spots. Kastmaster and leadhead jigs (in about 1 ounce) also produce as do Sassy Shad-type plastics. Generally, the first two and last two hours of daylight are the most productive. But in the early summer, the surface bite can go on all day long as the striper stuff themselves with shad.

Lake Mead largemouth bass fishing is covered in detail in Marketscope's *Bass Fishing in California*. Crappie and catfish angling is a popular nighttime activity at Mead, especially from houseboats and their fishing boat "tenders." Crappie lights attract crappie up to 1 1/2 pounds in Lake Mead coves. Channel cats averaging two to five pounds move into shallow coves to forage at night. Frozen anchovies, shrimp and nightcrawlers are top producers.

There are some consistently good fishing areas in massive Lake Mead. Look for striper in Las Vegas Bay, Las Vegas Wash, Government Wash, Gypsum Wash, Walker Wash (on the Arizona side where the Overton Arm and Temple Basin come together), Boulder Harbor, the Meat Hole (in the Overton Arm south of Heron Island) and around Fish Island (at the north end of the Overton Arm). Largemouth bass are often taken in Callville Bay, Las Vegas Marina, Las Vegas Wash, the Gypsum Beds, Grand Wash and Temple Bar. Crappie fishing is traditionally best in the coves of the Virgin and Muddy rivers in the Overton Arm.

Lake Mohave (map - p. 199)

Lake Mohave, located along the southernmost tip of Nevada, provides marvelous fishing grounds. This stretch of the Colorado River, between Hoover Dam and Davis Dam, is 71 miles long. Now that's a long lake! The widest point, south of Cottonwood, is about four miles. The upper part of the lake is characterized by narrow canyon waters, whereas the southern reaches offer a mosaic of secluded coves, rocky cliffs and sandy beaches. Most facilities are concentrated in the Cottonwood Cove and Lake Mohave Marina (near Davis Dam) areas of the lake. These include camping, boat rental, launch ramps, full-service marinas, etc. If one didn't know that Mohave was a Colorado River lake on the border between Nevada and Arizona, its prime fishing attractions would suggest that it was located in the Sierra somewhere. That's because rainbow trout, largemouth bass and catfish are the main bill-of-fare.

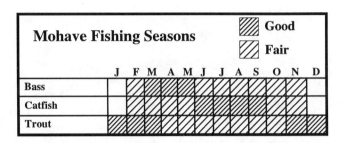

Mohave Fishing Seasons													Good / Fair
	J	F	M	A	M	J	J	A	S	O	N	D
Bass			▨	▨	▨	▨	▨	▨	▨	▨	▨	
Catfish		▨	▨	▨	▨	▨	▨	▨	▨	▨	▨	
Trout	▨	▨	▨	▨	▨	▨	▨	▨	▨	▨	▨	▨

Mohave Fishing Tips

The winter months of November, December, January and February are prime trout times at Mohave, although trout are taken all year long. The lake record rainbow is 16 lbs. 4 oz. Trolling, using leadcore line, is the most popular approach. Downriggers also work. Regular trout anglers score most consistently with Needlefish (both rainbow and frog patterns). Proper trolling depth depends on season and water temperatures. Bass anglers new to Mohave must make adjustments because of its exceptionally clear water. Approach casting targets quietly and slowly, and try your best to get that first cast exactly where you want it. Plastic worms (purple or brown) are popular, as is live bait fishing with water dogs. Most anglers hook them up through the lips, like a small bait fish. Catfishing peaks in the hot summer months. Frozen baits and commercial formulas score.

Lake Mohave Facts
Location: On the border between the southern tip of Nevada and Arizona
Size: Lake Mohave is 71 miles long and has hundreds of miles of shoreline
Species: Rainbow trout, largemouth bass, catfish and striped bass
Facilities: There are three major recreational access points on Lake Mohave. Each has extensive facilities.
11 Willow Beach Marina, (520) 767-4747
12 Cottonwood Cove Marina, Cottonwood Cove, Nevada 89046, (702) 297-1464
13 Lake Mohave Marina, Bullhead City, Arizona 86430, (520) 754-3245
* map key
Information: Lake Mead National Recreation Area, 601 Nevada Highway, Boulder City, Nevada 89005, (520) 754-3272

The north end of Mohave has long been the exclusive haunt of rainbow trout. But now the striped bass have moved into the Willow Beach area, with 20 pound-plus fish being taken. In the long run the stripers may harm the trout fishery, however, anglers are currently enjoying a double bounty. The north end of Mohave was once a trophy trout fishery. These days are gone, but planting programs have maintained a vibrant trout fishery all along the lake. Drifting bait in the current on a treble hook about 12 to 18 inches below a sinker is always a good approach. Another proven method is to cast plugs much like bass angling. Lures like Tennessee Shad worked near cliff drop-offs can produce many Mohave trout. The best daylight hours at Mohave are very early and late in the evening, but some summertime anglers chase trout in the cool of the night. Floating lights attract the shad and then the trout. Use light line and bait up with worms, cheese or commercial bait.

Lake Mohave's largemouth bass fishery is detailed in Marketscope's *Bass Fishing in California*. Largemouths can be found in almost all of the hundreds of coves of Lake Mohave. During the warm months catfish are taken in the coves after dark. Crappie fishing is best in the spring in coves in the southern half of the lake. There is very good all-around fishing action in the Willow Beach, Cottonwood Cove, and Mohave Marina sections of the lake.

Lake Havasu (map - p. 202)

Lake Havasu, the home of The London Bridge, is an immense and varied fishing and recreation locale. It is located in the desert between California and Arizona and extends from Davis Dam down to Parker Dam. In essence, Havasu is actually two distinct waters. First, there is the river portion from Davis Dam down to about Topock. Just below Davis Dam the water runs cold, even in summer, over a rock and rubble stream bed that is an excellent rainbow trout habitat. Down river, at about the state line, the stream bed changes to sand. These are good bass, catfish and crappie fishing areas. Lake Havasu itself from Topock south has a varied shoreline with marshlands and secluded coves. It varies in width from three miles to less than a half mile. There are abundant camping facilities, launch ramps and resorts.

Lake Havasu itself, as well as much of this region, is noted for its warm fall and winter weather. Rainfall is less than four inches annually so clear, dry, sunny days are the norm. Winter temperatures average in the mid-70's during the day from October through March. In contrast, summertime highs are often near 110°F.

Lake Havasu City is the hub of activity on the lake. This community, with a population in excess of 20,000, has a full range of facilities including marinas, resorts, restaurants, golf clubs, bait and tackle dealers, etc. Of course, in the Laughlin-Bullhead City area there is another concentration of recreation opportunities and amenities, including casinos on the Nevada side of the lake. There are also resorts, campgrounds, R.V. parks, marinas, etc. Most of the casinos have courtesy docks for boaters.

Havasu Fishing Seasons			Good — Fair										
	J	F	M	A	M	J	J	A	S	O	N	D
Bass			Fair	Good	Good	Good	Good	Good	Good	Good	Fair	
Catfish		Fair	Good	Good	Good	Good	Good	Good	Good	Good	Good	Good
Panfish	Fair	Good	Good	Good	Good	Good	Good	Good	Good	Good	Good	Good
Striped Bass	Fair	Fair	Good	Good	Good	Good	Good	Good	Good	Good	Good	Good
Trout	Fair	Fair		Good	Good	Good	Good	Good	Good	Good	Good	Good

Havasu Fishing Tips

In the winter, striped bass are usually concentrated in the deeper waters of the main lake. A traditional winter hot spot is the Havasu Spring area near Parker Dam. In early spring, striper start their move to shallower water. In March and April they are in the upper lake and lower river. By May, fishing is good all the way up to Davis Dam. In the warm summer months following the migration, stripers are spread out and fish are caught just about everywhere. Just below Davis Dam, surf casting equipment is used to reach the white water with larger jigs. Most of the river section is too shallow to troll, so bait angling and casting and retrieving are productive. Casters drift about 30 feet offshore and cast to shore like largemouth bass anglers. November, December and January are prime months for crappie in the Topock Marsh area. In Lake Havasu proper, trolling, casting and spoon jigging are productive methods of taking striper. Good striper spots include Grass Island, Skier's Island, Sod Farm, Pilot Rock, Red Rock and outside of Streamboat Bay.

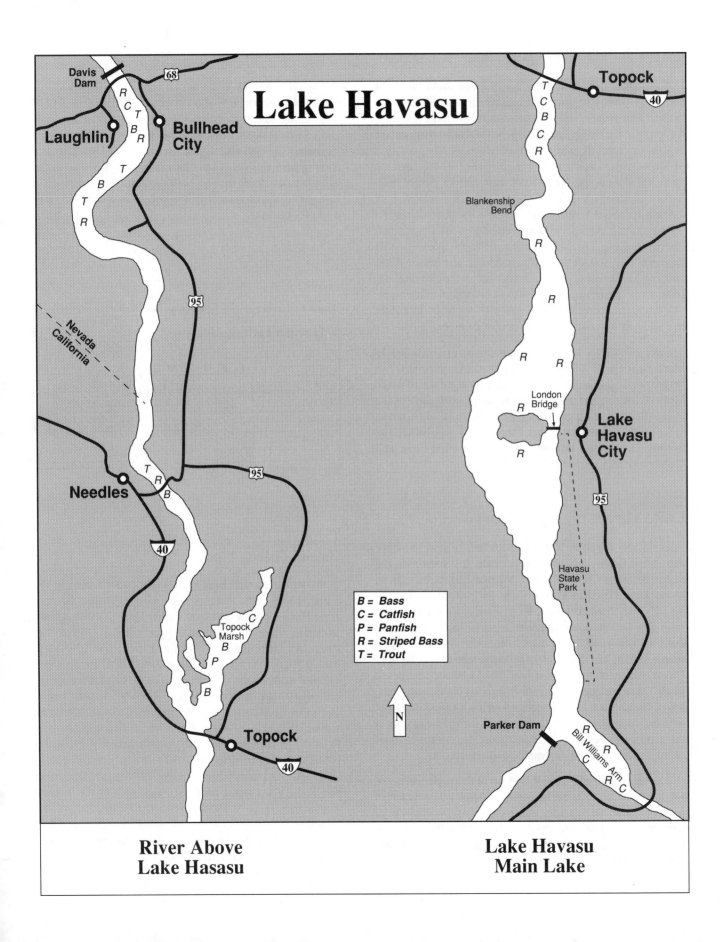

Lake Havasu

B = Bass
C = Catfish
P = Panfish
R = Striped Bass
T = Trout

**River Above
Lake Hasasu**

**Lake Havasu
Main Lake**

Bait fishing for stripers is maybe the most popular approach. Both shad and anchovies produce. Some anglers hook shad through the tail and pinch on a split shot a foot or so above the hook to get the bait down near structure or cover. Many anchovy anglers use a sliding sinker rig and either the front or back half of the bait fish. The use of anchovy chum is another way some anglers improve their bait fishing odds. This chum is made in Mexico and is available locally at Lake Havasu. By the way, most of the Havasu stripers run in the two to five pound range. Before the big 1983 flood, Havasu anglers hooked into 20 to 30 pound stripers regularly, but this is a rare occurrence now.

Havasu boasts both channel and flathead catfish. Most are in the two to five pound range, but some go up to 20 pounds. Channel cats are taken all over the lake, but flatheads are concentrated in the Bill Williams River area. Baits that produce include cut mackerel, anchovies, liver, nightcrawlers, and commercial products. Add catfish scent to any of these.

Lake Havasu Facts

Location: On the California-Arizona border

Size: The main lake is 45 miles long and covers 19,300 acres. Average depth is 40 feet.

Species: Striped bass, largemouth bass, rainbow trout, channel and flathead catfish, crappie, bluegill

Facilities: Extensive boating and onshore facilities are available at Lake Havasu. These are concentrated at the communities along the river and main lake.

Information: Lake Havasu Area Chamber of Commerce, 65 N. Lake Havasu Ave., Lake Havasu, AZ 86403, (520) 855-4115

Lake Havasu to the Mexico Border

(map - p. 197)

Lake Havasu is the southernmost of the string of famous Colorado River reservoirs. But it is by no means the end of great fishing on the Colorado River in California. As the crow flies, it's over 100 miles from Parker Dam at the south end of Lake Havasu down to the point where the Colorado River crosses the Mexico border near Yuma, Arizona. And as the Colorado flows, there are 140 miles of river angling for catfish, striped bass, largemouth bass, smallmouth bass, crappie and bluegill. The outstanding catfishing in these waters is well known, but very few Californians, besides the locals, are aware of the outstanding striper, bucketmouth and bronzeback possibilities.

Let's start with the catfishing. Flathead cats dominate the scene on the lower Colorado (from Parker Dam to Mexico). These are large, powerful fish, with many going from 20 to 40 pounds. They seem to prefer deeper pools and runs, especially those with sunken brush, rocks, etc. Flatheads are found most often immediately below and often just above all of the diversion dams on the river from Parker Dam on down. Some of the biggest cats, over 30 pounds, come out in the Yuma area. Below Laguna, Imperial and Morelos dams and at Pilot Knob are specific Yuma area hot spots.

Most large Colorado flatheads are caught in the summertime—from June through September. But large fish can and are taken throughout the year. Everyone agrees that nighttime angling is the most productive.

Live bait is the offering of choice. Goldfish are sold by the dozen at local bait shops. Personally caught bluegills or shad are also a popular choice, as are live crawdads. Most flathead chasers bait up on a sliding sinker rig. Use enough weight (usually from one to four ounces) to get the bait to the bottom depending on the current and the size of the bait. Line weight is a matter of choice, ranging from 12 to 50 pound test. Hook size depends on the bait size, but a 1/0 is probably about right. Rig with a 20 to 40 inch lead and a good swivel below the sinker. Most anglers hook the bait fish just behind the dorsal fin and below the spine. The largest cat recorded on the lower Colorado weighed in at over 60 pounds. And there are stories of fish being caught in the 80-90 pound class!

Some of the best striped bass fishing in the entire Colorado River system is available along the lower Colorado. The best bet for visitors is to come in spring or early summer and to concentrate on the waters immediately below one of six dams along the Colorado River. You see, these dams act as barriers to the natural upriver spring movement of stripers. So linesides congregate here feasting on schools of shad. The waters below Parker Dam probably get the most downriver action from anglers. The next dam south, Headgate Rock Dam, is also a fine striper producer, but these waters are almost completely overlooked. Next comes Palo Verde Diverson Dam, near Blythe. Anglers work the half-mile below the dam. Finally, there are three dams in the Yuma area (Imperial, Laguna and Morelos), each of which is a striper hot spot. Look for fish below all these dams to average four to six pounds with an occasional lunker going over 15 pounds.

Many anglers here like to fish a sliding sinker rig using netted live shad. Use just enough weight to get the shad bouncing along the bottom. Hook them through both lips.

When shad aren't available, some anglers substitute frozen shad or anchovies. Another approach is to catch some small (two to four inch) bluegills and use them for bait. This is legal in the lower Colorado River. Casting artificial lures into holding water from a drifting boat is another excellent approach.

Probably the most overlooked species along the Lower Colorado is the smallmouth bass. There's a good number of smallmouth bass all along the main channel of the river from Parker south to the Mexico border. Look for them at rockpiles and riprap in the main river, rather than in the pothole lakes favored by largemouths. Be sure to wear polaroid sunglasses to pick up the submerged rocks and stumps from your drifting boat. They are also useful in picking up navigational hazards in this river where water levels fluctuate frequently and widely. Tiny crayfish-shaped crankbait like those from Rebel are particularly effective, especially in fluorescent orange and chartreuse colors. Shad Raps, small Rapalas and crayfish-colored jigs also work. Fly anglers score best with Muddler Minnows that feature orange and brown color. Offerings that mimic the large resident flies and Wooly Buggers are also good. Most boat anglers prefer to fish when water flows are high (for east of launching), but wading or John-boat anglers often like low flow periods. Smallmouths are taken all year, but action peaks in spring and again in late fall.

Construction of Imperial Dam and other diversion and dike structures have created a number of placid backwaters that offer outstanding largemouth bass fishing. These include Martinez, Ferguson, Squaw, Taylor, Adobe, Walker, Three Fingers, Cibola and Palo Verde lakes. Sometimes called the "California Everglades," the sluggish river and sprawling marshes offer some of the best bass fishing in the entire state. The northern end of this bass paradise is at Walter's Camp at Palo Verde. From there for some 60 miles downstream, the Lower Colorado wanders through tule-lined shores and past hidden "lakes," secret sloughs, and brushy channels. These waters are best fished by flippin' plastic worms, grubs, and jigs into openings. A note of caution: boating in some areas can be hazardous and confusing. It's often best to stay close to your launch site or hire a guide. Spring and fall are the best seasons.

The Lower Colorado backwaters are also excellent crappie, bluegill and catfish fisheries. Catfishing for flatheads is also excellent in the All-American Canal which runs through the Imperial Valley north and west of Yuma.

Lower Colorado River Facts

Location: From Parker Dam at the south end of Lake Havasu to the Mexico border at Yuma, Arizona

Size: 140 miles of river with adjoining lakes

Species: Striped bass, flathead catfish, channel catfish, largemouth bass, smallmouth bass, crappie, bluegill

Facilities: There are a number of resorts, marinas, campgrounds, parks and communities along the Lower Colorado River.

Information: Parker Chamber of Commerce, (520) 669-2174; Blythe Chamber of Commerce, (760) 922-8166; Yuma County Chamber of Commerce, (520) 782-2567

Baja Fishing

Fishing in Southern California ocean waters is great. Inland regions would be thrilled to have it. But as it turns out, we've got it and even more. That's because there's Baja fishing too. Baja fishing is world-class fishing at its best. The fish are exotic, big and abundant. And the accommodations, whether they be on a long-range boat out of San Diego or at a seaside resort, are first class all the way.

It's impossible to cover everything about Baja fishing in the limited space of this section, so by necessity, only highlights and some basics are treated. More information is available in other books and magazines, from tackle stores, long-range trip operators and from conversations with people who have fished Baja. Since planning and preparation are important to making this type of an adventure a success, explore all these sources of Baja fishing insight before heading south.

Baja Trip Alternatives

There are several ways to enjoy Baja fishing. Some people cruise their ocean-going fishing boats down the Baja Peninsula. But this is a small minority of anglers. By far, a much more popular alternative is to fly or drive down to one of the outstanding resorts in Baja and fish in waters near that locale. Many of these resorts are relatively new and built to American standards, offering air conditioned rooms, swimming pools, tennis and many other amenities. Anglers who like to combine a plush resort vacation with some fine fishing will enjoy Baja resorts.

A third Baja alternative, one that is especially suited to dedicated anglers, is the long-range sport fishing boat trip. These trips are offered by several operators located in San

BAJA, MEXICO

Diego and are very popular. Part of the reason is the outstanding accommodations on the 90-115 foot aluminum-constructed boats. They feature air-conditioned staterooms, hot showers, sun decks, great food, and lounges complete with interior carpeting and video cassette television.

A final alternative for Baja-bound anglers is trailer boat fishing. This is also very popular. Boats ranging from outboard powered aluminum 14-footers to small flying bridge cruisers are towed by Californians to great fishing spots all along Baja.

Fly-in Fishing

An expensive and knowledgeable fishing-oriented travel agent is probably the single most important element for anglers wanting to fly to Baja's fishing destinations. They are familiar with airline schedules and fares, hotel and resort options, fishing charters, seasonal variations, Mexican travel regulations and everything else that goes into creating an enjoyable and successful trip. Make sure you deal with an agent who not only knows Baja travel, but also knows Baja fishing. Package deals that combine air travel, lodging and fishing often result in substantial savings and more time on the water. Here are some of the issues and questions to be concerned with when planning a fly-in Baja angling trip.

- Accommodations vary greatly both in proximity to the water and in amenities. There are many trade-offs to be made here. Discuss alternatives with your travel agent.

- Get up to speed on proof of citizenship documentation, luggage regulations, airport parking, options for bringing back fish, etc.

- There are seasonal trade-offs. For example, Cabo has lower hotel rates from about July 1 to about October 15 (considered off-season because of the heat) but this is when the marlin fishing is excellent.

- Consider the extra cost of sales and service taxes in Mexico. These can add 30% to hotel bills and hotel restaurant charges.

- Gather information on the proper types and quantity of tackle and equipment to take for a specific trip. Travel agents and Baja-oriented tackle dealers, as well as fishing books and outdoor magazines and newspapers, can all be helpful.

There are a number of good Baja fishing-oriented travel agents. These include the following:

- Baja Fishing Adventures, Long Beach, CA, (800) 451-6997

- Fishing International, Santa Rosa, CA, (800) 950-4242

Trailer Boat Fishing

Trailer boat anglers have the choice of an immense number of fishing locales along the over 2,000 miles of Baja coast. But don't expect the consistently good boat ramps that you've been used to in the United States. Many Baja ramps are extremely primitive and suitable only for aluminum boats. Sometimes a four-wheel drive tow vehicle is strongly recommended. Narrow and steep ramps are the norm. And watch out for the large tide swings in the upper Sea of Cortez area. Ramps here are only usable at higher tide levels.

Here is a brief rundown on some of the more popular trailer boating destinations:

- **Bahia Gonzaga Area**—This is a rapidly developing area that is only 230 miles south of the Mexicali border via Mex-5. Year-round fishing is good for spotted bay bass, corvina and grouper. In summer add yellowtail, barracuda and pompano. Fall brings dorado and skipjack. Much of the action takes place within a mile from shore.

- **Bahia de Los Angeles**—Not much farther down the Sea of Cortez coast is Bahia de Los Angeles. Facilities here are not what they once were, but the fishing is still better than anything along the California coast, despite the heavy pressure. Prominent species include barracuda, sierra, groupers, spotted bay bass, white sea bass, and yellowtail. Angling is good in the spring, summer and fall, but summertime air temperatures are intense. There can be long periods where the fishing is slow.

- **Santa Rosalia and Mulege**—The Transpeninsular highway (Mex-1) meets the Sea of Cortez at Santa Rosalia, about a 14 hour drive (600 miles) from the border. For the next 70 miles, anglers are treated to some of the finest fishing in the Gulf at places like San Lucas Cove, Punta Chivato, Mulege and Conception Bay. Small boat ramps are good here and the one at Punta Chivato can handle boats up to about 28 feet. Dominant fish here are yellowtail, grouper, and barracuda in the winter months, and dorado, skipjack and yellowfin in the summertime. Year-round residents include triggerfish, cabrilla, pargo, sargo, needlefish and pompano. Roosterfish sometimes show in summer and fall with occasional sailfish in summer.

- **East Cape**—For those who want to say that they've driven all the way down to the southern tip of Baja with a trailer boat, the East Cape, some 1,000 miles from the border, is the final destination. There is fine fishing year-round from Ventura to Los Frailes. Tuna, billfish and dorado are the main attraction, but don't overlook the outstanding action for snapper, grouper, triggerfish, pompano and roosterfish.

Trailer boat anglers driving down the Baja Peninsula need the following documentation:

- *A valid boat permit* which can be obtained by mail from the Mexican Department of Fisheries in San Diego, (619) 233-6956.

- *Valid fishing licenses* for all people 16 or over who are in a boat where fishing is taking place. These can also be obtained from the San Diego office noted in the above paragraph.

- *Current registration* for the boat and tow vehicle (to verify ownership).

- *Mexican insurance* for the boat and tow vehicle.

- *Valid passport or birth certificate* for each person in the party.

- *Mexican visa form.*

Long-Range Sportfishing Boats

Sportfishing boats began making multi-day trips into Baja waters in the late 1950s. In the early 1960s, the longest trip was about seven days and went to Guadalupe Island, a little over 200 miles south of San Diego. Sometimes boats also visited San Benito's and Cedros islands. It took 30-plus hours to reach these fertile fishing grounds where the quantity and size of species taken (mostly calico bass, giant sea bass, yellowtail and tuna) were outstanding.

Today, trips to these islands still operate. The main difference is that the boats are larger, more luxurious and twice as

fast. But, in addition, there are now trips that travel way down past the tip of Baja. There is a great deal of variability in the duration of these trips. They can extend from three days to almost three weeks. Of course, the length of the trip dictates the fishing grounds and the likely catch. Shorter trips (five to six days) concentrate mostly on larger fish of the same species as taken in Southern California waters. Eight to ten-day trips are needed to reach the truly exotic species (wahoo, dorado, etc.), and two-plus week trips to Clarion and the other islands in the Revilla Gigedo chain improve both the chance and size of these catches. Cost is another variable. A seven-day trip costs about $1,100 to $1,400, while a 16-day trip may run about $3,000. Expect trips to cost approximately $175 to $200 per day.

Miles	Trip Days	Fishing Grounds
250-300	5-6	Guadalupe San Benitos Cedros
500-600	7-8	Alijos Uncle Sam Banks
600-700	10-12	Alijos Cape San Lucas
900-1000	14-16	Clarion Roca Partida Socorro San Benedicto

A long-range Baja fishing trip on a modern boat out of San Diego can be one of the most exciting adventures of a lifetime. Anglers can catch over 1,000 pounds of fish per trip, and have a chance to hook monsters that weigh several hundred pounds. The trips are so good, in fact, that up to 90% of the passengers are repeat customers.

So what is the best way to get started? There are two schools of thought. Some experts suggest that anglers work their way up. Start with a short trip, about two to three days. Pick up some basic skills like casting, following your bait, managing the current, etc. With this method you'll know whether you like long-range trips, and you'll be more skillful before you spend big money on long trips. A second school of thought says that there is plenty of time to learn on a 16-day trip, for example. First-timers get free and friendly advice from seasoned long-rangers and deck hands. Serious anglers can pick up the tricks and techniques fairly quickly. Newcomers don't need to buy all the specialized equipment either. It can be rented. Plus there are long-range fishing seminars put on by tackle stores and boat operators that are extremely informative. No matter which approach you take, that first "long-ranger" will be an outstanding experience.

Three to five-day trips are popular for newcomers and regulars because they catch lots of fish with a minimum of travel time. The yellowtail caught off the SoCal coast are the northernmost edge of a population of fish that range south beyond Cedros Island. This species is the mainstay of the three to five-day trip. Cedros is as far south as a five-day trip will roam.

Three-day trips, often called San Martin Island trips, usually concentrate on water near this island which is off the Baja coast at San Quintin. But sometimes fish are found farther north at places such as Isolete and Colnett, two underwater reefs. Much of the travel on three-day trips is done at night, so their is close to two days of fishing action. A four-day trip to San Martin adds a third day of fishing. In addition to yellowtail, there are black sea bass, white sea bass, calico bass, halibut and rockfish. Many San Martin trips operate in spring and fall.

Four to five-day trips usually concentrate on Cedros, San Benitos and Guadalupe islands. It takes a full day of travel to reach this area. Look for big numbers of yellowtail in the 20 to 50 pound range, and calicos can go from five to eight pounds. Albacore are taken in the Guadalupe area in summertime. In the late summer and early fall, yellowfin and big-eye tuna are the main bill-of-fare on four to five-day trips at Cedros Island.

Seven to ten-day trips add variety and fishing time. Anglers take yellowfin tuna (up to 150 pounds), yellowtail, dorado, wahoo, grouper, black sea bass and calico bass. The maximum variety is on trips that depart from August and on into the fall, when weather and water temperatures bring warm water species farther north. Primary destinations include Alijos Rocks, San Pablo Bay, Ascuncion, Hippolito, the 13 and 23 Fathoms Banks and the Thetis Bank. Ten-day trips offer a good deal of fishing time since intermediate fishing stops provide action on three of the four travel days.

Today, the ultra long-range trips go from 16 to 23 days. Their destinations are places like the Revilla Gigedo chain and Clipperton Island. And their target is world-class yellowfin tuna, wahoo, black skipjack, rainbow runners and more.

The longer and farther south the trip, the larger the fish and variety of exotic species. Each day above 16 adds another fishing day. And operators typically decrease the number of passengers as they increase the days away from port, so fishing opportunity is improved. Some operators offer a fly-home-from-Cabo San Lucas option which shortens the trip by three days.

Seasons affect trip length. Usually the shortest trips, from three to four days, are in the summer and target yellowfin tuna. The longest trips are made in the winter to pursue wahoo and giant yellowfin tuna as far as 1,600 miles south of San Diego. An especially popular trip is the eight to ten day incursion in the fall. The warmest water temperatures of the year provide the opportunity for yellowtail, tuna, dorado, wahoo, giant sea bass and grouper all in one outing of less than two weeks.

There are many items to bring along on a long-range sportfishing boat: personal toiletries, medical supplies (ace bandages, band-aids, Q-tips, etc.), sunglasses, gloves, hand lotion, sun screen, room air freshener (to overcome the fish smell), laundry bag, and camera and film. Bring mostly old clothing . . . so old, in fact, that you can throw them away when you're home. Good footwear to avoid slipping on wet decks is also essential. Of course, many anglers bring along their own fishing gear.

All of the long-range sportfishing boats operate out of four landings in San Diego:

- Fisherman's Landing, (619) 221-8500
- H & M Landing, (619) 222-1144
- Lee Palm Long-Range Sportfishing, (619) 224-3857
- Point Loma Sportfishing, (619) 223-1627

Wahoo Fishing

Many feel that wahoo are the fastest, wildest and most exciting fish in Baja. They attain speeds of over 50 m.p.h. in the water and can jump 20 feet into the air. This sleek-snouted speedster is a far southern favorite. The best concentration are along the East Cape, at Cabo San Lucas, up the Pacific side of Baja to Thetis Bank, in the Revilla Gigedo chain and at Clarion Island. This super fighting game fish, actually a type of giant mackerel, weighs most often between 20 and 60 pounds, but 70 to 80 pounders aren't uncommon.

Wahoo are often located by trolling at a speed of about 8-9 knots. Oversized crankbait-like lures, like the Mako Marauder, are productive baits when trolled close in (50-100 feet) to the boat. Trollers use a medium-heavy to heavy 5 1/2 to 6 foot rod coupled to a Penn International 50 and 80 pound test line. This outfit can also be used for stand-up tuna fishing. Set the drag at about 25 pounds and be prepared for an unbelievable run.

Once located, wahoo can be taken by casting iron. Hopkins, Tady, Salsa and Krocodiles are thrown out and reeled in as fast as possible. Use 40 pound monofilament with a 18 to 24 inch wire leader. A final way to hook wahoo is with live bait. Collar-hooked anchovies on a 25 pound test line and a #2 live bait hook is one sure way to rig up. For baited sardines or mackerel, use a little larger hook and line. Don't forget the wire leader. You'll get more hook-ups with straight monofilament, but you'll lose more too. Consider yourself lucky to land half of the wahoo you hook, no matter what tackle and rigging you use—they're tough fighters.

Marlin Fishing

Striped marlin are caught virtually year-round at the tip of Baja. In late summer and early fall, this species ranges north along the Pacific side of Baja as far up as Southern California. In spring and summer, some striped marlin are taken as far north as Loreto and Mulege on the Sea of Cortez. But generally the best striped marlin fishing occurs south of La Paz off the stretch of coast extending about 150 miles to Cabo San Lucas. Specifically, good striped marlin fishing areas are found off Puerto Pescadaro, Buena Vista, Punta Colorado, San Jose del Cabo and Cabo San Lucas. Consistent areas out of Cabo include Golden Gate Banks, Jammie Banks, Lusitania Banks and Gordo Banks.

Blue and black marlin, the largest in the marlin family, visit the tip of Baja primarily in the fall and early winter months. Most are taken from La Paz south to Cabo San Lucas.

Most marlin are taken from local charter boats that originate from ports and harbors in southern Baja (e.g. Cabo San Lucas). Some are, however, taken incidentally by long-range sportfishing boats from San Diego at places like the Revilla Gigedo Islands.

The key to successful marlin fishing in Baja is finding the fish. The search is more than half the battle for these monsters (blues and blacks can weight up to five, six, seven, or even eight hundred pounds). Many wasted hours can be spent trolling. That's because knowledge of marlins' feeding habits, their hangouts, and the current and tidal movements that trigger the bite, all play a critical role. It's the charter boat captain's knowledge of subtle changes in conditions that often makes for a successful outing. By the way, most of these charter boat trips include the use of their tackle.

Yellowfin Tuna Fishing

Yellowfin tuna, ranging from 20 to 400 pounds, are one of the prime attractions in Baja. They are taken in Baja waters by both long-range sportfishing boats out of San Diego and by boats out of fishing centers in Baja. On the Pacific side of Baja, yellowfin tuna can range as far up as the lower waters of Southern California, when water temperatures reach their peak in the early fall. Yellowfin move as far north in the Sea of Cortez as the Midriff Islands, usually in the late summer and early fall. The best yellowfin tuna fishing is usually in the East Cape regions, at the South Cape, and at the farther south islands (i.e. Revilla Gigedo and Clipperton). For example, yellowfin tuna fishing is rated by experts to be either excellent or very good at Cabo San Lucas all year long, with the second six months of the year being the most outstanding.

Dorado Fishing

Dorado, or dolphin fish, are acrobatic fighters, brilliantly colored and delicious eating. They are generally a rich iridescent blue-green turning to bluish gold or silver gold on the lower flanks with white or yellow on the belly. Some dorado are caught in the southern portions of Baja practically year around. But the largest concentrations often appear in winter and spring. Dorado angling is good off Cabo San Lucas and along the San Jose del Cabo to La Paz coast during the summer. Large concentrations migrate north to the Midriff Islands in the Sea of Cortez in the warmer months.

Dorado are often caught on fall and winter long-range sportfishing boats out of San Diego on trips of eight to ten days, or longer. These beauties like to hang around floating kelp beds, logs or buoys. They are caught by trolling surface baits, small feathers, metal jigs or Rapala-type plugs. They also hit casted live bait or chunks of bait. A successful dorado stop on a long-range boat can yield over 100 fish in an hour or two.

Baja Travel and Angling Information

There are several basic Baja information sources that all southbound anglers should be aware of. Most public libraries have these publications. After looking them over, you may want to purchase the ones that best suit your needs.

- *The Baja Book III* (Baja Trails Publications)
- *Baja California Guide and Baja Map* (AAA)
- *Baja Boater's Guide ,Pacific Coast* (by Jack Williams)
- *Baja Boater's Guide , Sea of Cortez* (by Jack Williams)
- *Baja Catch* (Apples and Oranges, Inc.)
- *Long Range Fishing* (by Chuck Garrison)
- *Angler's Guide to Baja California* (by Tom Miller)

Southern California Sportfishing Landings

The following is an updated list of sportsfishing landings in Southern California (from north to south) along with phone numbers:

- Virg's Sportsfishing, Morro Bay, (805) 772-1222
- Patriot Sportfishing, Avila Beach, (805) 595-7200
- Sea Landing, Santa Barbara, (805) 963-3564
- Harbor Village Sportfishing, Ventura, (805) 658-1060
- CISCO Landing, Oxnard, (805) 985-8511
- Captain Hook's Sportfishing, Oxnard, (805) 382-6233
- Port Hueneme Sportfishing, Hueneme, (805) 488-2212
- Del Rey Sportfishing, Marina del Rey, (310) 822-3625
- Redondo Sportfishing, Redondo Beach, (310) 372-2111
- 22nd Street Landing, San Pedro, (310) 832-8304
- L.A. Harbor Sportfishing, San Pedro, (310) 547-9916
- Long Beach Sportfishing, Long Beach, (562) 432-8993
- Pierpoint Landing, Long Beach, (562) 983-9300
- Belmont Pier Sportfishing, Long Beach, (562) 434-6781
- Marina Sportfishing, Long Beach, (562) 598-6649
- Big Fish Sportfishing, Seal Beach, (562) 598-4700
- Newport Landing, Newport Beach, (949) 675-0550
- Davey's Locker, Newport Beach, (949) 673-1434
- Dana Wharf Sportfishing, Dana Point, (949) 496-5794
- Helgren's Sportfishing, Oceanside, (760) 722-2133
- Islandia Sportfishing, Mission Bay, (619) 222-1165
- Seaforth Sportfishing, Mission Bay, (619) 224-3383
- H & M Landing, San Diego, (619) 222-1144
- Point Loma Sportfishing, San Diego, (619) 223-1627
- Fisherman's Landing, San Diego, (619) 221-8500
- Lee Palm's Sportfishing, San Diego, (619) 224-3857

Launch Info

For complete information on the many public saltwater launch ramps see page 89.

Pacific Ocean Fishing

The coastal waters of the Pacific Ocean offer an immense variety of fishing opportunities. There are numerous sport fishing party boats, marinas and boat launching facilities for those who want to fish in the bays, islands and open ocean. Shore fishing facilities include miles of beaches and rocky coastlines, as well as numerous piers, jetties, breakwaters and harbors.

Fishing can and does go on all year long (see chart below). There's live bait fishing for bonito, barracuda, bass and yellowtail. There's also drift fishing for halibut and bottom fishing for lingcod and rockfish. Trollers pursue yellowfin, bonito and striped marlin. Surf casters work the breakers for perch, croaker and halibut, while more agile souls work rocky shores for the likes of opaleye, halfmoon, kelp bass and cabezon. And finally there are the pier, barge, jetty and breakwater anglers who catch a little bit of everything.

But ocean fishing can be dangerous. Anglers are lost every year. Breakers wash fishermen off rocks. People fall overboard. Wind warnings are foolishly ignored. Equipment fails. But don't let this scare you away from fishing. Do enjoy the marvelous experience of ocean fishing, but be prepared, be careful, and error on the side of caution.

The bite of most saltwater species is less predictable than that of their freshwater cousins. So success on an ocean fishing outing depends, to a great extent, on going at the proper time. There are many sources of fishing information that can be helpful to the saltwater angler. Ocean-oriented bait and tackle shops and party boat operators are always worth a phone call. There are several outdoor newspapers that are also very helpful, as are local daily papers. A drive to the shore to meet the party boats as they come in and to ask the pier anglers how they're doing is also worth considering.

Ocean bottom structure is also an important consideration, as shown on the next page.

Naturally occurring banks and reefs are highlighted on the maps in this chapter. But there are other reefs, many of which are closer to shore, that provide some outstanding angling. These manmade reefs, ranging from quarry rock piles to sunken ships, are scattered along the coast from San Luis Obispo all the way south to San Diego. In total, there are over

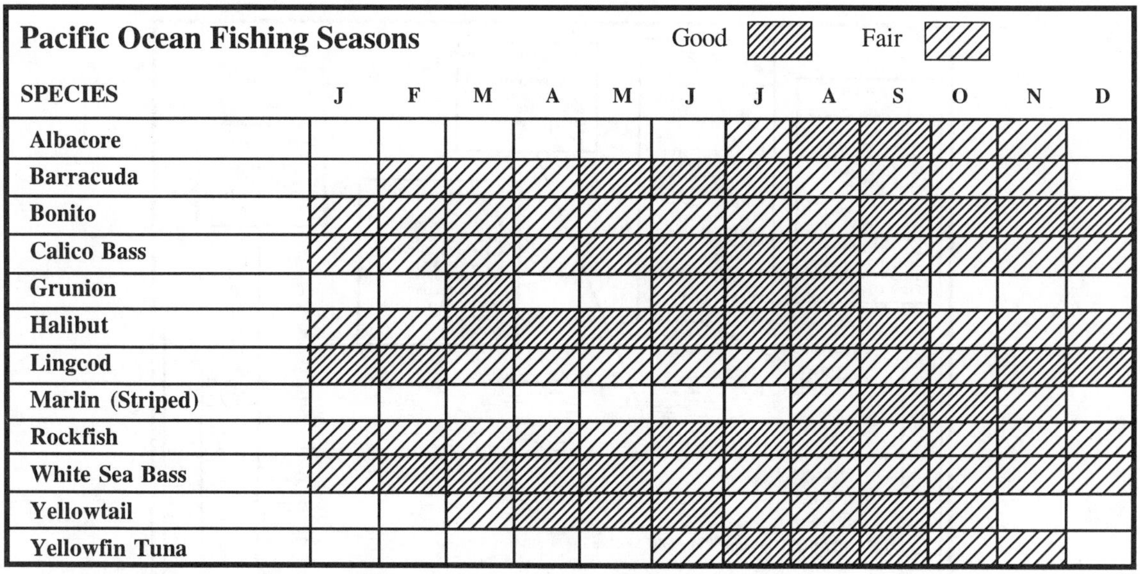

Pacific Ocean Fishing Seasons — Good ▨ Fair ▨

SPECIES	J	F	M	A	M	J	J	A	S	O	N	D
Albacore							▨	▨	▨	▨	▨	
Barracuda		▨	▨	▨	▨	▨	▨	▨	▨	▨		
Bonito	▨	▨	▨	▨	▨	▨	▨	▨	▨	▨	▨	▨
Calico Bass	▨	▨	▨	▨	▨	▨	▨	▨	▨	▨	▨	▨
Grunion			▨	▨	▨	▨	▨	▨				
Halibut	▨	▨	▨	▨	▨	▨	▨	▨	▨	▨	▨	▨
Lingcod	▨	▨	▨	▨	▨	▨	▨	▨	▨	▨	▨	▨
Marlin (Striped)							▨	▨	▨	▨		
Rockfish	▨	▨	▨	▨	▨	▨	▨	▨	▨	▨	▨	▨
White Sea Bass	▨	▨	▨	▨	▨	▨	▨	▨	▨	▨	▨	▨
Yellowtail				▨	▨	▨	▨	▨	▨	▨		
Yellowfin Tuna						▨	▨	▨	▨	▨	▨	

This section is based on *Angler's Guide to the United States Pacific Coast* (U.S. Dept. of Commerce).

two dozen. Recently, the California Department of Fish and Game published a booklet that describes each artificial reef in detail. Coordinates, maps and fish species that inhabit the reef are all presented. *A Guide to the Artificial Reefs of Southern California* is available from local Department of Fish and Game offices and at many public libraries. Review a copy and then head out for some shallow water reef fishing action.

San Diego Area (map - p. 213)

In the San Diego area the major offshore fishing grounds are about Mexico's Coronado Islands and near the Point Loma and La Jolla kelp beds. Some of the finest marine angling facilities for fishing in local and distant waters are to be found in San Diego Harbor and Mission Bay. San Diego is the principal port for long-range fishing trips to off the coast of

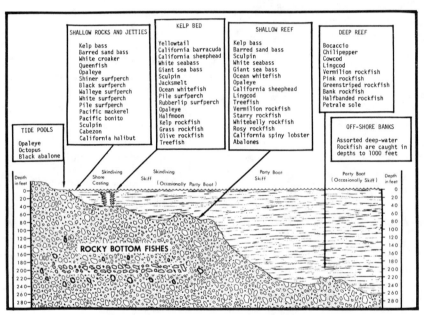

Species taken most commonly in rocky bottom habitats according to depth.

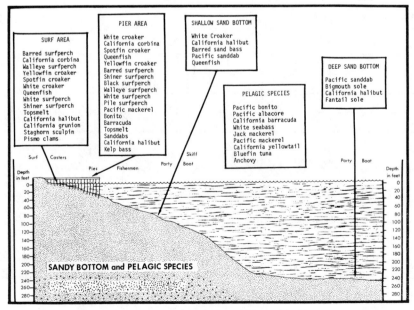

Species taken most commonly in sandy bottom and pelagic habitats according to depth.

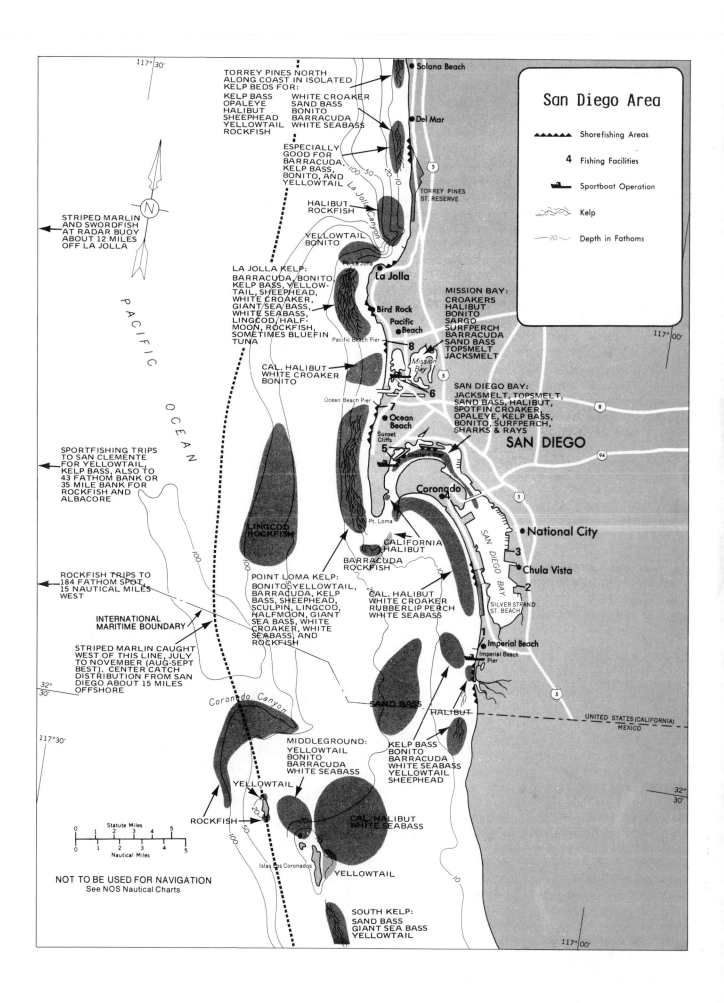

San Diego Area

⩗⩗⩗⩗ Shorefishing Areas

4 Fishing Facilities

⛴ Sportboat Operation

〰️ Kelp

—20— Depth in Fathoms

TORREY PINES NORTH
ALONG COAST IN ISOLATED
KELP BEDS FOR:
KELP BASS   WHITE CROAKER
OPALEYE   SAND BASS
HALIBUT   BONITO
SHEEPHEAD   BARRACUDA
YELLOWTAIL   WHITE SEABASS
ROCKFISH

● Solana Beach

● Del Mar

ESPECIALLY
GOOD FOR
BARRACUDA,
KELP BASS,
BONITO, AND
YELLOWTAIL

TORREY PINES
ST. RESERVE

HALIBUT
ROCKFISH

YELLOWTAIL
BONITO

STRIPED MARLIN
AND SWORDFISH
AT RADAR BUOY
ABOUT 12 MILES
OFF LA JOLLA

Pt. La Jolla

LA JOLLA KELP:
BARRACUDA, BONITO
KELP BASS, YELLOW-
TAIL, SHEEPHEAD,
WHITE CROAKER,
GIANT SEA BASS,
WHITE SEABASS,
LINGCOD, HALF-
MOON, ROCKFISH,
SOMETIMES BLUEFIN
TUNA

● La Jolla

● Bird Rock
Pacific
● Beach

Pacific Beach Pier

MISSION BAY:
CROAKERS
HALIBUT
BONITO
SARGO
SURFPERCH
BARRACUDA
SAND BASS
TOPSMELT
JACKSMELT

P A C I F I C

CAL. HALIBUT
WHITE CROAKER
BONITO

Mission
Bay

8

6

Ocean Beach Pier

7

SAN DIEGO BAY:
JACKSMELT, TOPSMELT,
SAND BASS, HALIBUT,
SPOTFIN CROAKER,
OPALEYE, KELP BASS,
BONITO, SURFPERCH,
SHARKS & RAYS

SPORTFISHING TRIPS
TO SAN CLEMENTE
FOR YELLOWTAIL,
KELP BASS, ALSO TO
43 FATHOM BANK OR
35 MILE BANK FOR
ROCKFISH AND
ALBACORE

O C E A N

● Ocean
Beach

Sunset
Cliffs

5

Shelter I. Bar

SAN DIEGO

● Corondo
4

LINGCOD
ROCKFISH

Pt. Loma

CALIFORNIA
HALIBUT

● National City

ROCKFISH TRIPS TO
184 FATHOM SPOT,
15 NAUTICAL MILES
WEST

BARRACUDA
ROCKFISH

CAL. HALIBUT
WHITE CROAKER
RUBBERLIP PERCH
WHITE SEABASS

SAN DIEGO BAY

3

● Chula Vista

INTERNATIONAL
MARITIME BOUNDARY

POINT LOMA KELP:
BONITO, YELLOWTAIL,
BARRACUDA, KELP
BASS, SHEEPHEAD,
SCULPIN, LINGCOD,
HALFMOON, GIANT
SEA BASS, WHITE
CROAKER, WHITE
SEABASS, AND
ROCKFISH

SILVER STRAND
ST. BEACH

2

STRIPED MARLIN CAUGHT
WEST OF THIS LINE, JULY
TO NOVEMBER (AUG-SEPT
BEST). CENTER CATCH
DISTRIBUTION FROM SAN
DIEGO ABOUT 15 MILES
OFFSHORE

● Imperial Beach

Imperial Beach
Pier

Coronado Canyon

SAND BASS

HALIBUT

UNITED STATES (CALIFORNIA)
MEXICO

MIDDLEGROUND:
YELLOWTAIL
BONITO
BARRACUDA
WHITE SEABASS

KELP BASS
BONITO
BARRACUDA
WHITE SEABASS
YELLOWTAIL
SHEEPHEAD

YELLOWTAIL

ROCKFISH

CAL. HALIBUT
WHITE SEABASS

| Statute Miles |
| 0 1 2 3 4 5 |
| Nautical Miles |
| 0 1 2 3 4 5 |

Islas Los Coronados

YELLOWTAIL

NOT TO BE USED FOR NAVIGATION
See NOS Nautical Charts

SOUTH KELP:
SAND BASS
GIANT SEA BASS
YELLOWTAIL

Baja California. It is also one of the ports for yellowfin sport fishing from July through October, with most fishing within 40 to 100 miles west and southwest of San Diego. Sometimes in early summer albacore will also appear near the Coronado Islands. Occasionally, trips by modern well-equipped sport fishing boats are made to San Clemente Island for yellowtail and kelp bass and to offshore banks for rockfish.

Variations in the bottom offshore topography have a pronounced influence on where different species are caught. The coastal shelf of San Diego is widest from Point Loma south to the Coronado Islands, averaging about 20 fathoms in depth. Here the bottom is sand, sand shell, and mud and sand, over which sand bass, white seabass, California halibut and sizeable quantities of forage fish such as the northern anchovy are frequently taken. Although the bottom is generally sandy from the Coronado Islands north, near-shore rocky reefs are to be found off Imperial Beach, Point Loma and La Jolla.

Off Point Loma the shelf is about three miles wide and becomes narrower off La Jolla and to the north; off shore the bottom depth descends to about 600 fathoms. The edge of the shelf is generally the inner limit of late summer fishing for striped marlin. Excellent fishing areas for rockfish can also be found along the shelf edge.

Several submarine canyons cut into the near-shore shelf; the two most prominent are the Coronado Canyon and the La Jolla Canyon. These canyons provide good habitats along their upper edges for rockfish, sheepheads, kelp bass and grouper.

The Coronado Islands are the property of Mexico, and a Mexican fishing license must be obtained before fishing about any of the three islands. When fishing from a commercial sport fishing boat, the foreign fishing license fee is usually included in the cost of the trip. These islands constitute a productive area in Southern California for fishing yellowtail, which are taken there during late spring through summer. The north end of the North Coronado Island is a traditional spot for yellowtail fishing, and anglers usually experience a morning bite. The "Middle Ground," between North Coronado and Middle Coronado, can also be good for yellowtail and for white seabass in spring. Other game fish taken by anglers around the Coronado Islands are as follows: Pacific barracuda, Pacific bonito, rockfish (olive, kelp and grass), lingcod, ocean whitefish, sculpin and kelp bass. Pacific barracuda are taken April through October (summer best), and Pacific bonito are caught in summer—the remaining species are taken year-round. Between the Coronado Islands and the mainland coast, fishing is good for white seabass in spring and early summer, when squid are spawning in this area. This is also a good fishing location for California halibut during the spring. North of the Coronado Islands along the edge of the Coronado Submarine Canyon in deep water, bottom anglers catch rockfish (chilipepper, bocaccio, vermillion, yellowtail, gopher and canary).

The Point Loma kelp beds and deep water immediately northwest of the Point are good fishing spots. Near shore, rockfish (olive, grass, vermillion and kelp) are commonly taken near the kelp beds; off shore in deeper water, bocaccio, chilipepper, gopher, canary and green-striped rock fish are caught.

Fishing the La Jolla kelp bed has become increasingly popular over the years. Statistics indicate there are more anglers catching greater numbers of fish from this area than from any other location along the California coast. Off Point La Jolla, California halibut sometimes are taken on the flats to the north and south of the La Jolla Submarine Canyon.

North of La Jolla begins a near continuous kelp bed that extends northward along the coast. There is a limited amount of fishing off the kelp beds at Del Mar and in adjacent areas to the north and south for kelp bass and rock fish (kelp, olive, grass and vermillion). Yellowtail and Pacific bonito sometimes are taken in and about these kelp beds.

Several public piers, located in bays or along the open coast, allow the marine anglers to catch resident fish and sometimes migratory species such as Pacific bonito and Pacific barracuda. The outer coast has two public piers. The Ocean Beach public fishing pier is a good place for surfperch (barred, pile, walleye and kelp), Pacific bonito, Pacific mackerel, white seabass, sharks (sand, brown smoothhound and leopard), queenfish, jacksmelt, California halibut and sculpin. To the south, the Imperial Beach fishing pier just north of the Mexican border has, at times, good fishing for pile and rubberlip surfperch in winter and spring, and walleye and

	San Diego Area Fishing Facilities				
Location	Sport Fishing Boats	Pier Fishing	Boat Rental	Launch Ramp	Jetty Fishing
Imperial Beach (1)*	X	X		X	
Chula Vista (2)				X	
National City (3)				X	
Coronado (4)				X	
Shelter Island (5)	X	X		X	
Mission Bay (6)	X		X	X	X
Ocean Bay Pier (7)		X			
Pacific Bay Pier (8)		X		X	

*Map fishing facilities

shiner surfperch all year. Sharks, rays, white croaker, Pacific sanddab, Pacific bonito, jacksmelt, Pacific barracuda, white seabass (small), cabezon, sculpin and "rock" crabs are also taken from this pier.

San Diego Bay has some fishing about the municipal piers for sculpin, jacksmelt, pile surfperch, topsmelt, sharks and rays. The major public sport fishing pier in San Diego Bay is on Shelter Island, near the entrance to the bay. Off the pier and along the nearby rocky shore, anglers catch surfperch (shiner, black, rubberlip and pile), jacksmelt, topsmelt, sand bass, sculpin, sharks, rays, Pacific bonito and California halibut. Anglers fish for the same array of shore species from the south side of Shelter Island and one mile east off Harbor Island.

Mission Bay offers excellent pier, shore or small-boat fishing. Bay fishermen frequently catch yellowfin and spotfin croaker, small Pacific bonito and Pacific barracuda, California halibut, shiner and rubberlip surfperch, topsmelt, jacksmelt, spotted sand bass, sharks and rays.

The open coast offers shore fishing along both rocky and sandy shores; the species caught depends upon which of these two shoreline types is being fished. Some of the better shore fishing areas are near Del Mar and Torrey Pines, and from Coronado to Imperial Beach.

The major sandy shore fish are surfperch, croaker, corbina and grunion. The barred surfperch is common and comprises about 70% of the shore angler's surfperch catch. It is taken throughout the year, but December through March is considered the best. Others such as shiner, white, rainbow, rubberlip and silver surfperch are available all year. The walleye surfperch is also taken most of the year over a sandy bottom, as well as around pier pilings and jetties. Catches of California corbina are taken off the sandy shore all year, but are greatest during July through September. Spotfin croaker are taken all year, but summer fishing is best, especially along beaches extending north from Imperial Beach. Yellowfin croaker are caught on some sandy shores during the summer run, but these locations will vary according to movements of the fish. The white croaker or kingfish is taken off most sandy beaches.

Grunion is one of the favorite fish on the open-coast sandy beach. This small silvery fish enters the surf during periods of high tide in late spring and summer from March to September. They may be captured by hand in such popular fishing areas such as La Jolla, Pacific Beach, Mission Beach, Ocean Beach, along the Coronado Strand (Silver Strand), and Imperial Beach. The best time to search for grunion is the second, third and fourth nights after a full moon and for a three-hour period after a high tide.

Along rocky portions of the coast at La Jolla, Bird Rock and Sunset Cliffs and about Point Loma, the species commonly taken are opaleye (best in spring), half moon, surf perch (black, shiner, walleye and pile), rockfish (kelp, grass and brown), kelp bass and occasionally sargo and cabezon. Opaleye, halfmoon and rockfish are available to the rocky-shore angler all year.

Solana Beach to Dana Point
(map - p. 216)

This fishing area, geographically between the population centers of San Diego and Los Angeles, is a growing one for marine sport operations. New facilities such the extensive small boat harbor at Dana Point (Dana Harbor), and the excellent small-boat basin at Oceanside now make many coastal fishing areas accessible to the small-boat angler. About 15 miles of coastline from Oceanside north to near San Mateo Point is the property of the U.S. Marine Corps and is part of the Camp Pendelton complex. Access to this area was very limited; however, in the north a portion of the coast (San Onofre Bluffs State Beach) and greater access to the shore is being given to the public.

The coastal shelf is very narrow off this section of coast, extending only two to three miles off shore before reaching a depth of 50 fathoms or more. Sand and gray sand predominate the bottom near shore, with some rocky areas such as those found north of Oceanside and along the coast of San Mateo Point northward. This hard bottom stratum allows for development of kelp, which in turn provides an attractive environment for kelp bass and the brown types of rockfish. Off shore in deeper water the bottom type is gray and green mud, and the coastal shelf descends to a depth of 300 to 400 fathoms within 8 to 10 miles offshore. Along the edge of the shelf, in the deep water, are several places where rockfish may be taken.

Sport fishing boats are available at the port of Dana Harbor and at Oceanside. These boats fish the coastal kelp beds and offshore in deep water for rockfish and other species. During albacore season they run offshore to 60 Mile Bank (60 miles southwest of Point Loma), to the 43 Fathom Bank (35 miles west of Point Loma), and sometimes beyond San Clemente Island. The 209 Bank, about 35 miles west of the mainland, is one of the better fishing areas for striped marlin and swordfish, and albacore occasionally are taken here during July or August.

Immediately offshore from Solana Beach north to Carlsbad and from San Mateo Point to San Clemente are substantial kelp beds. Although the kelp beds in this area are not as

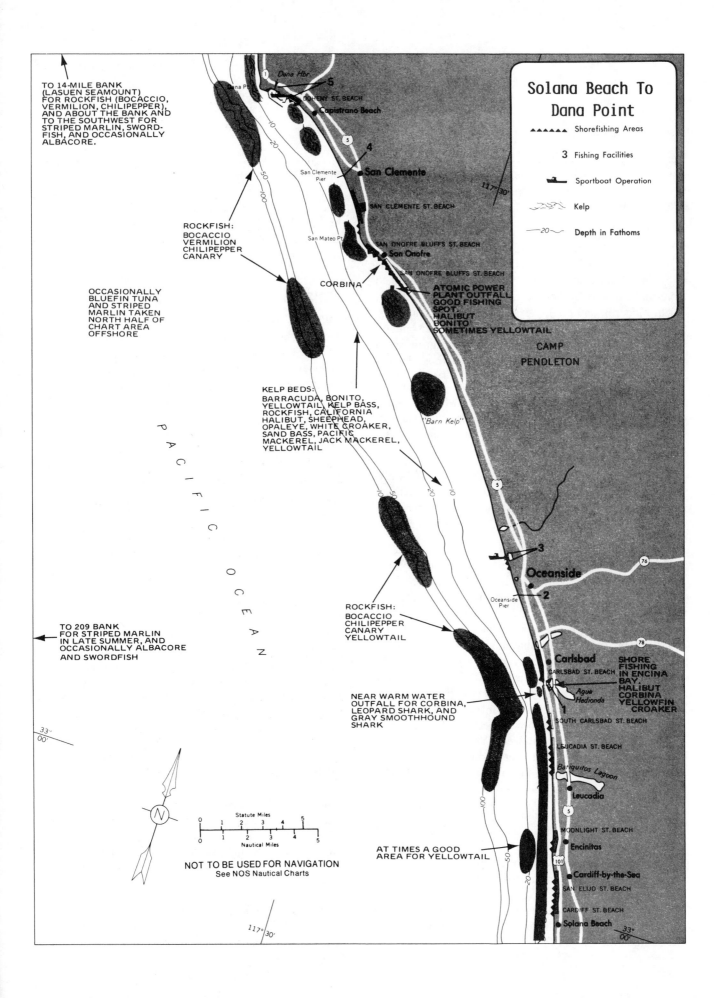

TO 14-MILE BANK
(LASUEN SEAMOUNT)
FOR ROCKFISH (BOCACCIO,
VERMILION, CHILIPEPPER),
AND ABOUT THE BANK AND
TO THE SOUTHWEST FOR
STRIPED MARLIN, SWORD-
FISH, AND OCCASIONALLY
ALBACORE.

ROCKFISH:
BOCACCIO
VERMILION
CHILIPEPPER
CANARY

OCCASIONALLY
BLUEFIN TUNA
AND STRIPED
MARLIN TAKEN
NORTH HALF OF
CHART AREA
OFFSHORE

KELP BEDS:
BARRACUDA, BONITO,
YELLOWTAIL, KELP BASS,
ROCKFISH, CALIFORNIA
HALIBUT, SHEEPHEAD,
OPALEYE, WHITE CROAKER,
SAND BASS, PACIFIC
MACKEREL, JACK MACKEREL,
YELLOWTAIL

PACIFIC OCEAN

TO 209 BANK
FOR STRIPED MARLIN
IN LATE SUMMER, AND
OCCASIONALLY ALBACORE
AND SWORDFISH

ROCKFISH:
BOCACCIO
CHILIPEPPER
CANARY
YELLOWTAIL

NEAR WARM WATER
OUTFALL FOR CORBINA,
LEOPARD SHARK, AND
GRAY SMOOTHHOUND
SHARK

AT TIMES A GOOD
AREA FOR YELLOWTAIL

Statute Miles
0 1 2 3 4 5

Nautical Miles
0 1 2 3 4 5

NOT TO BE USED FOR NAVIGATION
See NOS Nautical Charts

N

33°
00'

117° 30'

117° 30'

33°
00'

Solana Beach To
Dana Point

▲▲▲▲▲▲▲ Shorefishing Areas

3 Fishing Facilities

Sportboat Operation

Kelp

—20— Depth in Fathoms

Dana Hbr.
Dana Pt.
DOHENY ST. BEACH
5
Capistrano Beach
4
San Clemente
Pier
San Clemente
SAN CLEMENTE ST. BEACH
San Mateo Pt.
SAN ONOFRE BLUFFS ST. BEACH
San Onofre
SAN ONOFRE BLUFFS ST. BEACH
CORBINA
ATOMIC POWER
PLANT OUTFALL
GOOD FISHING
SPOT.
HALIBUT
BONITO
SOMETIMES YELLOWTAIL

CAMP
PENDLETON

"Barn Kelp"

3
Oceanside
2
Oceanside
Pier

76

78

Carlsbad
CARLSBAD ST. BEACH
Agua
Hedionda
SHORE
FISHING
IN ENCINA
BAY.
HALIBUT
CORBINA
YELLOWFIN
CROAKER
1
SOUTH CARLSBAD ST. BEACH

LEUCADIA ST. BEACH

Batiquitos Lagoon

Leucadia
5

MOONLIGHT ST. BEACH
Encinitas

101

Cardiff-by-the-Sea
SAN ELIJO ST. BEACH

CARDIFF ST. BEACH

Solana Beach
33°
00'

extensive as those off Point Loma to the south, or off the Santa Barbara coast farther north, they do provide a suitable habitat for kelp bass, sand bass and rockfish (kelp, grass, olive and vermillion), and also attract coastal migrants such as Pacific barracuda and Pacific bonito. Yellowtail and white seabass are sometimes taken near the kelp as are jack and Pacific mackerel (July to September), opaleye, white croaker and kelp rockfish. Near-shore rocky reefs provide a habitat suit-

Solano Beach to Dana Point Fishing Facilities					
Location	Sport Fishing Boats	Pier Fishing	Boat Rental	Launch Ramp	Jetty Fishing
Encina Bay (1)*					X
Oceanside Pier (2)		X			
Oceanside Harbor (3)	X			X	X
San Clemente (4)		X			
Dana Harbor (5)	X	X	X	X	X

*Map fishing facilities

able for many species such as opaleye, grass and kelp rockfish, halfmoon, cabezon and black surfperch.

Rockfishing is often productive along the edge of the narrow coastal shelf, in water 30 to 100 fathoms deep over rocky, sharp-sloping areas. Anglers fish off Carlsbad to Oceanside and north to Dana Point for bocaccio, chilipepper, canary and yellowtail species of rockfish.

Bluefin tuna and striped marlin are taken occasionally off the San Clemente Coast in late summer, even less frequently, however, in recent years.

Two public fishing piers are available along this stretch of coast. One is at San Clemente where surfperch (barred, walleye and rubberlip), California halibut, sculpin and the usual array of sharks and rays are caught. The second is the Oceanside fishing pier, good at times for runs of California halibut (spring and summer being best), sculpin, sargo, jacksmelt, white croaker (kingfish), queenfish, Pacific bonito, Pacific barracuda (in summer), kelp and sand bass, barred and walleye surfperch, and occasionally small white seabass. In addition, there is shore fishing from the jetty systems at Dana Harbor and Oceanside.

The extensive sandy shore beaches from Solana Beach to San Clemente are productive areas for the surf angler. Some of the better, or at least more popular, surf fishing areas are found near San Mateo Point where corbina are taken from July through September. Farther south there is excellent spotfin

croaker and barred surfperch fishing along San Onofre Bluffs State Beach near the northern boundary of Camp Pendelton. Fishing is good three miles south of Carlsbad, particularly about the entrance to the cooling-water inlet of the steam-electric generating plant, where because of a constant inflow of water from the ocean, the small bay has a high concentration of California halibut, corbina and yellowfin croaker. Other good shore fishing spots are north of Leucadia and near San Elijo Lagoon, just north of Solana Beach. Surfperch frequently taken along the sandy shores are the barred (best in winter and spring), walleye shiner, calico (best from December to March), and silver species. Other fish taken by the surf angler are the white and yellowfin croaker and California halibut. Grunion runs are known to occur on these beaches in late spring and early summer.

The shore from San Mateo Point to San Clemente has only a few isolated areas where rocky-shore species can be taken.

Los Angeles Area (map - p. 218)

A great diversity of fishing areas and facilities are available from Laguna Beach to Point Vicente. Many types of angling opportunities are available along rocky and sandy shores, from jetties and piers, in bays, and over offshore kelp beds and deep-water fishing grounds. The coastline is oriented generally in a northwest-southwest direction with about one-half composed of sandy beaches; the rest is a rocky shore interlaced with small sandy beaches.

Major sport fishing boat facilities are available at three locations in the Los Angeles-Long Beach Harbor area—one at Long Beach and two at San Pedro. Smaller sport boat operations are available at the Belmont Shore, Huntington Beach and Seal Beach piers. Newport Beach and Balboa have extensive sport boat and pier facilities.

South of Newport Beach to off Laguna Beach the coastal shelf is very narrow—about two miles, sometimes less—in width. The bottom near shore is mostly sand and mud interspersed with rocky areas. Because of the narrow shelf, open ocean species such as bluefin tuna and striped marlin sometimes migrate to within a short distance of the shore.

From about Newport Beach west towards Long Beach and Point Fermin, the coastal shelf widens to its greatest width in Southern California. The bottom near shore is primarily sand, gray sand and mud, and provides a good habitat for sand, shells, green sand and green mud. Along the outer edge of the coastal shelf, the bottom descends to a depth of 250 to 300 fathoms, providing good rockfishing locations. The bottom

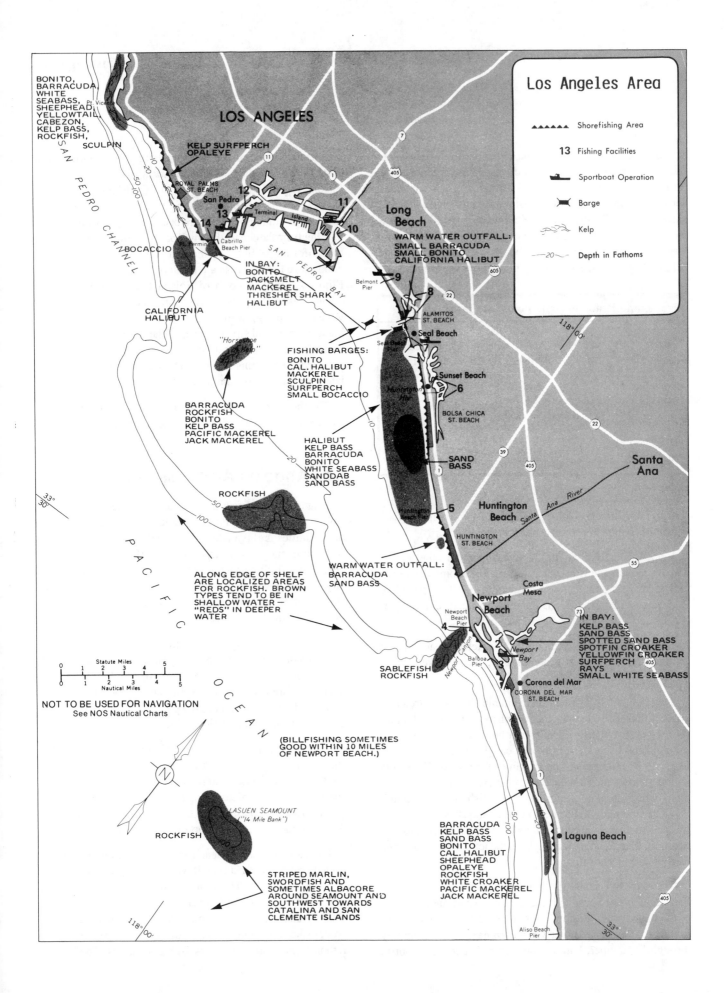

Los Angeles Area

- ▲▲▲▲ Shorefishing Area
- **13** Fishing Facilities
- 🚤 Sportboat Operation
- Barge
- Kelp
- —20— Depth in Fathoms

LOS ANGELES

BONITO,
BARRACUDA,
WHITE
SEABASS,
SHEEPHEAD
YELLOWTAIL,
CABEZON,
KELP BASS,
ROCKFISH,
SCULPIN

Pt Vicente

KELP SURFPERCH
OPALEYE

ROYAL PALMS
ST. BEACH

San Pedro

BOCACCIO

Pt. Fermin

Cabrillo
Beach Pier

CALIFORNIA
HALIBUT

SAN PEDRO CHANNEL

Terminal
Island

SAN PEDRO BAY

IN BAY:
BONITO
JACKSMELT
MACKEREL
THRESHER SHARK
HALIBUT

Long
Beach

WARM WATER OUTFALL:
SMALL BARRACUDA
SMALL BONITO
CALIFORNIA HALIBUT

Belmont
Pier

"Horseshoe
Kelp"

FISHING BARGES:
BONITO
CAL. HALIBUT
MACKEREL
SCULPIN
SURFPERCH
SMALL BOCACCIO

ALAMITOS
ST. BEACH

Seal Beach

BARRACUDA
ROCKFISH
BONITO
KELP BASS
PACIFIC MACKEREL
JACK MACKEREL

Sunset Beach

BOLSA CHICA
ST. BEACH

Huntington
Hbr.

HALIBUT
KELP BASS
BARRACUDA
BONITO
WHITE SEABASS
SANDDAB
SAND BASS

SAND
BASS

ROCKFISH

Santa
Ana

Huntington
Beach

Huntington
Beach Pier

HUNTINGTON
ST. BEACH

ALONG EDGE OF SHELF
ARE LOCALIZED AREAS
FOR ROCKFISH. BROWN
TYPES TEND TO BE IN
SHALLOW WATER —
"REDS" IN DEEPER
WATER

WARM WATER OUTFALL:
BARRACUDA
SAND BASS

Santa Ana River

Costa
Mesa

Newport
Beach

Newport
Beach Pier

IN BAY:
KELP BASS
SAND BASS
SPOTTED SAND BASS
SPOTFIN CROAKER
YELLOWFIN CROAKER
SURFPERCH
RAYS
SMALL WHITE SEABASS

Newport
Bay

Balboa
Pier

SABLEFISH
ROCKFISH

Newport Canyon

Corona del Mar

CORONA DEL MAR
ST. BEACH

PACIFIC OCEAN

Statute Miles
0 1 2 3 4 5
0 1 2 3 4 5
Nautical Miles

NOT TO BE USED FOR NAVIGATION
See NOS Nautical Charts

(BILLFISHING SOMETIMES
GOOD WITHIN 10 MILES
OF NEWPORT BEACH.)

N

LASUEN SEAMOUNT
("14 Mile Bank")

ROCKFISH

STRIPED MARLIN,
SWORDFISH AND
SOMETIMES ALBACORE
AROUND SEAMOUNT AND
SOUTHWEST TOWARDS
CATALINA AND SAN
CLEMENTE ISLANDS

BARRACUDA
KELP BASS
SAND BASS
BONITO
CAL. HALIBUT
SHEEPHEAD
OPALEYE
ROCKFISH
WHITE CROAKER
PACIFIC MACKEREL
JACK MACKEREL

Laguna Beach

Aliso Beach
Pier

reaches depths greater than 400 fathoms near the middle of the San Pedro Channel.

South of Newport are scattered small kelp beds where a number of coastal species such as barracuda, kelp bass, sand bass, white croaker, bonito, California halibut, sheephead and rockfish (kelp, olive, grass, and vermillion) are caught. Occasionally, yellowtail and white seabass are landed. Off Laguna Beach, over deep-water rocky areas, anglers fish for boccaccio, chilipepper and canary rockfish. Southeast of Newport Beach and northwest of Laguna Beach over the coastal shelf is a kelp area where several of the brown species of rockfish are commonly taken. Bluefin tuna and striped marlin have been caught just offshore a short distance from Laguna Beach, although not very often in recent years.

Farther offshore to the west is Lasuen Seamount, widely known as "14 Mile Bank" or "58 Fathom Spot." This is an excellent bottom fishing area for rockfish (bocaccio, vermillion and chilipepper), and in summer striped marlin and swordfish are taken near the surface about the Seamount and to the southwest. Albacore are also caught here during the summer, but like bluefin tuna, only occasionally in recent years.

Off Newport in the Newport Submarine Canyon, sablefish (black cod), a species usually associated with more northern latitudes, can be taken in deep water. On rare occasions during the spring, coho (silver) salmon have been caught off Newport. Since deep water is close to shore off Newport, striped marlin are taken on occasion only a short distance south of the Newport Harbor entrance.

From Huntington Beach west over sandy bottom near shore, there is good fishing for many of the bottom species. California halibut is one of the more important fish caught in this area.

The "horseshoe kelp" bed south of Los Angeles Harbor has been reduced in size over the years, and the kelp growth is now under the surface. However, this spot sometimes is good for Pacific barracuda, Pacific bonito, kelp bass, yellowtail, jack and Pacific mackerels and rockfish (olive, kelp and vermillion).

The greater Los Angeles Harbor-San Pedro Bay area, being readily accessible to large numbers of people, is a popular place for fishing from shore and small boats. Good locations for catching bay fish can be found within the harbor itself, along the extensive jetties, or about piers that are on open channels in the outer harbor area. Bay fishing is also popular in Alamitos and Seal Beach bays where jacksmelt, surfperch, skates, sharks, rays, sargo and turbot are taken by anglers along with an occasional small mackerel or Pacific bonito.

Numerous fishing piers (public and commercial) and open bulkhead areas provide many thousands of recreational fishing hours each month for only the cost of bait and tackle. In addition to the many commercial piers and marina floats available for fishing in Los Angeles Harbor, there are piers built specifically for fishing at Cabrillo Beach (near Point Fermin), Belmont Shore, Seal Beach, Huntington Beach, Newport Beach (two piers), and south of Laguna Beach at Aliso Beach. From these piers, anglers catch California halibut, kingfish (white croaker), sharks, rays, jacksmelt, queenfish, surfperch (barred, black, walleye, pile and shiner) and Pacific and jack mackerels.

Surf fishing takes place along rocky shores from point Fermin to Point Vicente. Southwest from Newport Bay to Dana Point there is fishing from the manmade jetties at Los Alamitos Bay and Newport Bay for opaleye, grass and kelp rockfish, halfmoon, cabezon and black perch. The San Pedro Channel entrance is accessible from shore; the rest of the breakwater to the east can be reached by boat. Here there is good fishing for opaleye, halfmoon, kelp bass and rockfish (brown types).

Los Angeles Area Fishing Facilities					
Location	Sport Fishing Boats	Pier Fishing	Boat Rental	Launch Ramp	Jetty Fishing
Aliso Pier (1)*		X			
Newport Bay (2)	X		X	X	X
Balboa Pier (3)		X			
Newport Pier (4)		X			
Huntington Pier (5)		X		X	
Huntington Harbor (6)				X	
Seal Beach Pier (7)	X	X			
Alamitos Bay (8)				X	X
Belmont Pier (9)	X	X	X		
Golden Shores (10)				X	
Long Beach (11)	X				
San Pedro (12)	X		X	X	
22nd St. Landing (13)	X				
Cabrillo Beach (14)		X			X

*Map fishing facilities

Sandy-shore fishing is available from Newport Beach to Long Beach. One of the more popular places for surf fishing is Bolsa Chica State Beach. Species most commonly taken off sandy beaches are surfperch (barred, walleye, shiner, calico and silver), croakers (spotfin, white and yellowfin), California halibut, and corbina. Grunion are also caught during their periodic spawning runs.

Santa Monica Area (map - p. 221)

The coast from Point Vicente to Solromar borders one of the most populated areas along the West coast and is intensively fished, particularly from Redondo Beach to Santa Monica. Sandy shore, rocky shore, pier and jetty fishing as well as excellent facilities for boat fishing are found from Point Vicente to Solromar.

The coastline is rocky from near Point Vicente to Malaga Cove, south of Redondo Beach. Northward from Malaga Cove to northwest of Santa Monica is an extensive stretch of sandy beach. From Santa Monica, the coast swings westward and the coastal shore begins to get rocky once again, with occasional offshore reefs. The first substantial concentrations of kelp near shore, which are common from here to Point Conception, are found just west of Malibu Point to near Point Dume, and again west of Zuma Beach.

The offshore coastal shelf is very narrow from Point Fermin to Point Vicente, and these waters are frequented many times by schools of bait fish such as anchovy and jack and Pacific mackerels. Depths of 200 fathoms or more are found two to three miles offshore. The bottom then descends to its greatest depth in the San Pedro Channel—over 400 fathoms. Bottom types, aside from rocky areas, are generally green sand; in deeper water, green mud predominates. Along the edge of the shelf are rocky areas that attract sizeable concentrations of red rockfish.

Santa Monica Bay is relatively shallow (less than 50 fathoms deep) and cut by two prominent submarine canyons, the Redondo and Santa Monica canyons. Rocky areas are found near the edges of these canyons as well as along the edge of the coastal shelf, and these places usually provide some of the better rockfishing. A number of shallow reefs are offshore in lower Santa Monica Bay between Point Vicente and Redondo Beach. The coastal shelf is about three miles wide from Santa Monica to near Point Dume, and it is about two miles wide to the west beyond Point Dume. Again, the bottom types are usually sand near shore, grading to mud and sand farther offshore, and green mud at the greater depths.

Excellent facilities for sport fishing are located at the small-boat harbors of Redondo Beach, Marina del Rey, Santa Monica, and to the west at Malibu and Paradise Cove. Sport fishing boats operate locally or travel from these ports to distant waters to fish around Catalina, Santa Barbara, or San Nicolas islands. Special offshore trips for yellowfin and occasionally albacore are made during the summer. The boats fish southwest of Redondo Beach along the edges of the Redondo Canyon (the south edge in particular) where there is good deep-water fishing for rockfish (vermillion, canary, bocaccio, gopher and chilipepper). Rockfishing is also productive off Point Dume where vermillion, olive and bocaccio species enter the catch. Along the kelp beds west of Zuma Beach, olive, grass and kelp rockfish are taken frequently, along with occasional bonito and yellowtail during summer.

Rocky-shore fishing is popular from Point Vicente to near Malaga Cove, just south of Redondo Beach. Several species of surfperch are commonly taken here along with olive, grass and kelp rockfish. Opaleye fishing is excellent along this rocky stretch of coast.

Rocky-shore species caught in the area west of Santa Monica are the opaleye, surfperch (black and shiner), rockfish (grass, kelp and olive), halfmoon, cabezon, sargo and occasionally kelp bass.

From Redondo Beach north to Manhatten Beach are several public fishing piers. These piers are popular for fishing California halibut (spring and summer best) and surfperch (barred, black, walleye, pile and shiner). Mackerel sometimes are taken from these piers as are the usual action-

Santa Monica Area Fishing Facilities					
Location	Sport Fishing Boats	Pier Fishing	Boat Rental	Launch Ramp	Jetty Fishing
Redondo Beach (1)*	X	X	X	X	X
Hermosa Pier (2)		X			
Manhatten Pier (3)		X			
Marina del Rey (4)	X		X	X	X
Venice Pier (5)		X			
Santa Monica Pier (6)	X	X		X	
Malibu Pier (7)	X	X			
Paradise Cove Pier (8)	X	X			

*Map fishing facilities

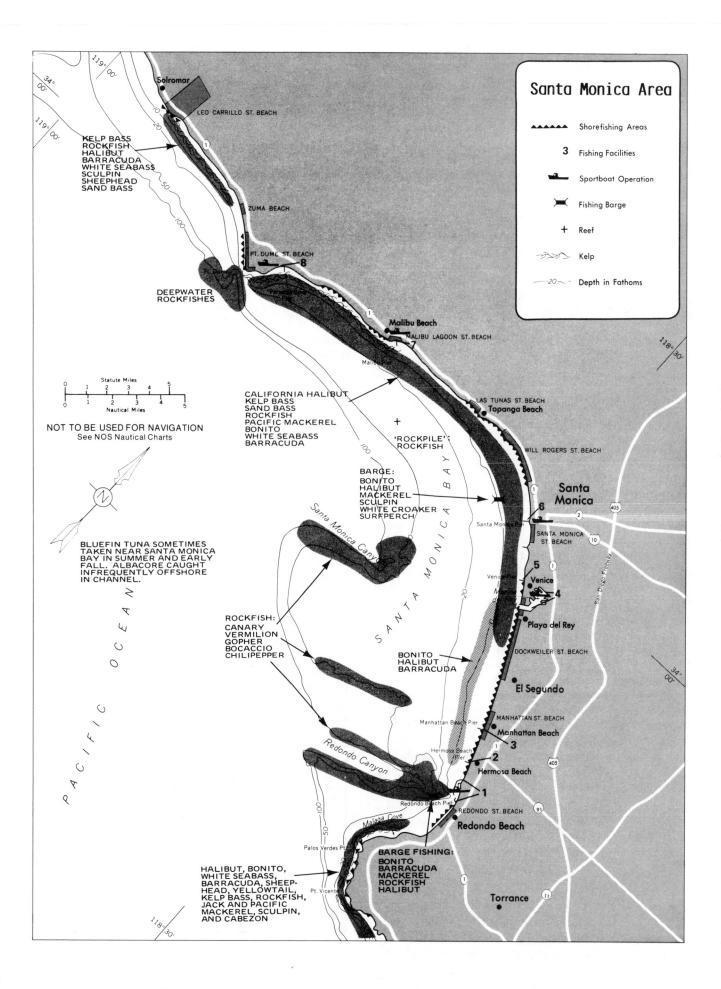

Santa Monica Area

- ▲▲▲▲ Shorefishing Areas
- **3** Fishing Facilities
- Sportboat Operation
- Fishing Barge
- **+** Reef
- Kelp
- --20-- Depth in Fathoms

Solromar

LEO CARRILLO ST. BEACH

KELP BASS
ROCKFISH
HALIBUT
BARRACUDA
WHITE SEABASS
SCULPIN
SHEEPHEAD
SAND BASS

ZUMA BEACH

PT. DUME ST. BEACH

DEEPWATER
ROCKFISHES

Malibu Beach

MALIBU LAGOON ST. BEACH

Malibu Pier

CALIFORNIA HALIBUT
KELP BASS
SAND BASS
ROCKFISH
PACIFIC MACKEREL
BONITO
WHITE SEABASS
BARRACUDA

LAS TUNAS ST. BEACH
Topanga Beach

'ROCKPILE'
ROCKFISH

WILL ROGERS ST. BEACH

BARGE:
BONITO
HALIBUT
MACKEREL
SCULPIN
WHITE CROAKER
SURFPERCH

Santa Monica Pier

Santa
Monica

SANTA MONICA
ST. BEACH

Statute Miles
0 1 2 3 4 5
Nautical Miles
0 1 2 3 4 5

NOT TO BE USED FOR NAVIGATION
See NOS Nautical Charts

N

BLUEFIN TUNA SOMETIMES
TAKEN NEAR SANTA MONICA
BAY IN SUMMER AND EARLY
FALL. ALBACORE CAUGHT
INFREQUENTLY OFFSHORE
IN CHANNEL.

Santa Monica Canyon

SANTA MONICA BAY

Venice Pier

Venice

Marina del Rey

Playa del Rey

DOCKWEILER ST. BEACH

ROCKFISH:
CANARY
VERMILION
GOPHER
BOCACCIO
CHILIPEPPER

BONITO
HALIBUT
BARRACUDA

El Segundo

MANHATTAN ST. BEACH
Manhattan Beach Pier
Manhattan Beach

3

Redondo Canyon

Hermosa Beach Pier

2

Hermosa Beach

1

Redondo Beach Pier

Malaga Cove

REDONDO ST. BEACH

Redondo Beach

Palos Verdes Pt.

HALIBUT, BONITO,
WHITE SEABASS,
BARRACUDA, SHEEP-
HEAD, YELLOWTAIL,
KELP BASS, ROCKFISH,
JACK AND PACIFIC
MACKEREL, SCULPIN,
AND CABEZON.

Pt. Vicente

BARGE FISHING:
BONITO
BARRACUDA
MACKEREL
ROCKFISH
HALIBUT

Torrance

PACIFIC OCEAN

405

2

10

405

91

1

11

getters—sharks and rays. At the Redondo Piers, excellent bonito fishing is available; these fish are apparently attracted by the warm water discharged by a steam-electric power plant.

Excellent surf fishing is available along the extensive sandy beaches from south of Redondo Beach to north of Santa Monica, especially between Redondo Beach and Playa del Rey. Sandy-shore species taken by surf anglers are barred surfperch (best from January through March), walleye surfperch, California halibut (spring and summer best), jacksmelt and shovelnose guitarfish. In some years fishing is good for corbina, spotfin croaker and yellowfin croaker, particularly along the sandy shore from Playa del Rey to Venice and from Manhatten Beach to Redondo Beach. Grunion are sometimes gathered along Malibu, Santa Monica, Venice and Hermosa beaches during periods of evening high tides in the spring and summer. Zuma Beach's sandy shores offer good fishing for barred surfperch, with occasional catches of corbina and croakers.

Ventura Area (map - p. 223)

The principal sport fishing ports in the Ventura area are Port Hueneme, Channel Islands Harbor and Ventura Harbor. These are the principal ports that specialize in fishing about the Santa Barbara Channel Islands and offshore south of the islands for albacore during the summer fishing season. On isolated occasions, catches of coho salmon are made in late winter and early spring by party boats fishing southeast of Point Mugu and south and west of Ventura. The catches during this time are not large, but represent the southern extension of salmon sport fishing.

About 11 miles offshore from Port Hueneme and the Channel Islands Harbor is Anacapa Island, one of the more important islands for marine sport fishing. The island is the eastward extension of the chain of Santa Barbara Channel Islands and is less than one-half mile wide in most places, rising to an elevation of 930 feet above sea level. There is excellent fishing around Anacapa for kelp bass and black seabass, as well as for boccaccio and canary rockfish. Occasional catches of Pacific barracuda and yellowtail are made here in summer. Broadbill swordfish and striped marlin are taken south of Anacapa Island during summer and early fall.

The coastal shelf east of Port Hueneme is very narrow—from Point Mugu eastward it is no more than one mile wide. Immediately west of Point Mugu, the Mugu Submarine Canyon cuts through the coastal shelf, and water depths plunge to 250 to 300 fathoms. The coastal shelf widens slightly between Point Mugu and Port Hueneme before being interrupted by another submarine canyon, Hueneme Canyon. Northwest of Hueneme, the shelf becomes several miles wide, an area commonly known as the Ventura Flats. The shelf narrows slightly west of Ventura, and the more offshore rocky reefs provide good rockfishing.

The bottom types range from rock to sand and shells in the southeast, and from mud to sand and shells in the Mugu-Hueneme area. Sand and mud predominate on the Ventura Flats, which has good fishing for flatfish such as California halibut. In deeper water, the typical mud and green mud bottom predominates. The offshore bottom becomes shallower west of Hueneme Canyon, and adjacent to Ventura Flats the depth at mid-Santa Barbara Channel is only about 130 fathoms.

Immediately offshore of the area from Solromar to Point Mugu, anglers fish along the edge of the kelp beds for rockfish (grass, olive and kelp) and occasionally bonito. About four miles offshore of Solromar there is a shallow area approximately 45 fathoms deep. This is a good fishing spot for chilipepper rockfish and sometimes yellowtail and Pacific barracuda. Limited catches of coho and king salmon are made occasionally in the early spring.

The coast is rocky from Leo Carrillo State Beach to Point Mugu. The shore borders the coast highway and is readily accessible to the fishing public. This rocky coast offers good fishing for opaleye, kelp bass, surfperch and rockfish (grass, kelp and olive). From about Point Mugu to near Port Hueneme, access is restricted since it is part of the Point Mugu Naval Air Station and Pacific Missile Range. The sandy shore starts at Point Mugu and extends up along the coast all the way to Ventura; from Ventura west to Rincon Point, sandy beaches are interspersed with rocky points of land. Along the sandy beaches extending from Point Mugu northward, the following species are taken from shore: walleye and barred surfperch (excellent fishing area for barred with January to March being

Ventura Area Fishing Facilities					
Location	Sport Fishing Boats	Pier Fishing	Boat Rental	Launch Ramp	Jetty Fishing
Port Hueneme (1)*	X				X
Hueneme Pier (2)		X			
Channel Isl. Har. (3)	X	X		X	X
Ventura Harbor (4)	X			X	X
Ventura Pier (5)		X			

*Map fishing facilities

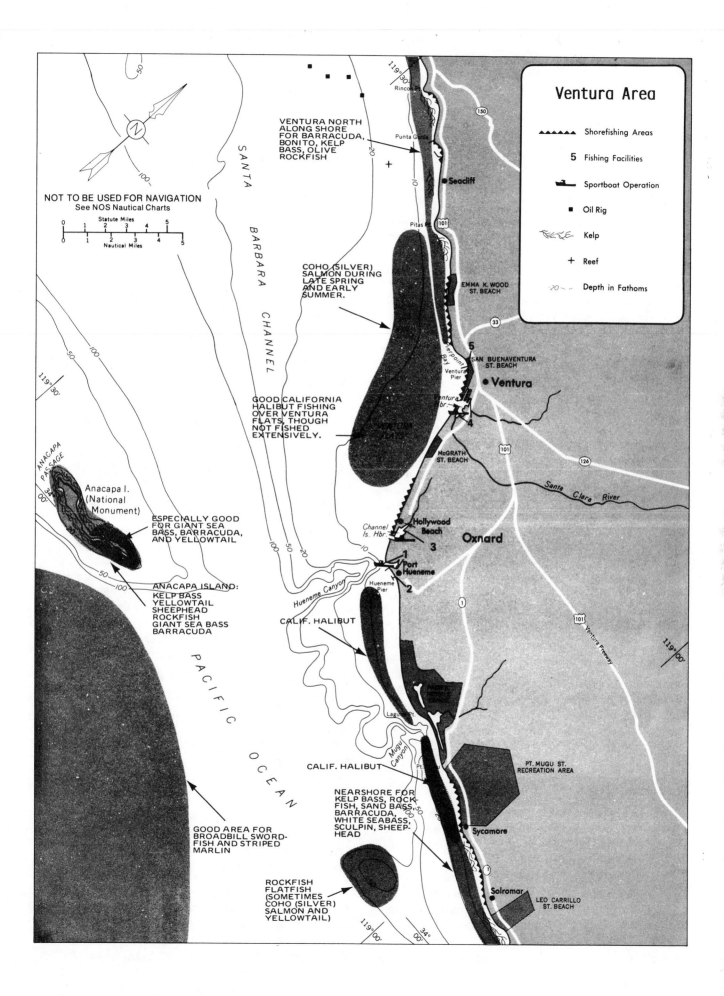

NOT TO BE USED FOR NAVIGATION
See NOS Nautical Charts

Statute Miles
0 1 2 3 4 5

Nautical Miles
0 1 2 3 4 5

Ventura Area

- ▲▲▲ Shorefishing Areas
- **5** Fishing Facilities
- 🚤 Sportboat Operation
- ■ Oil Rig
- 〰 Kelp
- ✛ Reef
- ～20～ Depth in Fathoms

SANTA BARBARA CHANNEL

VENTURA NORTH ALONG SHORE FOR BARRACUDA, BONITO, KELP BASS, OLIVE ROCKFISH

COHO (SILVER) SALMON DURING LATE SPRING AND EARLY SUMMER.

GOOD CALIFORNIA HALIBUT FISHING OVER VENTURA FLATS, THOUGH NOT FISHED EXTENSIVELY.

ANACAPA I.
(National Monument)

ESPECIALLY GOOD FOR GIANT SEA BASS, BARRACUDA, AND YELLOWTAIL

ANACAPA ISLAND:
KELP BASS
YELLOWTAIL
SHEEPHEAD
ROCKFISH
GIANT SEA BASS
BARRACUDA

PACIFIC OCEAN

GOOD AREA FOR BROADBILL SWORD-FISH AND STRIPED MARLIN

ROCKFISH FLATFISH (SOMETIMES COHO (SILVER) SALMON AND YELLOWTAIL)

CALIF. HALIBUT

CALIF. HALIBUT

NEARSHORE FOR KELP BASS, ROCK-FISH, SAND BASS, BARRACUDA, WHITE SEABASS, SCULPIN, SHEEP-HEAD

Rincon Pt.

Punta Gorda

Seacliff

Pitas Pt.

EMMA K. WOOD ST. BEACH

SAN BUENAVENTURA ST. BEACH

Ventura Pier

Ventura

Ventura Hbr.

McGRATH ST. BEACH

Channel Is. Hbr.

Hollywood Beach

Oxnard

Port Hueneme

Hueneme Pier

Hueneme Canyon

Laguna Pt.

Mugu Canyon

Pt. Mugu

PT. MUGU ST. RECREATION AREA

Santa Clara River

Ventura Freeway

Sycamore

Solromar

LEO CARRILLO ST. BEACH

ANACAPA PASSAGE

best), California halibut (spring and summer being best), jacksmelt, sharks (several species), corbina, spotfin croaker, yellowfin croaker and occasionally kelp bass.

Anglers fish about the jetties and docks at Port Hueneme and from the sport fishing pier (actually a fishing float) in the Channel Islands Harbor. About the Port Hueneme jetties, anglers will likely find opaleye, surfperch (black and shiner), rockfish (grass, kelp and olive), halfmoon and cabezon. Some of the fish caught from the public fishing float at Channel Islands Harbor are walleye and barred surfperch, staghorn sculpin, California halibut (spring and summer), lingcod (winter), kelp bass, several species of sharks and rays, and occasionally croakers.

Santa Barbara Area (map - p. 225)

This coastline, which encompasses the major Southern California sport fishing port of Santa Barbara is oriented in an east-west direction. This is the only sizable coastal segment of the U.S. Pacific coast to have this orientation other than the south side of the Strait of Juan de Fuca in Washington. The area is distinguished by the most extensive and best-developed kelp beds along the California coast. Lush kelp beds are present throughout the region, but are best developed from about Goleta Point to Point Conception.

At the west end of this area is one of the most notable of coastal geographical features—Point Conception. This if often called the "Cape of Good Hope of the West Coast" because of the wide variation in winds and weather found about the point. Many times the waters south and east of Point Conception may be relatively smooth and have low wind speeds over them. However, immediately north and west of the point and offshore only a shore distance the seas may be rough and the wind near gale force. The coastline south of Point Conception is protected by a coastal mountain range that parallels the shore and provides a dampening influence on the prevailing northwest winds which are most intense from spring to early fall.

Point Conception is often described as an ecological dividing point for marine life. South of the point is the subtropical zone; north of it is the temperate zone. Many coastal open-ocean fish, such as Pacific barracuda and yellowtail that are common to the waters off Southern California and Baja California, Mexico, are taken only rarely north of Point Conception. Conversely, some northern marine and anadromous species such as coho salmon are taken only in small numbers southeast of Point Conception in late winter and early spring.

The shoreline from Carpenteria to Point Conception and Point Arguello is predominantly a sandy one, broken occasionally by a few prominent points with shallow reefs close to shore. Along most of the coast, the shore is backed by cliffs 50 to 150 feet high.

Offshore the coastal shelf is quite broad when compared to the coastal areas to the south. The shelf is about five miles wide south of Santa Barbara, narrowing westward to about two to three miles wide off Point Conception. The depths in the center of the Santa Barbara Channel range from about 200 fathoms off Santa Barbara to 250 fathoms south of Point Conception.

From Santa Barbara, sport fishing boats travel to grounds along the coast to the west and east and offshore to the Santa Barbara Channel Islands.

A number of reefs along the coast are excellent fishing spots, as are the extensive kelp beds. West of Santa Barbara, near and amid the kelp, are resident populations of kelp bass, rockfish (olive, grass and vermillion), sheephead, and cabezon. During summer, anglers also catch Pacific barracuda and an occasional yellowtail or white seabass. Pacific barracuda generally work up the coast toward Point Conception from September to November and down the coast from January to April. Pacific bonito sometimes show along the coast in summer and fall.

Good drift-fishing locations for California halibut and kelp bass are found off the Goleta Beach pier; other good halibut grounds are just east of Point Conception, where fishing is best in spring and summer. This area also yields occasional summer catches of bonito and yellowtail.

Pier fishing is available at Santa Barbara (Sterns Wharf) and at the Goleta Beach and Gaviota public piers. The Goleta Beach pier is noted for sizable catches of surfperch. Walleye surfperch are abundant, and barred surfperch fishing is excellent in winter and spring. Best California halibut fishing is in spring and early summer, and tomcod, spotfin croaker, sand shark and jacksmelt enter the pier angler's catch mostly during July, August and September.

At the Santa Barbara pier, anglers also catch a variety of surfperch (rubberlip, shiner, walleye and barred), sharks, California halibut (in spring and summer), lingcod (in winter), kelp bass, rockfish and occasionally croakers.

The beaches west of Capitan to north of Point Conception are especially good for surf fishing. Sandy-shore species include the barred surfperch (January through March being best), walleye and rubberlip surfperch, spotfin croaker (usually a brief summer run in this area) and California halibut

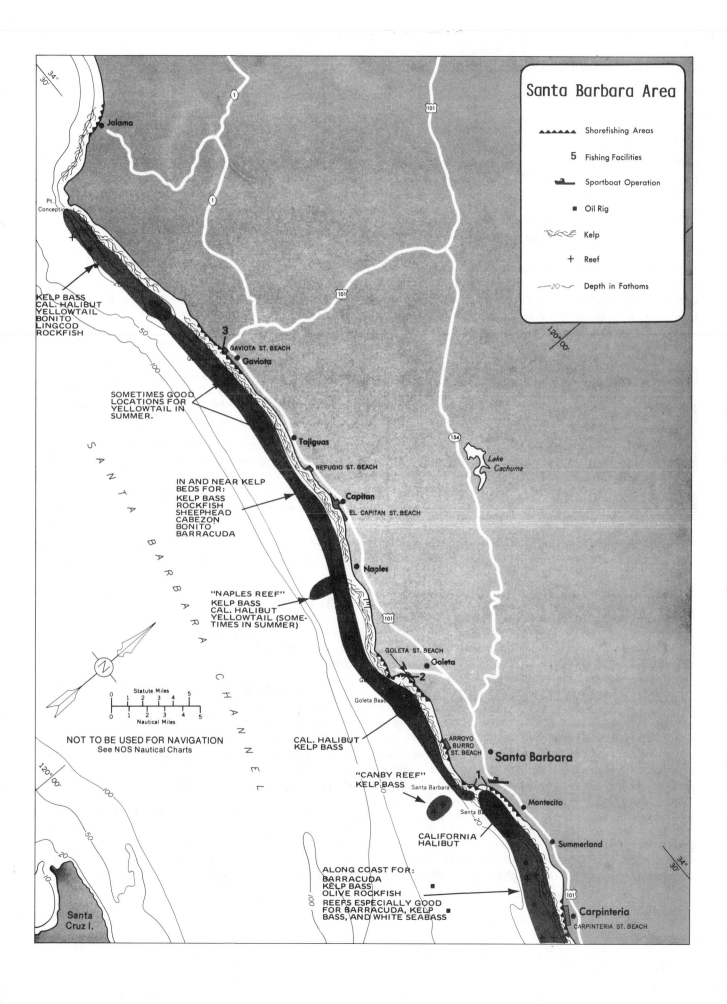

Santa Barbara Area

Legend:
- ▲▲▲▲▲ Shorefishing Areas
- **5** Fishing Facilities
- ⛵ Sportboat Operation
- ■ Oil Rig
- ～～ Kelp
- ✛ Reef
- ～20～ Depth in Fathoms

Jalama

Pt. Conception

**KELP BASS
CAL. HALIBUT
YELLOWTAIL
BONITO
LINGCOD
ROCKFISH**

3 GAVIOTA ST. BEACH
Gaviota

**SOMETIMES GOOD
LOCATIONS FOR
YELLOWTAIL IN
SUMMER.**

Tajiguas

REFUGIO ST. BEACH

Lake Cachuma

**IN AND NEAR KELP
BEDS FOR:
KELP BASS
ROCKFISH
SHEEPHEAD
CABEZON
BONITO
BARRACUDA**

Capitan

EL CAPITAN ST. BEACH

Naples

**"NAPLES REEF"
KELP BASS
CAL. HALIBUT
YELLOWTAIL (SOME-
TIMES IN SUMMER)**

SANTA BARBARA CHANNEL

GOLETA ST. BEACH
Goleta

2

Goleta Beach

NOT TO BE USED FOR NAVIGATION
See NOS Nautical Charts

Statute Miles
0 1 2 3 4 5

Nautical Miles
0 1 2 3 4 5

**CAL. HALIBUT
KELP BASS**

ARROYO
BURRO
ST. BEACH

Santa Barbara

**"CANBY REEF"
KELP BASS**

Santa Barbara

1

Santa B.

Montecito

**CALIFORNIA
HALIBUT**

Summerland

**ALONG COAST FOR:
BARRACUDA
KELP BASS
OLIVE ROCKFISH**

**REEFS ESPECIALLY GOOD
FOR BARRACUDA, KELP
BASS, AND WHITE SEABASS**

Santa
Cruz I.

Carpinteria

CARPINTERIA ST. BEACH

34° 30'

120° 00'

(late spring and summer being best). Rocky-shore anglers most often encounter cabezon, black surfperch, and olive, kelp and grass rockfish.

Immediately north of Point Conception at Jalama, anglers cast into the surf for barred, silver and walleye surfperch and kelp greenling. Farther north, from Point Arguello north to Point Sal, the coastal area is usually closed to civilian use due to Navy and Air Force missile-launching facilities, with the exception of a small beach at the town of Surf. Here there is good surf fishing for barred, silver, calico and walleye surfperch and California halibut.

Santa Barbara Area Fishing Facilities					
Location	Sport Fishing Boats	Pier Fishing	Boat Rental	Launch Ramp	Jetty Fishing
Santa Barbara Harbor (1)*	X	X	X	X	X
Goleta Beach (2)		X	X	X	
Gaviota Bch Pier (3)		X		X	

*Map fishing facilities

Santa Barbara Channel Islands

(map - p. 227)

Sport fishing boats visit all these islands from Port Hueneme, Channel Islands Harbor, Ventura Harbor and Santa Barbara. During the summer, albacore boats occasionally travel farther offshore near the edge of the continental shelf, southwest of Santa Rosa and San Miguel Islands and below San Nicolas Island.

The climate about the Santa Barbara Channel Islands is usually influenced by northwest winds from spring through summer, though the wind intensity if moderated slightly owing to their distance south and east of Point Conception. Fog and low stratus clouds are common about the western-most islands during late spring and summer.

The western-most island, San Miguel, is seven miles long, three miles wide, and rises to a height of 831 feet. The island coastline is predominately rocky with many shoal areas along the west and north sides. Sandy beaches are scattered about the island; the beach at the west end contains one of the largest seal and sea lion rookeries in Southern California. About the island are several good places for fishing lingcod and rockfish.

Santa Rosa Island has a rocky shore along the northwest and southwest sides; however, the east end has a number of sandy beaches. Good fishing for rockfish and lingcod can be found near shore about the northern and western ends of the island.

The western islands (Santa Rosa and San Miguel) have not been fished as extensively as the islands closer to the ports in the Ventura and Santa Barbara areas. The distance that sport fishing boats are required to travel is an important factor. Additionally, wind, weather, and sea conditions about these islands are usually more severe than at the islands to the east.

Santa Cruz is the largest of the Channel Islands. It and Anacapa Island have the most sport fishing pressure. Rock-fishing is good all about the island; fishing is usually best on the southeast side, which is protected from the westerly winds. Sometimes this lee side of the island has excellent fishing for yellowtail and bonito. Bluefin tuna have been taken off the southwest end commercially during the summer, so this area has a potential for a sport fish catch of this species.

San Nicolas Island (map - p. 227)

San Nicolas is 25 miles southwest of Santa Barbara Island. The nearest point on the mainland is Point Vicente, 55 miles to the northeast.

The island is 8 1/2 miles long, and the highest point is 907 feet above sea level. A sizable shoal area extends around it, principally on the northwest and north sides. The bottom types are scattered rocky areas on the north and west ends, with shallow areas of sand and white and green shells. The shore is rocky, except for isolated sandy beaches, and the east end has the greatest predominance of sand.

Fishing is good about the entire island, but only a small amount of fishing effort is expended in the area. Sport fishing boats from Port Hueneme and Channel Islands Harbor as well as from the Los Angeles area sometimes fish here. No one section is noted for being distinctively better than others.

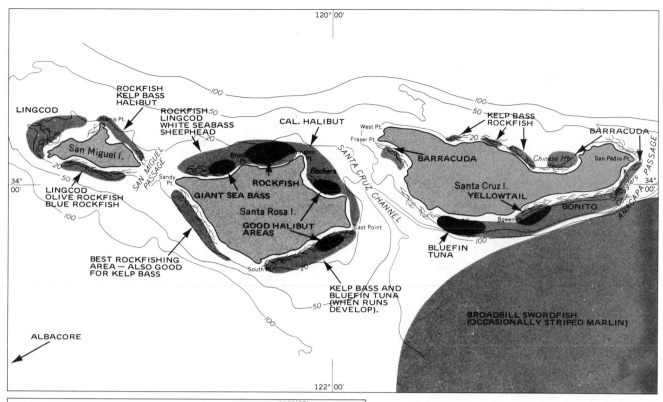

ROCKFISH
KELP BASS
HALIBUT

ROCKFISH
LINGCOD
WHITE SEABASS
SHEEPHEAD

LINGCOD

CAL. HALIBUT

LINGCOD
OLIVE ROCKFISH
BLUE ROCKFISH

Harris Pt.

San Miguel I.

SAN MIGUEL PASSAGE

Sandy Pt.

100

50

20

50

20

100

34°
00'

BEST ROCKFISHING
AREA — ALSO GOOD
FOR KELP BASS

Brockway

Carrington Pt.

Bechers

ROCKFISH

GIANT SEA BASS

Santa Rosa I.

GOOD HALIBUT
AREAS

South Pt.

East Point

20

50

KELP BASS AND
BLUEFIN TUNA
(WHEN RUNS
DEVELOP).

West Pt.

Fraser Pt.

SANTA CRUZ CHANNEL

100

KELP BASS
ROCKFISH

BARRACUDA

Santa Cruz I.
YELLOWTAIL

50

20

Chinese Hbr.

BARRACUDA

San Pedro Pt.

BONITO

Smuggler's Cove

ANACAPA PASSAGE

34°
00'

Bowen Pt.

100

BLUEFIN
TUNA

BROADBILL SWORDFISH
(OCCASIONALLY STRIPED MARLIN)

ALBACORE

120° 00'

122° 00'

100

50

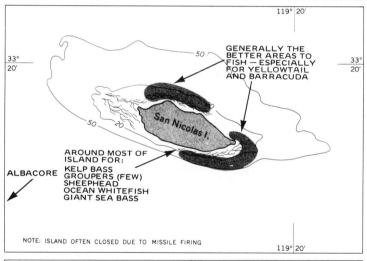

119° 20'

33°
20'

50

GENERALLY THE
BETTER AREAS TO
FISH — ESPECIALLY
FOR YELLOWTAIL
AND BARRACUDA

33°
20'

50

20

San Nicolas I.

AROUND MOST OF
ISLAND FOR:
KELP BASS
GROUPERS (FEW)
SHEEPHEAD
OCEAN WHITEFISH
GIANT SEA BASS

ALBACORE

NOTE: ISLAND OFTEN CLOSED DUE TO MISSILE FIRING

119° 20'

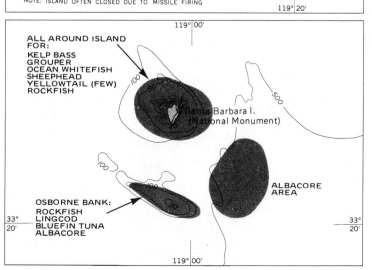

119° 00'

ALL AROUND ISLAND
FOR:
KELP BASS
GROUPER
OCEAN WHITEFISH
SHEEPHEAD
YELLOWTAIL (FEW)
ROCKFISH

100

50

500

Santa Barbara I.
(National Monument)

100

100

20

ALBACORE
AREA

OSBORNE BANK:
ROCKFISH
LINGCOD
BLUEFIN TUNA
ALBACORE

33°
20'

33°
20'

119° 00'

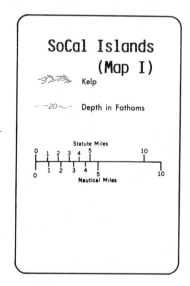

SoCal Islands
(Map I)

Kelp

20 Depth in Fathoms

Statute Miles

0 1 2 3 4 5   10

0 1 2 3 4 5   10
Nautical Miles

N

NOT TO BE USED FOR NAVIGATION
See NOS Nautical Charts

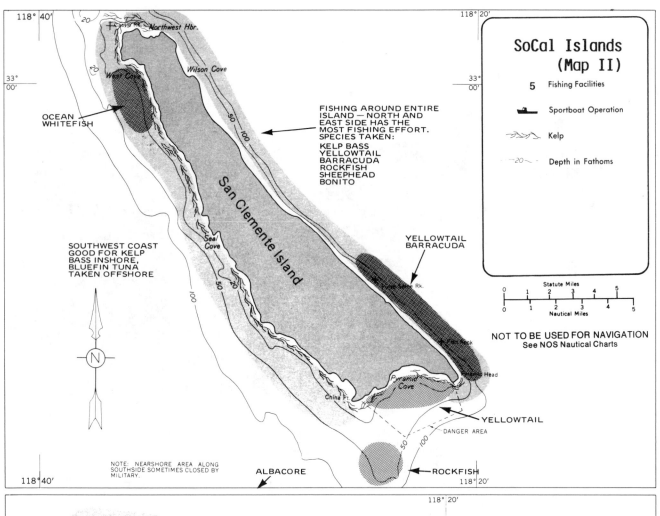

118° 20'

33° 00'   33° 00'

Eagle Rk.   Northwest Hbr.

Wilson Cove

West Cove

OCEAN
WHITEFISH

**SoCal Islands
(Map II)**

5   Fishing Facilities

   Sportboat Operation

   Kelp

—20—   Depth in Fathoms

FISHING AROUND ENTIRE
ISLAND — NORTH AND
EAST SIDE HAS THE
MOST FISHING EFFORT.
SPECIES TAKEN:
KELP BASS
YELLOWTAIL
BARRACUDA
ROCKFISH
SHEEPHEAD
BONITO

San Clemente Island

Seal
Cove

SOUTHWEST COAST
GOOD FOR KELP
BASS INSHORE,
BLUEFIN TUNA
TAKEN OFFSHORE

YELLOWTAIL
BARRACUDA

Castle Rock

N

Statute Miles
0   1   2   3   4   5
0   1   2   3   4   5
Nautical Miles

NOT TO BE USED FOR NAVIGATION
See NOS Nautical Charts

Fish Rock

Pyramid Head

China Pt.   Pyramid
Cove

YELLOWTAIL

DANGER AREA

NOTE: NEARSHORE AREA ALONG
SOUTHSIDE SOMETIMES CLOSED BY
MILITARY.

ALBACORE

ROCKFISH

118° 40'   118° 20'

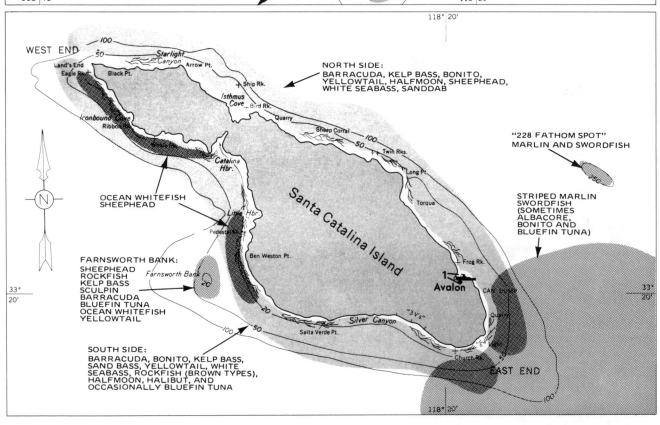

118° 20'

WEST END   100
50   Starlight
Canyon   Arrow Pt.

Land's End
Eagle Rk.   Black Pt.

Ship Rk.

NORTH SIDE:
BARRACUDA, KELP BASS, BONITO,
YELLOWTAIL, HALFMOON, SHEEPHEAD,
WHITE SEABASS, SANDDAB

Isthmus
Cove   Bird Rk.

Ironbound Cove
Ribbon   Quarry

Sheep Corral   100
50   Twin Rks.

"228 FATHOM SPOT"
MARLIN AND SWORDFISH

N

Catalina
Hbr.

OCEAN WHITEFISH
SHEEPHEAD

Long Pt.

Torqua

STRIPED MARLIN
SWORDFISH
(SOMETIMES
ALBACORE,
BONITO AND
BLUEFIN TUNA)

Little Hbr.
Pedestal Rk.

Ben Weston Pt.

Santa Catalina Island

Frog Rk.

FARNSWORTH BANK:
SHEEPHEAD
ROCKFISH
KELP BASS
SCULPIN
BARRACUDA
BLUEFIN TUNA
OCEAN WHITEFISH
YELLOWTAIL

Farnsworth Bank   20

1
Avalon   CAN DUMP

33° 20'   33° 20'

20
100   50   Silver Canyon
Salta Verde Pt.

"3 V's"

Quarry

SOUTH SIDE:
BARRACUDA, BONITO, KELP BASS,
SAND BASS, YELLOWTAIL, WHITE
SEABASS, ROCKFISH (BROWN TYPES),
HALFMOON, HALIBUT, AND
OCCASIONALLY BLUEFIN TUNA

E. Light

Church Rk.   EAST END

118° 20'

Santa Barbara Island (map - p. 227)

The small island of Santa Barbara is 20 miles west of the "west end" of Catalina Island. It is about one mile long and a half mile wide, and it rises abruptly to a peak of 635 feet above sea level. The shore is rocky, and kelp areas are common about the entire island; the heaviest kelp growth is along the north side.

Fishing boats from the Los Angeles area and from Port Hueneme and Channel Islands Harbor frequent Santa Barbara Island. Anglers fish all about the island, and no one area is noted for having better fishing than another. Albacore are sometimes taken about five miles southeast of the island. To the south about six miles is Osborne Bank. This is a good fishing area for rockfish, lingcod and occasionally bluefin tuna and albacore. But the tuna are increasingly rare.

Santa Catalina Island (map - p. 228)

Because of its proximity to metropolitan Los Angeles, Santa Catalina Island has been fished intensively by marine game fish anglers for a great number of years. Santa Catalina Island is one of the largest of the eight Southern California islands. Although the island points in a northwest-southeast direction, common terminology results in the northwest end being called the "west end" and the southeast end, near Avalon, being called the "east end." The island is about six miles wide and 18 miles long. The northwest third is constricted, and the narrowest point is called the "isthmus." Here the island is only about one-third of a mile wide with Isthmus Cove on the northeast side and Catalina Harbor on the southwest side. The island rises to an altitude of about 2,000 ft.; much of it is over 1,000 ft. high.

The coastline about Catalina is rocky in most places, and patches of kelp frequently are found near shore. Sizable kelp areas occur near the west end and near the entrance to Catalina Harbor. Some patchy areas occur south of the isthmus towards the east end. The south end (southwest) has good fishing for number of species, and white seabass are frequently caught while night fishing. Kelp bass are fished inshore, and the sandy coves offer good fishing for California halibut and ocean whitefish.

Excellent billfishing for striped marlin and broadbill swordfish can be found off the east end during the summer. Bluefin tuna are sometimes taken south and west of the island, between Santa Catalina and San Clemente Islands. The "228-fathom spot," five miles northeast of Avalon Harbor, is good during late summer for marlin and swordfish. The "58-fathom spot" (also known as "14 Mile Bank" and Lasuen Seamount), about midway between Avalon Harbor and Dana Point on the mainland, is good for striped marlin, swordfish and albacore (July through September). This bank also provides good fishing for rockfish. Southwest of the 58-fathom spot, towards Catalina and San Clemente Islands, is another good fishing area for striped marlin and swordfish.

San Clemente Island (map - p. 228)

The large island of San Clemente is about 70 miles west of the mainland off Oceanside and about 45 miles south of Long Beach. The entire island is the property of the U.S. Navy and there are no civilian marinas or public access. Portions of the surrounding waters are restricted because of naval operations.

The island is about 18 miles long and from 2 1/2 to 3 1/2 miles wide; its highest elevation is about 1,900 feet. The coastal shelf is narrow, particularly on the northeast side. The shore is rocky, and the bottom types near shore are a mixture of rock, mud and sand. This type of substrate allows kelp to attach, and kelp patches are common with the most prominent growths at the north end. Kelp is also found along the west side with concentrations around China Point and just west of Pyramid Head at the southern end. Along the northeast side, to about 20 fathoms in depth, there is kelp. The kelp growth is close to shore owing to the sharp slope of the bottom.

Sport fishing boats from the Los Angeles area frequent the island, and most of the fishing is at about the north end and along the east side. Three well-known grounds are "Slide Area," "Purse Seine Rock," and "Fish Hook"—all on the east side. Good fishing is also found along the southwest side, although it is more exposed to the northwest winds and rough seas. Bluefin tuna sometimes are found along the southwest side, and albacore were once caught south and southwest of the island during the summer, but that almost never happens now.

Santa Catalina Island Fishing Facilities					
Location	Sport Fishing Boats	Pier Fishing	Boat Rental	Launch Ramp	Jetty Fishing
Avalon, Catalina Island (1)*	X	X	X		

*Map fishing facilities

Fish Cleaning

There's a syndrome among some anglers that I like to call, "The Fear of Filleting." It's not unlike "The Fear of Flying." But fortunately, it's a lot easier to overcome. It just takes a little knowledge, a little willingness and an extra sharp filleting knife.

But don't be mislead, filleting is not the end-all or be-all of fish cleaning. It's only one of several basic approaches (all are presented here, in detail), and filleting is not even desirable or appropriate for some fish.

Field Dressing

Actually, the word dressing is not accurate, but we're stuck with it. Field dressing means removing the entrails and gills of a fish just after catching. This process is generally reserved for large fish (several pounds or more). It's purpose is to preserve the fish at its height of freshness. Field dressing, for example, is quite common among ocean salmon anglers. It's the kind of thing that's desirable but not absolutely necessary—especially if your catch is kept cold.

Here's how it's done. With the fish pointing away from you, put the tip of your knife in the anal vent and cut through the belly (leaving the intestines as undisturbed as possible) up to where the gills come together under the chin of the fish.

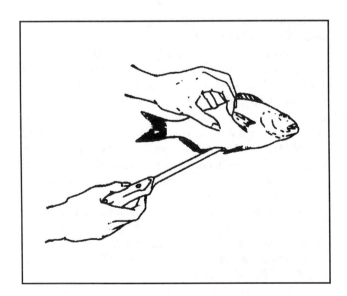

Next, with short cuts, free the bottom of the gills from the chin flesh and from the belly flesh, as illustrated in the following diagram.

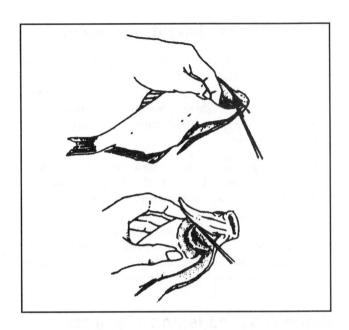

Now, pull open the gill cover on each side of the fish and cut the top of the gills free from the head. The gills and entrails can now be lifted or slid out of the fish in one unit. Now, remove the strip of reddish tissue near the backbone in the intestinal cavity. You may have to cut through a thin layer of tissue covering this area. As a last step, rinse off the fish. It is now ready for icing down.

Traditional Fish Cleaning

This approach is basically an extension of field dressing. As a young boy, my earliest memory of fish cleaning was the assembly line my dad set up with my brother and myself to clean a stringer of well over 100 Lake Michigan perch (about 1/2 to 1 pound each). Here are the steps:

1. **Scaling**—Using a knife (not necessarily real sharp) or a fish scaler, scrape from the tail towards the head. This is best done out-of-doors since the scales fly around. Actually some fish (like salmon and sanddabs) can be scaled with the spray from a garden hose nozzle. It's quick and easy.

2. **Gutting**—This is actually the same as the beginnings of field dressing. Open the belly from anal vent to gills.

3. **Be-Heading**—The entrails are slid forward and out of the body cavity, and then with a sharp knife, cut perpendicular to the backbone at the top of the gill cover, cut off the entrails, gills and head.

4. **Rinsing**—Rinse inside and outside of fish after removing red flesh in body cavity (see Field Dressing section).

5. Fish is now ready for cooking or preserving.

Filleting

Filleting is simple and has many advantages. For example, scaling is not necessary since the skin (and scales) will be removed. It can and often is done without even gutting or field dressing the fish first. It produces boneless or almost bone-free slabs of meat. And filleting works great on fish of all sizes and both round-bodied and flat-bodied fish.

Here are the steps in filleting:

1. Make the first cut just behind the gills. Cut down to the backbone, then turn the knife toward the tail of the fish and slice above the spine (feeling for it as you proceed) all the way to the tail. One flank of the fish will now be removed. Flip the fish over and repeat the process. This step is illustrated below.

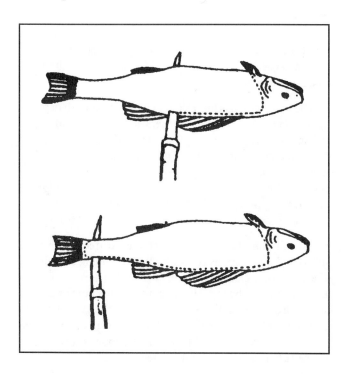

2. Now cut away the rib cage from each fillet. Insert the knife at the top of the rib cage and slice down following close to ribs.

3. Lastly, remove the skin. Lay fillet skin side down on cutting board. Insert the knife just about one-half inch from the tail and cut down to the skin. Now, firmly holding the tail end, turn the blade forward and work the knife along the skin, "lifting" the meat from the skin all the way to the large end of the fillet.

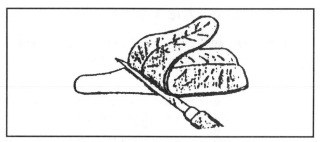

With a little practice, filleting becomes second nature. For a great visual display, watch the pros do it when a party boat docks after a day of fishing. You'll be amazed. Successful filleting depends on two things once you understand the principles: 1) Use a good fish fillet knife; and 2) keep the knife very sharp.

Steaking

Steaking simply means cutting a fish into similar-sized parts by making parallel cuts that are all perpendicular to the spine! Just joking! I know only math freaks and geometry teachers could understand that definition.

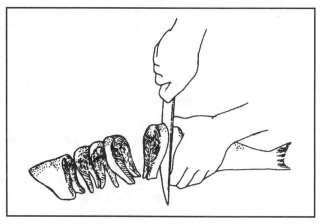

The first step in steaking (which, by the way, is usually reserved only for large fish) is to remove the head (this is done after field dressing) right at the gill cover. Now just lay the fish flat and divide it into about one-inch thick pieces. The tail section (where the steaks are small) can be filleted. Some varieties need to be scaled before steaking.

Keeping Fish Fresh

Fish is delicious. But it is also one of the most perishable of foods. So, from the time a fish is caught until it is served, care must be taken to preserve its freshness.

Freshness on the Water

If possible, the best way to keep a fish fresh, while continuing to fish, is to keep your catch alive. This can be done in several ways:

- For pan fish, use a collapsible basket. A fully submerged burlap bag will also serve the purpose.

- The best stringers are those that have large safety pin type clasps, and some type of swivel mechanism so fish are less likely to get twisted up.

- The proper stringing technique is to run the stringer through both the upper and lower lip. This allows the fish to open and close its mouth, thereby forcing water through its gills to breathe. Never run a stringer through the fishes' gills. This prevents it from closing its mouth and therefore starving it of oxygen.

- Let out the full stringer. Even add a rope if extra length is needed to keep the fish down deep in the water. The water is cooler and more oxygenated down deeper.

- If you move your boat quickly, lift the stringer out of the water during a short trip.

- Surf and river anglers who use a stringer move the fish along with them, always placing the fish back into the deepest water available.

- When using a creel, bed and surround fish in dry grass. Canvas creels or fishing vests should be moist to maintain coolness.

There are some hazards to be aware of when keeping fish in water:

- Fish on stringers have been known to be eaten by turtles. Never string fish in warm lake water. Summertime surface water temperatures in some Southern California lakes are in the 80's!

- Stringers are taboo in salt waters. It's just feeding the sharks. Rather, use a cooler or fish box, preferably with ice in it.

Freshness During Travel

If you're traveling for any length of time, follow these simple steps to ensure freshness:

- Field dress the fish.

- Dry the fish thoroughly.

- Cover each fish with foil or plastic.

- Surround each package of fish in a cooler with crushed or cubed ice.

Refrigeration

Fish do not do particularly well under prolonged refrigeration. So it's best to either eat fresh caught fish, or freeze them. Refrigerated fish should be covered with heavy foil, freezer paper or plastic to prevent moisture from escaping.

Freezing

There are basically two ways to freeze fresh fish. With either approach you can freeze whole-field cleaned fish, fish fillets, steaks or chunks.

The first method is more conventional. Wrap fish in packaging materials with high barriers to moisture and vapor transmission. A good quality freezer wrapping paper or heavy foil is recommended. Wrap tightly and tape securely. This method is adequate. Defrost slowly in a refrigerator. Better flavor and preservation can be achieved by repeatedly dipping and freezing unwrapped fish in water until a layer of ice is formed. Then wrap securely.

Actually, the best and simplest way to freeze fish is to utilize old milk cartons or similar liquid holding containers. Fresh and well-cleaned fish can be placed in the container up to an inch from the top. Now, simply fill the container with water (or a brine solution of 1/3 cup of table salt to one gallon of water) and shake to make sure there are no air bubbles. Seal up container and freeze. Thawing is best done on a drain rack so the fish does not sit in cold water.

Date fish packages you put in the freezer. Store them at 0°F or lower, and plan to use within 2 months for best flavor.

Cooking Fish

There are numerous fish cookbooks jam-packed with recipes. But matching your favorite catch to an unfamiliar or inappropriate recipe often leads to less than enjoyable eating. Rather than special recipes, successful fish cooking depends on adhering to two simple principles:

1. Know when the fish is done—too often fish is overcooked.

2. Match cooking method to the fish flavor, fish size and fat level.

First, let's address the "when fish is done" issue. Fish by its very nature is more tender than red meat or poultry. It doesn't contain fibers that need to be broken down by extensive cooking. Some cooking experts say fish should be considered more like egg than like meat. So, as in cooking egg, just enough heat needs to be applied to firm up the protein. Overcooking makes eggs tough and dry; it does the same for fish.

So how dow you tell when fish is cooked for just the right length of time? It's easy. Fish is cooked properly when it flakes when probed with a fork. By flaking, I mean separated into its natural layers or divisions. This test should be done often at the center, or thickest part of the fish fillet, steak or whole fish.

Matching Fish to Cooking Method

Now the second key principle of successful fish cooking: matching the specific fish to the specific cooking method. Fish caught in Southern California have a wide variety of flavor levels, fish size and fat level. Typically, all fish is considered a low-fat source of protein. But there are pronounced differences in fat content that do affect taste and texture. Flavor level also varies generally from very mild to quite pronounced. This influences cooking method and seasoning selection. Fortunately, all these fish can be grouped into four cooking categories.

Category One. In this category are the delicate, mild flavored, lean and generally small cuts of fish. Specific examples include sole, sanddabs, flounder and halibut. Cuts of fish in this category are generally thin and oval shaped. The exception is halibut which is thicker and has a heavier texture.

Category One fish are very good sauteed. Sole fillets are so delicate that some only need to be cooked on one side. A flour coating promotes browning. Thicker cuts can have a flour,

crumb, cornmeal or egg-wash coating before frying. Oven frying or foil baking also works well, as does poaching.

Category Two. Fish in this second group are generally of medium density, yet still light in flavor. We're talking about lingcod, the whole family of rockfish, surfperch, salmon, trout, catfish, striped bass and yellowtail. Both steaks and fillets from larger fish in this category are good poached, cooked in foil or oven-fried. Pan frying is good with a coating like crumbs or egg-wash to add flavor, texture and enhance browning. Small, whole fish are good baked or foil cooked. The most oily fish in this category, salmon, is very good barbecued.

Category Three. Here we have the Southern California fish that are more dense with a darker meat and more pronounced flavor. Three ocean-going fish—the tunas (albacore, yellowfin, etc.), bonito, mackerel and barracuda—make up this third category. To be honest with you, many fishermen don't even like the robust (some say strong) flavor of these fish. But those who do usually barbecue them. Fresh caught barbecued tuna is quite tasty, but some would say that it's not as good as "good old Charlie The Tuna."

Category Four. Now we're into the large fish that result in thick cuts (1 to 1 1/2 inch) of dense meat. Southern California fish in this category are the sharks, swordfish and giant sea bass. Cuts of these fish brown nicely in a frying pan without any coating, and you can barbecue them directly on a greased grill. In fact, cubes can be skewered for kabobs. Meal-sized pieces are good baked, poached or cooked in foil.

The preceding categories and guidelines have wide latitude. That's why for each fish covered in the "How to Catch" chapter, specific cooking information is given.

Sauteing

This method is often called frying, but frying is quite distinct. More on this in the pan frying section below. Sauteing is cooking fish in a frying pan, usually in a small amount of melted butter, over moderate or high heat.

This is one of the fastest and simplest ways to prepare fish. And, it is well suited for either lean or fat fish. The fish is sprinkled with salt and pepper and dipped in flour on both sides. Cooking time per side varies from 1 minute to 3 minutes. A sauce can be prepared in the pan after the fish are removed to a warm platter.

Frying (both Pan and Deep)

Frying fish means immersing either partially or completely in cooking oil. This process results in a thicker, more crusty covering of the fish than with sauteing or oven frying. Frying usually involves a batter made with a beaten egg and a small amount of milk. The dipped fish pieces are rolled in bread crumbs, cracker crumbs or a purchased coating mix.

One eighth inch of shortening or salad oil should be heated to between 350 and 375 degrees in a substantial frying pan. Or, if deep-frying, use enough shortening or salad oil in a deep fryer to cover the fish. Heat to the same temperature. Finished fish should be golden brown and flake when tested.

Some pitfalls to avoid: Don't let the oil temperature fall; it results in a greasy or soggy coating. Too much fish put in the oil at one time can lower the cooking temperature where the fish can't cook properly. Too high an oil temperature will result in a dark coating or burnt flavor. If batter falls off, the fish pieces may have been too wet. So, pat dry before battering.

Oven Frying

Everybody knows how to oven-fry chicken, so everybody knows how to oven-fry fish. This method is simple and doesn't cause fat spattering, if that's a problem with you.

Fish should be serving-sized pieces. Dip each piece in milk, drain, sprinkle with salt and pepper, then roll in bread crumbs or cracker crumbs. Melt enough butter or margarine in a shallow baking pan to generously coat the bottom. Now, turn the crumb-coated fish over in the melted butter or margarine and arrange the pieces in the pan. Bake in a hot oven (about 500ºF) until the fish flakes (from 5 to 15 minutes). Turn each piece one time so it browns evenly.

Baking

Foil wrapped or covered-dish oven cooking is the typical fish baking approach. The covering or enclosure is needed to prevent the fish from drying out. This is an ideal method for baking fish with vegetables, herbs or tomato sauce. The steam that is developed helps produce a tasty sauce. Oven temperature is usually about 450ºF.

Barbecuing or Grilling

Rich, full-flavored fish such as salmon, trout or tuna are most desirable for barbecuing since they're fatter and the smoke enhances the taste. Milder-tasting fish might be overcome by the smoke flavor. Serving-sized fillets, steaks and whole fish can be barbecued.

Some people like to grill directly over the coals, while others put the fish on a sheet of heavy aluminum foil. The foil method works well in a covered grill because it prevents any sticking or turning problems.

Some helpful hints: Make sure the coals are hot and the grill is hot—fish stick like magnets to a cold grill. Start fillets skin side up (if no foil is used) and turn only once. If foil is used, fillet skin should be down (that is, touching foil). While cooking, the fish is basted with melted butter or your favorite sauce.

Broiling

Broiling, of course, is much akin to barbecuing, except that the heat is above the fish. Any fish can be broiled, but leaner fish must be basted often to prevent it from drying out. Fillets are often broiled on only one side, while steaks are turned once. Broil 2 to 3 inches from the heat.

Poaching

Poaching is simmering fish gently in a flavorful liquid. The liquid is never boiled, however. Fish prepared this way is very good served hot with a fish sauce made from the poaching liquid. Any fish with a low fat content, and salmon of course, is delicious prepared this way. And as an extra bonus, cold, poached fish like tuna is great.

Pieces of fish are often poached in cheese cloth while large, whole fish are done in a poaching pan that has a special rack for lowering and removing the fish. Again, the flake test will reveal when the fish is cooked properly. Fillets should be tested after about 5 minutes.

An easy way to poach a steak or fillet is to put it in lightly salted water in a wide saucepan or skillet on top of the stove (it's much less fuss than the classic oven poach). Frozen fish pieces can even be defrosted and poached at the same time.

Poaching is complete (for frozen or fresh fish) when the meat has turned from translucent to opaque, and it feels somewhat springy rather than squishy. Cooked pieces are patted dry and served with melted butter or in other more elaborate ways.

Smoking

Many avid, and some not so avid, anglers own and use fish smokers. They are simple to use and quite modestly priced. And they produce delicious smoked fish. All commercially available smokers come with detailed instruction manuals. It is also possible to convert such items as 55 gallon drums, or a discarded refrigerator and a hot plate into a smoker. Instructions for these do-it-yourself projects can be found in smoking-oriented cookbooks in your local library.

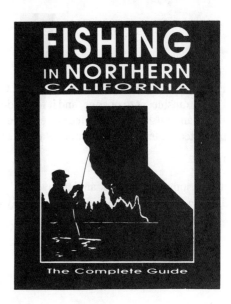

Pier Fishing In California

- Complete coast and bay guide
- How to catch 100 game fish
- Specific info on every pier
- 256 pages, 8 1/2 "x 11"

Fishing in Northern California

- How to catch all game fish
- The best techniques, lures and bait, rigging
- Complete coverage of streams, rivers, lakes, ocean
- Many illustrations and maps
- 256 pages, 8 1/2"x11"

OUR BESTSELLERS -in detail

Pier Fishing In California
By Ken Jones

There are many marvelous ocean and bay fishing opportunities on California's piers. And now there is a book that covers each and every one of them — from San Diego to San Francisco Bay to Crescent City. Learn how to fish each pier, the species, best baits, proper timing, the underwater environment, fishing tips, and more. Plus, find out about the best techniques, baits, lures, and necessary equipment from an expert who has fished all these piers all his life. There is also an extensive pier fish identification section and cleaning and cooking info.

This is the first guide to fishing the vast number of piers in the ocean and bays of California. It covers every pier on the California coast and in the bay waters. The opening chapters explain the basics of pier fishing including techniques, tackle, bait and lures, underwater environment, casting and landing, cleaning and cooking, timing and much, much more.

This Guide is perfect - it's the most comprehensive, accurate, well organized and filled with sound advice. Just right for all anglers who want to successfully fish California's many piers from Oregon to Baja."

--Larry Green
KCBS Fisherman's Forecast

"PIER FISHING IN CALIFORNIA is an outstanding guide. It provides a first hand, insiders view to every pier in California. It's eminently useful to everyone from the beginning angler to the expert."

--Jim Matthews, Editor
CALIFORNIA ANGLER MAGAZINE

Ken Jones has fished the piers of California for decades. He has lived in both Southern and Northern California and traveled the state extensively, fishing the piers as he goes along. He has fished many piers more than 50 times and has kept detailed records of each outing. Ken is a high school social sciences teacher and athletic director. He lives with his wife and children in Boonville, Ca.

8 1/2 x 11 inches, 256 pages

Expanded and Updated Edition
Fishing in Northern California
By Ken Albert

Here is an enlarged and updated version of the premier book for NorCal anglers.

- **More lakes, rivers & streams**
- **More "how-to" info**
- **More "where-to-go" info**
- **More illustrations & maps**

"FISHING IN NORTHERN CALIFORNIA is a must for those seeking fishing oppurtunities in Northern California's vast and varied waters."

—Bob Reeves—Co-Publisher
RECREATION LAKES OF CALIFORNIA

"FISHING IN NORTHERN CALIFORNIA greatly clarifies the complexities of fishing in the North State. I highly recommend it."

—Larry Green -- Outdoor Writer,
Syndicated Columnist and KCBS
Fisherman' Forecast

Yes, outdoor writers and fishing experts are enthusiastically recommending FISHING IN NORTHERN CALIFORNIA because it details the nitty-gritty of Northern and Central California fishing; How to rig up, When to fish, Where to fish, Equipment and guidelines,Fish freshness and cleaning, Fish cooking, and more.

It covers 50 NorCal lakes (with complete fishing information and full page maps for each), mountain trout streams and lakes (with maps), the Delta (with 4 pages of fishing maps), coastal rivers, Central Valley rivers, the Pacific Coast (with detailed info and 6 full page fishing maps), San Francisco Bay as well as Bay Area Hot Spots, party boat fishing, surf fishing,drift fishing, pier fishing, rock fishing and more.

Both Veteran anglers and beginners are finding FISHING IN NORTHERN CALIFORNIA an information bonanza. It explains how, when and where to catch salmon, trout, sturgeon, striper, steelhead, shark, shad, rock crab,rock cod, panfish, lingcod, kokanee, halibut, crawdads,catfish, bass, albacore, abalone.

8 1/2 x11 inches, 256 pages

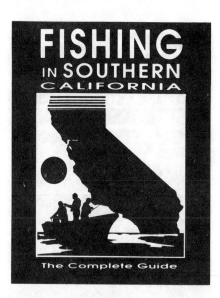

Fishing in Southern California
- How to catch all game fish
- The best techniques, lures and bait, rigging
- Complete coverage of streams, rivers, lakes, ocean
- 63 maps, many illustrations
- 256 pages, 8 1/2"x11"

Bass Fishing in California
- Secrets of the Western Pros
- Best techniques. What? Where? Why?
- "How to fish" the top 40 lakes in the state
- 40 maps, many illustrations
- 256 pages, 8 1/2" x 11"

OUR BESTSELLERS -in detail

Expanded and Updated Edition
Fishing in Southern California
By Ken Albert

Here is a new enlarged and updated version of the premier SoCal fishing book.

- **More lakes**
- **More maps**
- **More "where to go" info**
- **More tips**

> "At last, a basic information book for Southern California ...every angler should have a copy."
> —UNITED ANGLERS OF CALIF.

> "Southern California should delight in...FISHING IN SOUTHERN CALIFORNIA."
> —The Editors
> CALIFORNIA ANGLER MAGAZINE

Both the veteran anglers and beginners are finding this book an information bonanza. It explains in detail how, when and where to catch SoCal abalone, barracuda, largemouth bass, bluegill, bonito, calico bass, catfish, crappie, grunion, halibut, marlin, rockfish, striped bass, trout (in streams, in lakes and golden) and yellowtail.

This book covers SoCal lakes (44 of the best with full page fishing maps), mountain trout streams and lakes (with maps), the Salton Sea, Colorado river lakes (with full page fishing maps), the Pacific coast (with detailed info and 8 full page maps) as well as surf fishing, pier fishing, rockfishing, party boat fishing, Baja fishing trips, fish cleaning and fish cooking.

This book has become a bestseller because it details the nitty-gritty of SoCal fishing; how to rig up, when to fish, equipment and tackle, best techniques, lures and bait and more.

8 1/2 x 11 inches, 256 pages

Expanded and Updated Edition
Bass Fishing in California
By Ron Kovach

Here is the expanded and updated edition of the bible of bass fishing in California.

At last, a bass fishing book just for California anglers—both beginners and veterans. Bass fishing inCalifornia is unique and special, and now there's a book that tells it all. How? What? Where? and Why?

This book explains in detail how to catch bass using crankbaits, plastic worms, top-water lures, spinner baits, spoons, jigs and live bait. Plus there are chapters on equipment, electronics, tips and tricks, and more. There is also a chapter detailing sure-fire ways to catch smallmouth bass.

> "This book really does detail the secrets of the Western pros. These are the tricks we use out there every day."
> —Bobby Garland
> Top Touring Pro and Lure Manufacturer

> "This book is a must for any bass angler who would like to learn what it takes to catch fish in our manmade waters. It has more about finesse fishing with worms and other baits than any other book."
> —Don Iovino
> Top Touring Pro and Professional Guide

But most valuable to Caiifornians, this is a guide to over 3 dozen of the best bass lakes, up and down the state. Two full pages are devoted to each lake, including a large fishing map and numerous fishing tips. Ron Kovach is highly successful professional bass fisherman and outdoor writer. In this book he tells, in simple terms, exactly how the Western bass pros catch so many big fish. And how the weekend angler can do it too.

8 1/2 x 11 inches, 256 pages

more ....

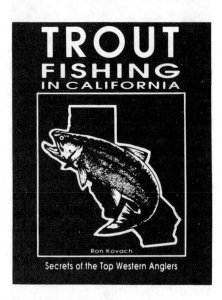

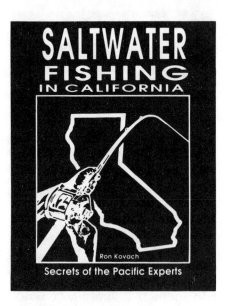

Trout Fishing in California
- Secrets of the Top Western anglers
- Best techniques. What? Where? Why?
- Major "Where to fish" sections
- 50 maps, many illustrations
- 240 pages, 8 1/2" x 11"

Saltwater Fishing in California
- Secrets of the Pacific Experts
- Best techniques. What? Where? Why?
- Complete Mexico-Oregon "Where-to" sections
- 15 full - page maps; many illustrations
- 256 pages, 8 1/2" x 11"

OUR BESTSELLERS -in detail

Expanded and Updated Edition
Trout Fishing in California
Secrets of the Western Anglers
by Ron Kovach

Trout fishing is special in California. And now there is a special book for the California trout angler - both veteran and beginner. Trout fishing is number one all up and down California. This book answers all the"Hows", "Whats", "Wheres", and "Whys" for angling, from the Oregon border down to San Diego.

It covers, in detail, how to catch trout in lakes or streams, with lures or bait, or flies, by trolling, casting or still fishing, from boat or shore. Plus there are chapters on reading the water, tips and tricks, cleaning and cooking, and more. There are also chapters on pack-in trout fishing and ice fishing. And even better for California anglers, this is a guide to the best trout waters all over California. Detailed information and precise maps are featured. The entire state is devided into manageable regions, and then specific trout fishing particulars are presented for highly productive waters in each region.

"There are more secrets and tricks in this book than a person will ever be able to use in a lifetime."
—Jon Minami
California Record Holder, 1983-1987

"It will give you that edge in catching the trophy of a lifetime."
—Bob Bringhurst
World Record Holder, 1977-1984

Ron Kovach is a highly successful professional angler and outdoor writer. *Trout Fishing in California* follows on the heels of his best selling *Bass Fishing in California*, also proudly published by Marketscope Books.

And now, this essential book has been expanded and updated!

8 1/2 x 11 inches, 240 pages

Saltwater Fishing in California
Secrets of the Pacific Experts
By Ron Kovach

California is blessed with over 800 miles of Pacific Ocean coastline. This is a marvelous resource for all Golden State anglers. And now there is a book that covers it all. Surf fishing. Kelp fishing. Harbor and Bay fishing. Poke poling. And more. Don't go saltwater fishing without it.

Both veteran anglers and beginners are finding this book a necessity. It explains, in detail, how to catch albacore, barracuda, bass, bonito, halibut, rockfish,sharks, salmon, stripers, yellowtail and striped marlin. And there is a large "How-To and Where-To" Guide for hot spots all along the coast. And don't be without the Saltwater Sportfish I.D. Section.

"Saltwater Fishing in California belongs in every angler's tackle box"
—Bob Robb, Editor
Peterson's Fishing Magazine

"Finally - a comprehensive, informative book that addresses all aspects...of saltwater angling."
—Larry Green
KCBS

This book has become a standard because it explains in simple, straightforward language how to catch fish in the Pacific, off California.

8 1/2 x 11 inches, 256 pages

Special: Barrett Lake

Fishing Barrett Lake is a trip back in time. This San Diego City 811-acre water reservoir is located just north of the Mexico border in remote foothills. The lake is predominately a northern-strain largemouth fishery and anglers can experience what fishing must have been like in the good-old days. During April through September, it is not uncommon to catch over 50 large-mouths a day, most in the 1 1/2 to 3 pound range, but some 6 to 7 pounds are caught almost daily. There are also bluegill and bullheads to be taken during this same time period.

The fishing stays exceptional for the bass because anglers must release all the bass they catch and fish with barbless artificials. There are virtually no facilities at the lake except the boat dock where anglers get rental aluminum boats and motors. You can't launch your own boat and entry is strictly limited to 25 parties per fishing day. Those parties are chosen through an application lottery, and you are allowed to submit only one application per season. Each reservation includes a row boat rental and you can also reserve a motor or bring your own. The reservation also gives you the right to bring up to three fishing chums, and float tubes are allowed. The lake is open on a Wednesday, Saturday, Sunday schedule from mid-April through September.

Barrett is the lake for anglers to learn how to fish for bass or experiment with new techniques. Why? Because everything will catch fish. These northern-strain bass are aggressive and most anglers use spinnerbaits or crankbaits for the fish. But plastic worms, jigs, surface poppers, fly rod streamers and poppers, trout spinners, spoons, and just about any other lure you can think of will get eaten by the bass here.

This is not to say that the fishing is always easy here. It can get tough late in the season, but there is always very good surface action early and late in the day. Pop-R-type baits are preferred then. If the fish can't be taken on spinnerbaits and cranks, most anglers simply fish deeper with plastics and jigs off the points. There is also good bluegill fishing but most are small. You can keep the bluegill, however.

Light spinning or baitcasting tackle with six- or eight-pound test is adequate, and fly rods that throw from six- to eight-weight lines are preferred. If you bring a full complement of four with your reservation, it is a good idea to have at least a couple in your party bring float tubes. It makes for a less-crowded boat.

To get to Barrett Lake, from the Los Angeles area, take Interstate 5 or 15 south to I-8. Go east on I-8 to Japatul Road. Take that road south and west 5 1/2 miles to Lyon Valley Road. Take Lyon Valley south about six miles to the large pullout at the road to the lake. Those with reservations will be met by a City Lakes employee and escorted through the locked gate and down a dirt road three miles to the lake.

For information contact The San Diego Water Utilities Department, (619) 668-2050

Special: Eastside Reservoir

The Eastside Reservoir project in Southern California is nearing completion and water began filling the lake in late 1999. Within five years, it will be the region's premier fishing lake because of an intensive fishery management and habitat enhancement plan designed from the inception of the lake.

Coming soon under a bass boat near you, the state's greatest largemouth bass lake where a world record is possible. Probable even! About to be released for the downrigger and lead-core crowd, a rainbow trout fishery that will put Montana to shame. For the fly-rod popper crowd, rejoice, the smallmouth are coming. Hawg panfish hunters take note, two-pound bluegill on tap.

These could all be marquees for the Eastside Reservoir project, the Metropolitan Water District's (MWD) new water storage facility that is nearing completion. The reservoir is located near Hemet in western Riverside County in Southern California. It could be opened to the public as early as the fall of 2,000. Most importantly, it won't take long before Eastside Reservoir will become the fishery all others in the region are judged against, living up to its marquee billing.

How are officials so sure Eastside will become the premier freshwater fishery in the region? Because it is being built that way.

It's not very often you get to build a fishery from the bare ground up, but that is exactly what the Department of Fish and Game's (DFG) Mike Giusti has been doing with the Eastside Reservoir project. In fact, it has never been done before, and the MWD contracted with the DFG to have Giusti devote 100 percent of his time to designing a fishery enhancement and management plan for the reservoir. And they gave Giusti a hefty budget to work with in creating this model fishery.

Eastside Reservoir will be the largest body of fresh water in Southern California. Giusti said that Silverwood, Perris, Skinner, and Castaic all would fit inside of the new lake. Eastside Reservoir will have 26 miles of shoreline and will span 4,500 surface acres. It will store up to 800,000 acre feet of water and be over 200 feet deep at its deepest points.

The reservoir will be contained by two main dams constructed on the east and west ends of the Domenigoni Valley southwest of Hemet. There will also be a small, third dam in a pass on the hills on the north side of the project. Recreation areas will be located below both main dams and smaller recreation lake complexes will be made in these two areas, with 105 surface acres of water in the west area and 70 acres in the east area. There will be two, full-service marinas and launch ramps, one at each end of the reservoir. Stay tuned!

MJ Carpet Specialist

Riverside, California 92505

Mr. Ken Albert,

Prior to the 1996 trout season I purchased your book "Fishing in Southern California." I have much success because of it.

I also purchased "Trout Fishing in California," as suggested in your book in which I have read numerous times. There is so much information—I don't want to overlook any tips.

To go back for a moment, I am a thirty-two year-old man and I had fished only twice in my life. Many years ago at that. I must admit I hated it.

Seventeen years later I am married with two kids—a five year-old boy and four year-old girl. My son wanted a fishing pole this past Christmas so my wife and I thought it would be a good idea to get him one. What I didn't anticipate was that he actually wanted to use it.

This is when I bought your book. I figured if we're gonna do it, we might as well do it right. You made fishing sound so simple. Both my kids are actually catching fish and I really enjoy it. Yes, they are both fishing now. They are using floating bait and myself a lure. Recently my Kastmaster has been just killing 'em, or should I say, catching 'em.

My point is, I may still hate fishing had there not been such an easy to understand and apply book on the market. You have given me some knowledge and a technique to use and pass on to my kids where otherwise I wouldn't have. We have spent unforgettable moments that no one can take away and it can only get better.

To you and your staff, I am truly grateful. Well wishes to you and your family.

Mike Juarez

P.S. I am really looking forward to this summer's catfishing.